library wars

9

Love & War

STORY & ART BY Kiiro Yumi   ORIGINAL CONCEPT BY Hiro Arikawa

library
wars
Love & War

Contents

The Library Freedom Act

Libraries have the freedom to acquire their collections.

Libraries have the freedom to circulate
materials in their collections.

Libraries guarantee the privacy of their patrons.

Libraries oppose any type of censorship.

When libraries are imperiled,
librarians will join together
to secure their freedom.

library wars
Love & War

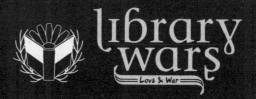

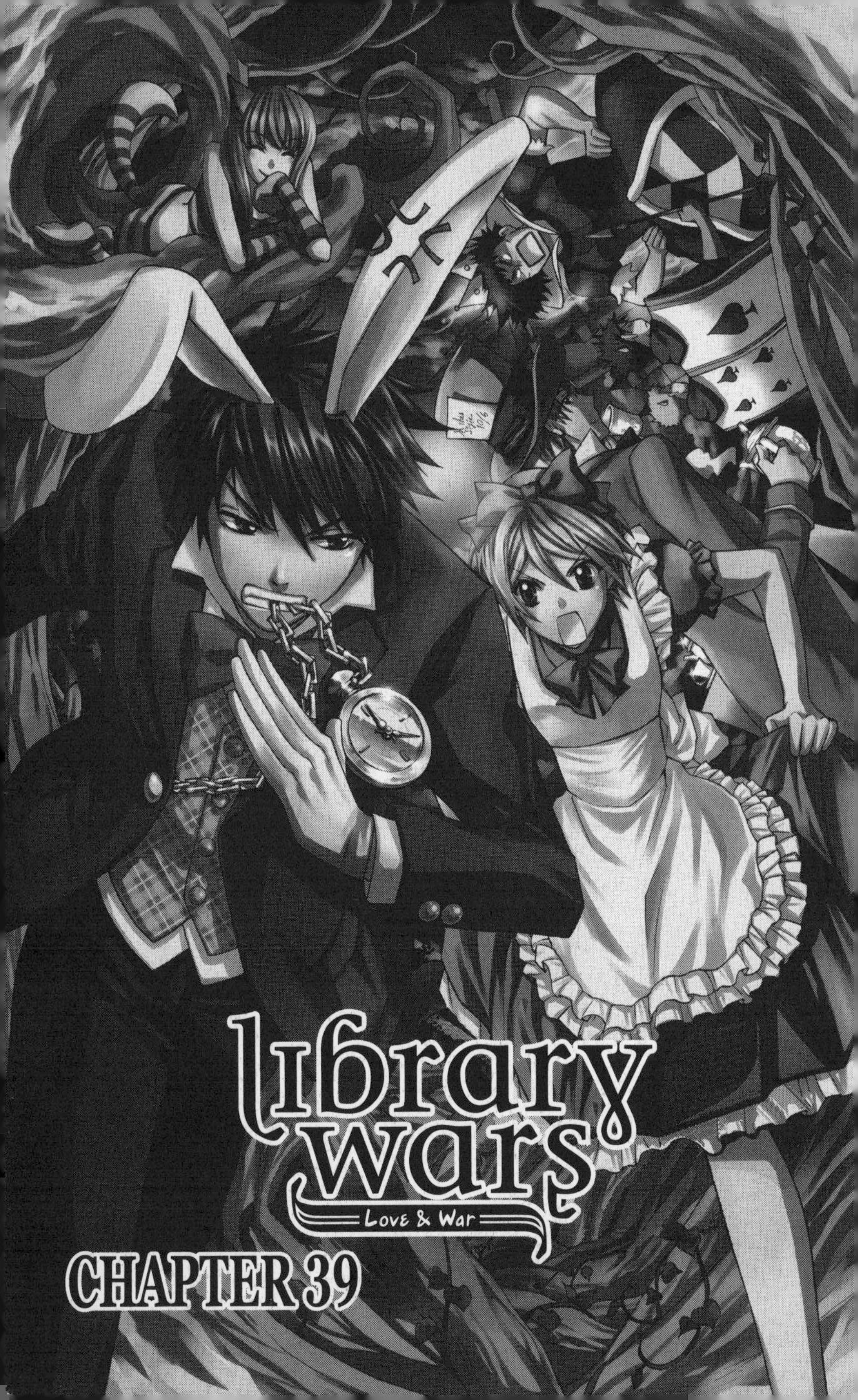
library wars
Love & War
CHAPTER 39

Library Wars Love & War Volume 9

Let's do it!

Hope you enjoy the story.

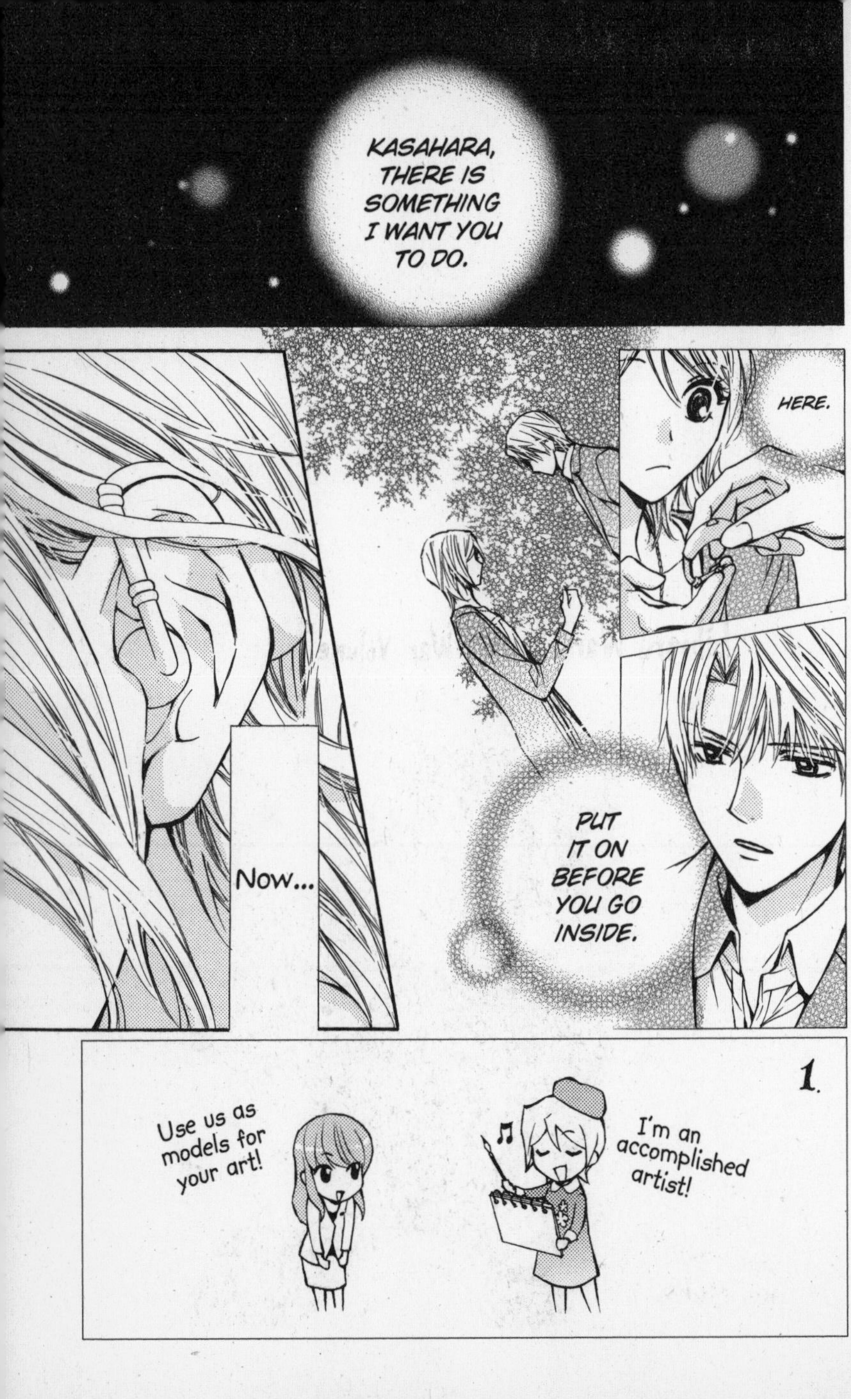
KASAHARA, THERE IS SOMETHING I WANT YOU TO DO.
HERE.
PUT IT ON BEFORE YOU GO INSIDE.
Now...
1.
I'm an accomplished artist!
Use us as models for your art!

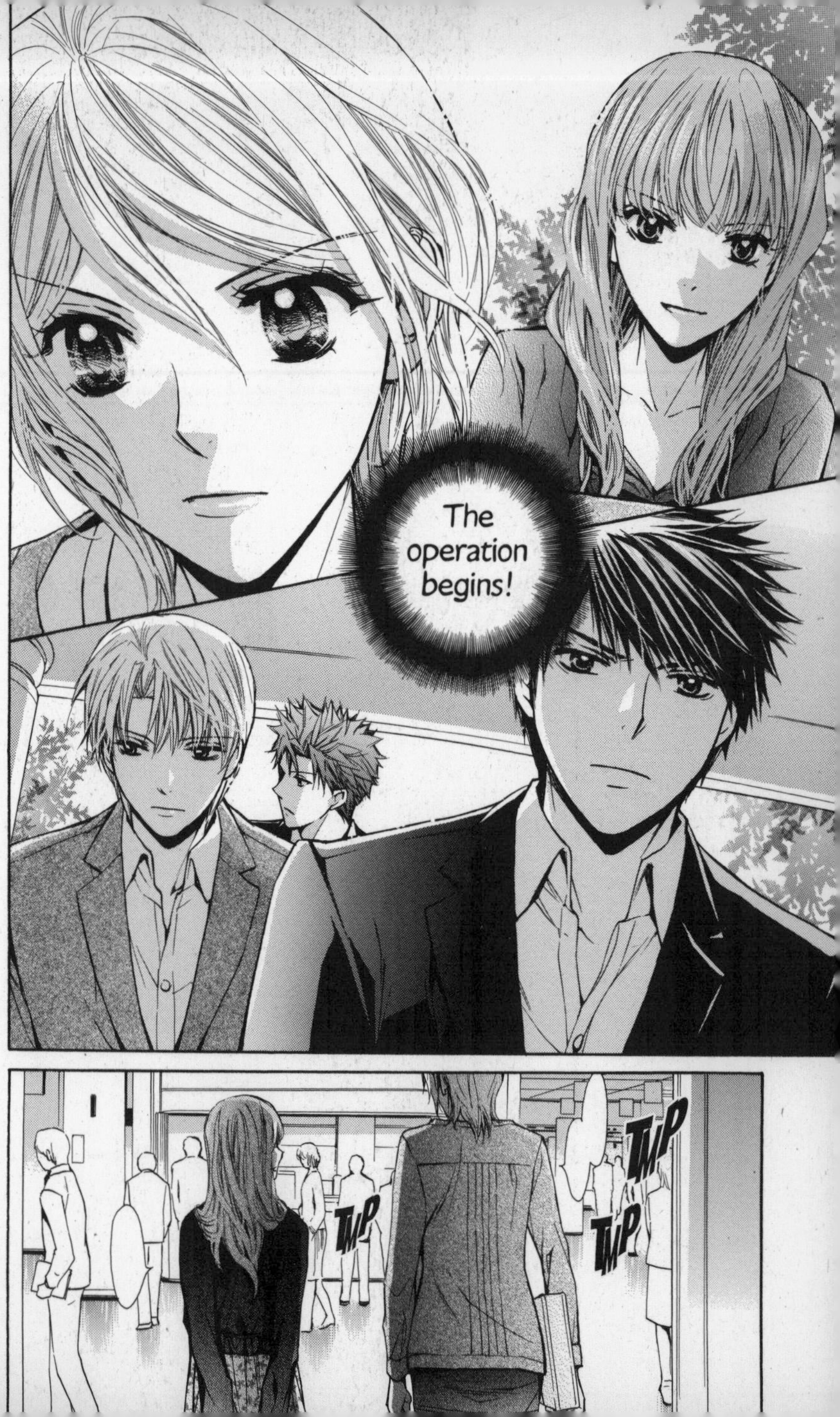
The operation begins!
TMP
TMP
TMP

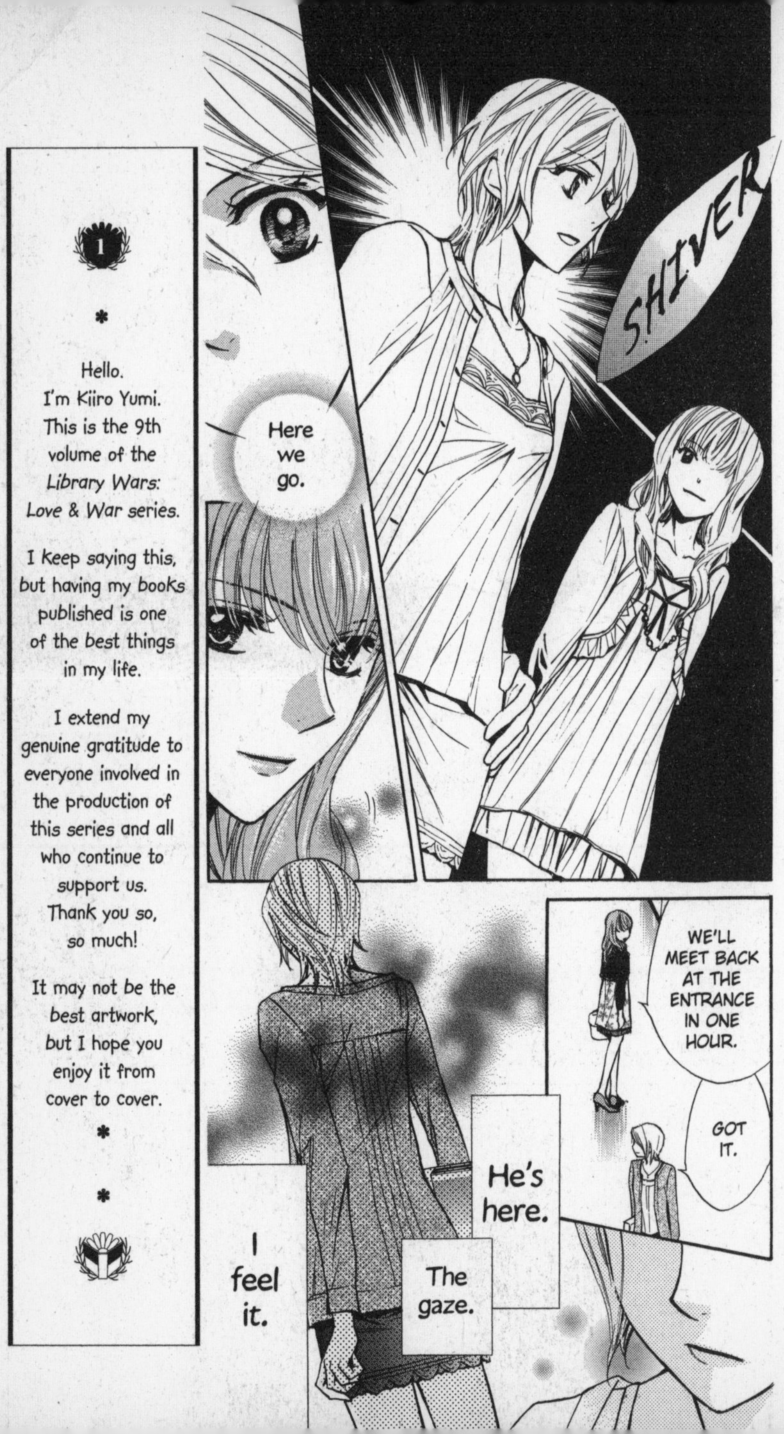
SHIVER
Here we go.
WE'LL MEET BACK AT THE ENTRANCE IN ONE HOUR.
GOT IT.
He's here.
The gaze.
I feel it.

1

*

Hello.
I'm Kiiro Yumi.
This is the 9th volume of the *Library Wars: Love & War* series.

I keep saying this, but having my books published is one of the best things in my life.

I extend my genuine gratitude to everyone involved in the production of this series and all who continue to support us.
Thank you so, so much!

It may not be the best artwork, but I hope you enjoy it from cover to cover.

*

*

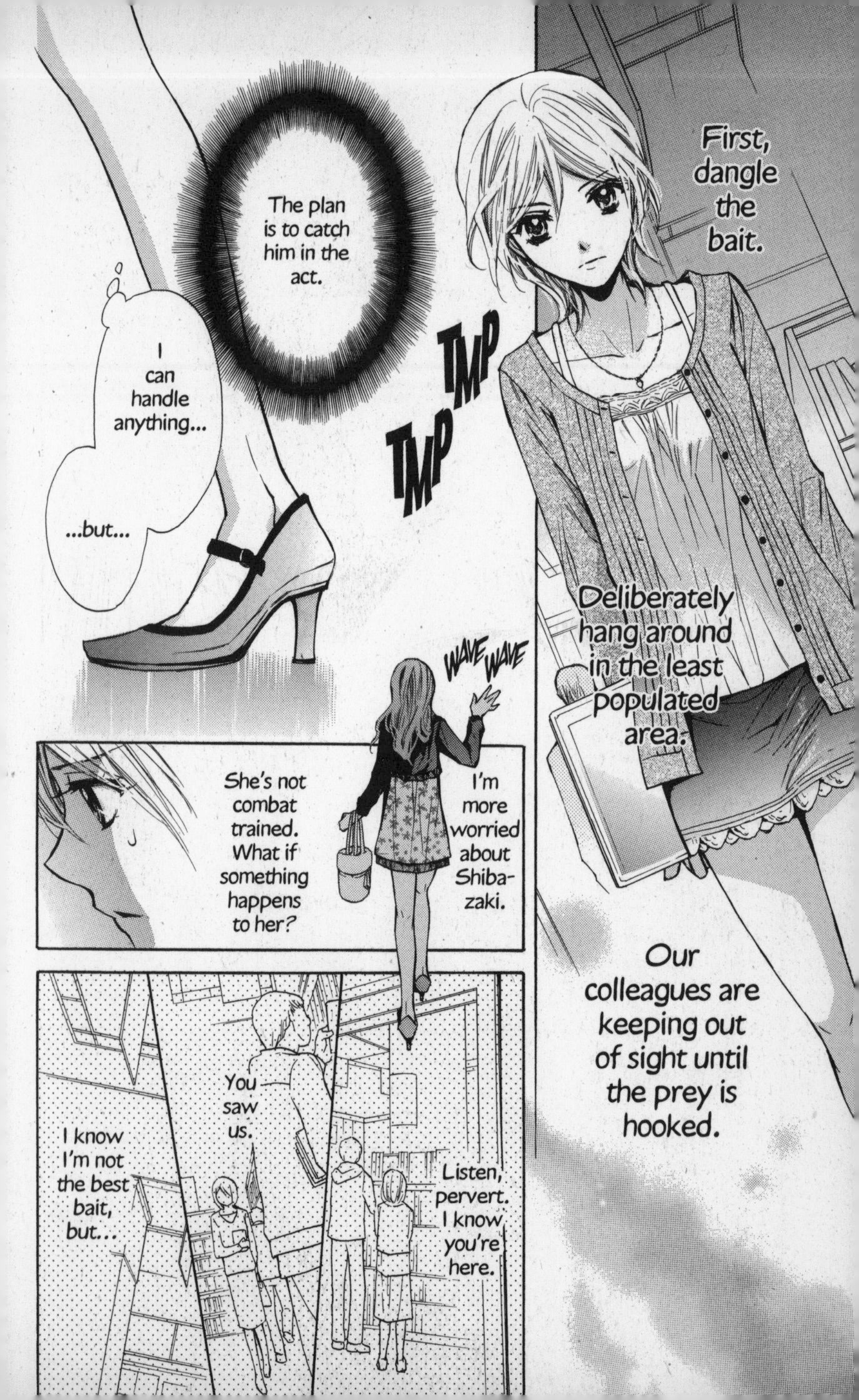
First, dangle the bait.
Deliberately hang around in the least populated area.
Our colleagues are keeping out of sight until the prey is hooked.
The plan is to catch him in the act.
TMP TMP
I can handle anything...
...but...
WAVE WAVE
I'm more worried about Shiba-zaki.
She's not combat trained. What if something happens to her?
Listen, pervert. I know you're here.
You saw us.
I know I'm not the best bait, but...

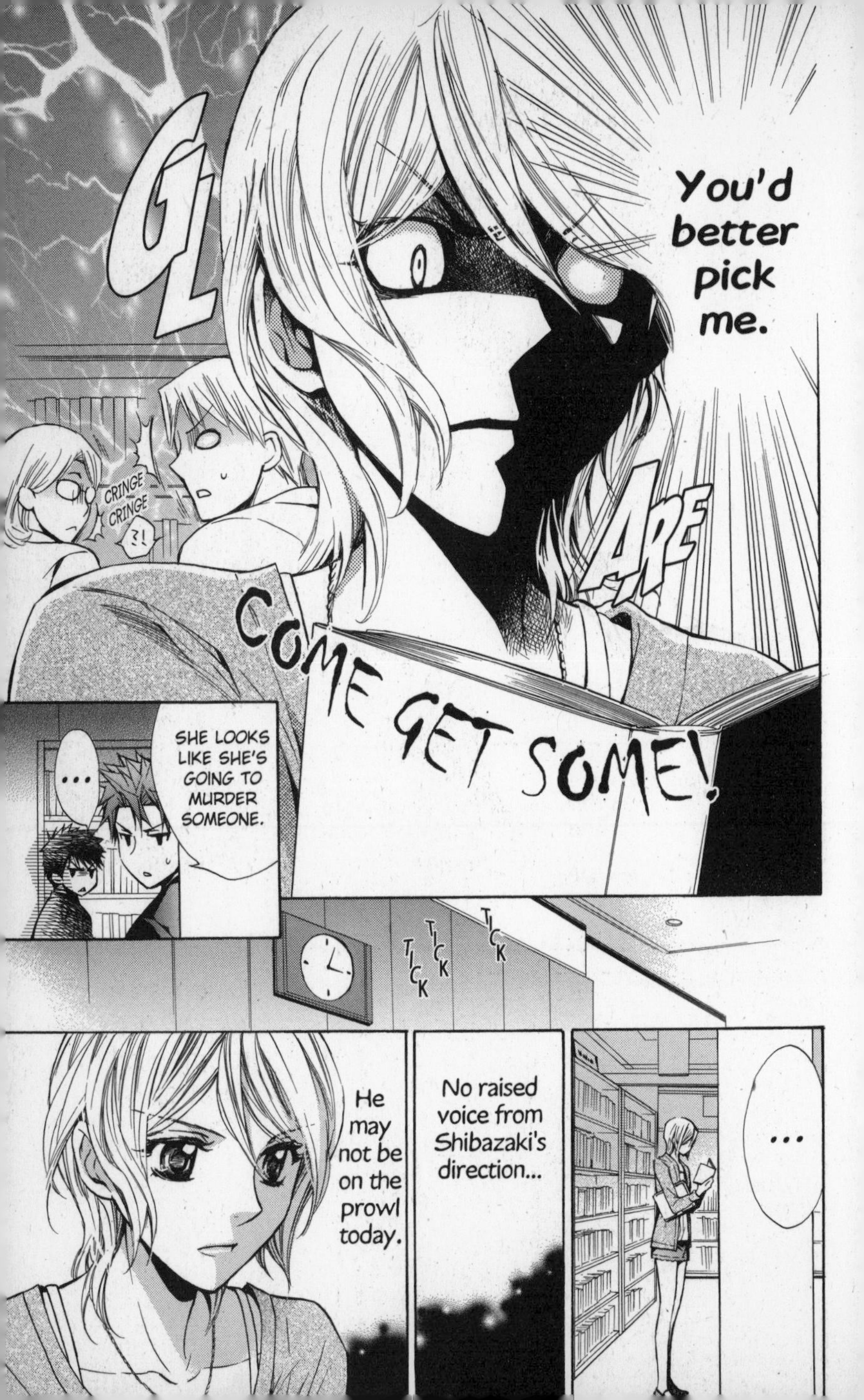
You'd better pick me.
GL
ARE
COME GET SOME!
CRINGE
CRINGE
?!
SHE LOOKS LIKE SHE'S GOING TO MURDER SOMEONE.
...
TICK
TICK
TICK
...
No raised voice from Shibazaki's direction...
He may not be on the prowl today.

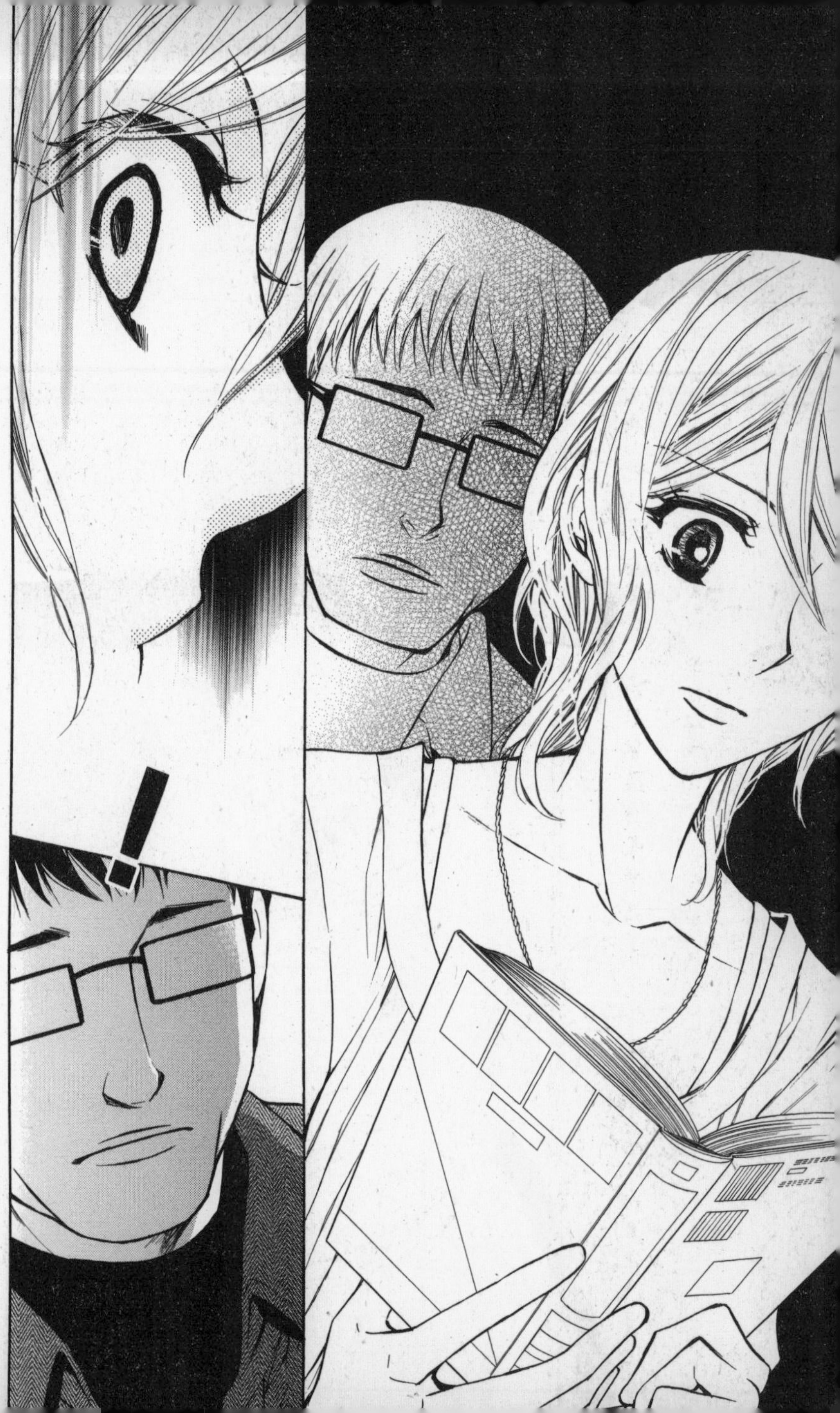
!

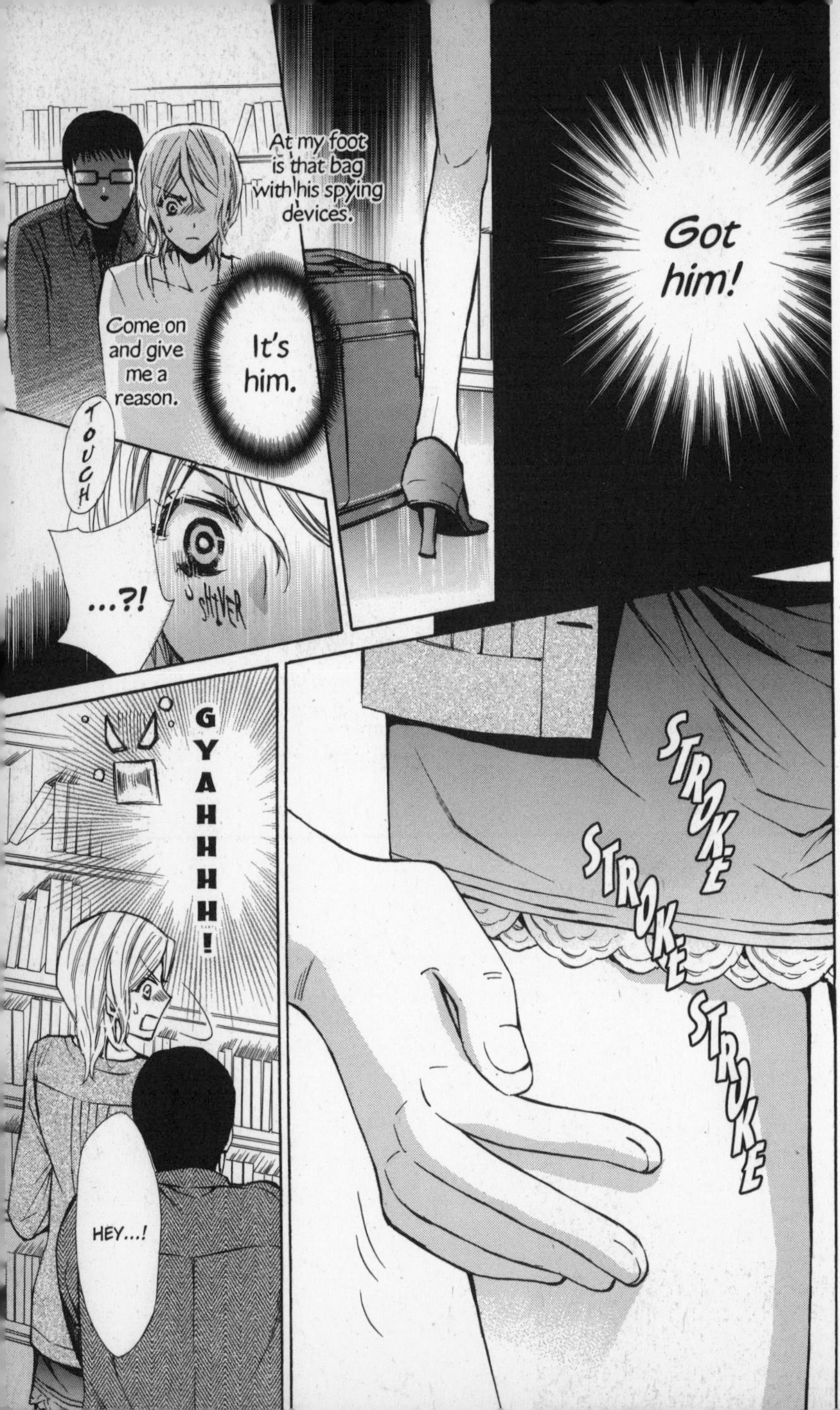
Got him!
At my foot is that bag with his spying devices.
It's him.
Come on and give me a reason.
TOUCH
...?!
SHIVER
STROKE STROKE STROKE STROKE
GYAHHHHH!
HEY...!

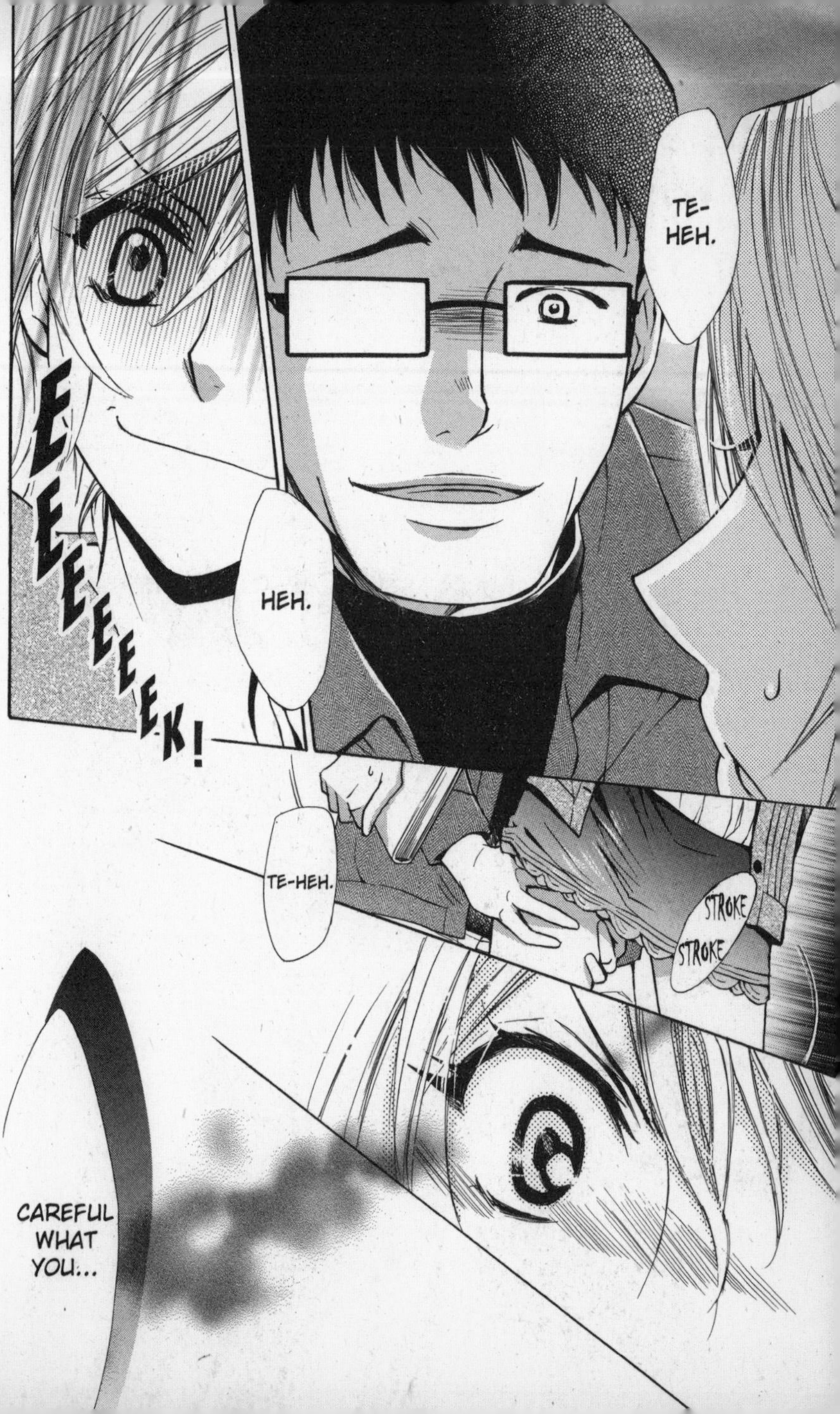
TE-HEH.
HEH.
EEEEEEEK!
STROKE STROKE
TE-HEH.
CAREFUL WHAT YOU...

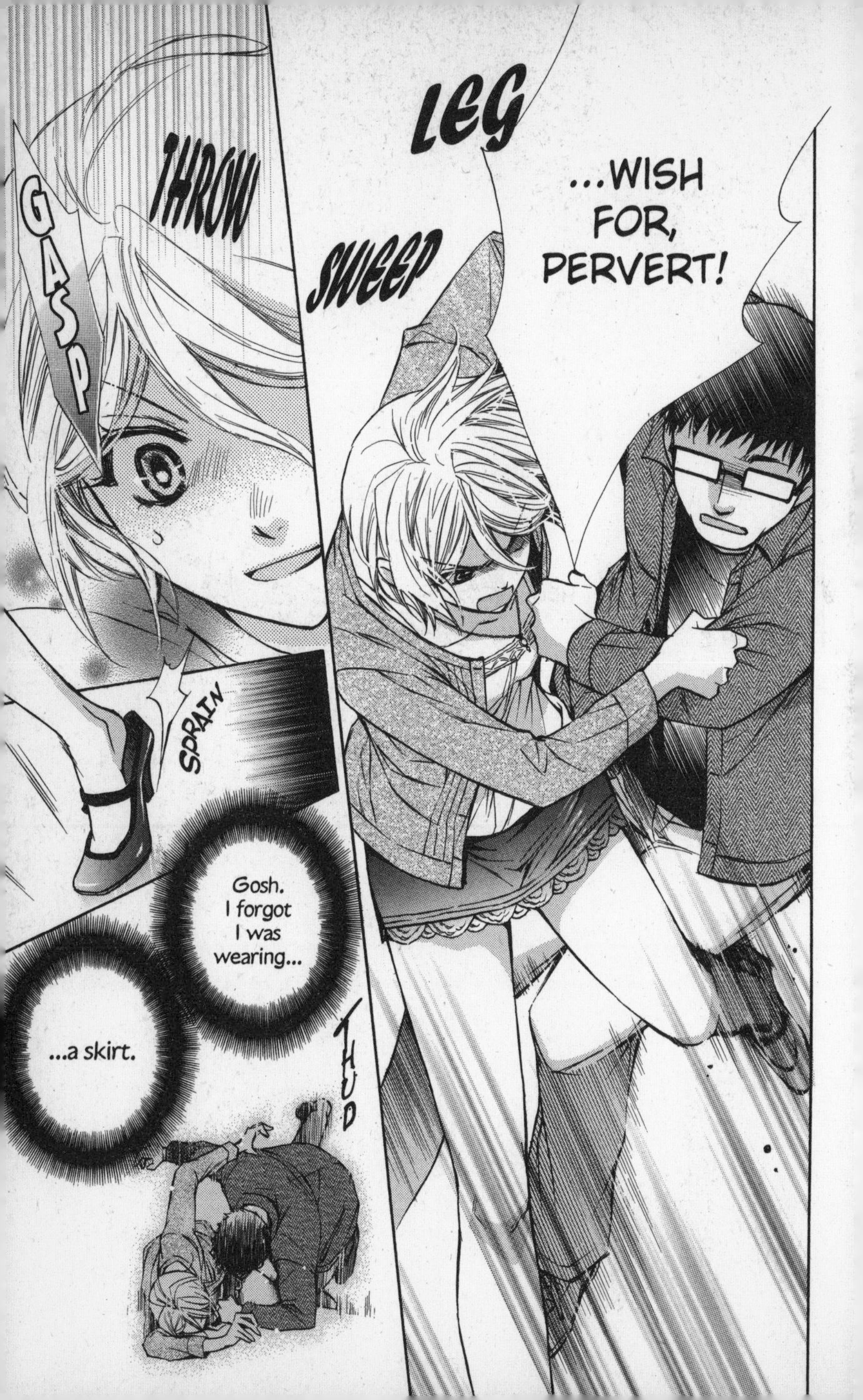
...WISH FOR, PERVERT!
LEG
SWEEP
GASP
THROW
SPRAIN
Gosh. I forgot I was wearing...
...a skirt.
THUD

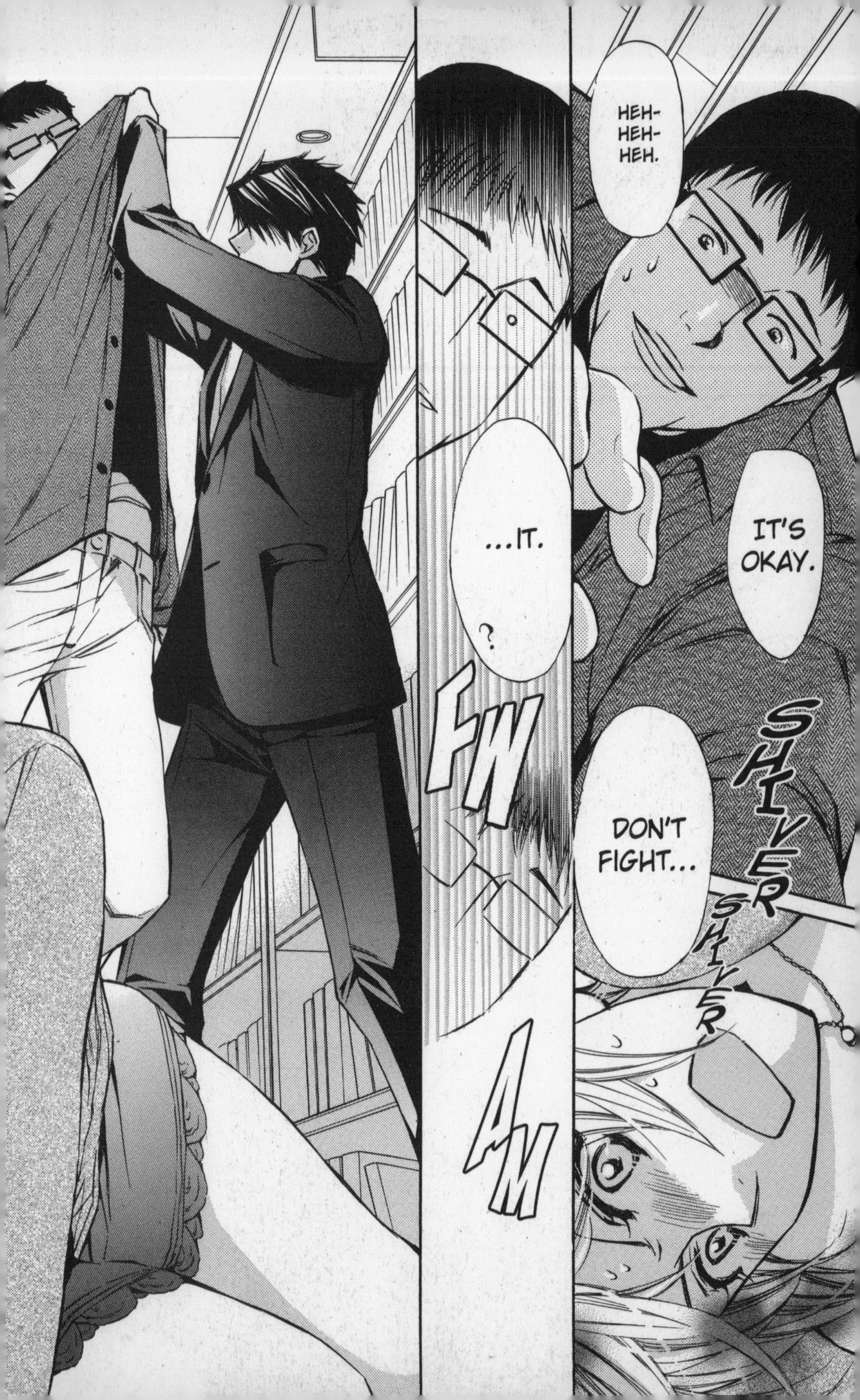
HEH-HEH-HEH.
IT'S OKAY.
DON'T FIGHT...
SHIVER
SHIVER
...IT.
?
FW
AM

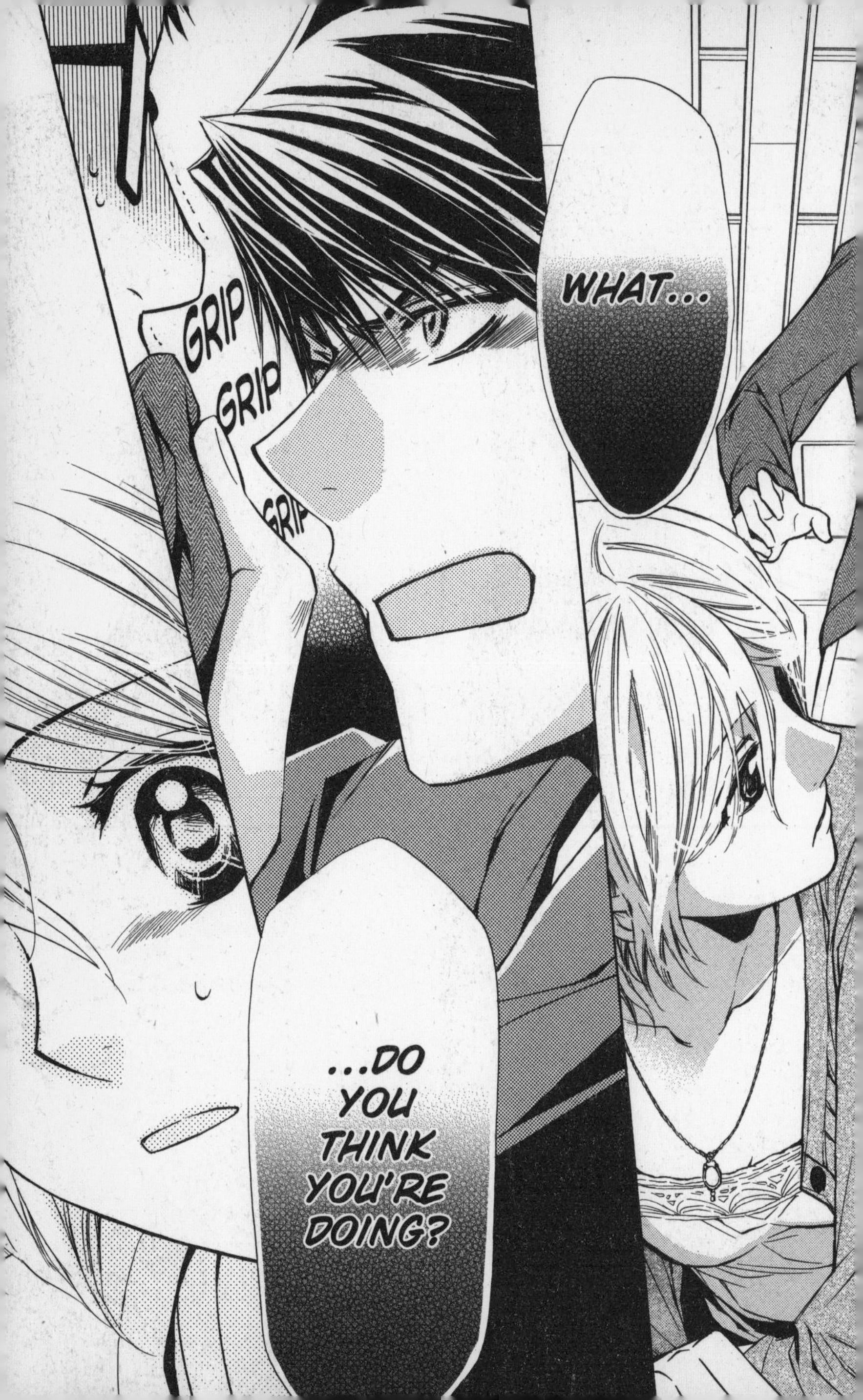
WHAT...
GRIP
GRIP
GRIP
...DO YOU THINK YOU'RE DOING?

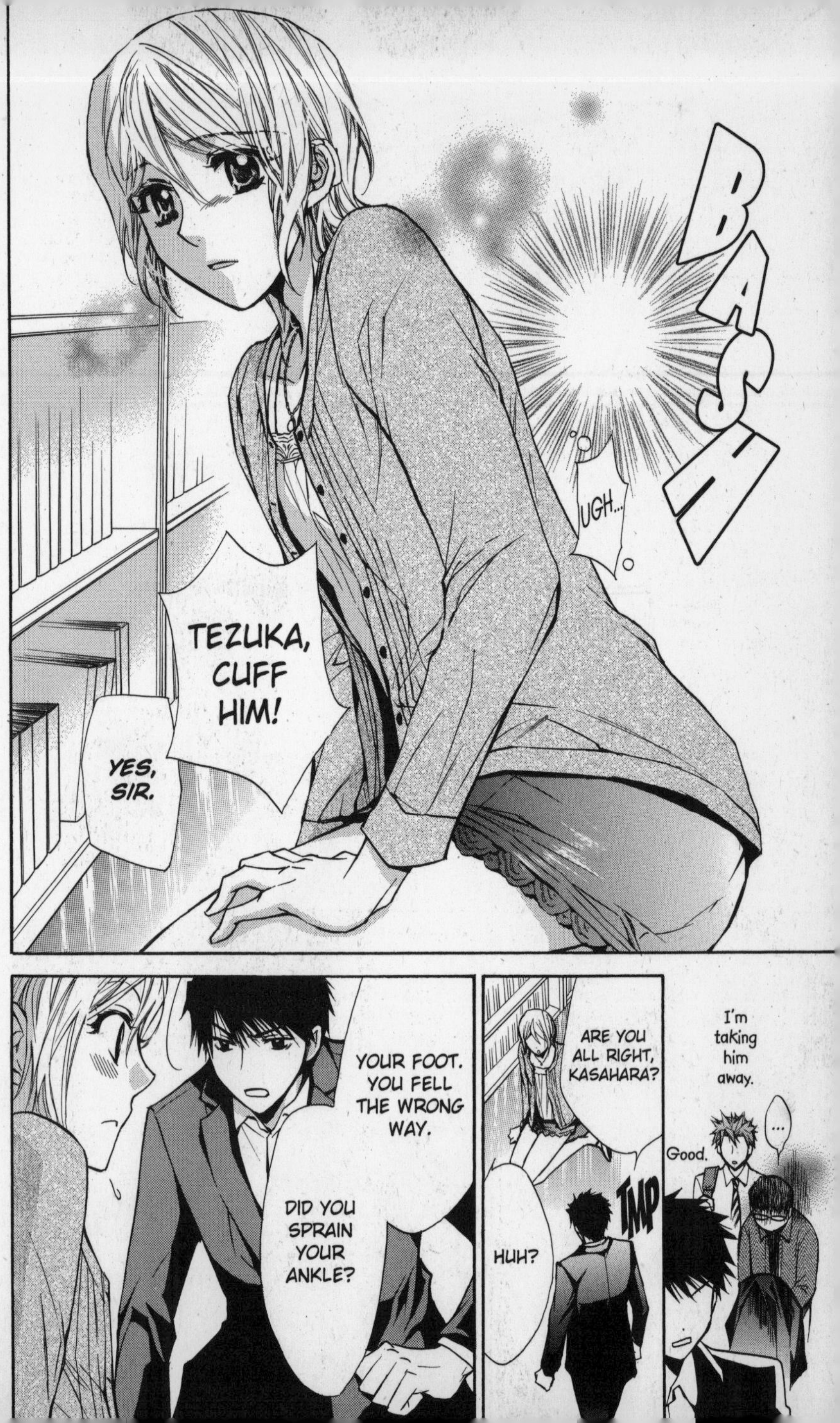
BASH
UGH...
TEZUKA, CUFF HIM!
YES, SIR.
I'm taking him away.
...
Good.
ARE YOU ALL RIGHT, KASAHARA?
TMP
HUH?
YOUR FOOT. YOU FELL THE WRONG WAY.
DID YOU SPRAIN YOUR ANKLE?

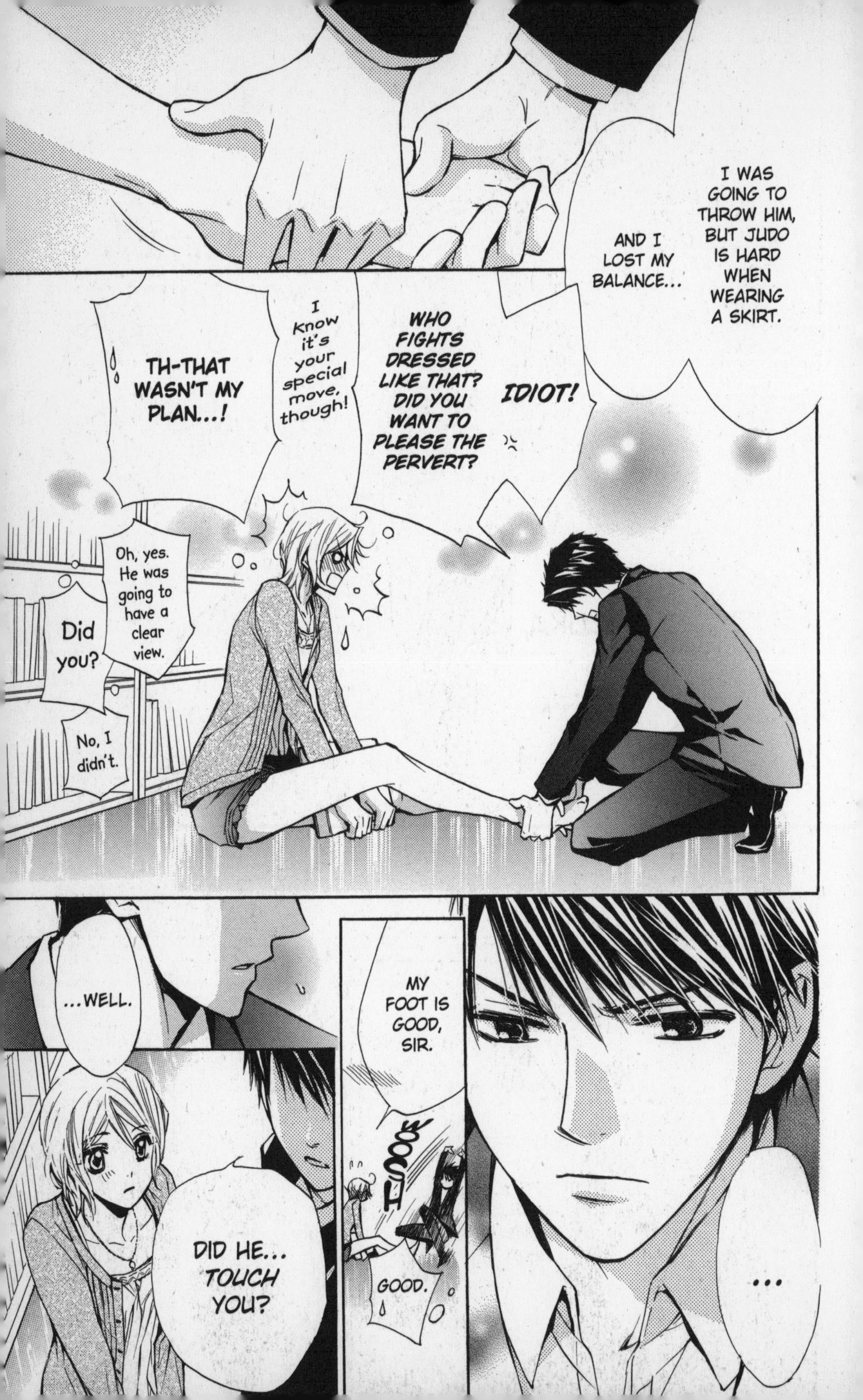
I WAS GOING TO THROW HIM, BUT JUDO IS HARD WHEN WEARING A SKIRT.
AND I LOST MY BALANCE...
IDIOT!
WHO FIGHTS DRESSED LIKE THAT? DID YOU WANT TO PLEASE THE PERVERT?
I know it's your special move, though!
TH-THAT WASN'T MY PLAN...!
Oh, yes. He was going to have a clear view.
Did you?
No, I didn't.
...
MY FOOT IS GOOD, SIR.
WOOSH
GOOD.
...WELL.
DID HE... TOUCH YOU?

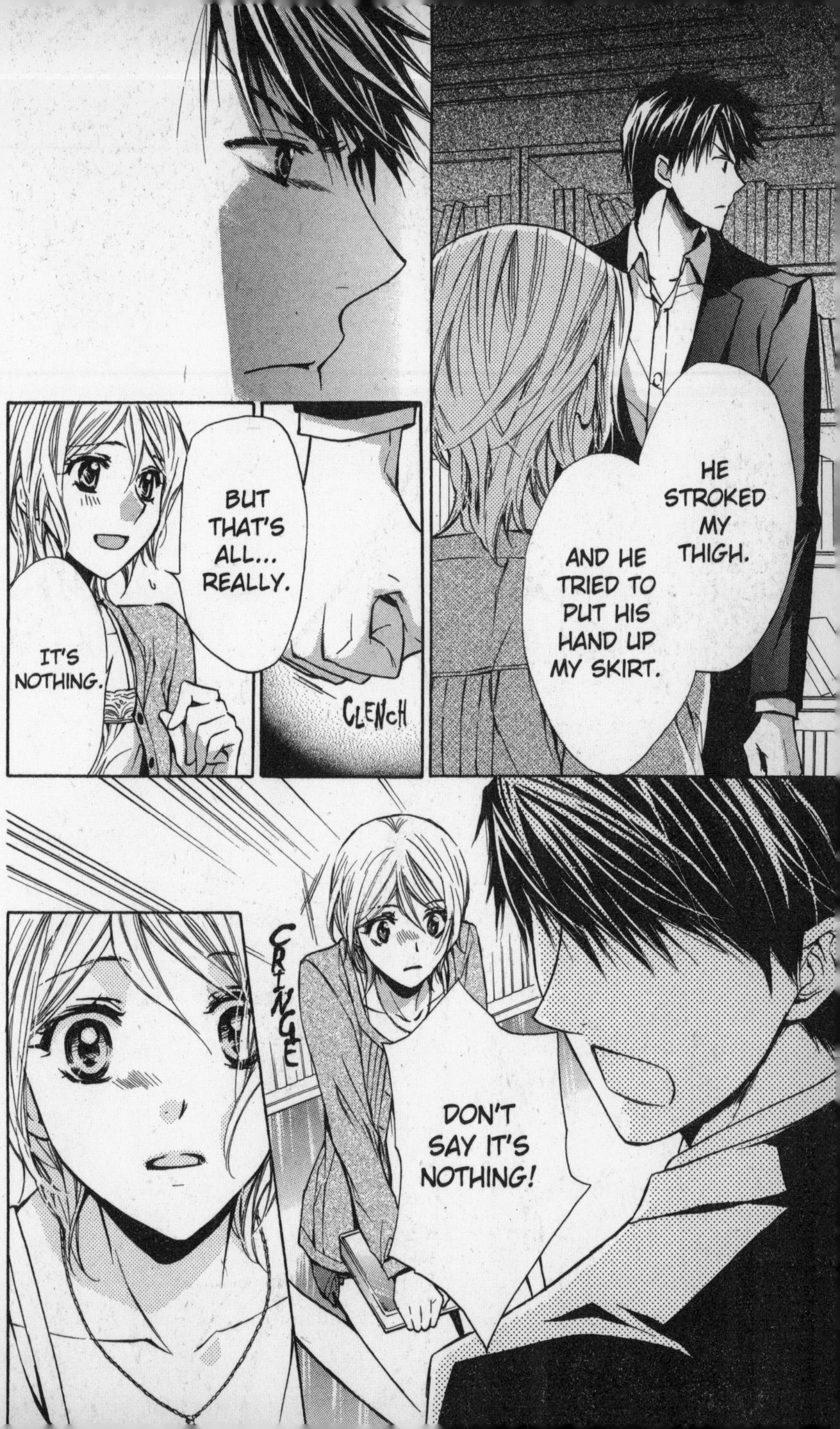
HE STROKED MY THIGH.
AND HE TRIED TO PUT HIS HAND UP MY SKIRT.
CLENCH
BUT THAT'S ALL... REALLY.
IT'S NOTHING.
DON'T SAY IT'S NOTHING!
CRINGE

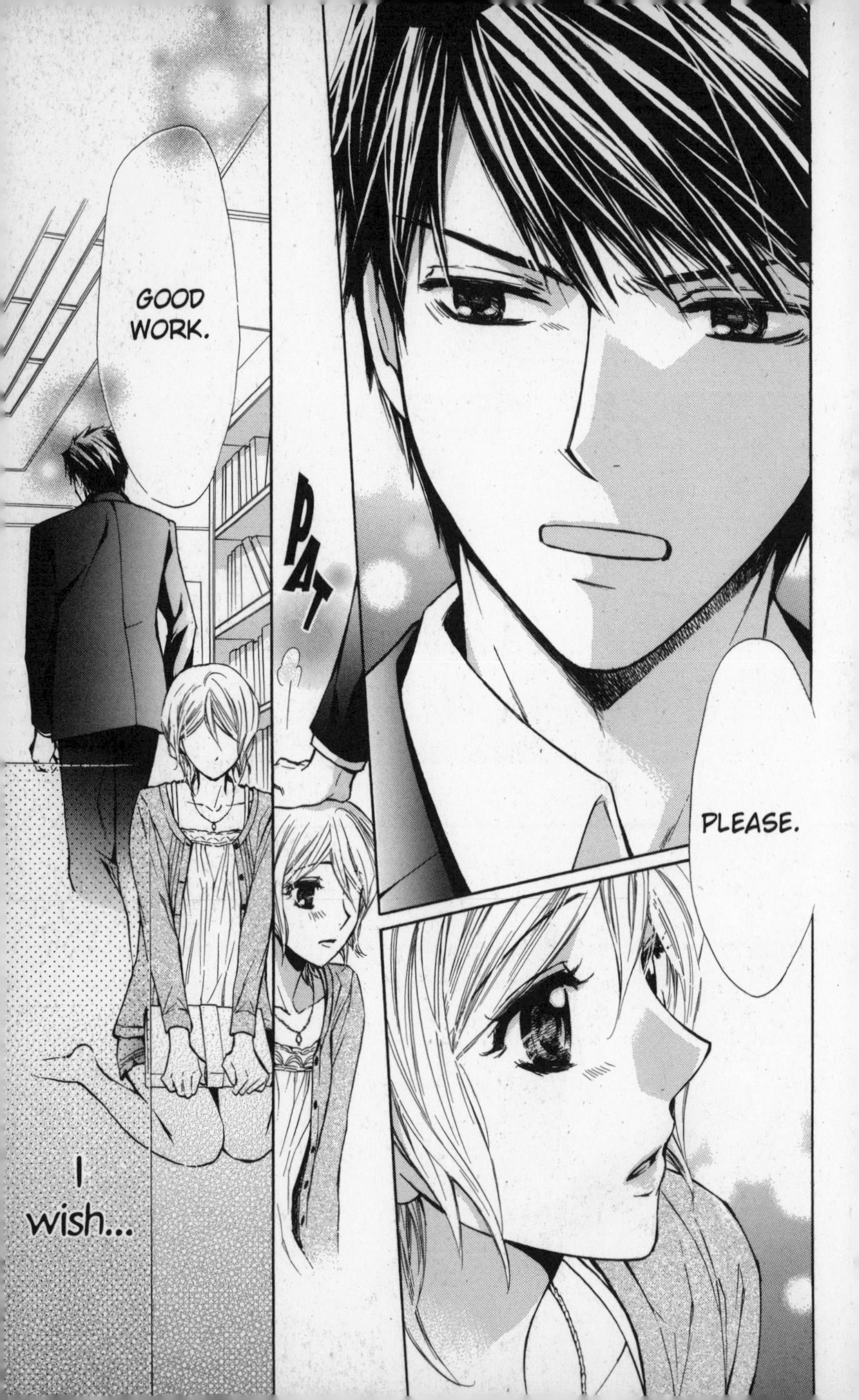
PLEASE.
PAT
GOOD WORK.
I wish...

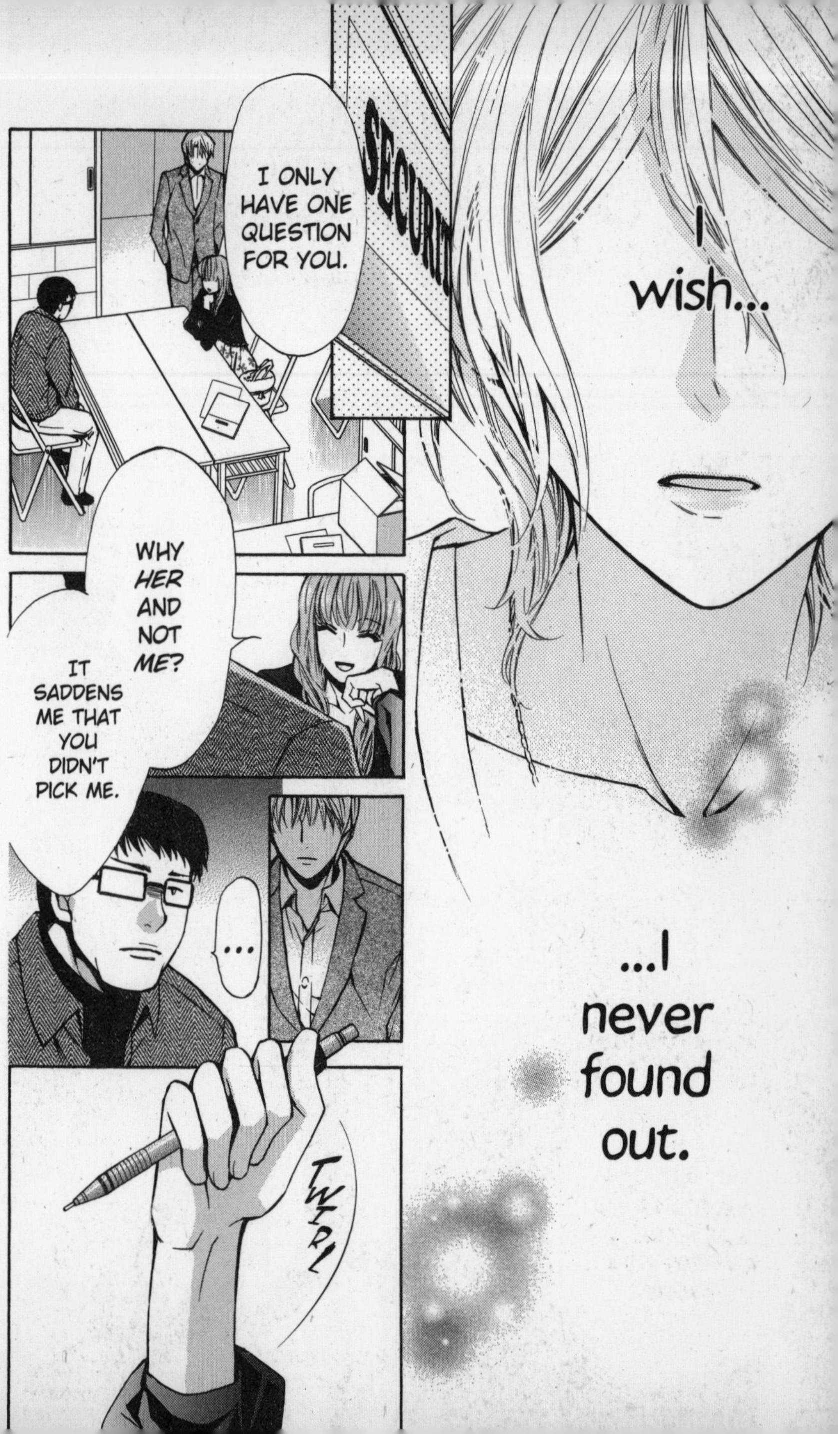
I wish...
...I never found out.
SECURIT
I ONLY HAVE ONE QUESTION FOR YOU.
WHY HER AND NOT ME?
IT SADDENS ME THAT YOU DIDN'T PICK ME.
...
TWIRL

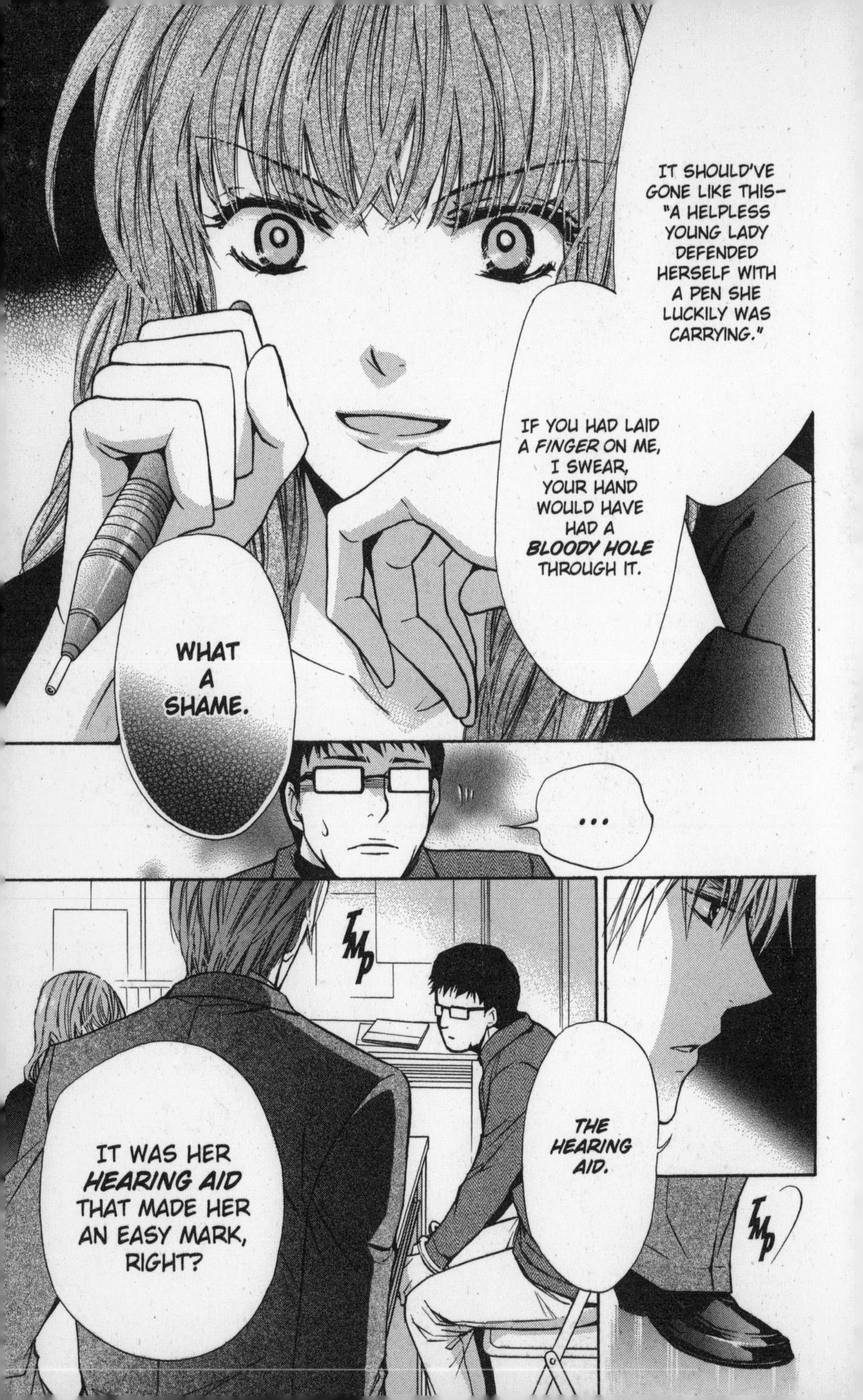

IT SHOULD'VE GONE LIKE THIS– "A HELPLESS YOUNG LADY DEFENDED HERSELF WITH A PEN SHE LUCKILY WAS CARRYING."
IF YOU HAD LAID A *FINGER* ON ME, I SWEAR, YOUR HAND WOULD HAVE HAD A ***BLOODY HOLE*** THROUGH IT.
WHAT A SHAME.
...
TMP
THE HEARING AID.
TMP
IT WAS HER ***HEARING AID*** THAT MADE HER AN EASY MARK, RIGHT?

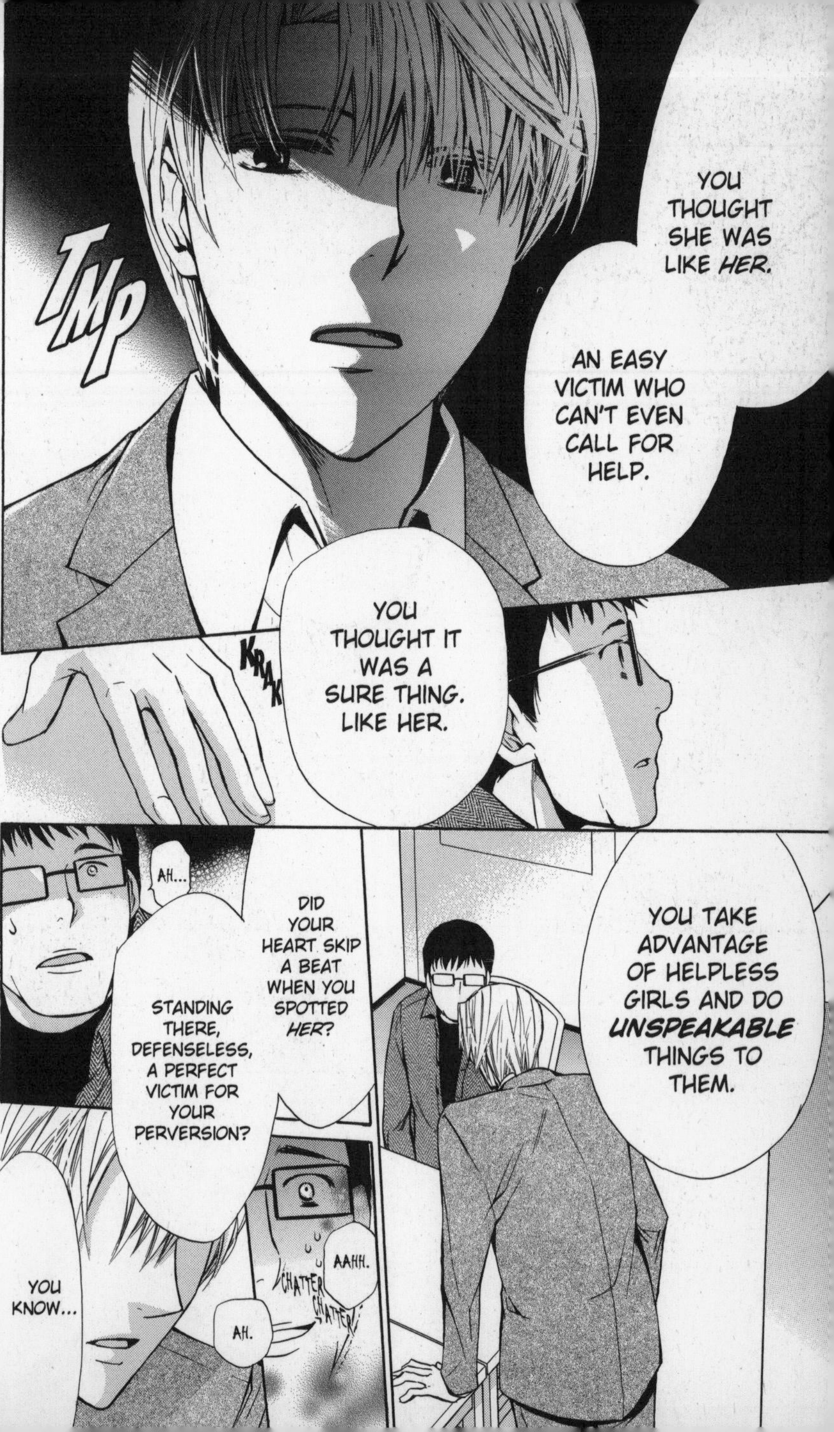
YOU THOUGHT SHE WAS LIKE *HER*.
AN EASY VICTIM WHO CAN'T EVEN CALL FOR HELP.
TMP
YOU THOUGHT IT WAS A SURE THING. LIKE HER.
KRAK
YOU TAKE ADVANTAGE OF HELPLESS GIRLS AND DO ***UNSPEAKABLE*** THINGS TO THEM.
DID YOUR HEART SKIP A BEAT WHEN YOU SPOTTED *HER*?
AH...
STANDING THERE, DEFENSELESS, A PERFECT VICTIM FOR YOUR PERVERSION?
AAHH.
CHATTER CHATTER
AH.
YOU KNOW...

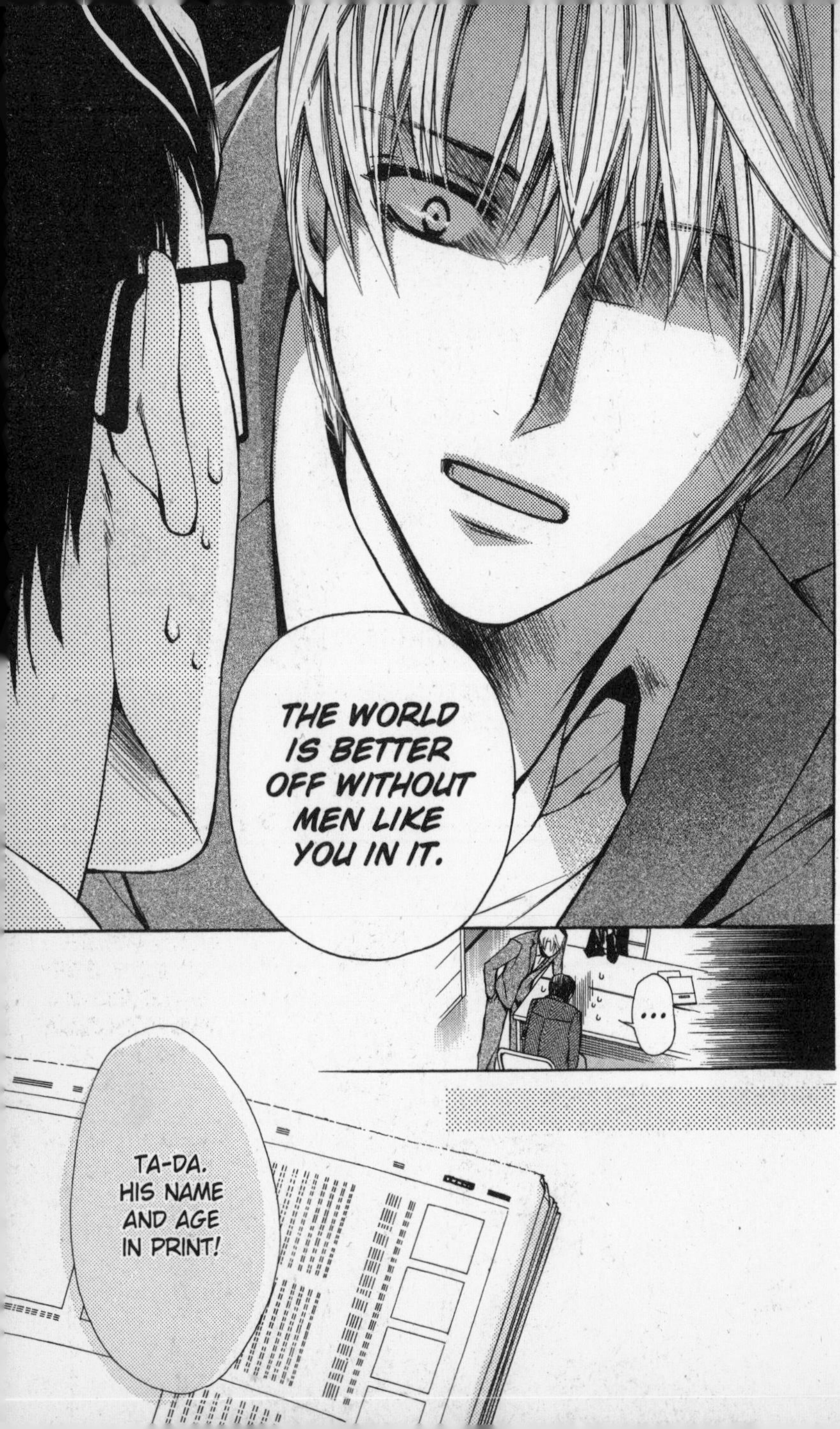
THE WORLD IS BETTER OFF WITHOUT MEN LIKE YOU IN IT.
...
TA-DA. HIS NAME AND AGE IN PRINT!

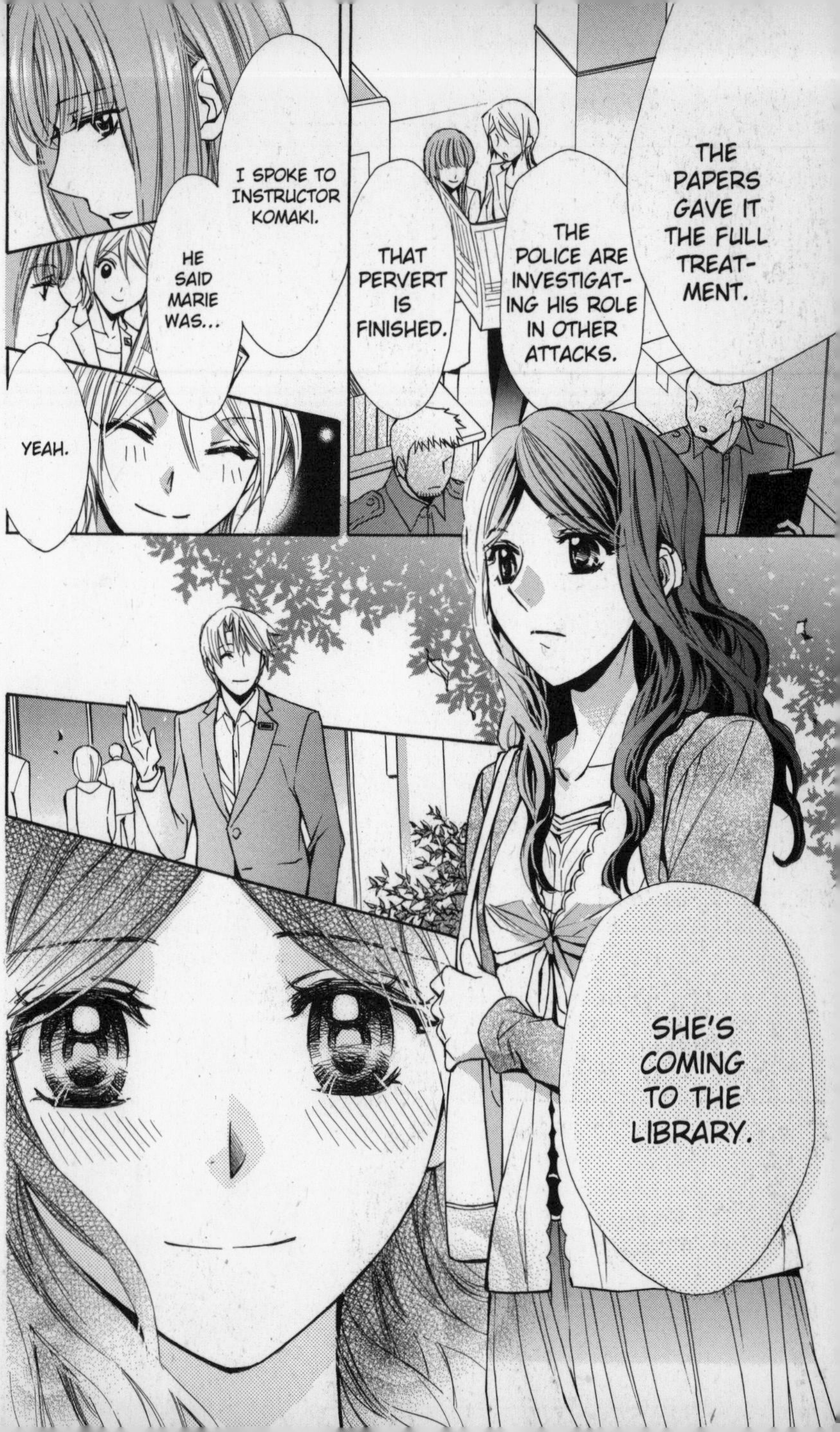
THE PAPERS GAVE IT THE FULL TREAT-MENT.
THE POLICE ARE INVESTIGAT-ING HIS ROLE IN OTHER ATTACKS.
THAT PERVERT IS FINISHED.
I SPOKE TO INSTRUCTOR KOMAKI.
HE SAID MARIE WAS...
YEAH.
SHE'S COMING TO THE LIBRARY.

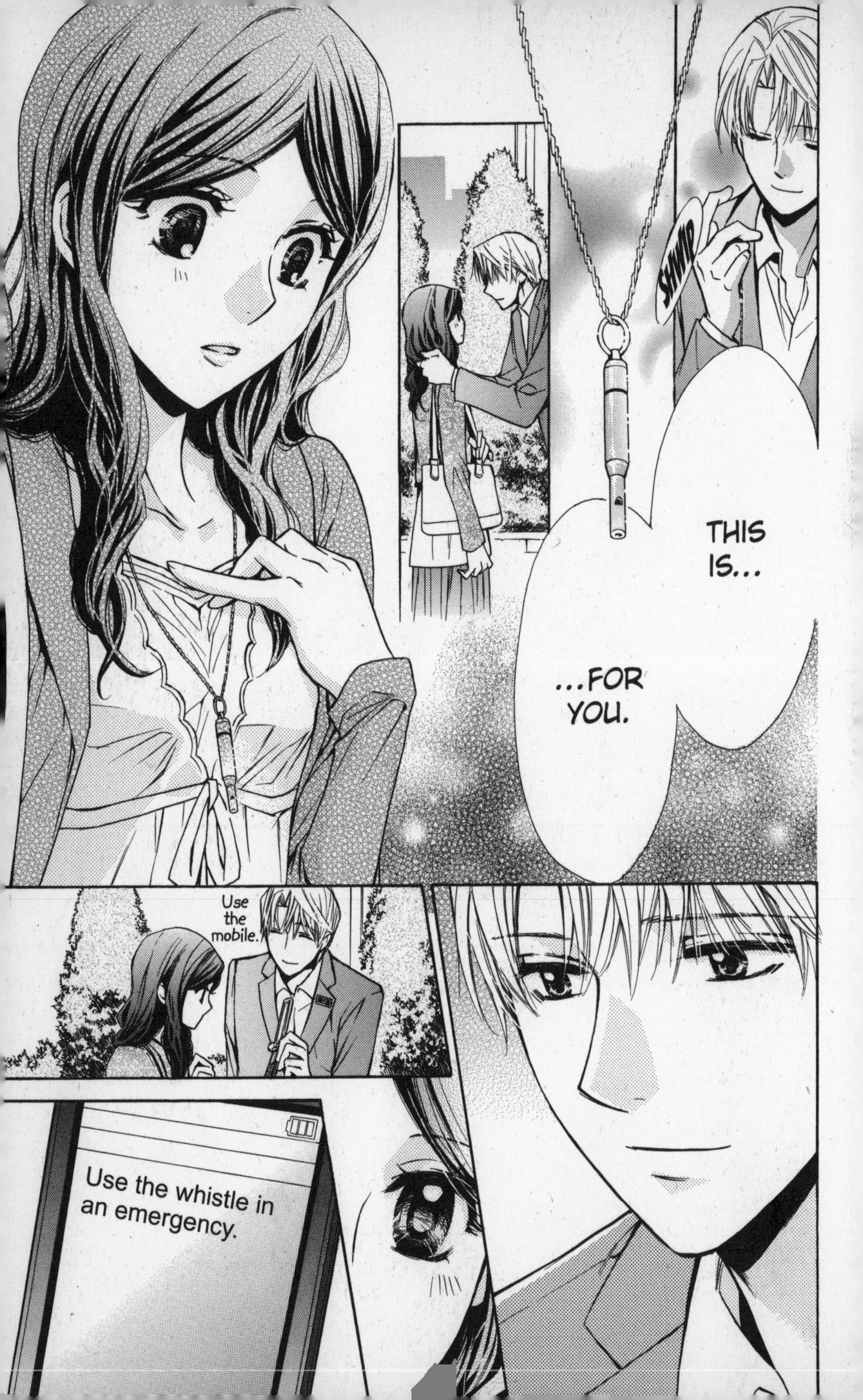
SHWIP
THIS IS...
...FOR YOU.
Use the mobile.
Use the whistle in an emergency.

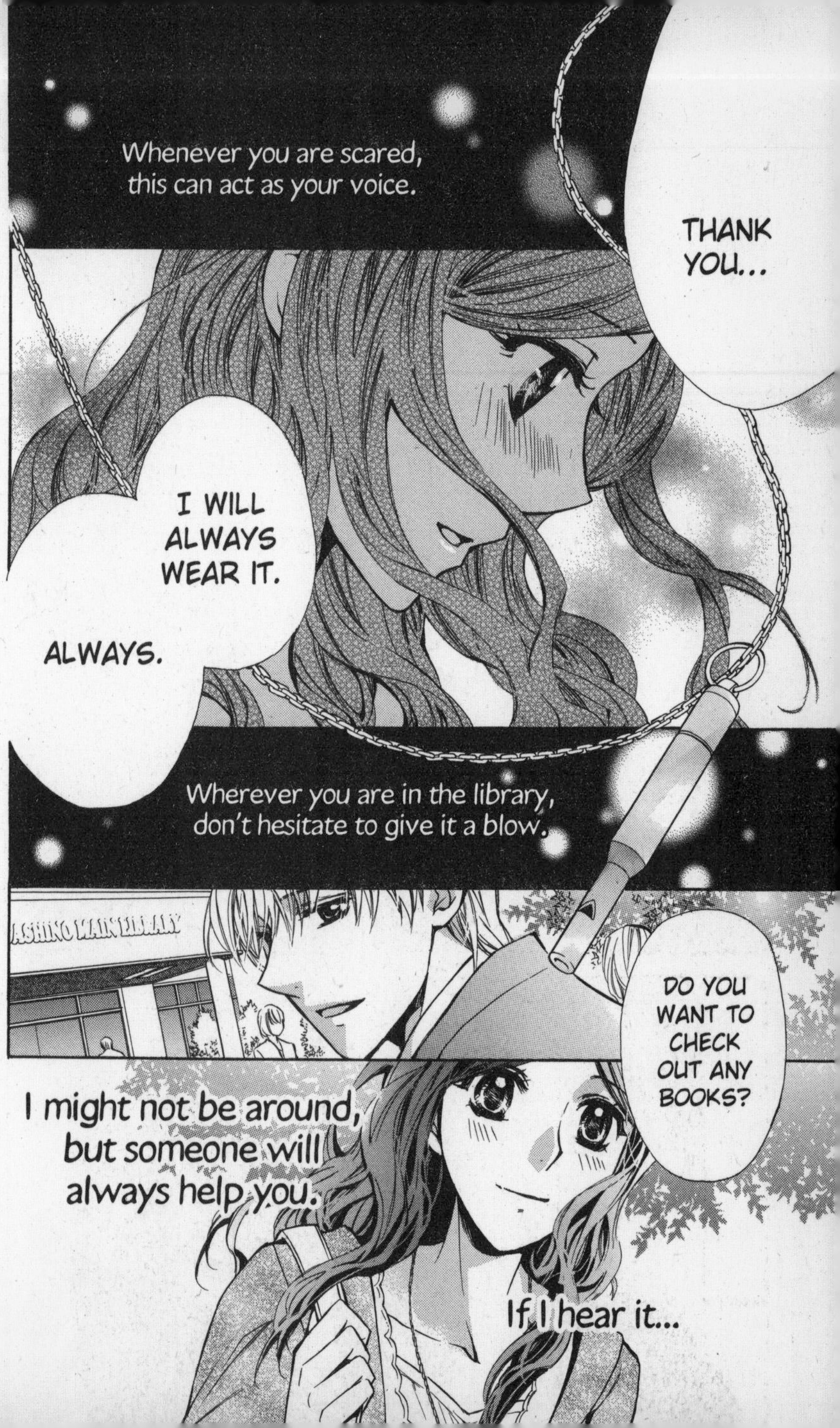
Whenever you are scared, this can act as your voice.
THANK YOU...
I WILL ALWAYS WEAR IT.
ALWAYS.
Wherever you are in the library, don't hesitate to give it a blow.
ASHINO MAIN LIBRARY
DO YOU WANT TO CHECK OUT ANY BOOKS?
I might not be around, but someone will always help you.
If I hear it...

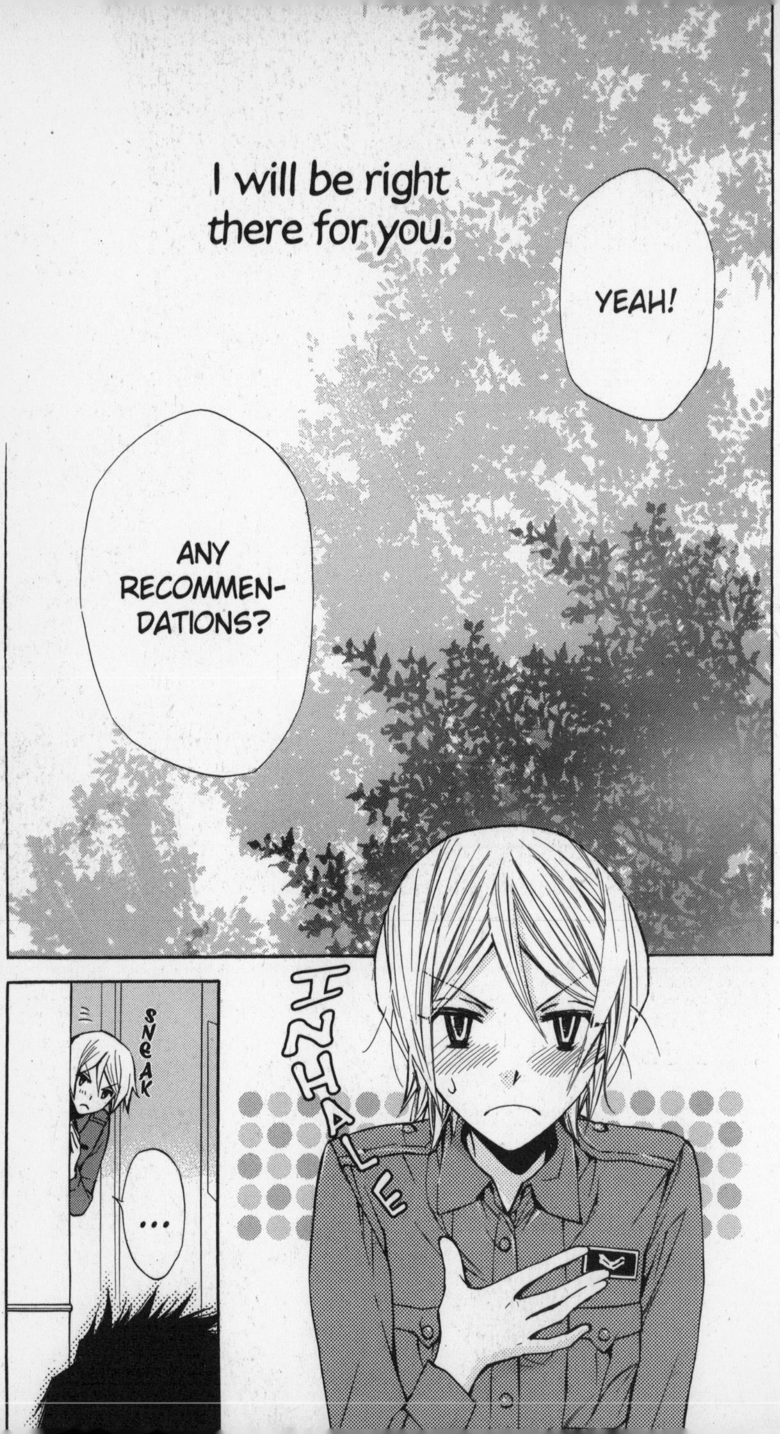

I will be right there for you.
YEAH!
ANY RECOMMEN-DATIONS?
INHALE
SNEAK
...

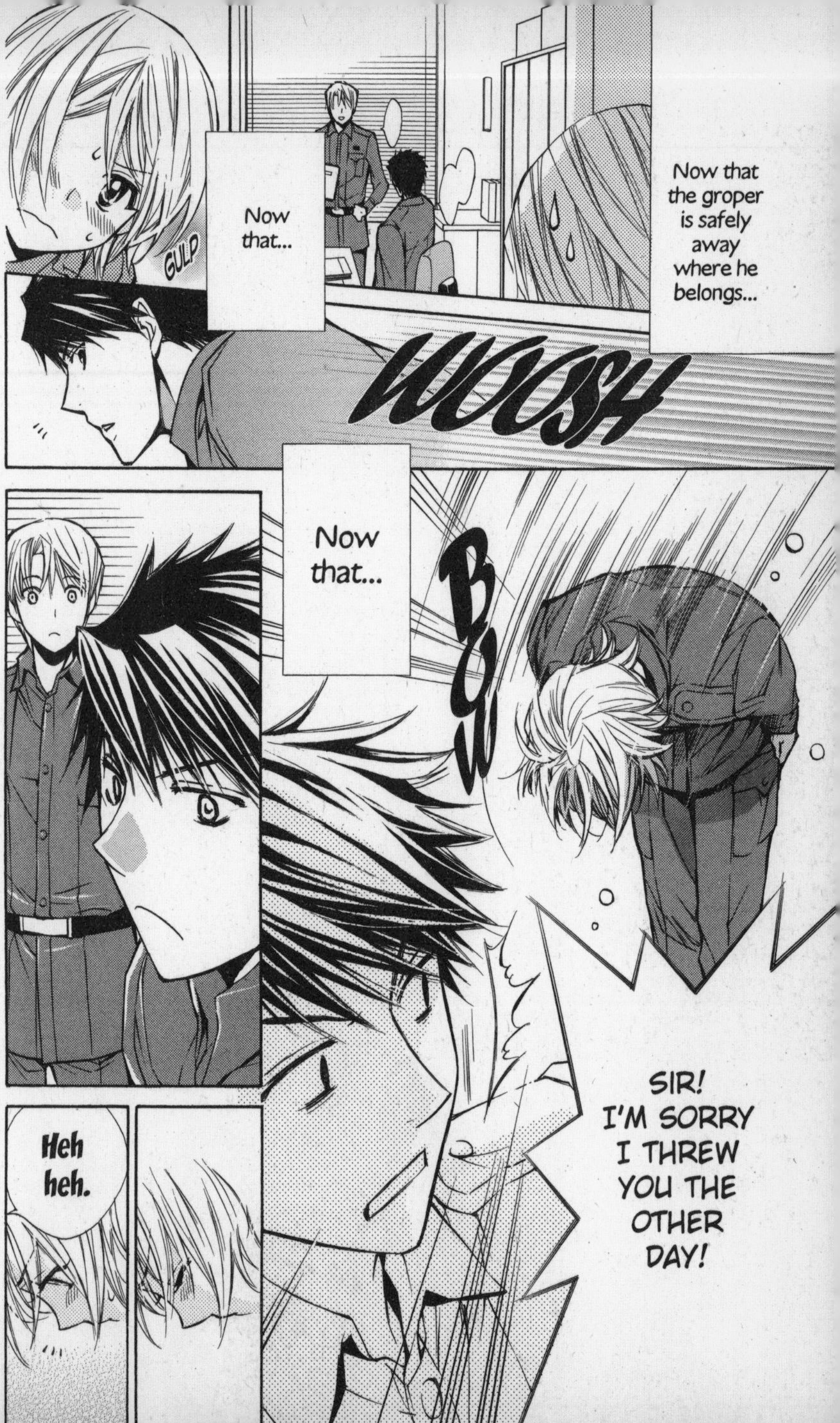
Now that the groper is safely away where he belongs...
Now that...
GULP
WOOSH
Now that...
BOW
SIR! I'M SORRY I THREW YOU THE OTHER DAY!
Heh heh.

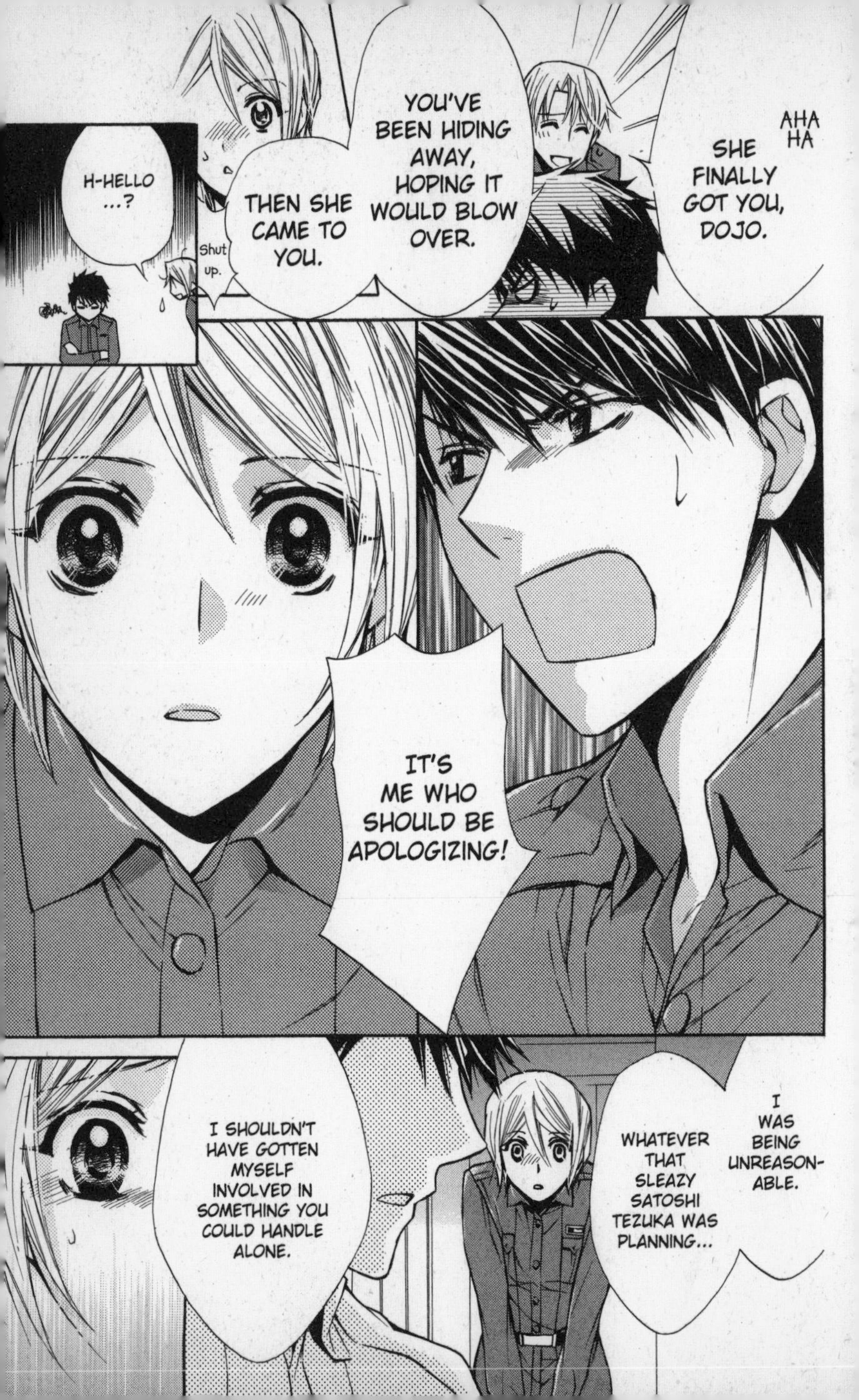
AHA HA
SHE FINALLY GOT YOU, DOJO.
YOU'VE BEEN HIDING AWAY, HOPING IT WOULD BLOW OVER.
THEN SHE CAME TO YOU.
Shut up.
H-HELLO ...?
IT'S ME WHO SHOULD BE APOLOGIZING!
I WAS BEING UNREASON-ABLE.
WHATEVER THAT SLEAZY SATOSHI TEZUKA WAS PLANNING...
I SHOULDN'T HAVE GOTTEN MYSELF INVOLVED IN SOMETHING YOU COULD HANDLE ALONE.

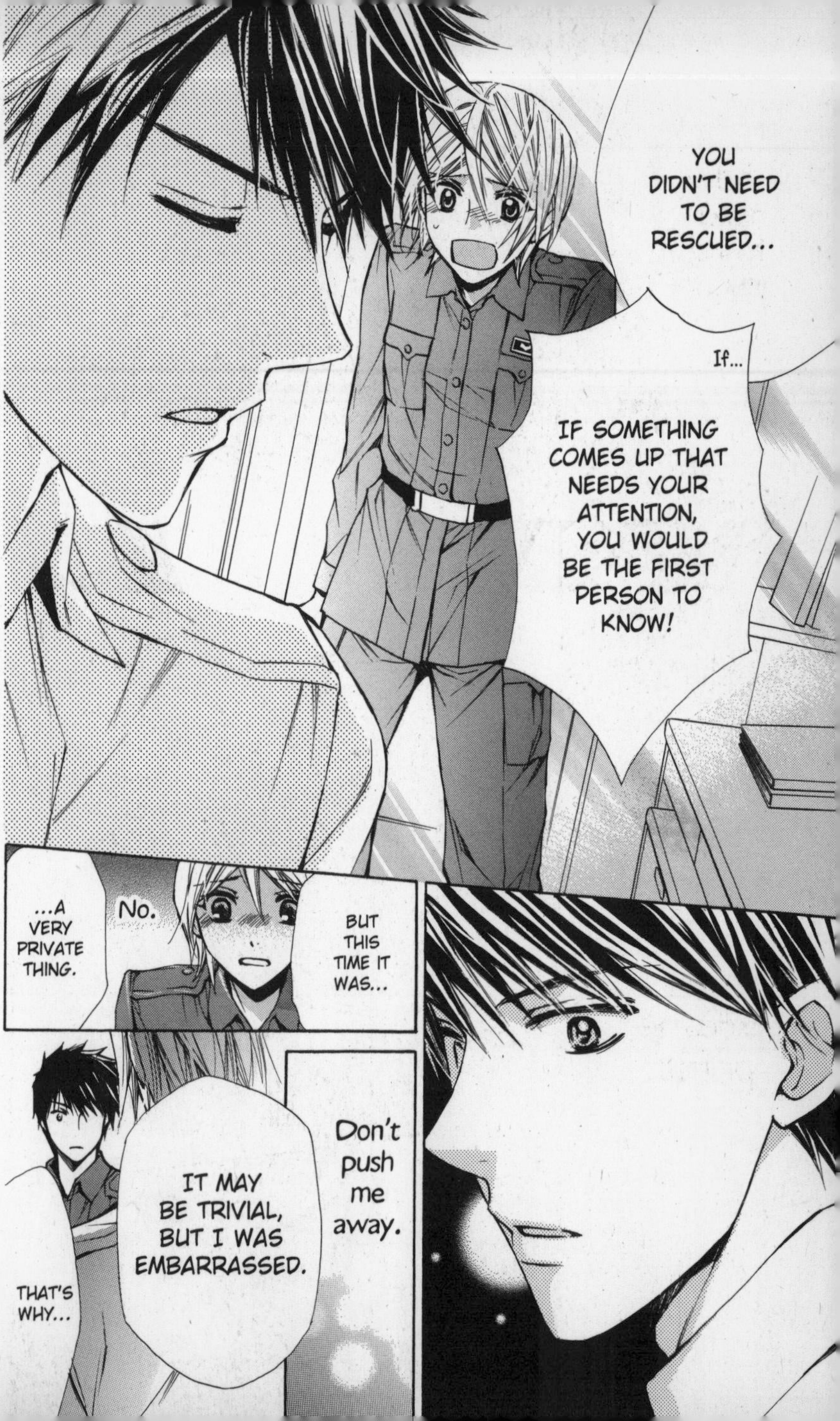
YOU DIDN'T NEED TO BE RESCUED...
If...
IF SOMETHING COMES UP THAT NEEDS YOUR ATTENTION, YOU WOULD BE THE FIRST PERSON TO KNOW!
BUT THIS TIME IT WAS...
No.
...A VERY PRIVATE THING.
Don't push me away.
IT MAY BE TRIVIAL, BUT I WAS EMBARRASSED.
THAT'S WHY...

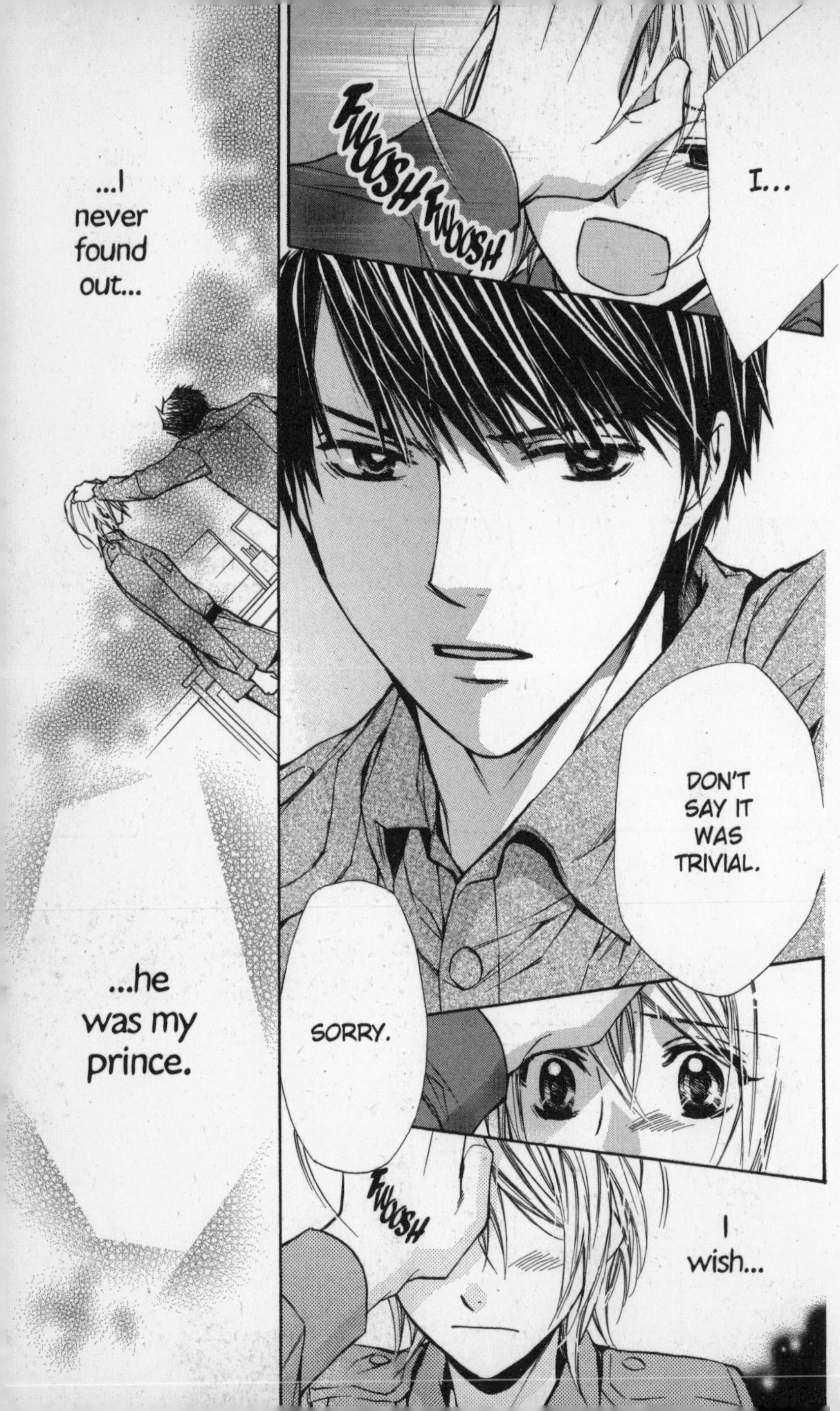
FWOOSH FWOOSH
I...
DON'T SAY IT WAS TRIVIAL.
SORRY.
FWOOSH
I wish...
...I never found out...
...he was my prince.

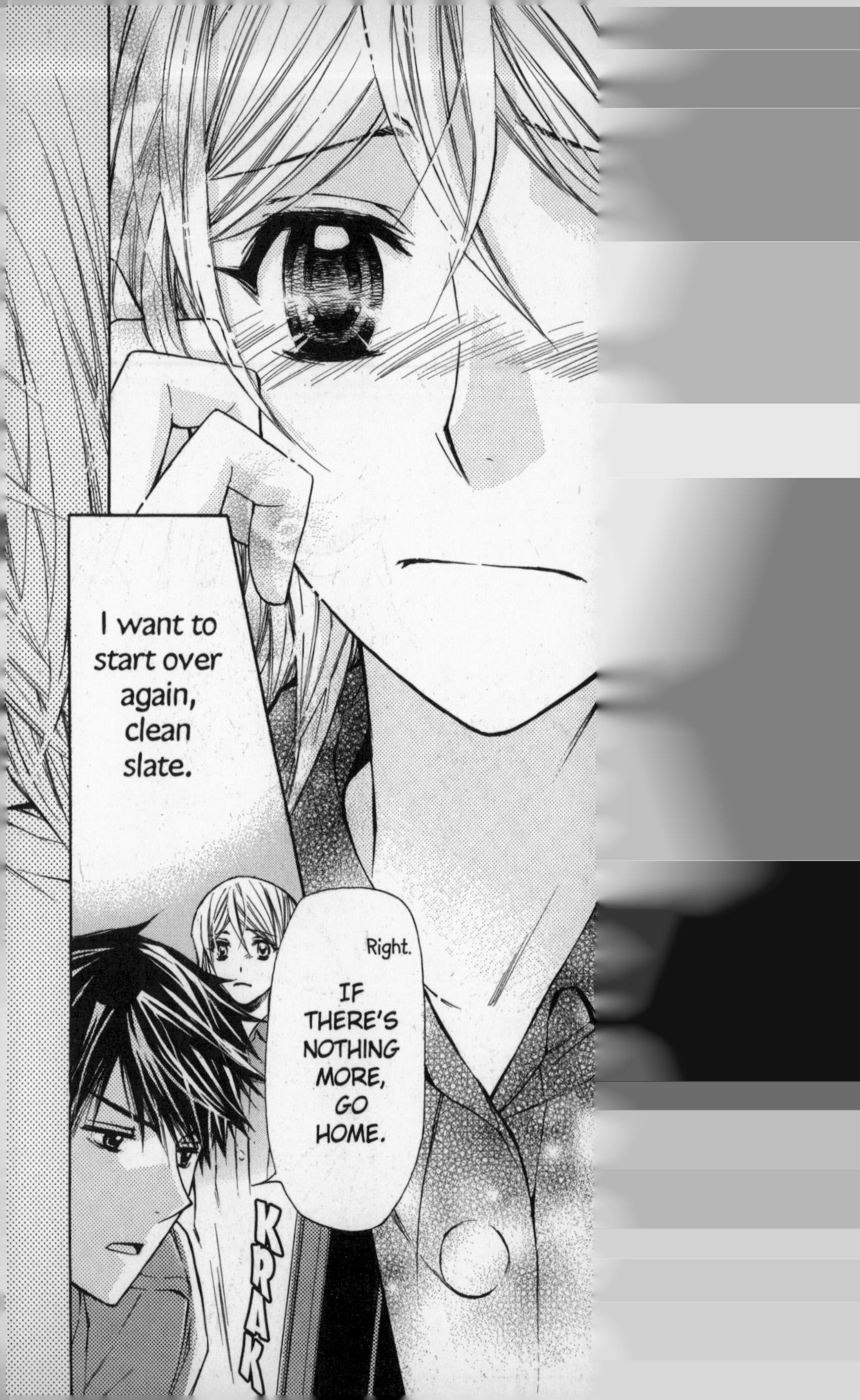
I want to start over again, clean slate.
Right.
IF THERE'S NOTHING MORE, GO HOME.
KRAK

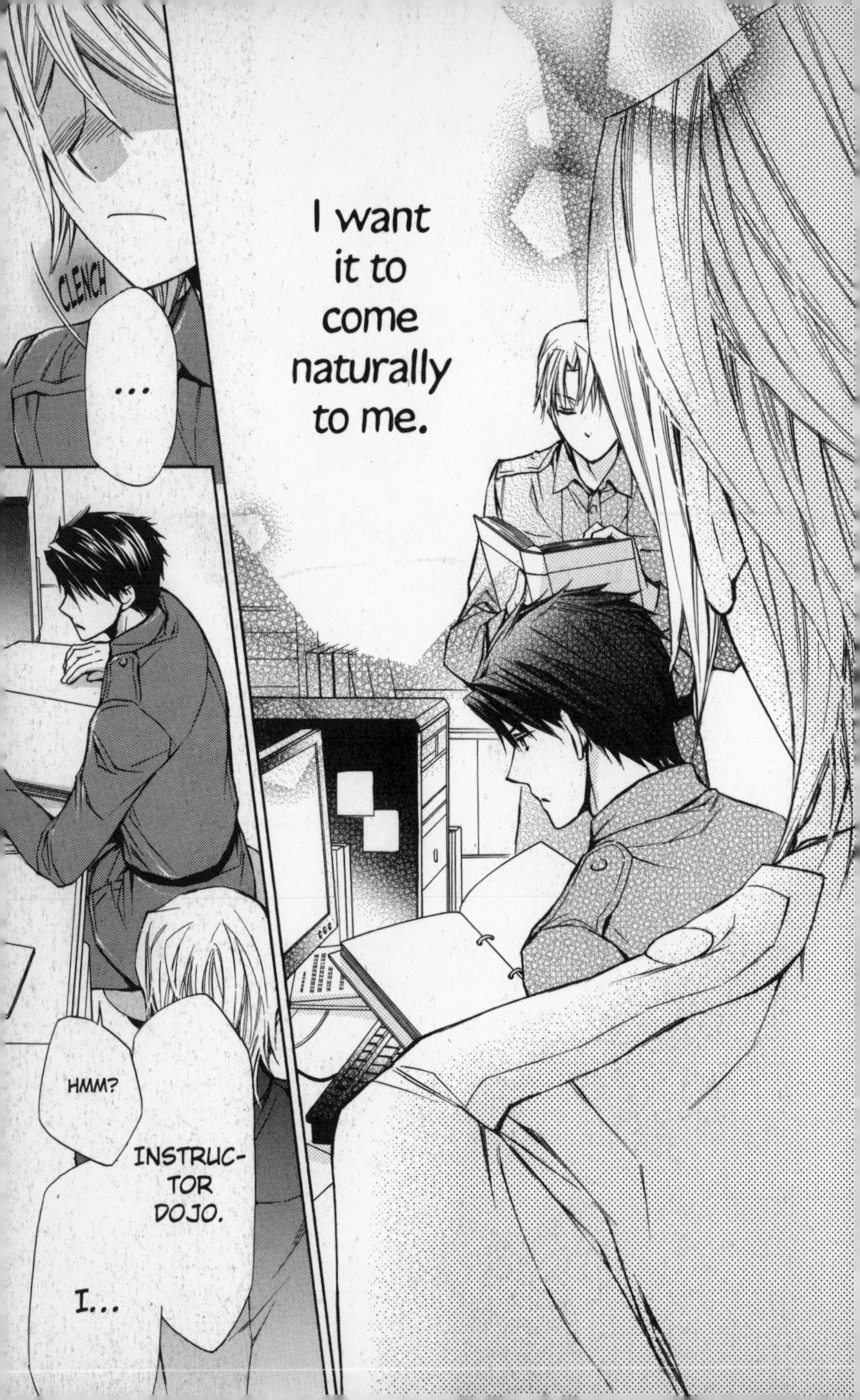
I want it to come naturally to me.
CLENCH
...
INSTRUC-TOR DOJO.
HMM?
I...

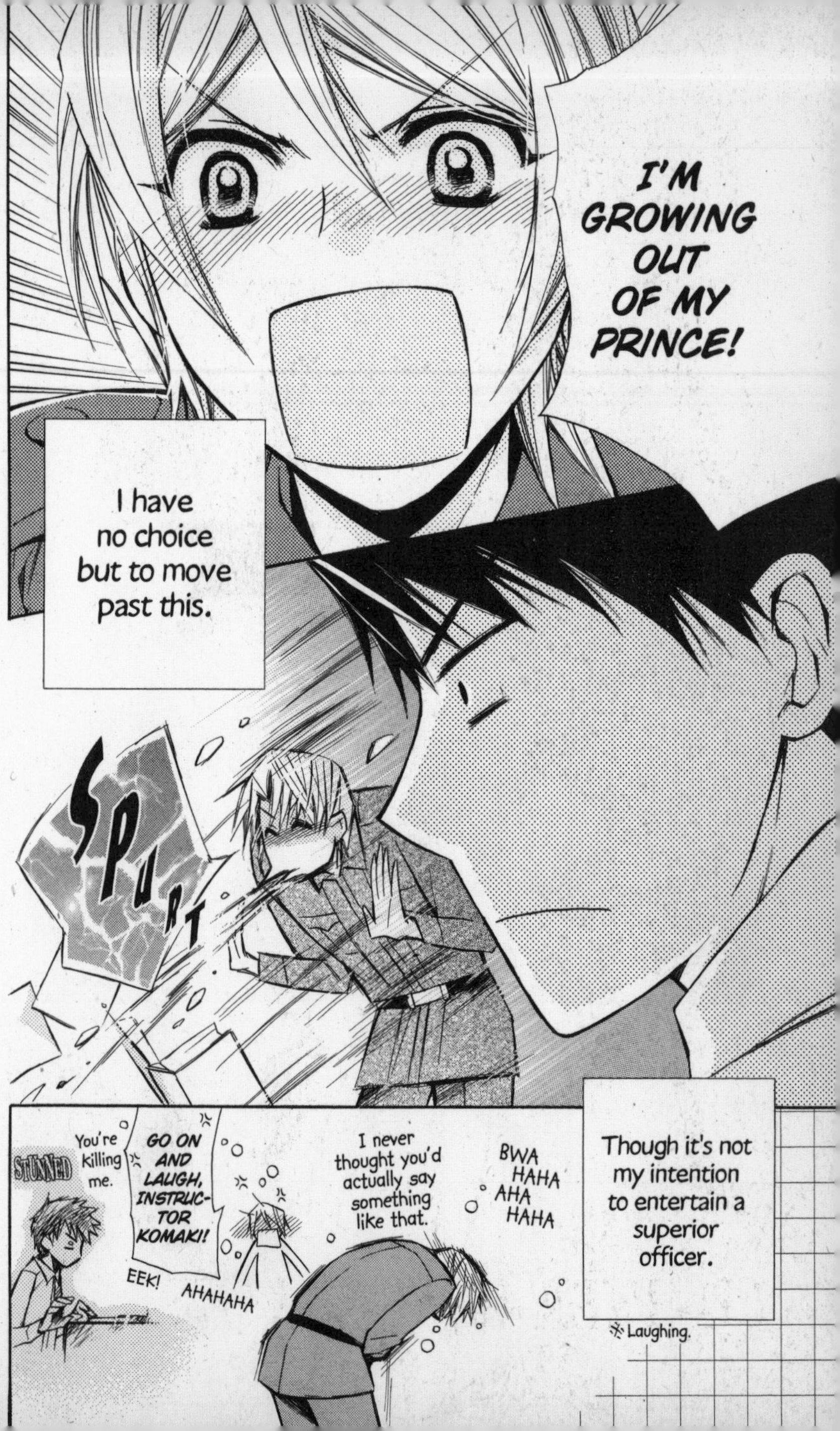
I'M GROWING OUT OF MY PRINCE!
I have no choice but to move past this.
SPURT
Though it's not my intention to entertain a superior officer.
BWA HAHA AHA HAHA
I never thought you'd actually say something like that.
GO ON AND LAUGH, INSTRUCTOR KOMAKI!
You're killing me.
STUNNED
EEK!
AHAHAHA
※Laughing.

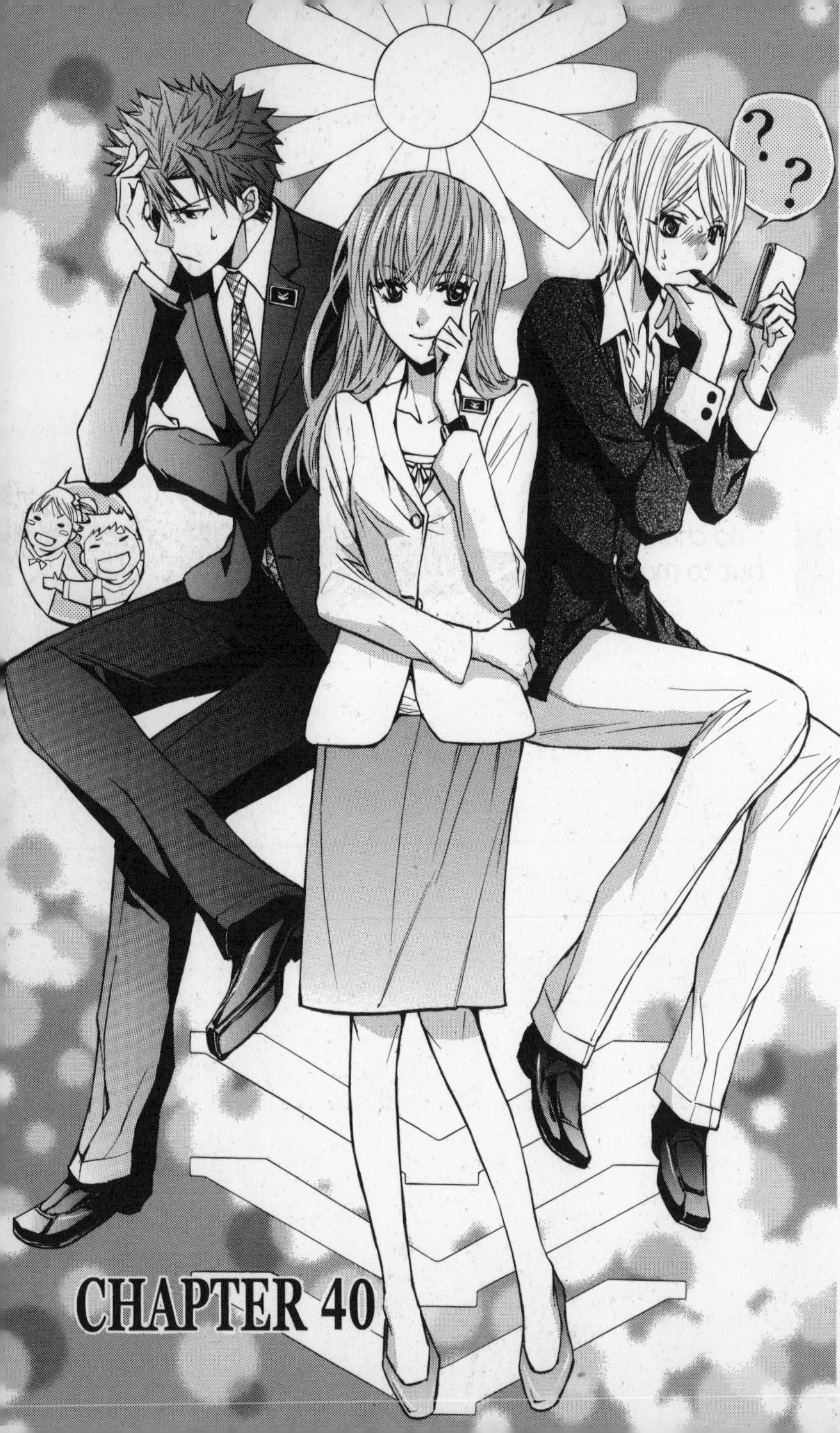
??

CHAPTER 40

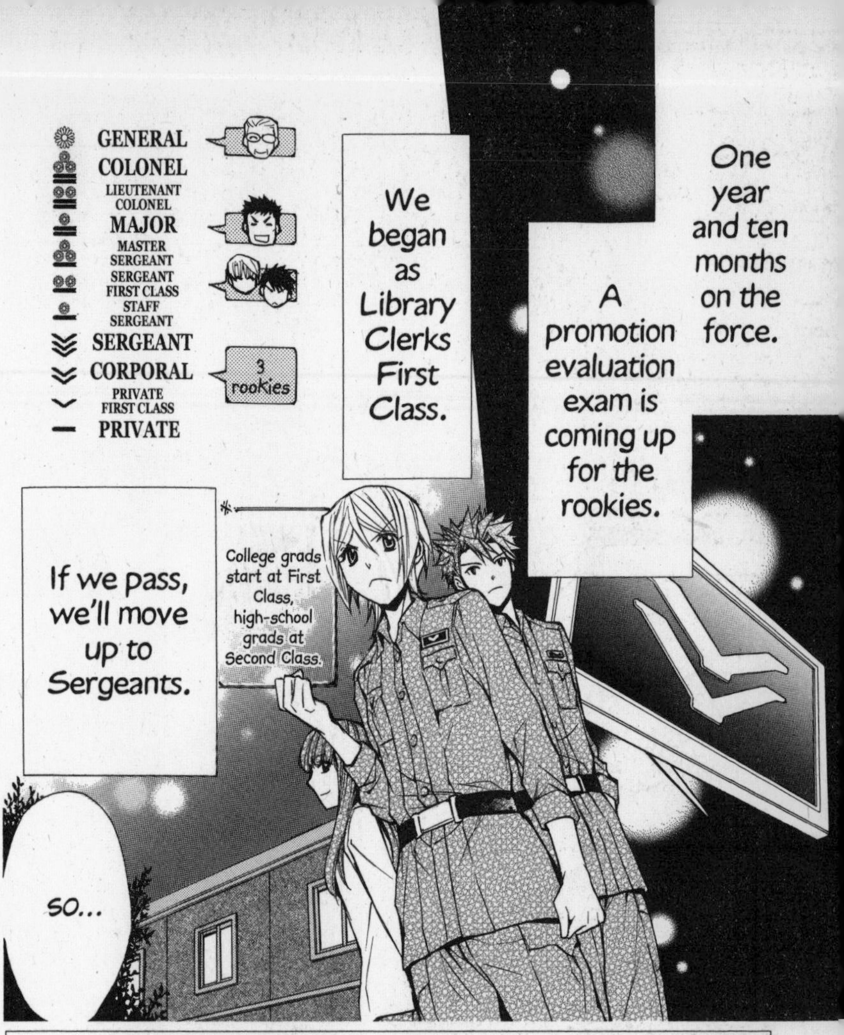
One year and ten months on the force.
A promotion evaluation exam is coming up for the rookies.
We began as Library Clerks First Class.
GENERAL
COLONEL
LIEUTENANT COLONEL
MAJOR
MASTER SERGEANT
SERGEANT FIRST CLASS
STAFF SERGEANT
SERGEANT
CORPORAL
PRIVATE FIRST CLASS
PRIVATE
3 rookies
If we pass, we'll move up to Sergeants.
※ College grads start at First Class, high-school grads at Second Class.
so...

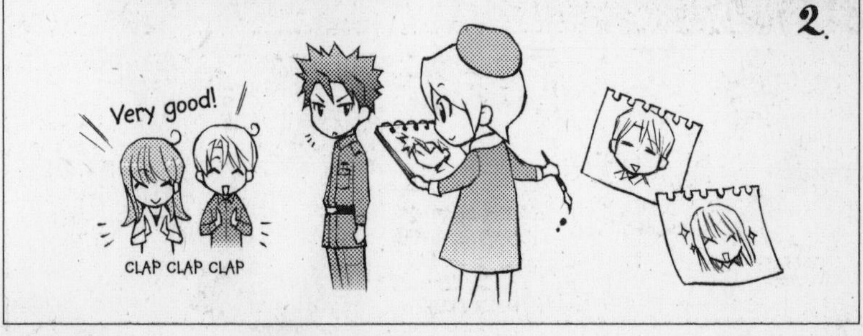
2.
Very good!
CLAP CLAP CLAP

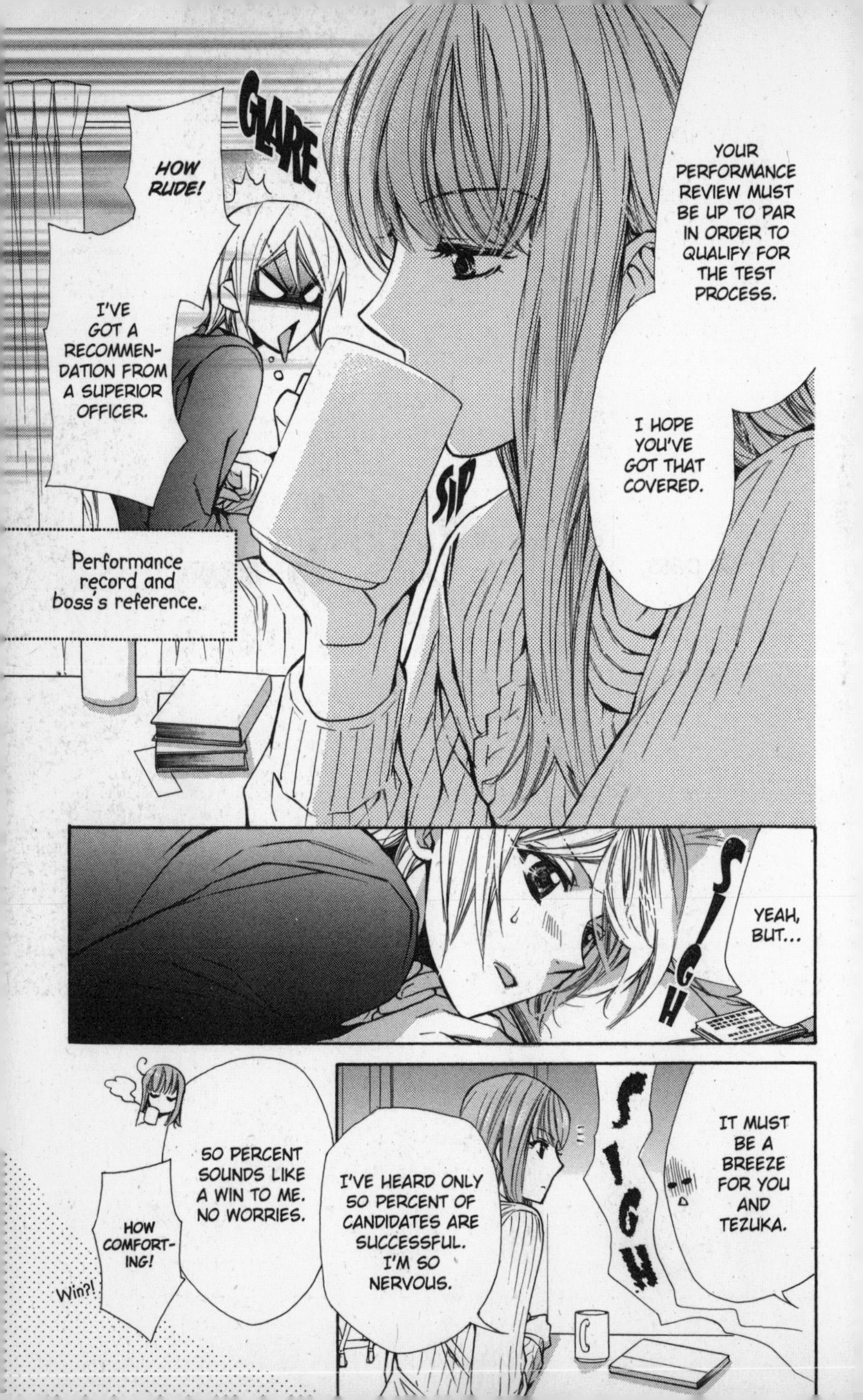
YOUR PERFORMANCE REVIEW MUST BE UP TO PAR IN ORDER TO QUALIFY FOR THE TEST PROCESS.
I HOPE YOU'VE GOT THAT COVERED.
SIP
GLARE
HOW RUDE!
I'VE GOT A RECOMMEN-DATION FROM A SUPERIOR OFFICER.
Performance record and boss's reference.
SIGH
YEAH, BUT...
IT MUST BE A BREEZE FOR YOU AND TEZUKA.
SIGH
I'VE HEARD ONLY 50 PERCENT OF CANDIDATES ARE SUCCESSFUL. I'M SO NERVOUS.
50 PERCENT SOUNDS LIKE A WIN TO ME. NO WORRIES.
HOW COMFORT-ING!
Win?!

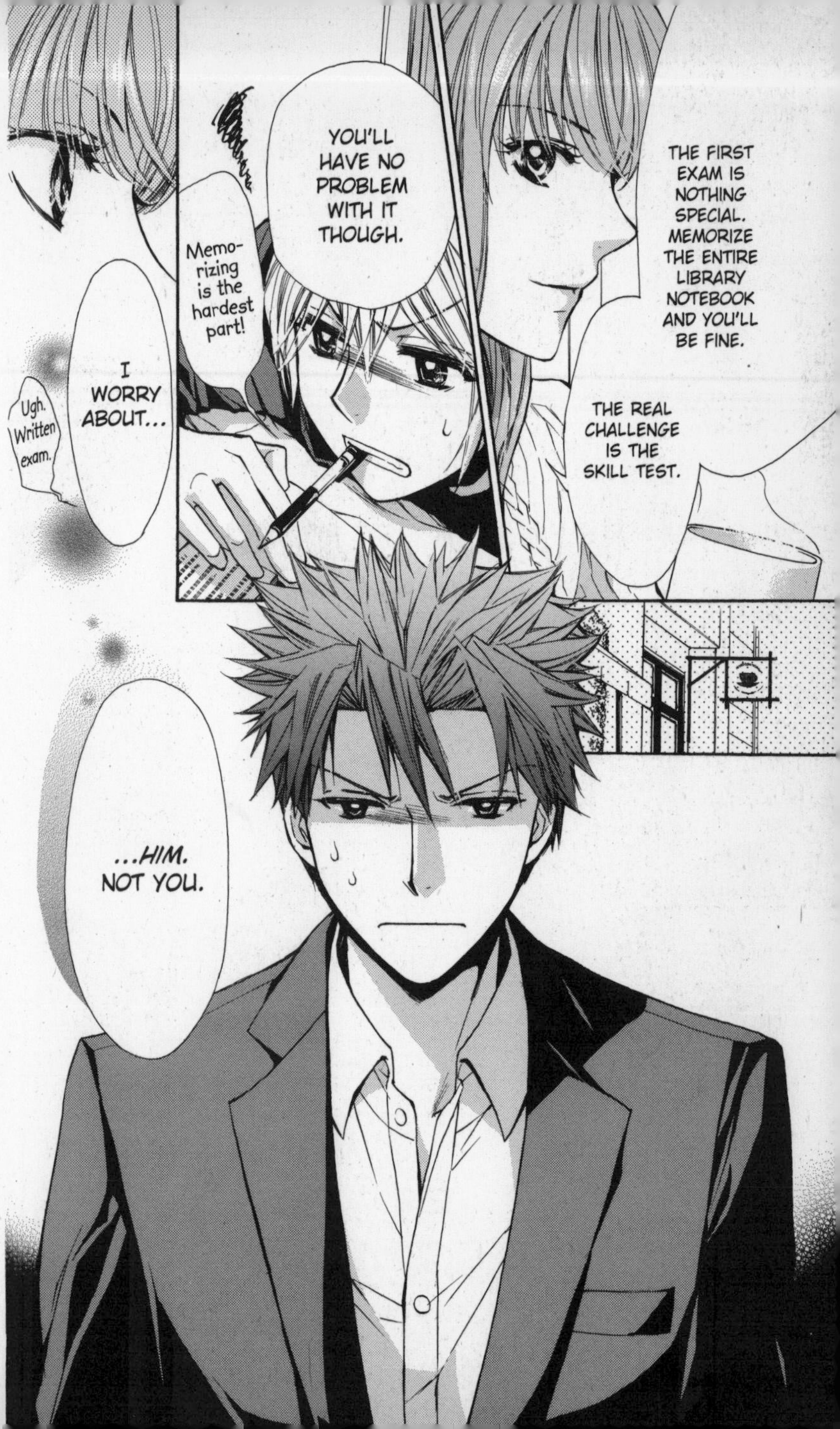
THE FIRST EXAM IS NOTHING SPECIAL. MEMORIZE THE ENTIRE LIBRARY NOTEBOOK AND YOU'LL BE FINE.
THE REAL CHALLENGE IS THE SKILL TEST.
YOU'LL HAVE NO PROBLEM WITH IT THOUGH.
Memo-rizing is the hardest part!
I WORRY ABOUT...
Ugh. Written exam.
...HIM. NOT YOU.

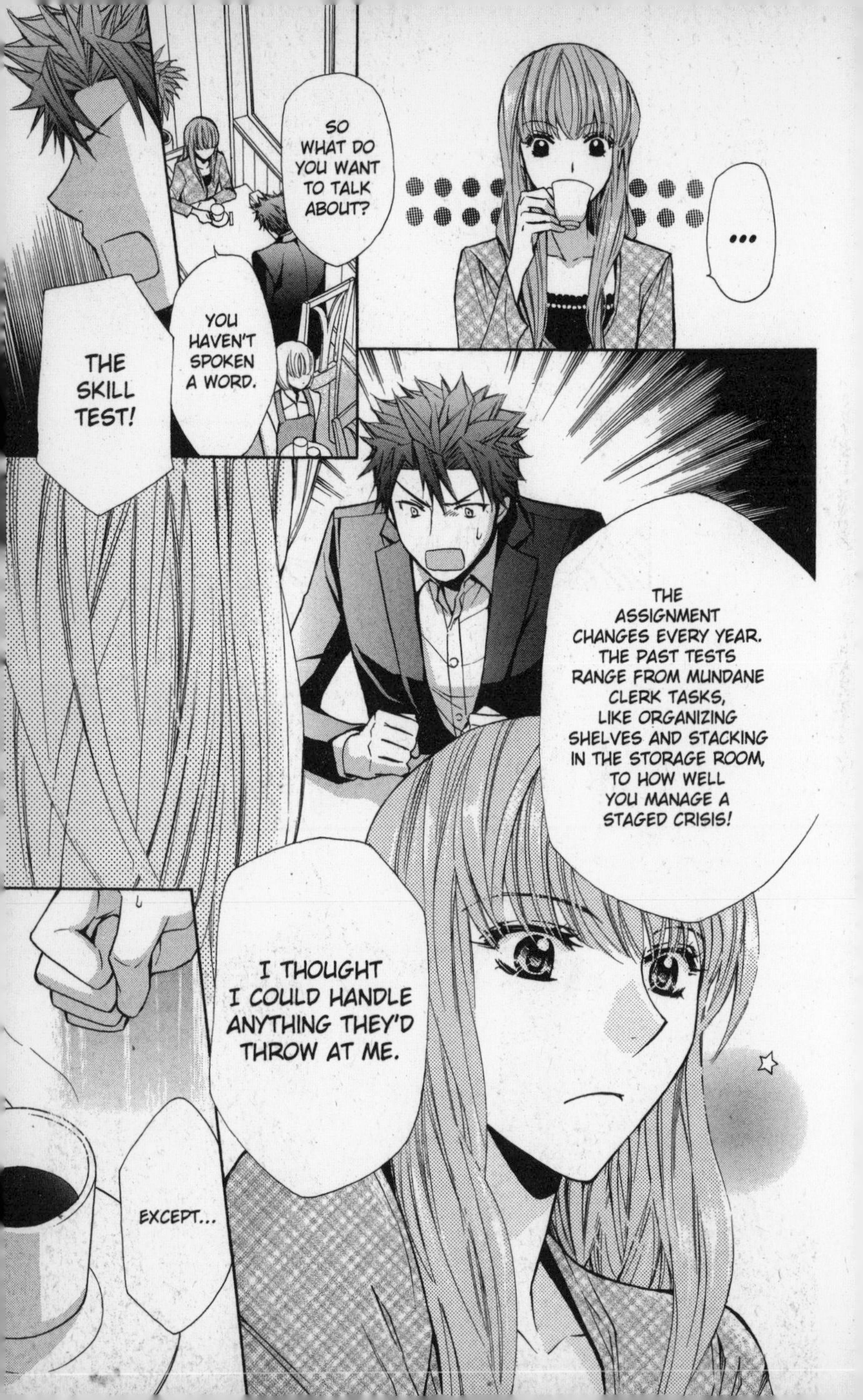
...
SO WHAT DO YOU WANT TO TALK ABOUT?
YOU HAVEN'T SPOKEN A WORD.
THE SKILL TEST!
THE ASSIGNMENT CHANGES EVERY YEAR. THE PAST TESTS RANGE FROM MUNDANE CLERK TASKS, LIKE ORGANIZING SHELVES AND STACKING IN THE STORAGE ROOM, TO HOW WELL YOU MANAGE A STAGED CRISIS!
I THOUGHT I COULD HANDLE ANYTHING THEY'D THROW AT ME.
EXCEPT...

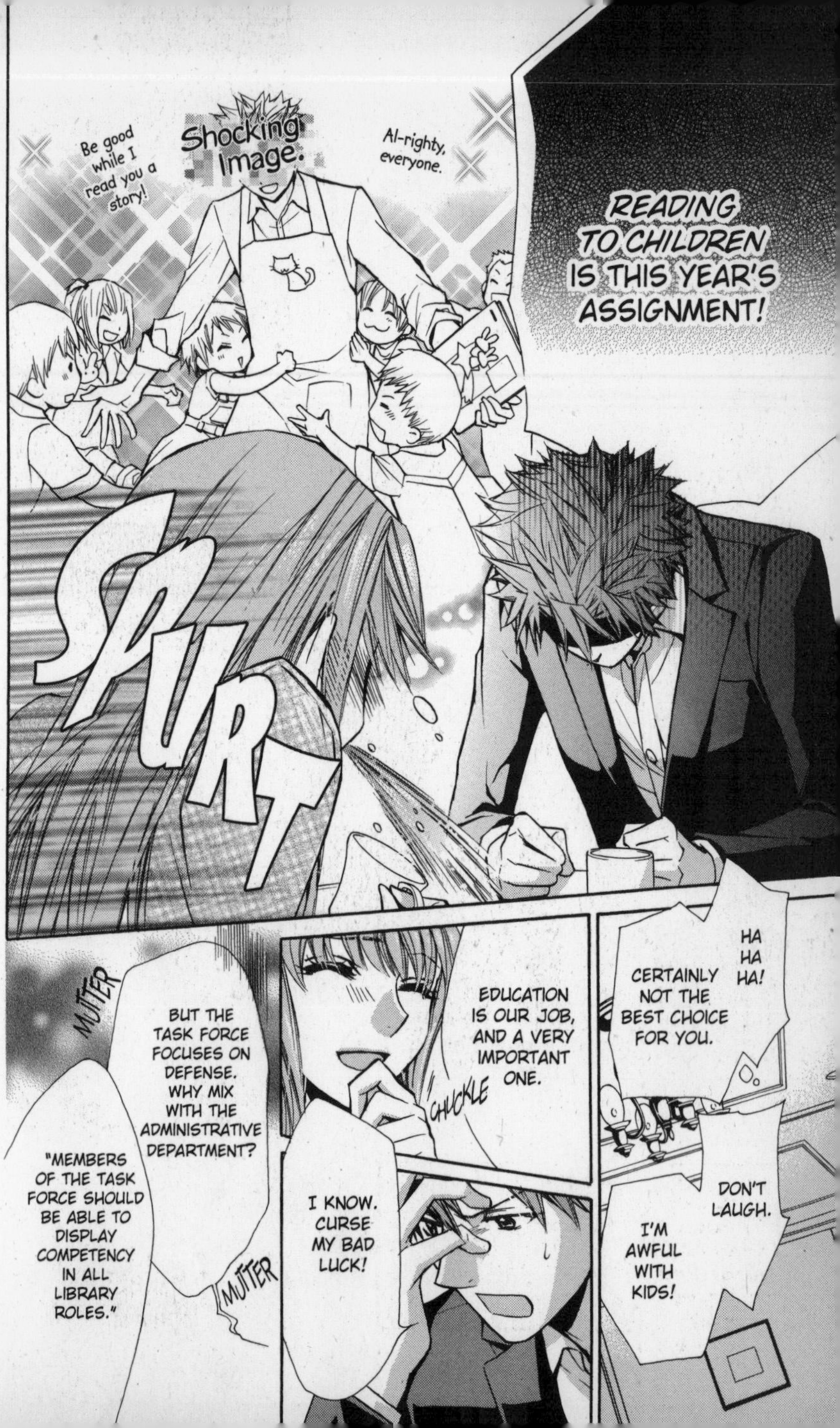
READING TO CHILDREN IS THIS YEAR'S ASSIGNMENT!
Al-righty, everyone.
Shocking Image.
Be good while I read you a story!
SPURT
HA HA HA!
CERTAINLY NOT THE BEST CHOICE FOR YOU.
EDUCATION IS OUR JOB, AND A VERY IMPORTANT ONE.
CHUCKLE
MUTTER
BUT THE TASK FORCE FOCUSES ON DEFENSE. WHY MIX WITH THE ADMINISTRATIVE DEPARTMENT?
DON'T LAUGH.
I'M AWFUL WITH KIDS!
I KNOW. CURSE MY BAD LUCK!
"MEMBERS OF THE TASK FORCE SHOULD BE ABLE TO DISPLAY COMPETENCY IN ALL LIBRARY ROLES."
MUTTER

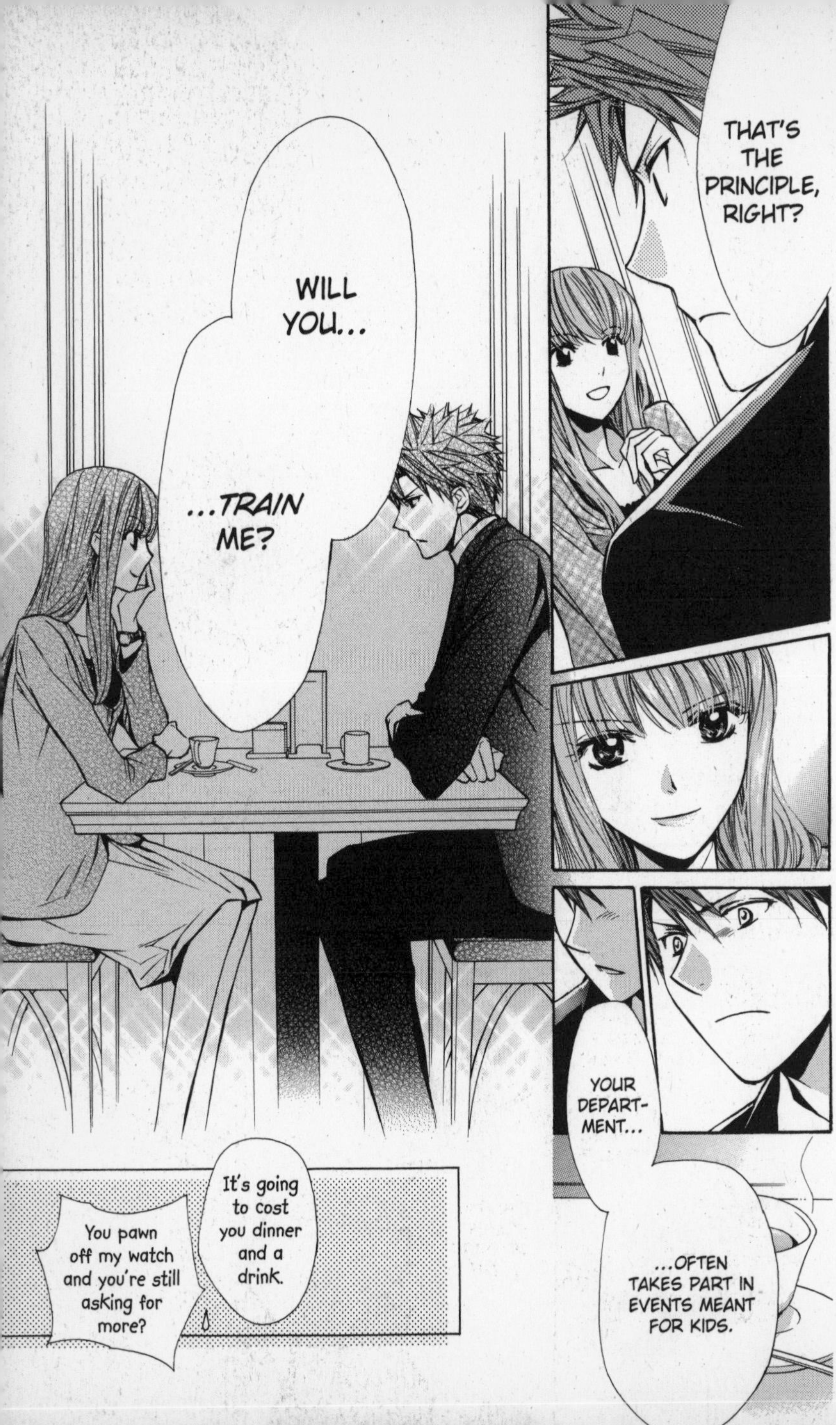
THAT'S THE PRINCIPLE, RIGHT?
YOUR DEPARTMENT...
...OFTEN TAKES PART IN EVENTS MEANT FOR KIDS.
WILL YOU...
...TRAIN ME?
It's going to cost you dinner and a drink.
You pawn off my watch and you're still asking for more?

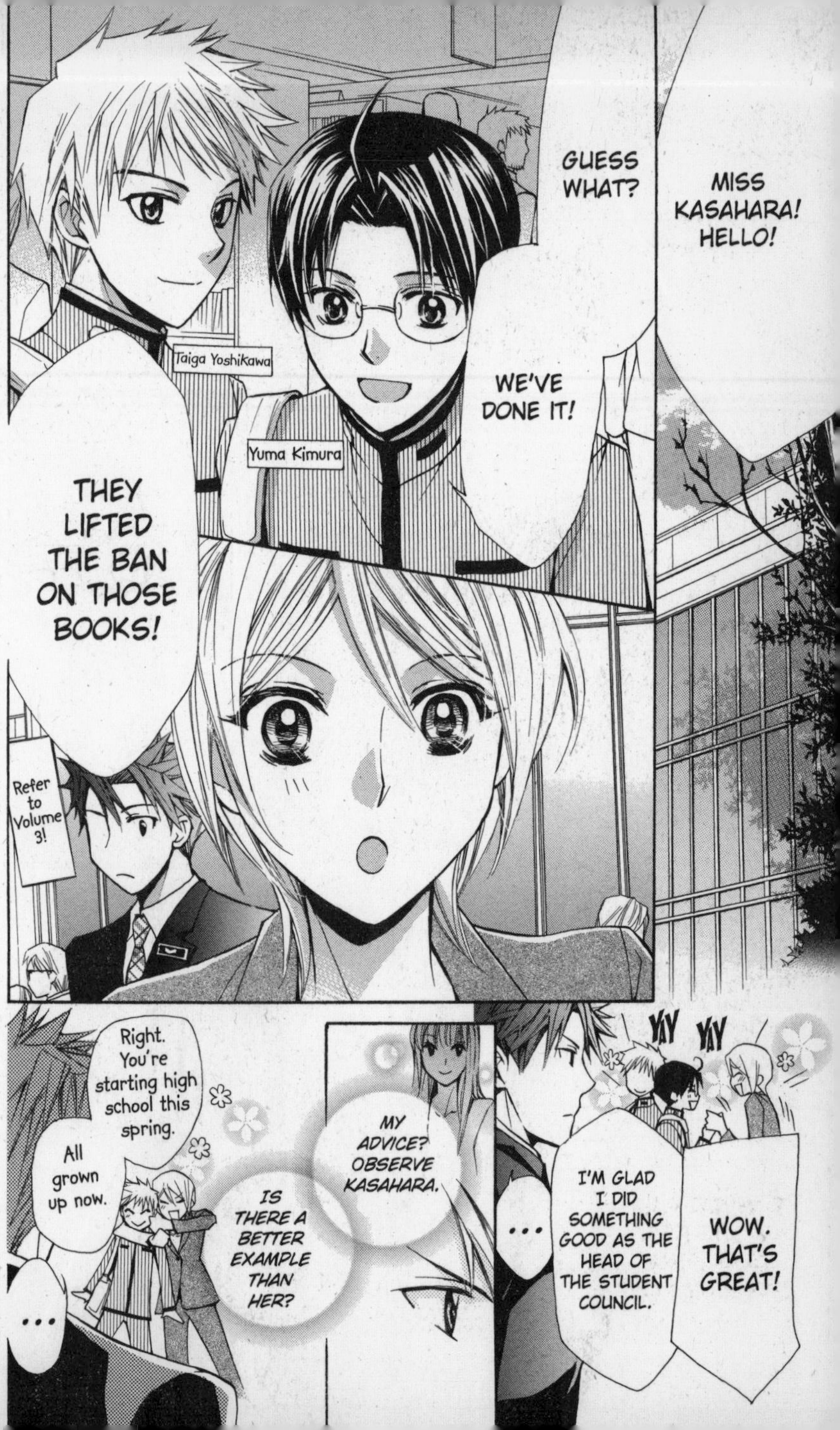
MISS KASAHARA! HELLO!
GUESS WHAT?
WE'VE DONE IT!
Taiga Yoshikawa
Yuma Kimura
THEY LIFTED THE BAN ON THOSE BOOKS!
Refer to Volume 3!
YAY
YAY
WOW. THAT'S GREAT!
I'M GLAD I DID SOMETHING GOOD AS THE HEAD OF THE STUDENT COUNCIL.
...
MY ADVICE? OBSERVE KASAHARA.
IS THERE A BETTER EXAMPLE THAN HER?
Right. You're starting high school this spring.
All grown up now.
...

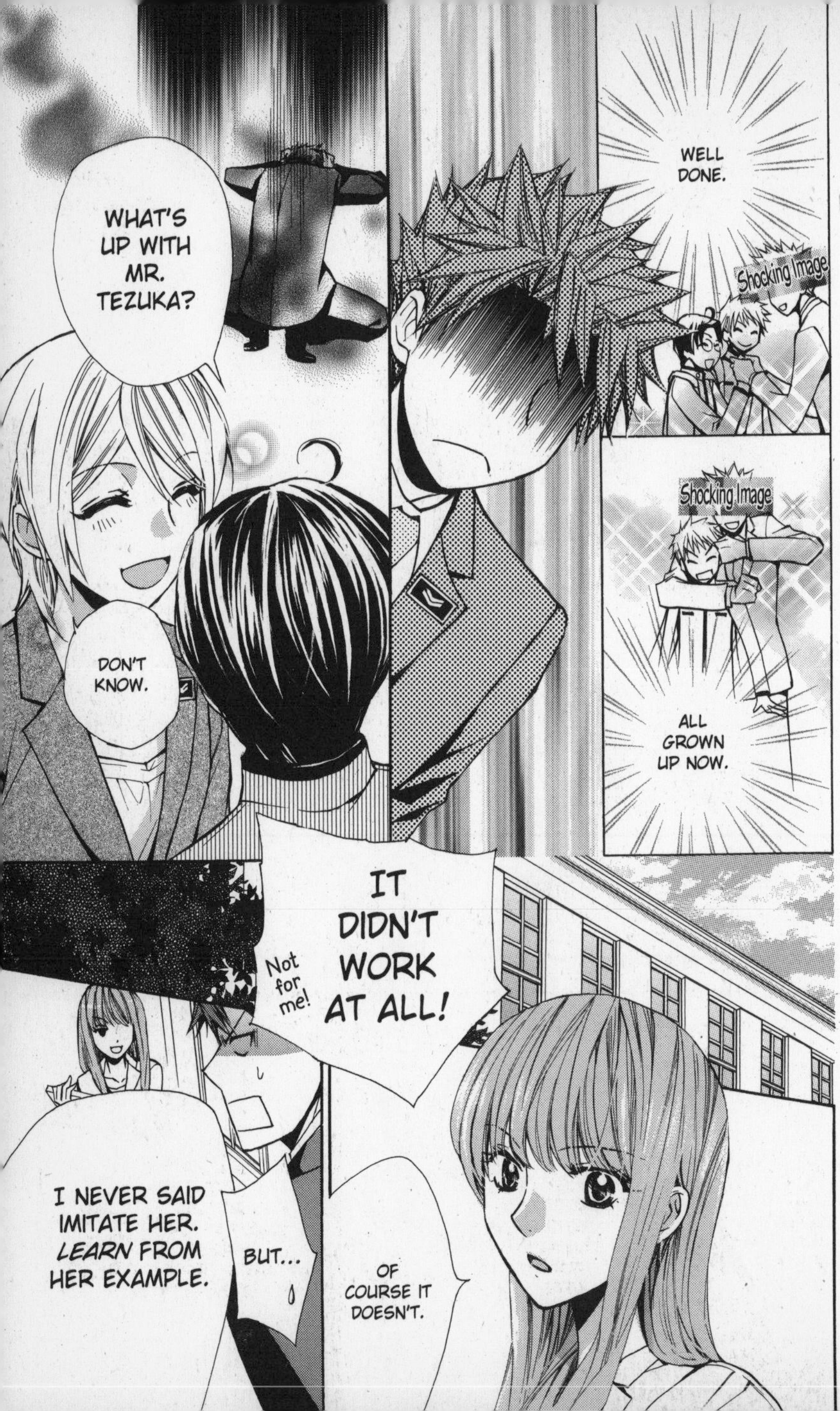
WELL DONE.
Shocking Image
Shocking Image
ALL GROWN UP NOW.
WHAT'S UP WITH MR. TEZUKA?
DON'T KNOW.
IT DIDN'T WORK AT ALL!
Not for me!
OF COURSE IT DOESN'T.
BUT...
I NEVER SAID IMITATE HER. *LEARN* FROM HER EXAMPLE.

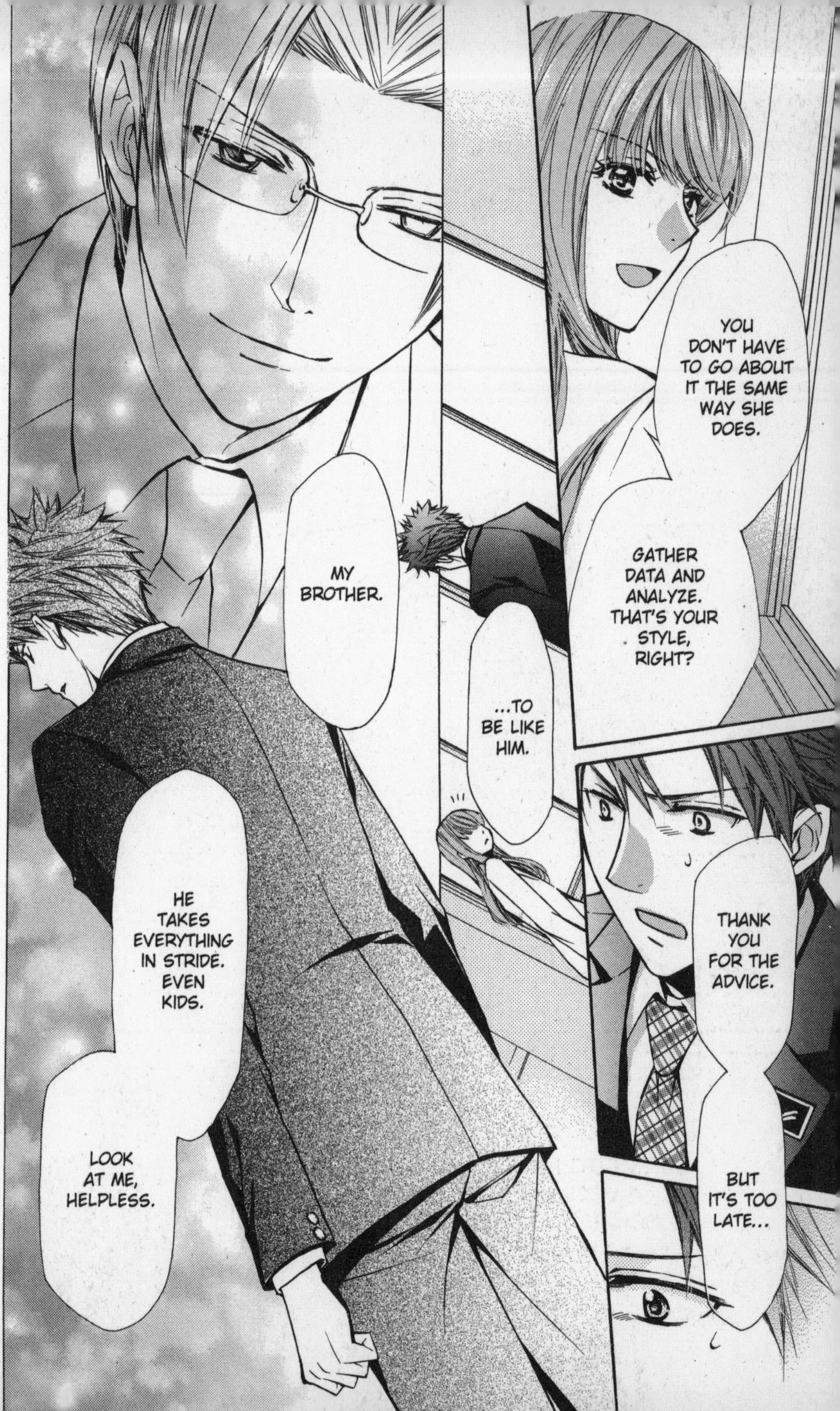
YOU DON'T HAVE TO GO ABOUT IT THE SAME WAY SHE DOES.
GATHER DATA AND ANALYZE. THAT'S YOUR STYLE, RIGHT?
THANK YOU FOR THE ADVICE.
BUT IT'S TOO LATE...
...TO BE LIKE HIM.
MY BROTHER.
HE TAKES EVERYTHING IN STRIDE. EVEN KIDS.
LOOK AT ME, HELPLESS.

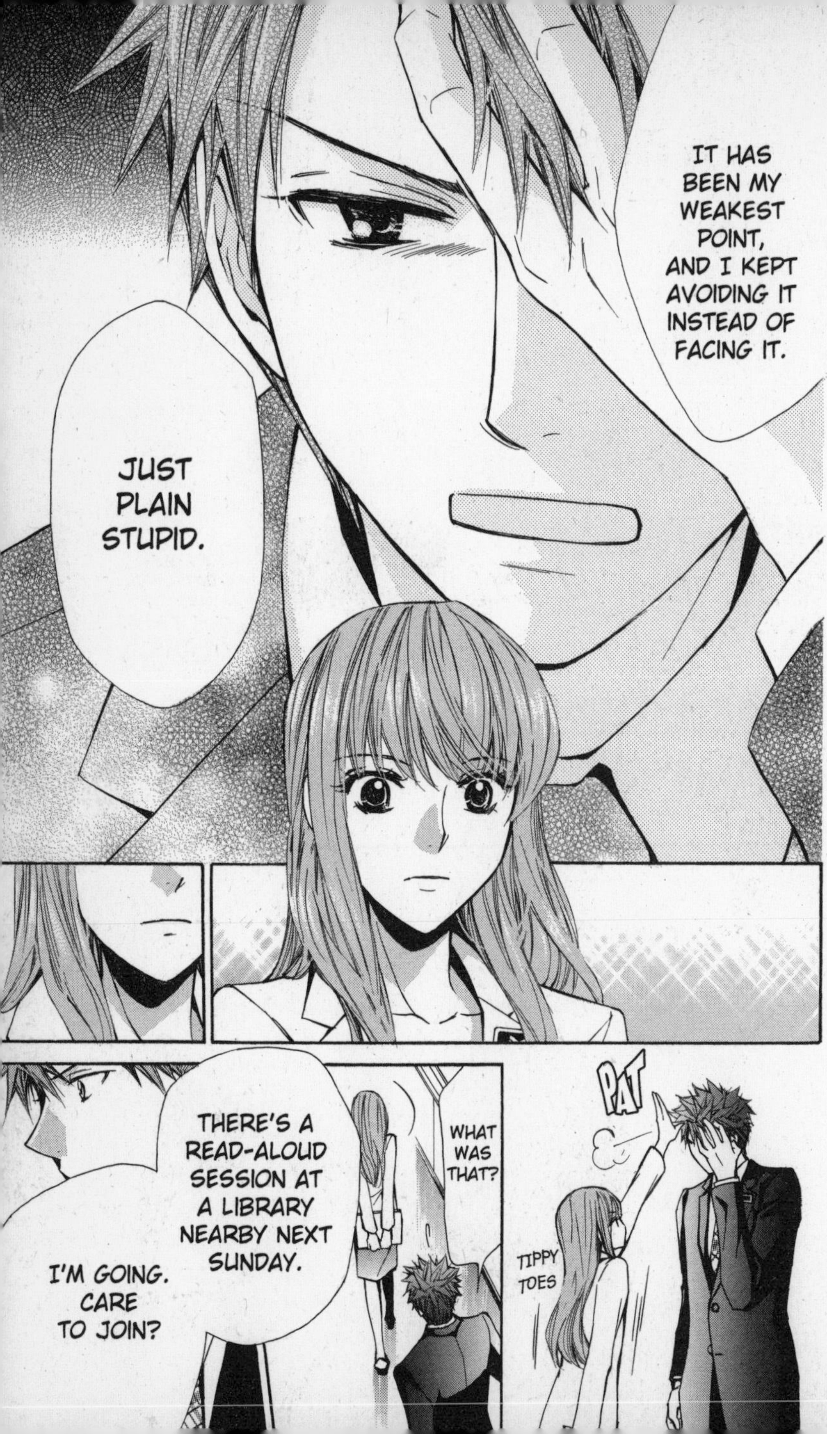
IT HAS BEEN MY WEAKEST POINT, AND I KEPT AVOIDING IT INSTEAD OF FACING IT.
JUST PLAIN STUPID.
PAT
TIPPY TOES
WHAT WAS THAT?
THERE'S A READ-ALOUD SESSION AT A LIBRARY NEARBY NEXT SUNDAY.
I'M GOING. CARE TO JOIN?

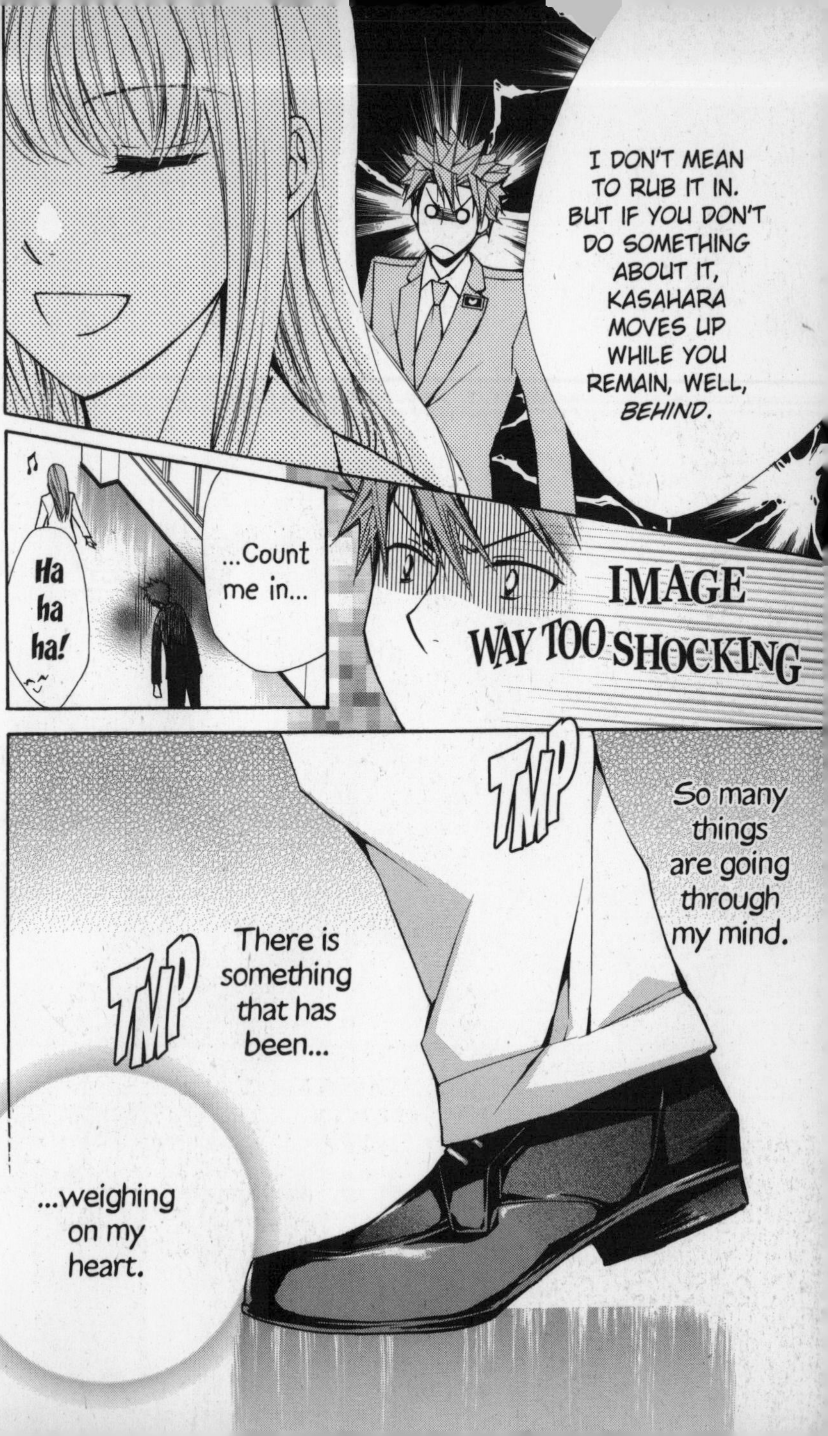
I DON'T MEAN TO RUB IT IN. BUT IF YOU DON'T DO SOMETHING ABOUT IT, KASAHARA MOVES UP WHILE YOU REMAIN, WELL, *BEHIND*.
IMAGE
WAY TOO SHOCKING
...Count me in...
Ha ha ha!
TMP
So many things are going through my mind.
TMP
There is something that has been...
...weighing on my heart.

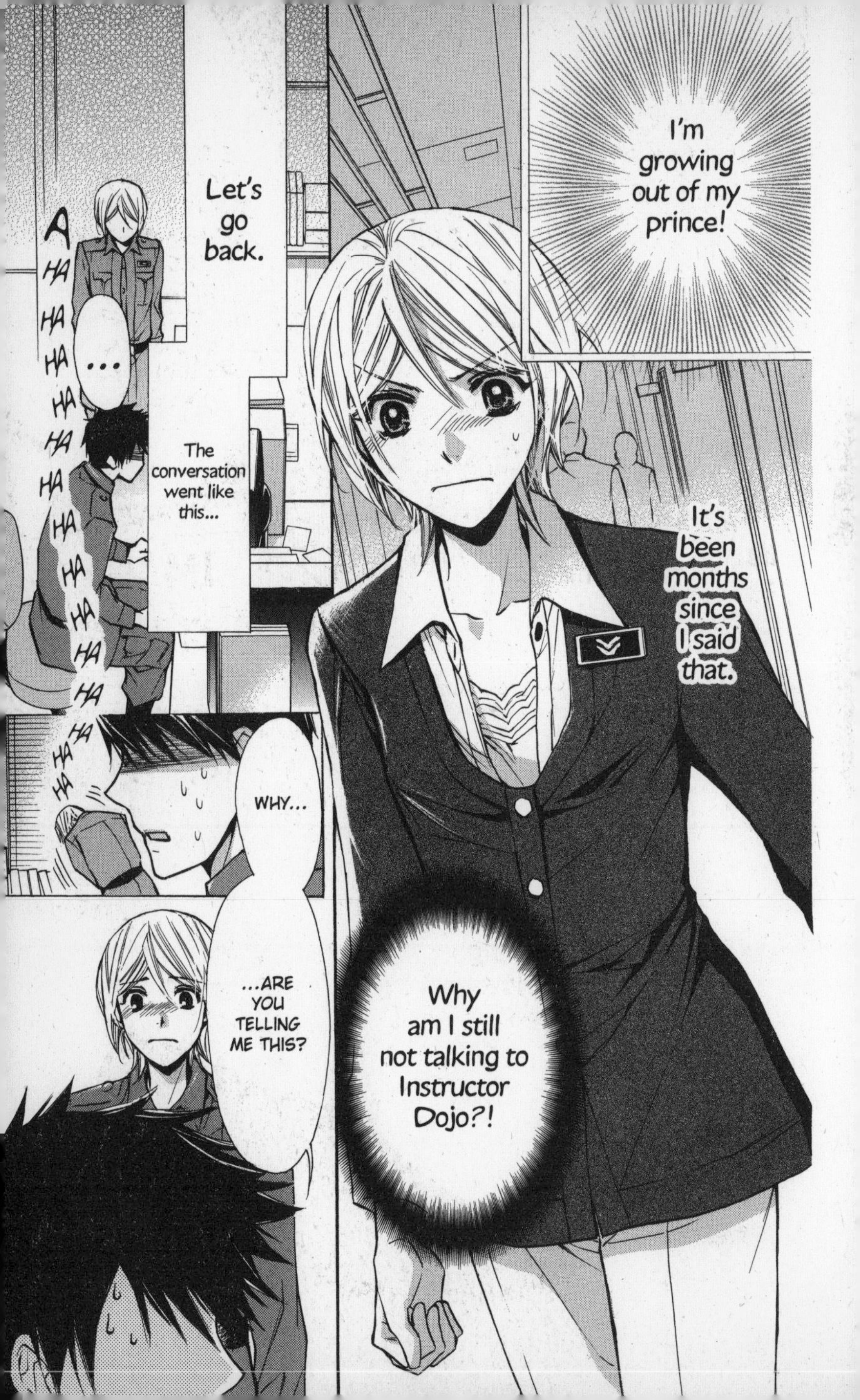
I'm growing out of my prince!
It's been months since I said that.
Why am I still not talking to Instructor Dojo?!
Let's go back.
The conversation went like this...
A HA HA HA HA HA HA HA HA HA HA HA HA HA HA HA
...
WHY...
...ARE YOU TELLING ME THIS?

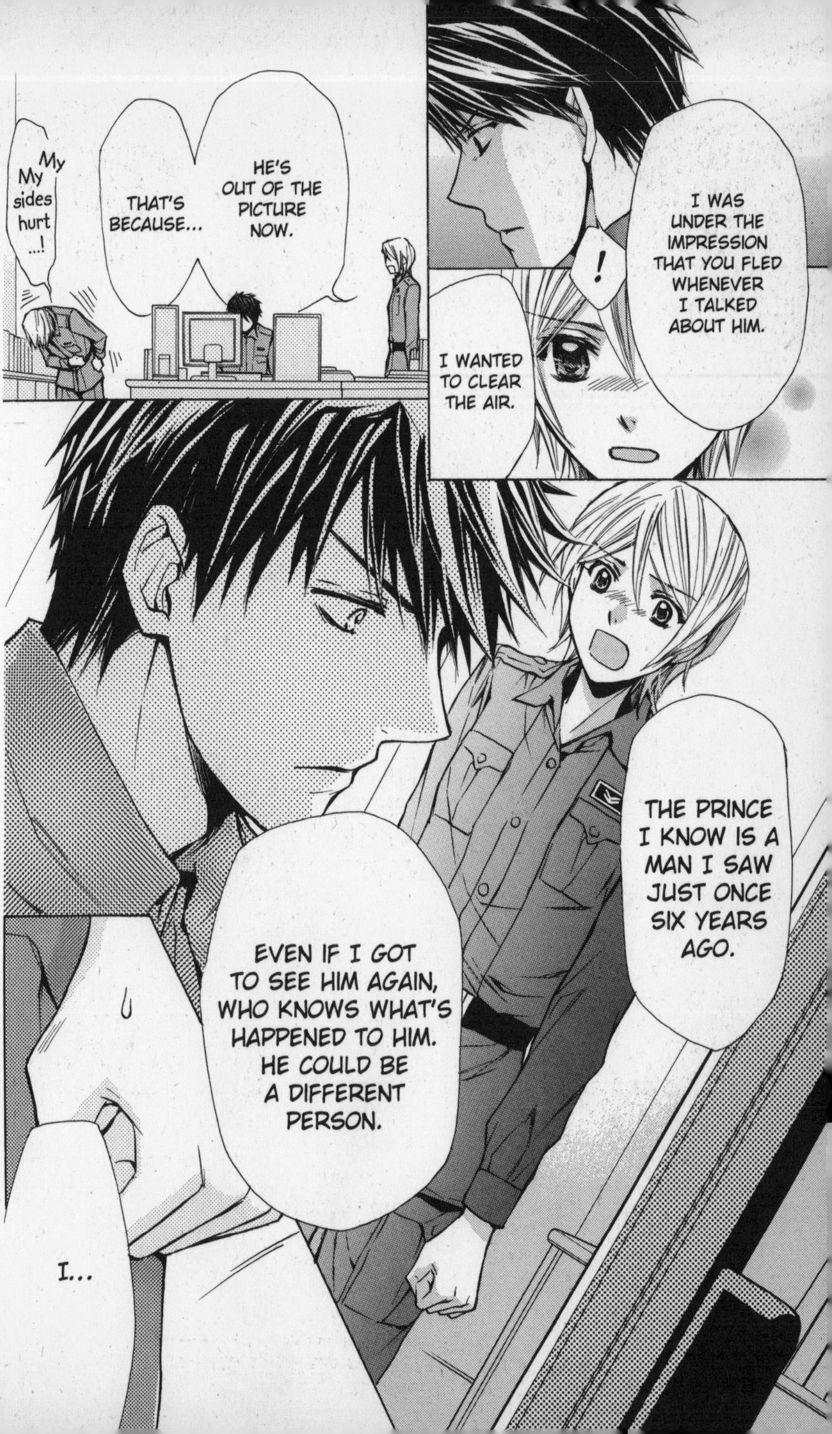
I WAS UNDER THE IMPRESSION THAT YOU FLED WHENEVER I TALKED ABOUT HIM.
!
I WANTED TO CLEAR THE AIR.
HE'S OUT OF THE PICTURE NOW.
THAT'S BECAUSE...
My My sides hurt ...!
THE PRINCE I KNOW IS A MAN I SAW JUST ONCE SIX YEARS AGO.
EVEN IF I GOT TO SEE HIM AGAIN, WHO KNOWS WHAT'S HAPPENED TO HIM. HE COULD BE A DIFFERENT PERSON.
I...

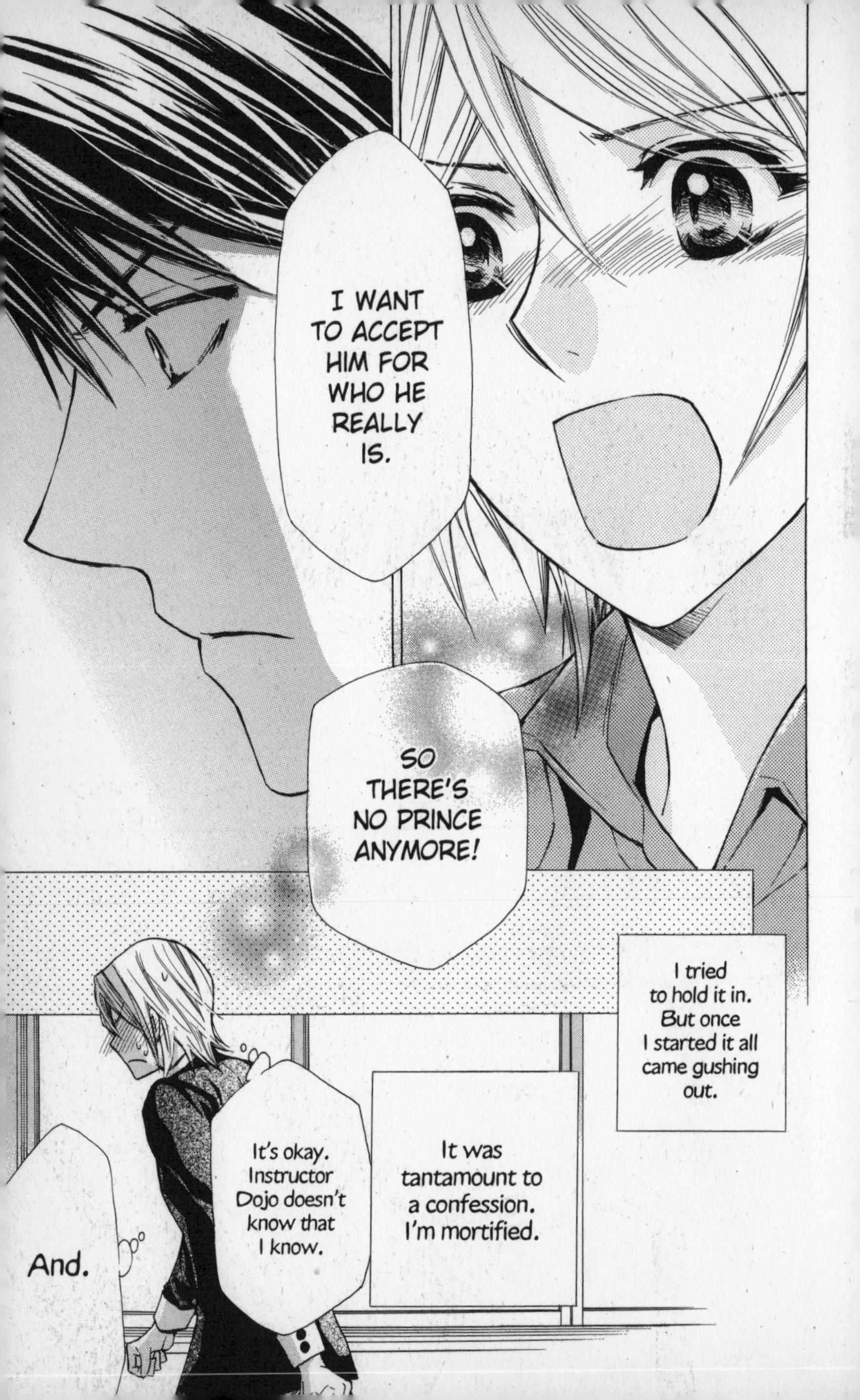
I WANT TO ACCEPT HIM FOR WHO HE REALLY IS.
SO THERE'S NO PRINCE ANYMORE!
I tried to hold it in. But once I started it all came gushing out.
It was tantamount to a confession. I'm mortified.
It's okay. Instructor Dojo doesn't know that I know.
And.

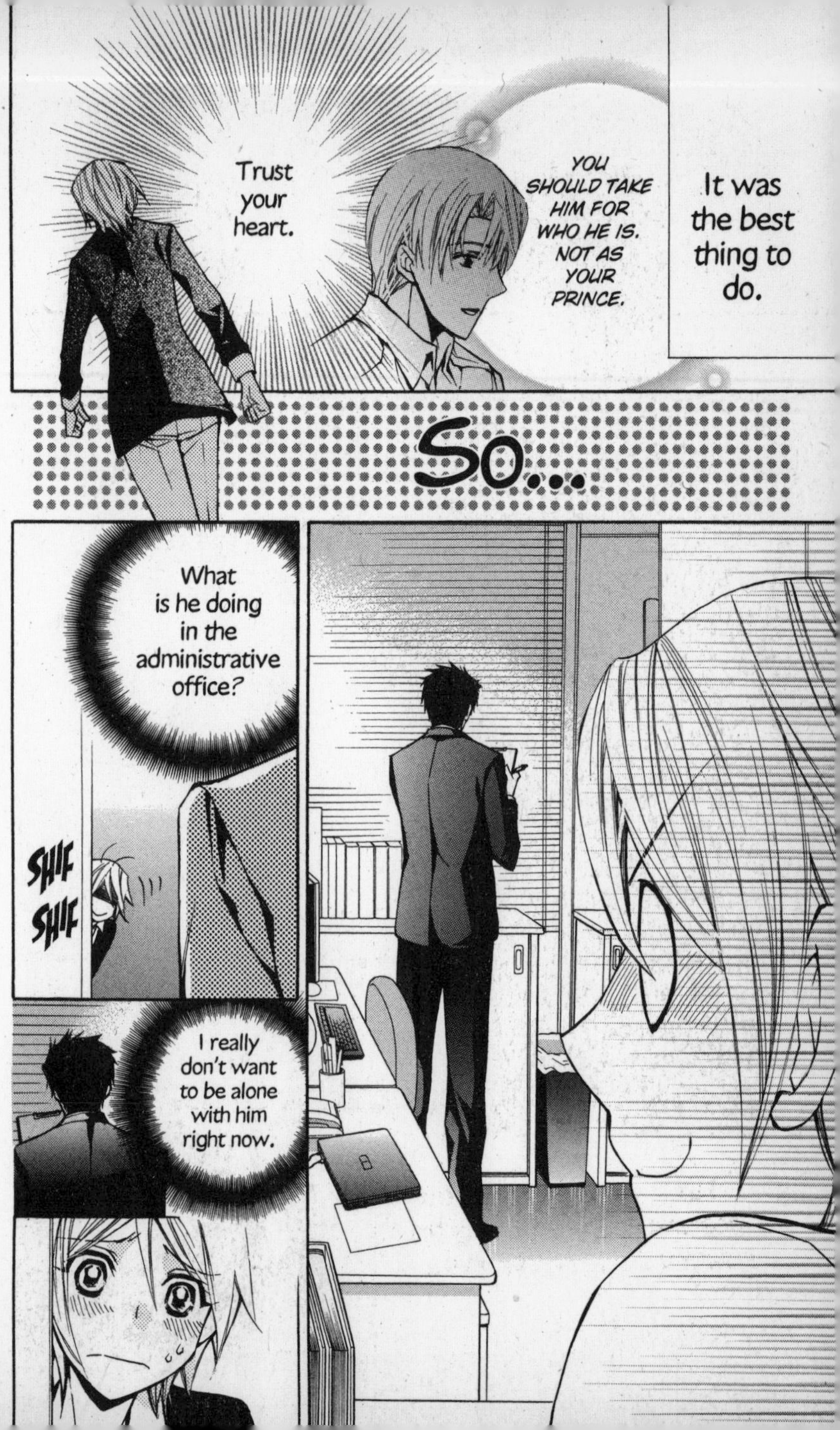
It was the best thing to do.
YOU SHOULD TAKE HIM FOR WHO HE IS. NOT AS YOUR PRINCE.
Trust your heart.
So...
What is he doing in the administrative office?
SHIF SHIF
I really don't want to be alone with him right now.

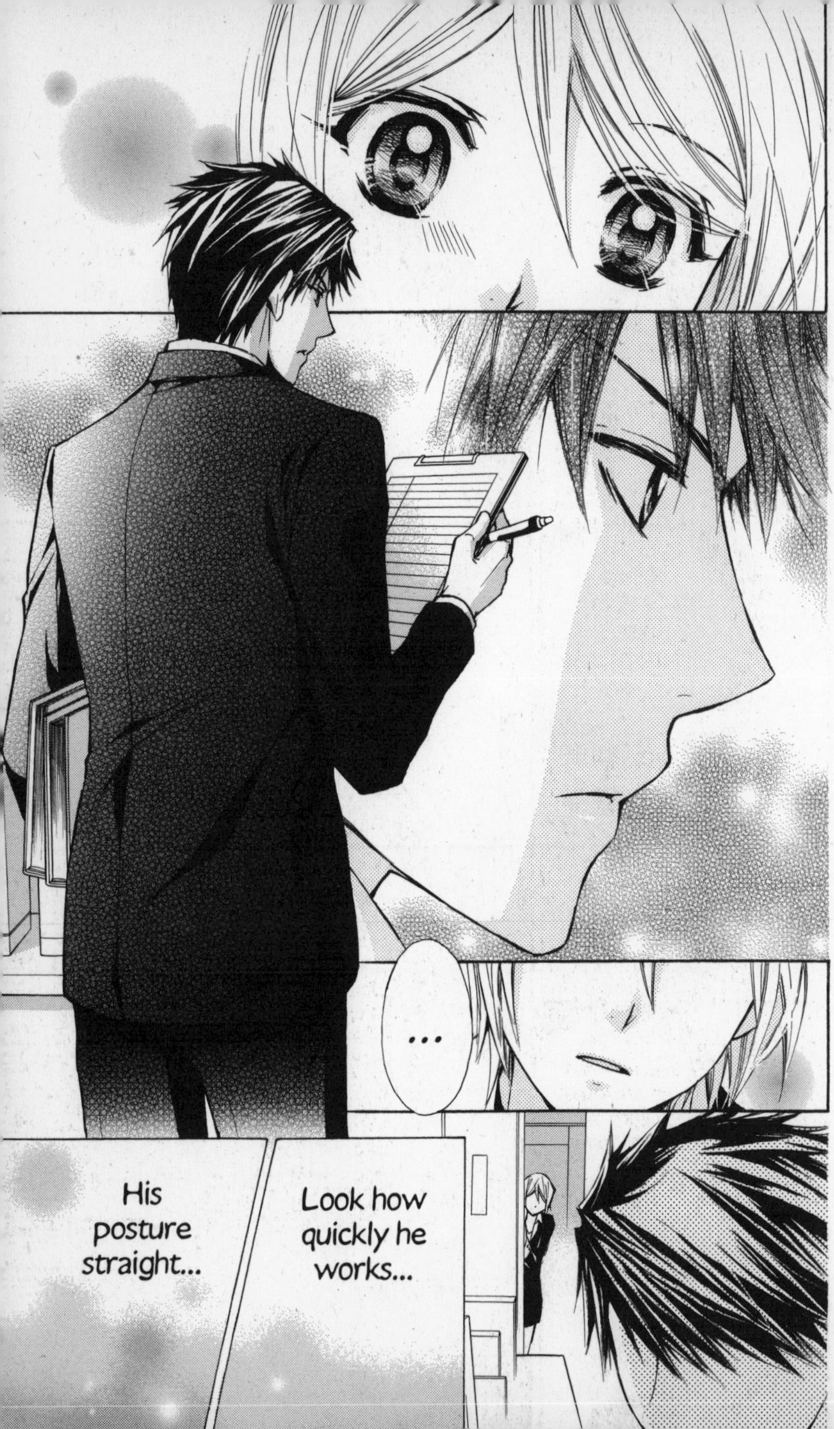
...
Look how quickly he works...
His posture straight...

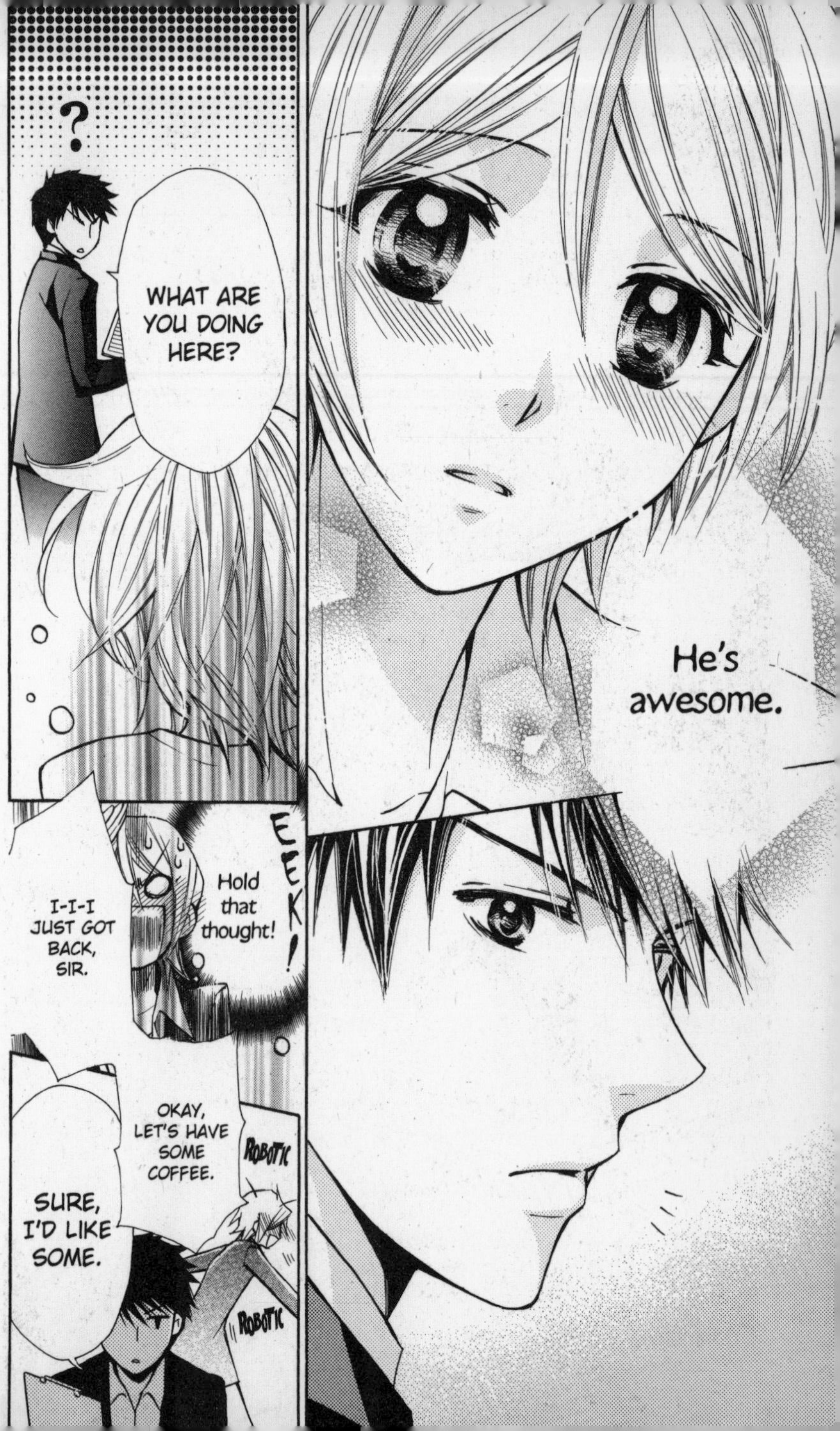
He's awesome.
?
WHAT ARE YOU DOING HERE?
EEK!
Hold that thought!
I-I-I JUST GOT BACK, SIR.
ROBOTIC
OKAY, LET'S HAVE SOME COFFEE.
SURE, I'D LIKE SOME.
ROBOTIC

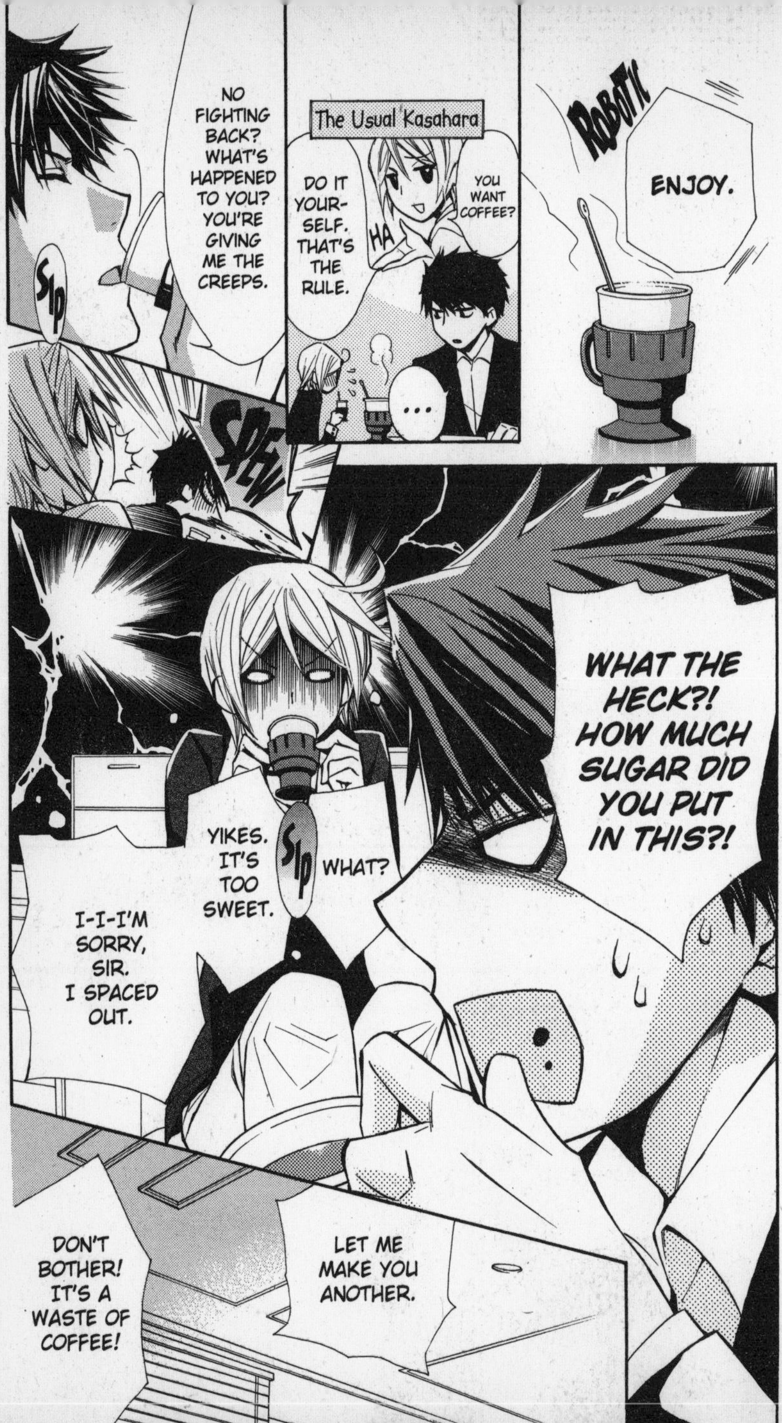
ROBOTIC
ENJOY.
The Usual Kasahara
YOU WANT COFFEE?
HA
DO IT YOURSELF. THAT'S THE RULE.
...
NO FIGHTING BACK? WHAT'S HAPPENED TO YOU? YOU'RE GIVING ME THE CREEPS.
SIP
SPEW
WHAT THE HECK?! HOW MUCH SUGAR DID YOU PUT IN THIS?!
WHAT?
SIP
YIKES. IT'S TOO SWEET.
I-I-I'M SORRY, SIR. I SPACED OUT.
LET ME MAKE YOU ANOTHER.
DON'T BOTHER! IT'S A WASTE OF COFFEE!

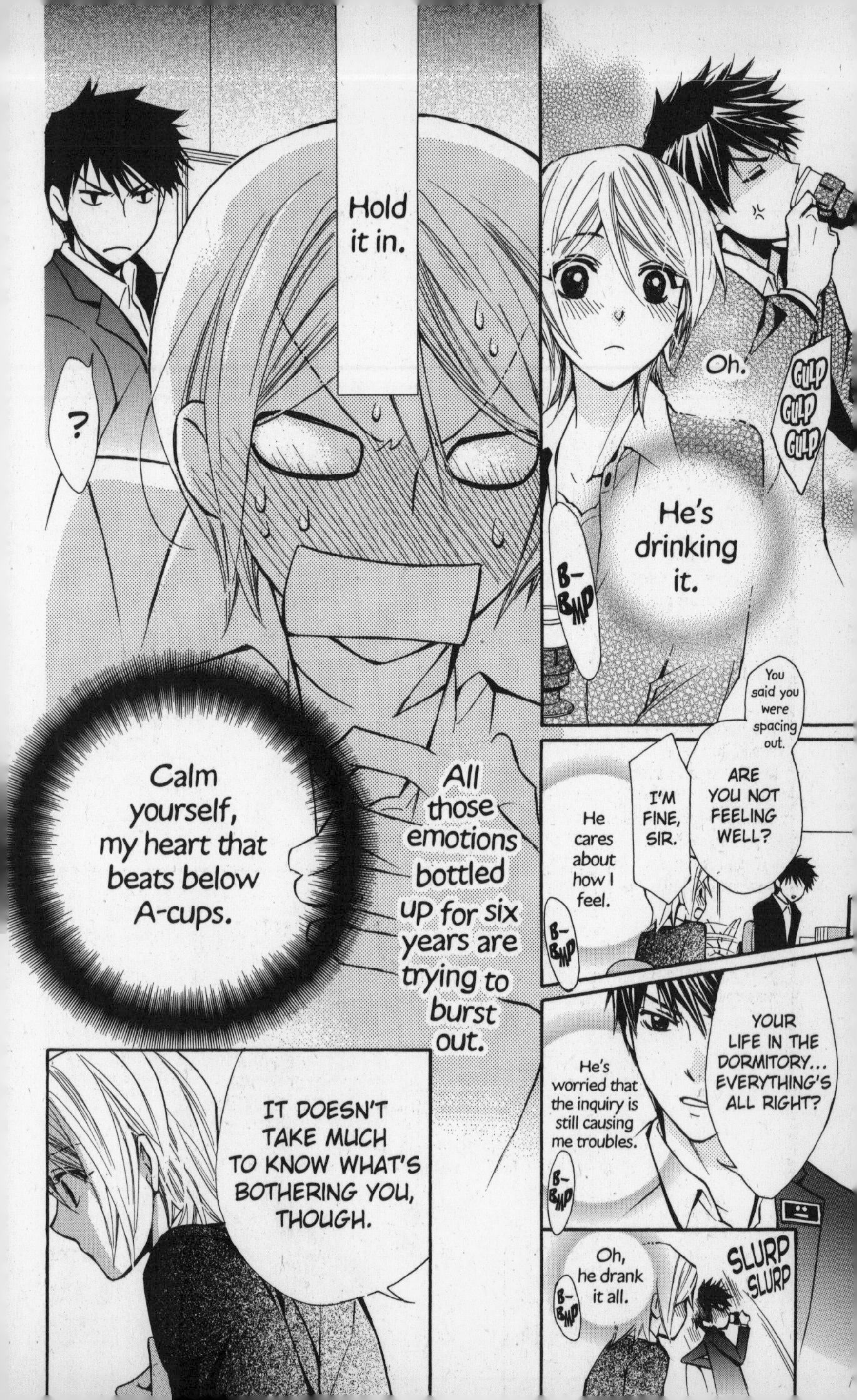
Oh.
GULP GULP GULP
He's drinking it.
B-BMP
You said you were spacing out.
ARE YOU NOT FEELING WELL?
I'M FINE, SIR.
He cares about how I feel.
B-BMP
YOUR LIFE IN THE DORMITORY... EVERYTHING'S ALL RIGHT?
He's worried that the inquiry is still causing me troubles.
B-BMP
SLURP SLURP
Oh, he drank it all.
B-BMP
Hold it in.
?
All those emotions bottled up for six years are trying to burst out.
Calm yourself, my heart that beats below A-cups.
IT DOESN'T TAKE MUCH TO KNOW WHAT'S BOTHERING YOU, THOUGH.

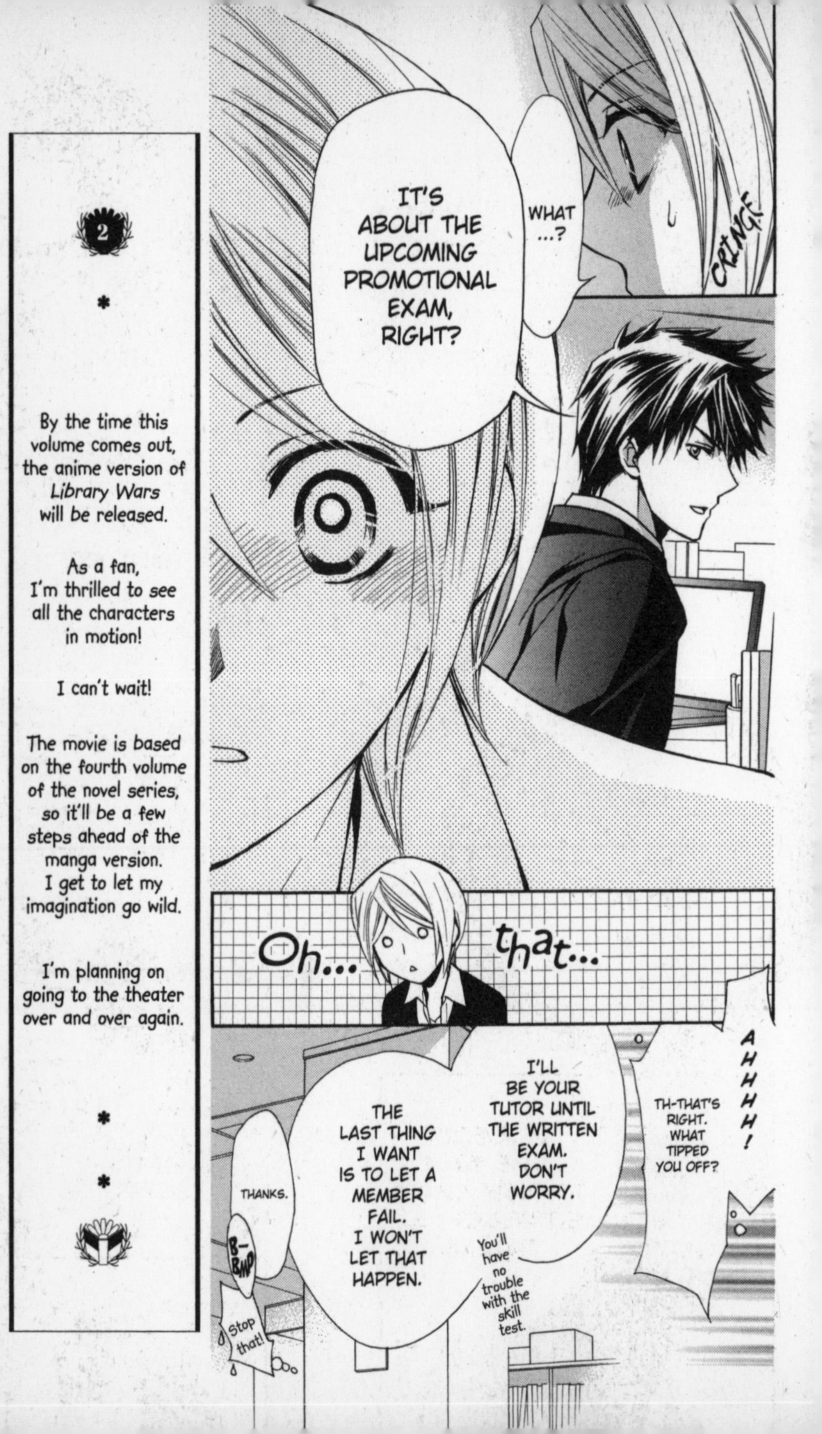
WHAT ...?
CRINGE
IT'S ABOUT THE UPCOMING PROMOTIONAL EXAM, RIGHT?
Oh... that...
AHHHHH!
TH-THAT'S RIGHT. WHAT TIPPED YOU OFF?
I'LL BE YOUR TUTOR UNTIL THE WRITTEN EXAM. DON'T WORRY.
You'll have no trouble with the skill test.
THE LAST THING I WANT IS TO LET A MEMBER FAIL. I WON'T LET THAT HAPPEN.
THANKS.
B-BMP
Stop that!

2

*

By the time this volume comes out, the anime version of *Library Wars* will be released.

As a fan, I'm thrilled to see all the characters in motion!

I can't wait!

The movie is based on the fourth volume of the novel series, so it'll be a few steps ahead of the manga version. I get to let my imagination go wild.

I'm planning on going to the theater over and over again.

*

*

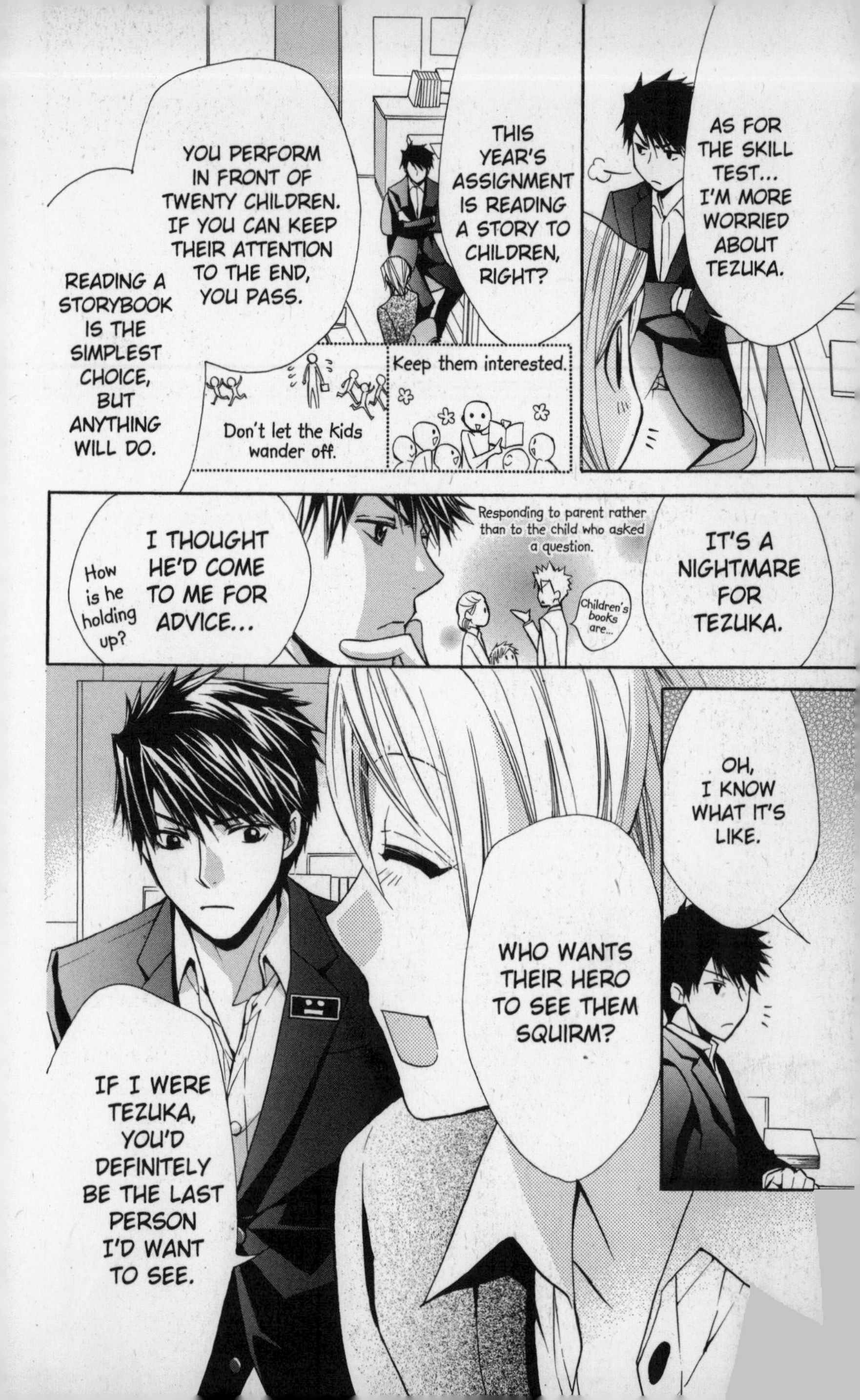
AS FOR THE SKILL TEST... I'M MORE WORRIED ABOUT TEZUKA.
THIS YEAR'S ASSIGNMENT IS READING A STORY TO CHILDREN, RIGHT?
YOU PERFORM IN FRONT OF TWENTY CHILDREN. IF YOU CAN KEEP THEIR ATTENTION TO THE END, YOU PASS.
READING A STORYBOOK IS THE SIMPLEST CHOICE, BUT ANYTHING WILL DO.
Keep them interested.
Don't let the kids wander off.
IT'S A NIGHTMARE FOR TEZUKA.
Responding to parent rather than to the child who asked a question.
Children's books are...
I THOUGHT HE'D COME TO ME FOR ADVICE...
How is he holding up?
OH, I KNOW WHAT IT'S LIKE.
WHO WANTS THEIR HERO TO SEE THEM SQUIRM?
IF I WERE TEZUKA, YOU'D DEFINITELY BE THE LAST PERSON I'D WANT TO SEE.

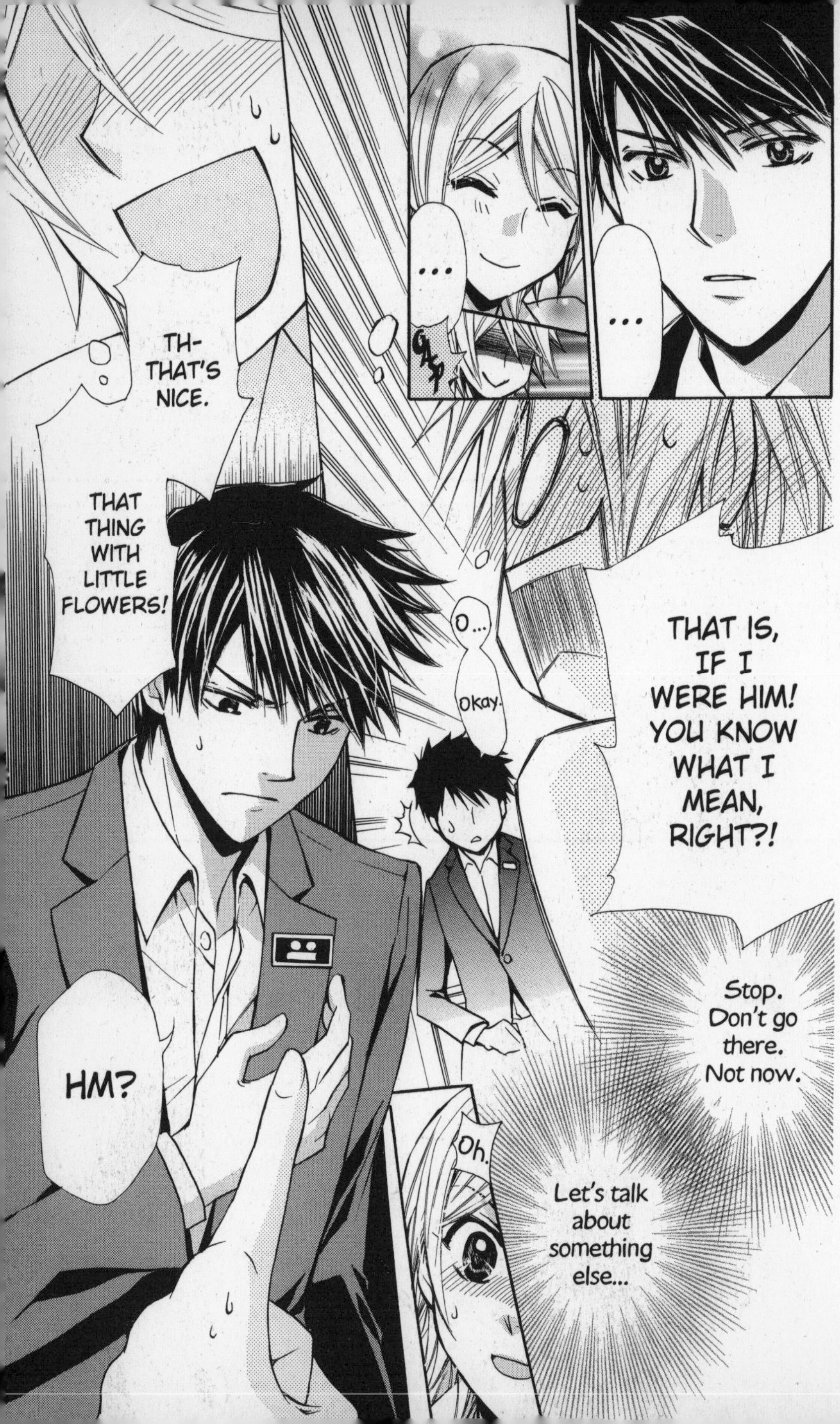
...
...
GASP
TH- THAT'S NICE.
THAT THING WITH LITTLE FLOWERS!
THAT IS, IF I WERE HIM! YOU KNOW WHAT I MEAN, RIGHT?!
O...
Okay.
HM?
Stop. Don't go there. Not now.
Oh.
Let's talk about something else...

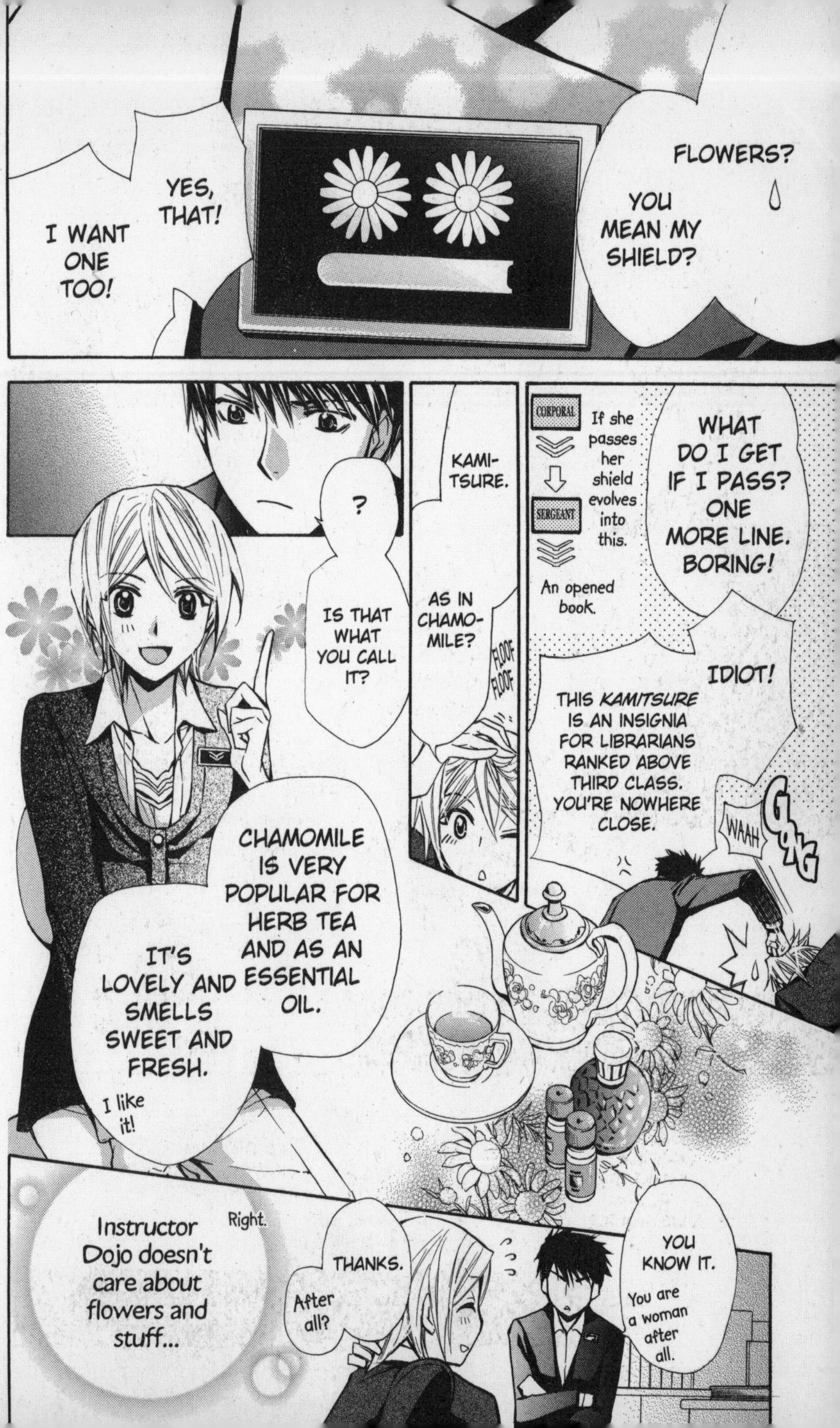
FLOWERS?
YOU MEAN MY SHIELD?
YES, THAT!
I WANT ONE TOO!
WHAT DO I GET IF I PASS? ONE MORE LINE. BORING!
CORPORAL
SERGEANT
If she passes her shield evolves into this.
An opened book.
IDIOT!
THIS KAMITSURE IS AN INSIGNIA FOR LIBRARIANS RANKED ABOVE THIRD CLASS. YOU'RE NOWHERE CLOSE.
WAAH
GONG
KAMI-TSURE.
AS IN CHAMO-MILE?
FLOOF FLOOF
?
IS THAT WHAT YOU CALL IT?
CHAMOMILE IS VERY POPULAR FOR HERB TEA AND AS AN ESSENTIAL OIL.
IT'S LOVELY AND SMELLS SWEET AND FRESH.
I like it!
YOU KNOW IT.
You are a woman after all.
THANKS.
After all?
Right.
Instructor Dojo doesn't care about flowers and stuff...

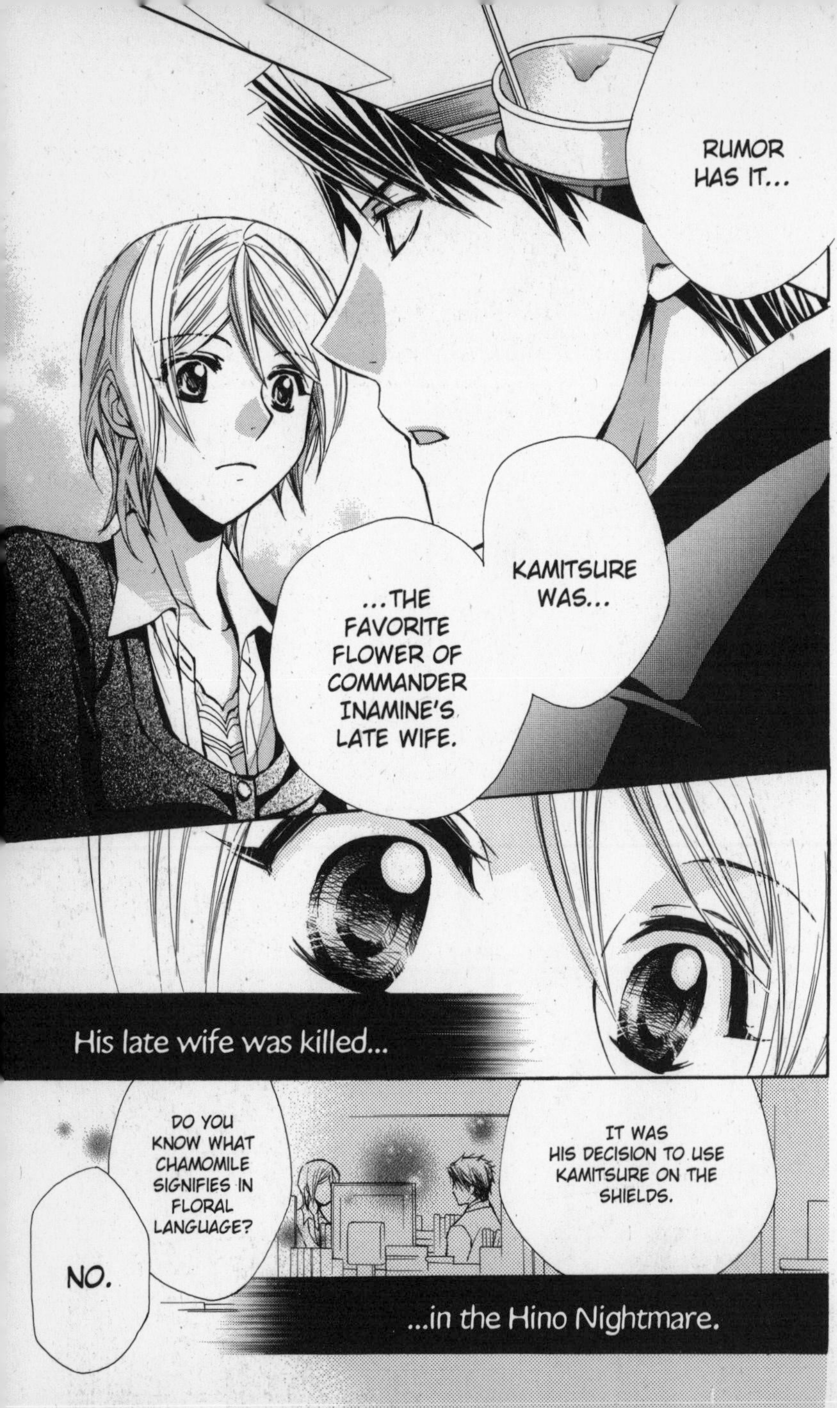
RUMOR HAS IT...
KAMITSURE WAS...
...THE FAVORITE FLOWER OF COMMANDER INAMINE'S LATE WIFE.
His late wife was killed...
IT WAS HIS DECISION TO USE KAMITSURE ON THE SHIELDS.
DO YOU KNOW WHAT CHAMOMILE SIGNIFIES IN FLORAL LANGUAGE?
NO.
...in the Hino Nightmare.

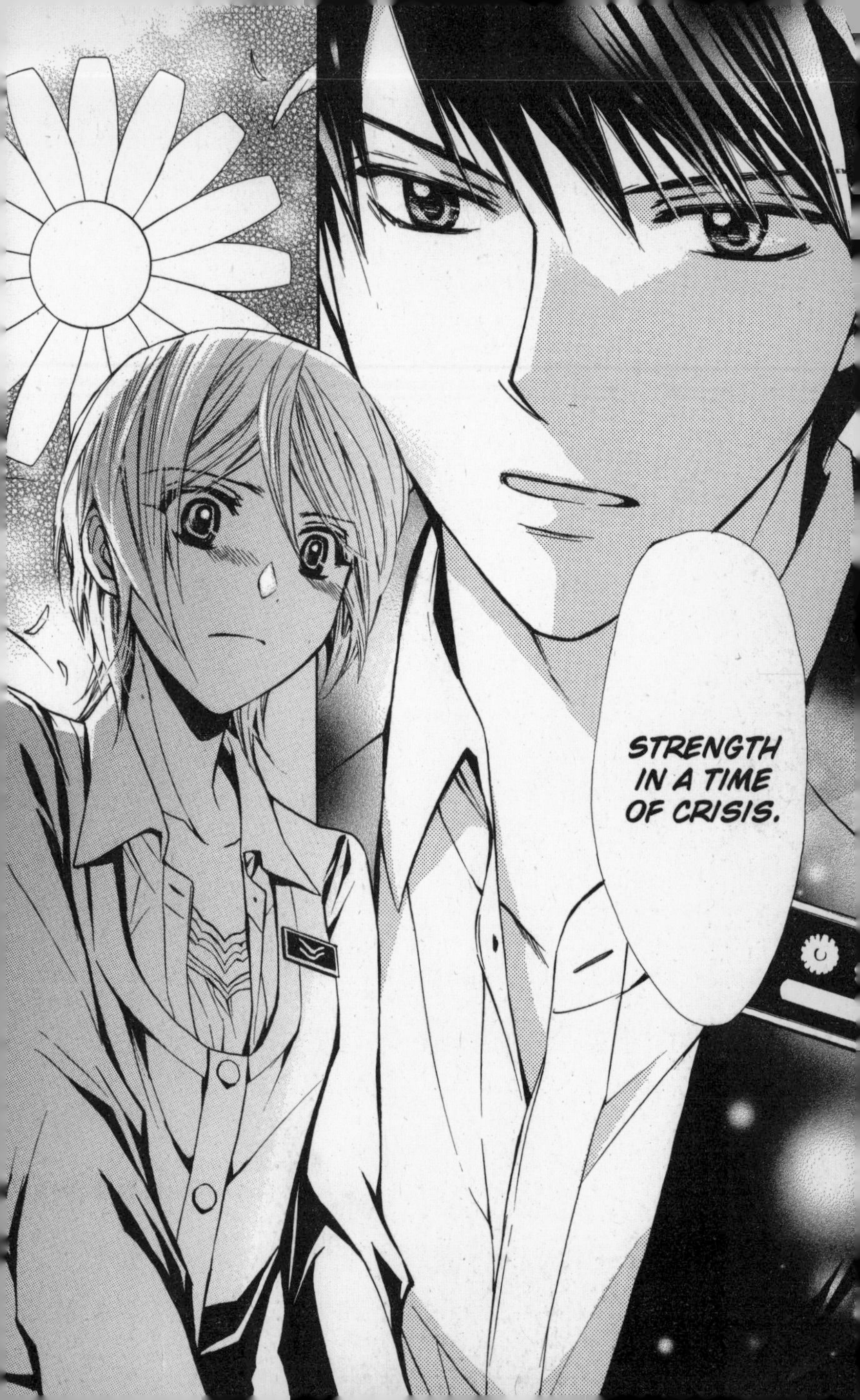
STRENGTH IN A TIME OF CRISIS.

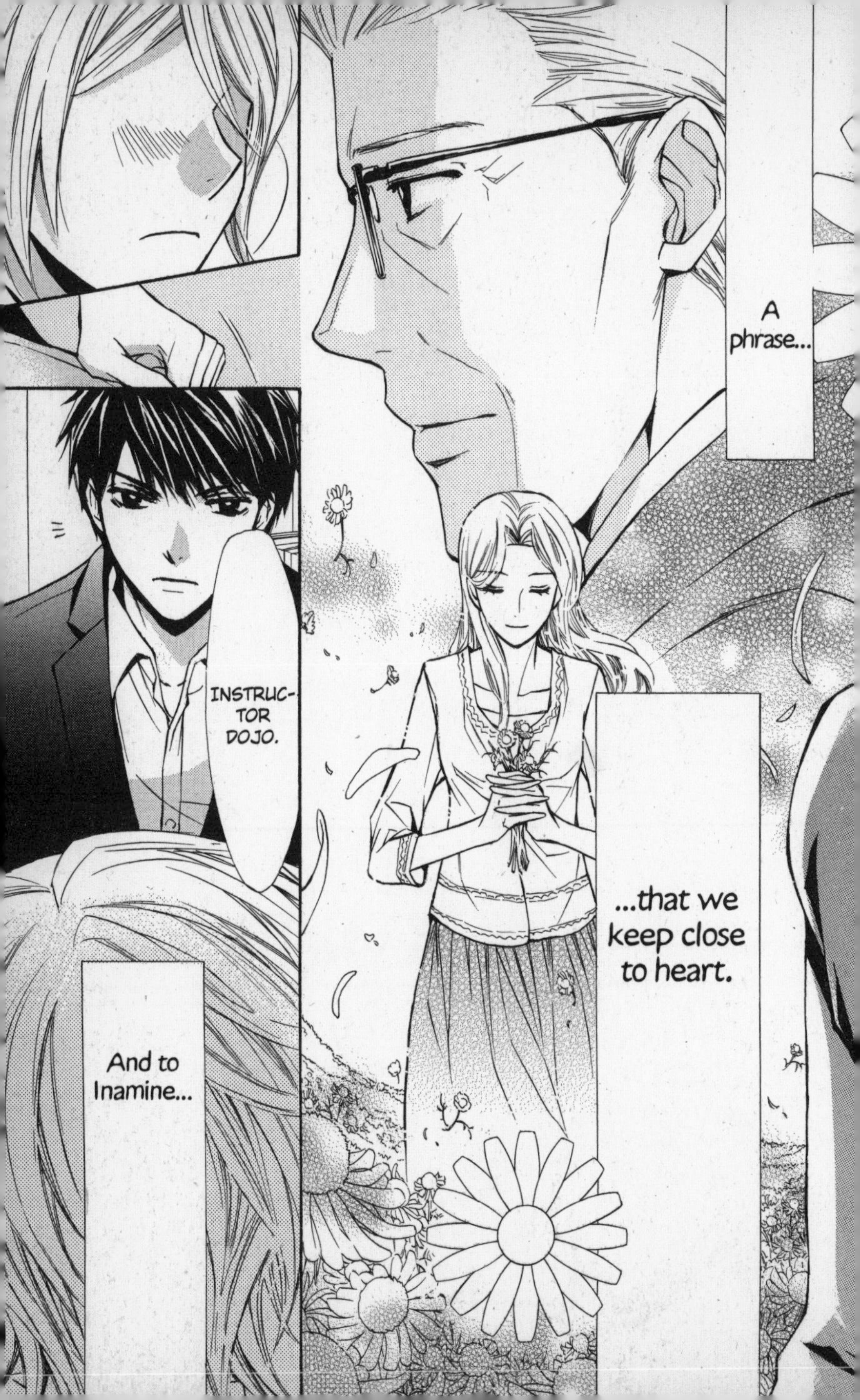
A phrase...
...that we keep close to heart.
INSTRUC-TOR DOJO.
And to Inamine...

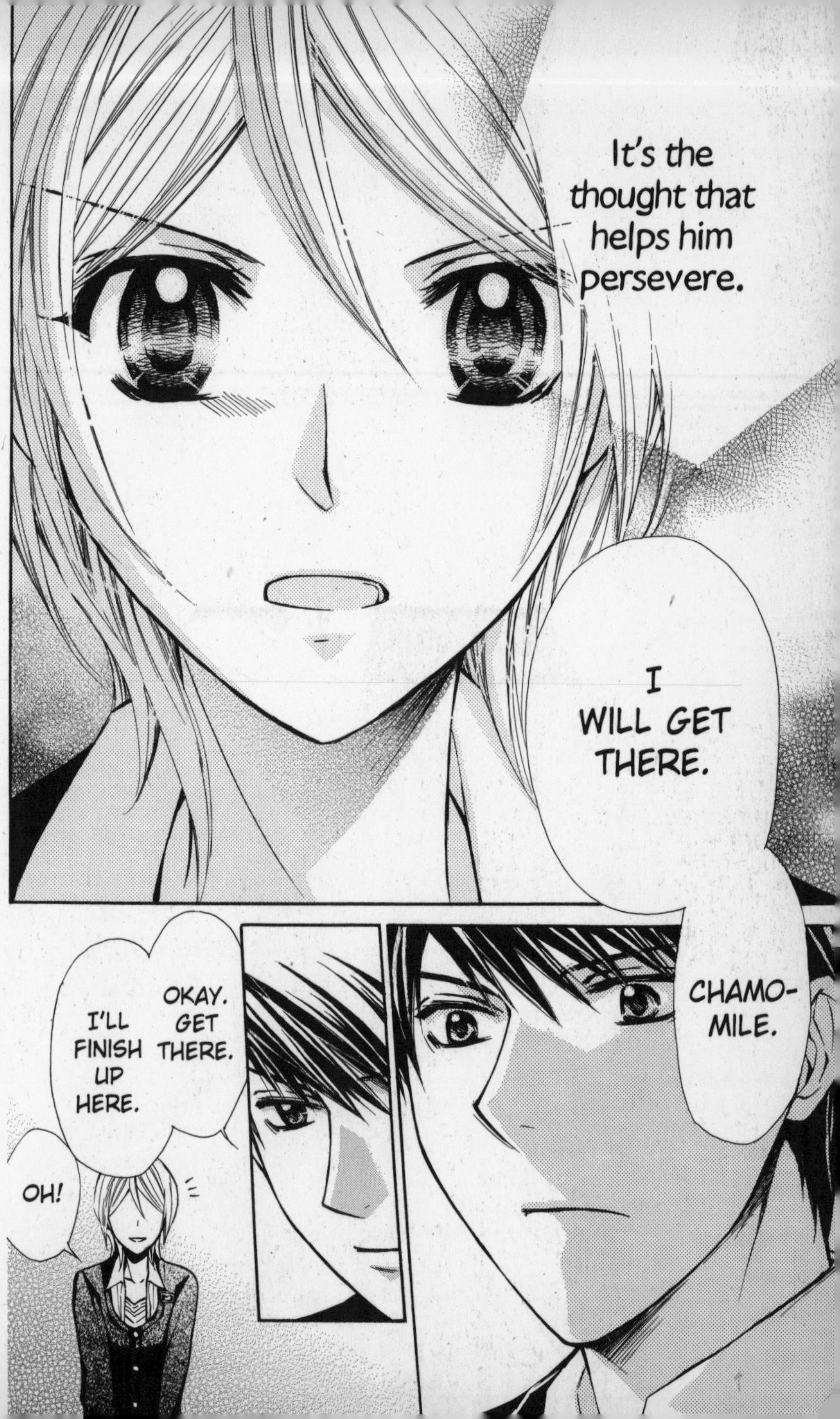
It's the thought that helps him persevere.
I WILL GET THERE.
CHAMO-MILE.
OKAY. GET THERE.
I'LL FINISH UP HERE.
OH!

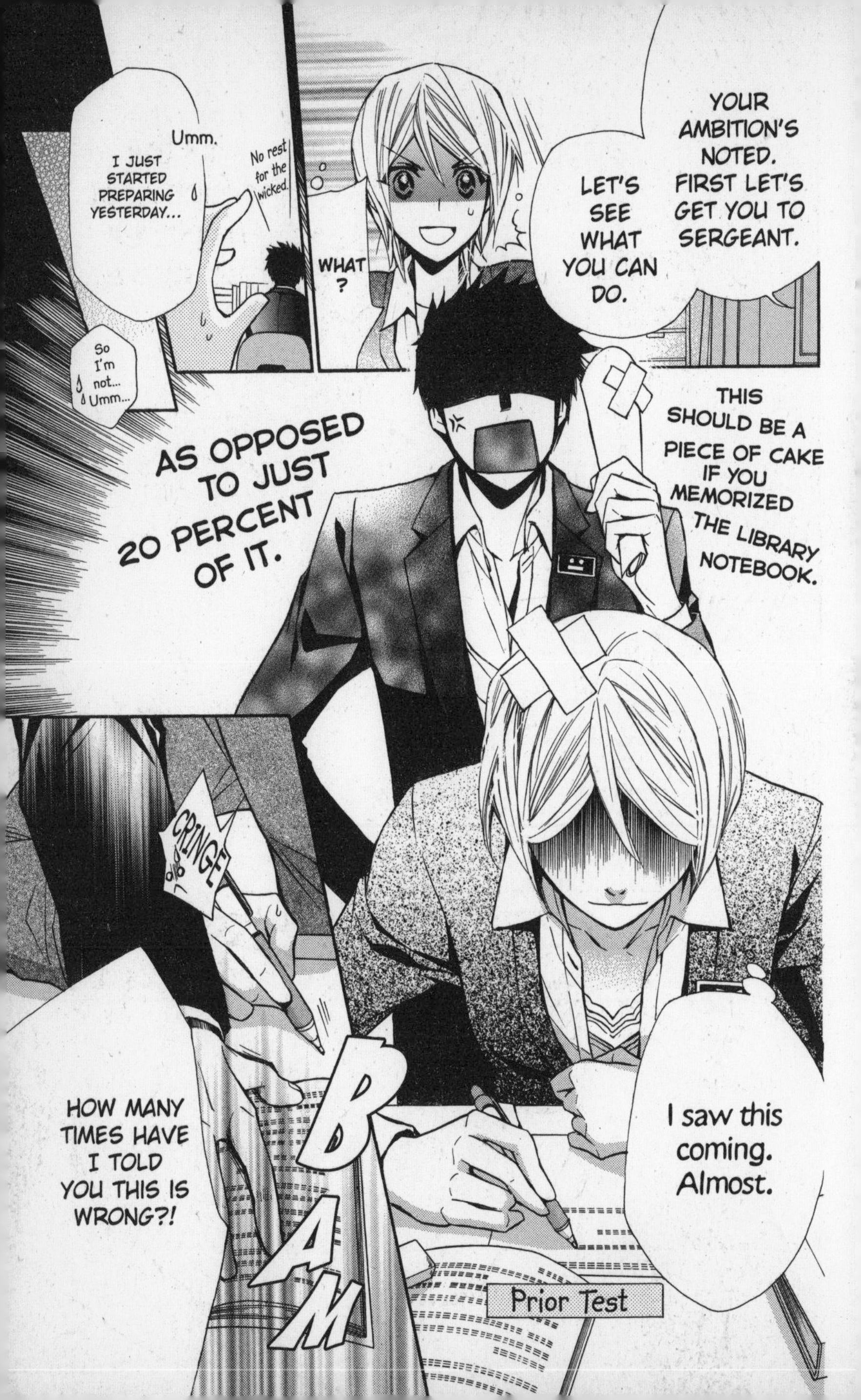
YOUR AMBITION'S NOTED. FIRST LET'S GET YOU TO SERGEANT.
LET'S SEE WHAT YOU CAN DO.
WHAT?
No rest for the wicked.
Umm.
I JUST STARTED PREPARING YESTERDAY...
So I'm not... Umm...
THIS SHOULD BE A PIECE OF CAKE IF YOU MEMORIZED THE LIBRARY NOTEBOOK.
AS OPPOSED TO JUST 20 PERCENT OF IT.
I saw this coming. Almost.
Prior Test
BAM
CRINGE
HOW MANY TIMES HAVE I TOLD YOU THIS IS WRONG?!

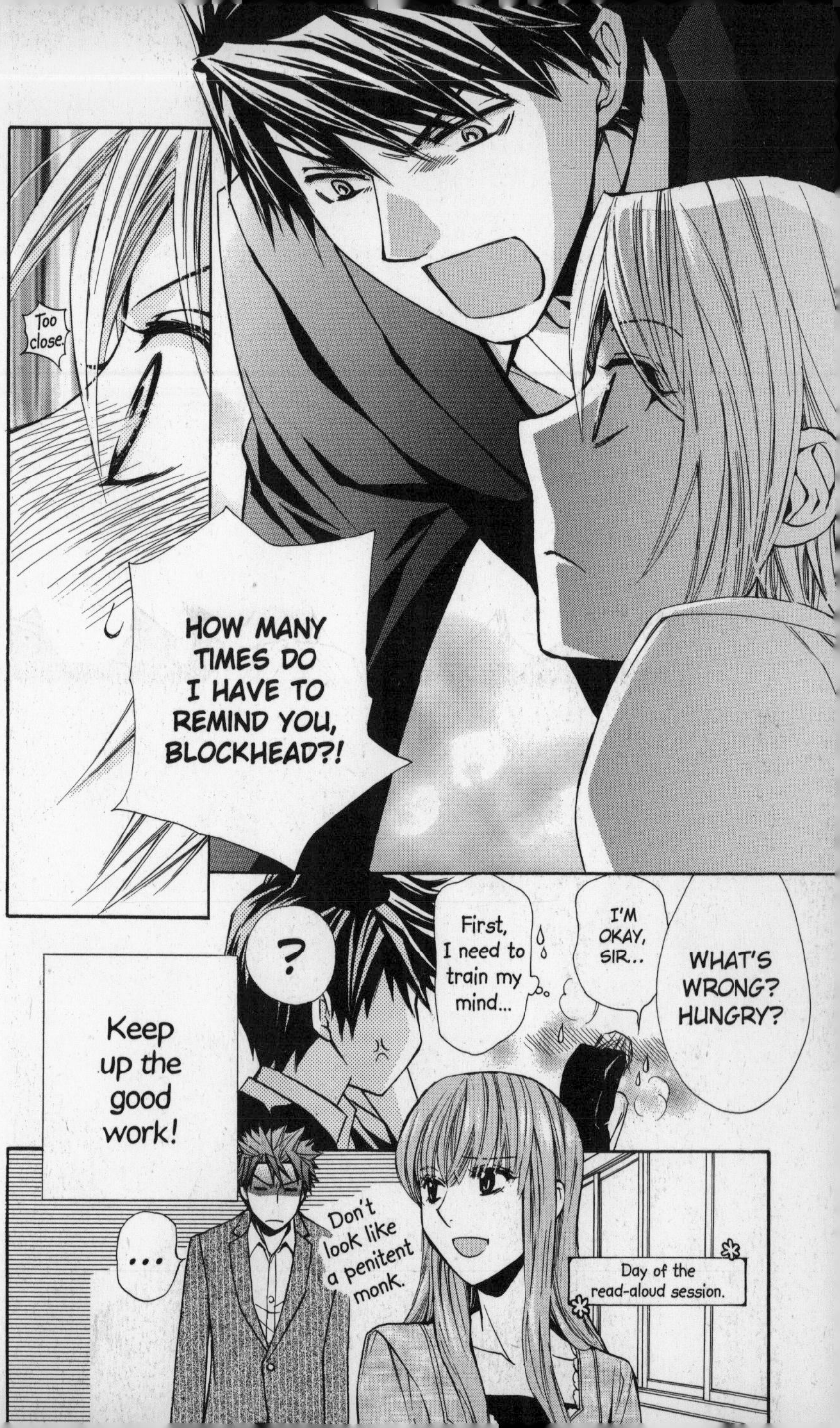
HOW MANY TIMES DO I HAVE TO REMIND YOU, BLOCKHEAD?!
Too close.
WHAT'S WRONG? HUNGRY?
I'M OKAY, SIR...
First, I need to train my mind...
?
Keep up the good work!
Day of the read-aloud session.
Don't look like a penitent monk.
...

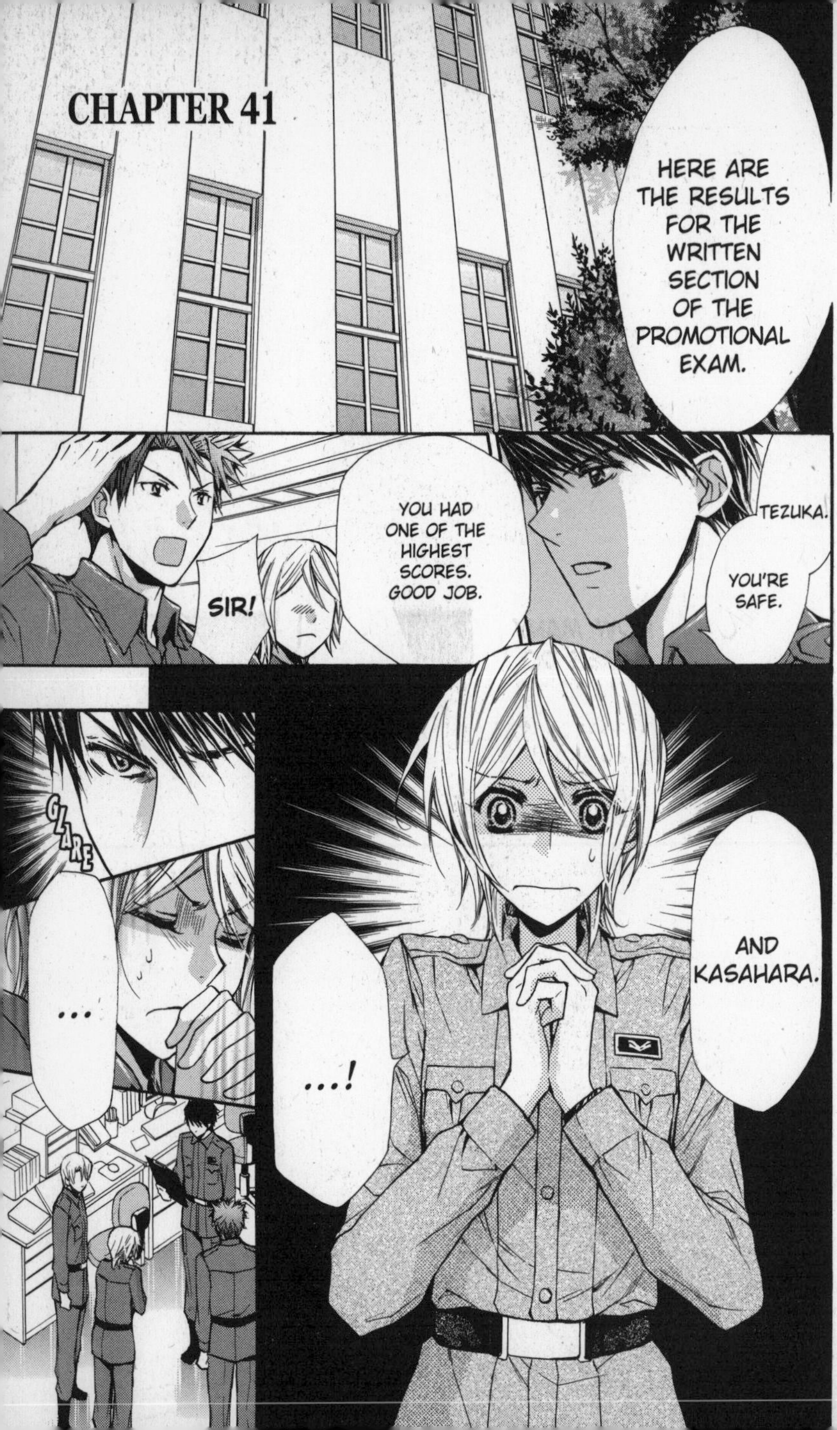
CHAPTER 41
HERE ARE THE RESULTS FOR THE WRITTEN SECTION OF THE PROMOTIONAL EXAM.
TEZUKA.
YOU'RE SAFE.
YOU HAD ONE OF THE HIGHEST SCORES. GOOD JOB.
SIR!
AND KASAHARA.
...!
GLARE
...

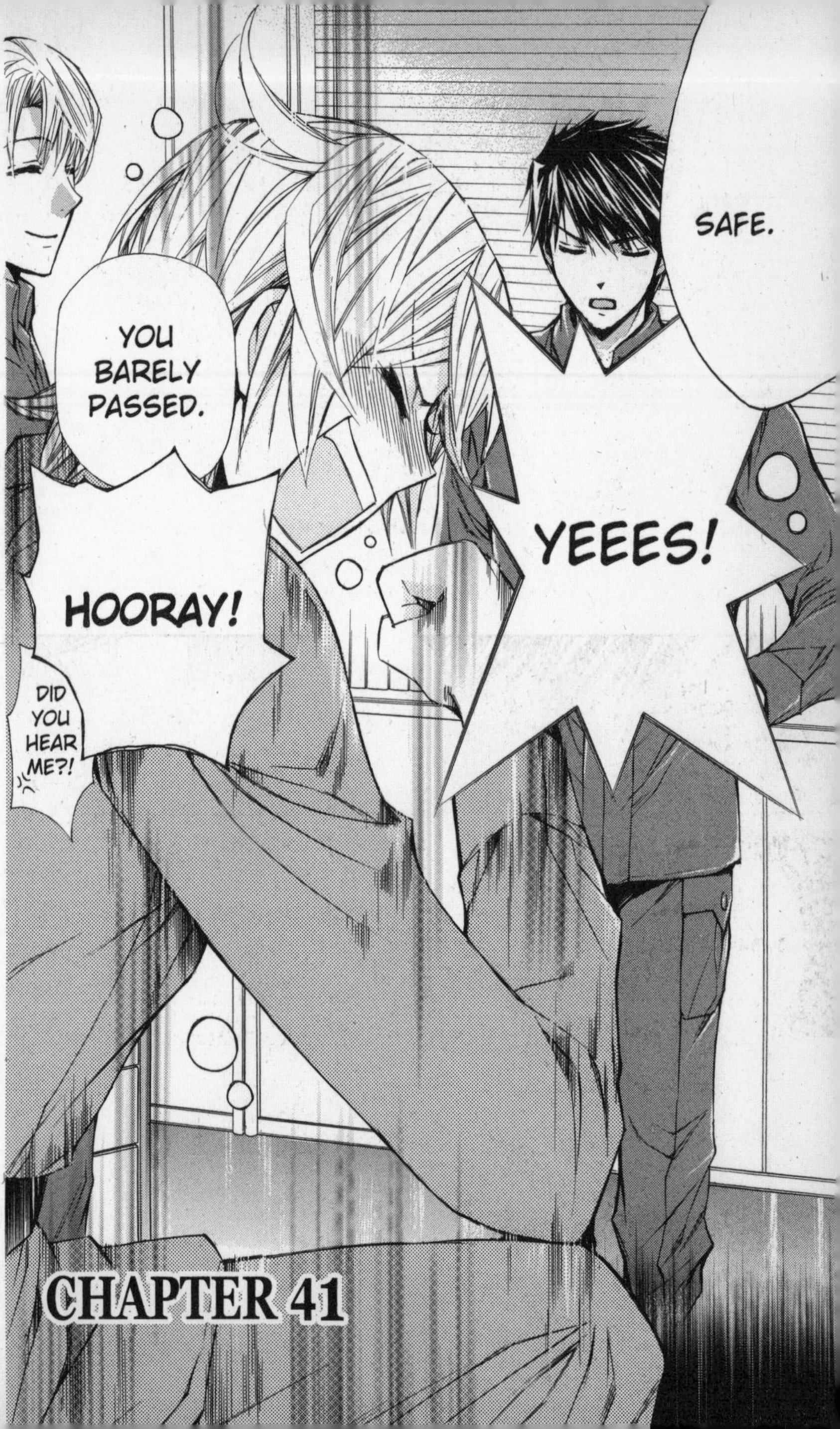
SAFE.
YOU BARELY PASSED.
YEEES!
HOORAY!
DID YOU HEAR ME?!

CHAPTER 41

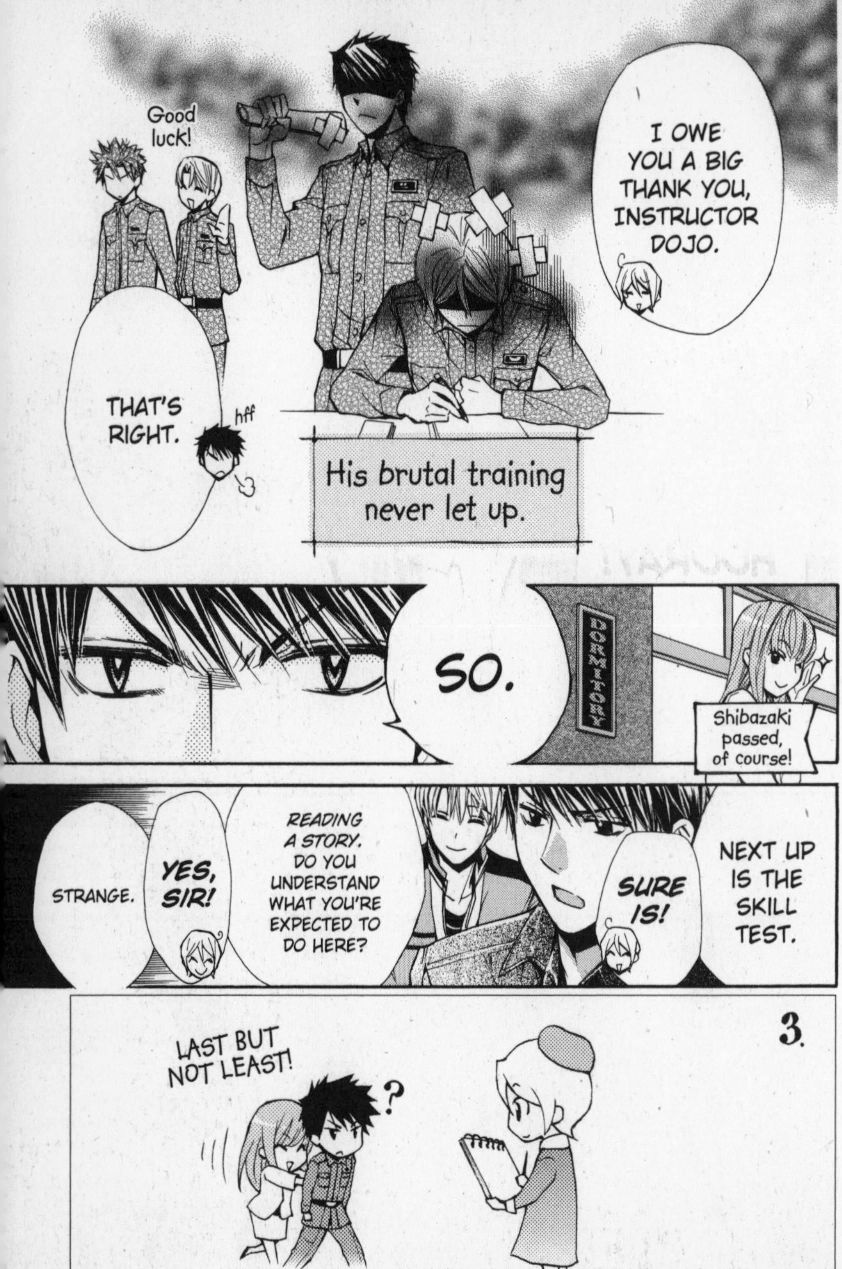
I OWE YOU A BIG THANK YOU, INSTRUCTOR DOJO.
Good luck!
His brutal training never let up.
THAT'S RIGHT.
hff
Shibazaki passed, of course!
DORMITORY
SO.
NEXT UP IS THE SKILL TEST.
SURE IS!
READING A STORY. DO YOU UNDERSTAND WHAT YOU'RE EXPECTED TO DO HERE?
YES, SIR!
STRANGE.
3.
LAST BUT NOT LEAST!
?

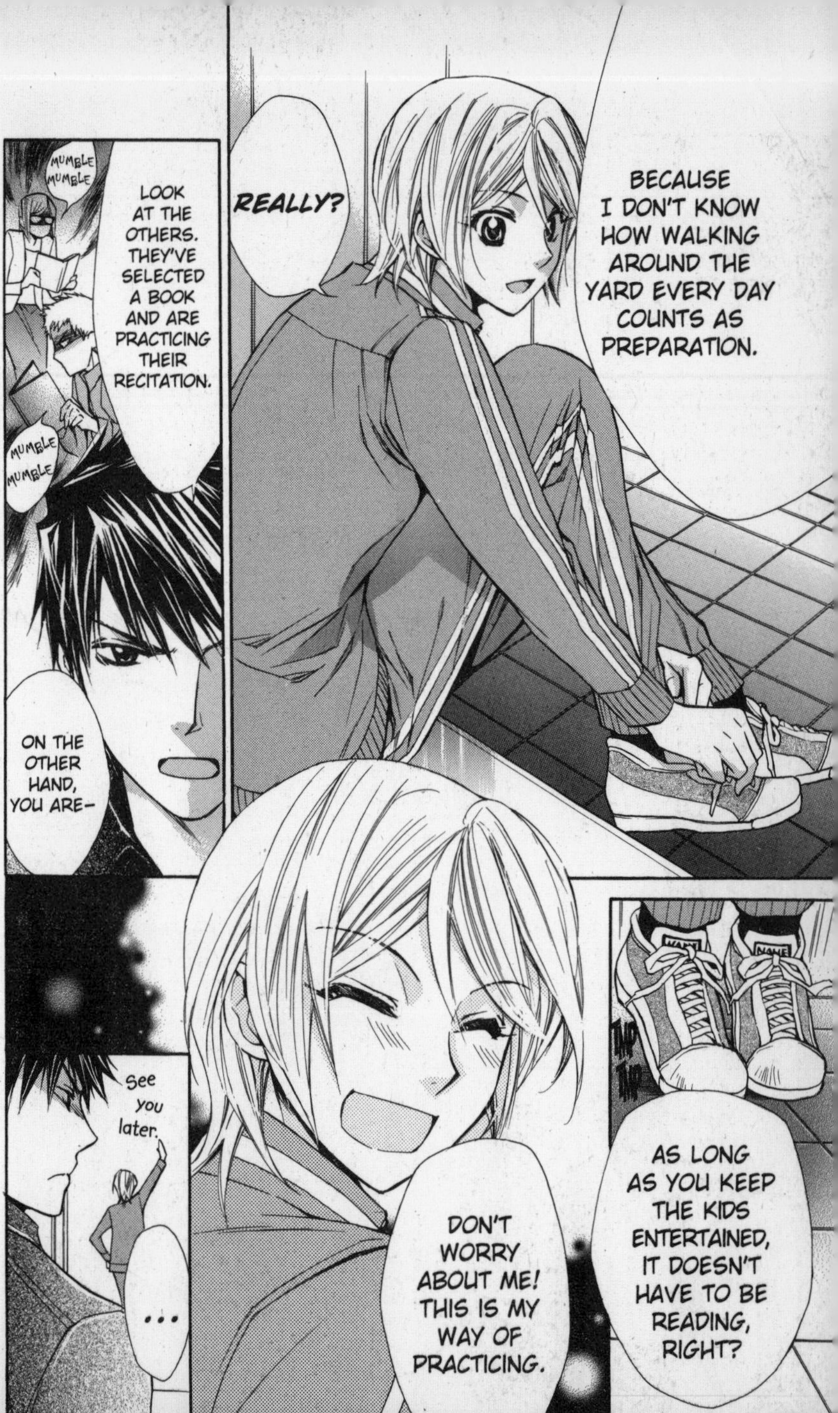
BECAUSE I DON'T KNOW HOW WALKING AROUND THE YARD EVERY DAY COUNTS AS PREPARATION.
REALLY?
MUMBLE MUMBLE
LOOK AT THE OTHERS. THEY'VE SELECTED A BOOK AND ARE PRACTICING THEIR RECITATION.
MUMBLE MUMBLE
ON THE OTHER HAND, YOU ARE–
TAP TAP
AS LONG AS YOU KEEP THE KIDS ENTERTAINED, IT DOESN'T HAVE TO BE READING, RIGHT?
DON'T WORRY ABOUT ME! THIS IS MY WAY OF PRACTICING.
See you later.
...

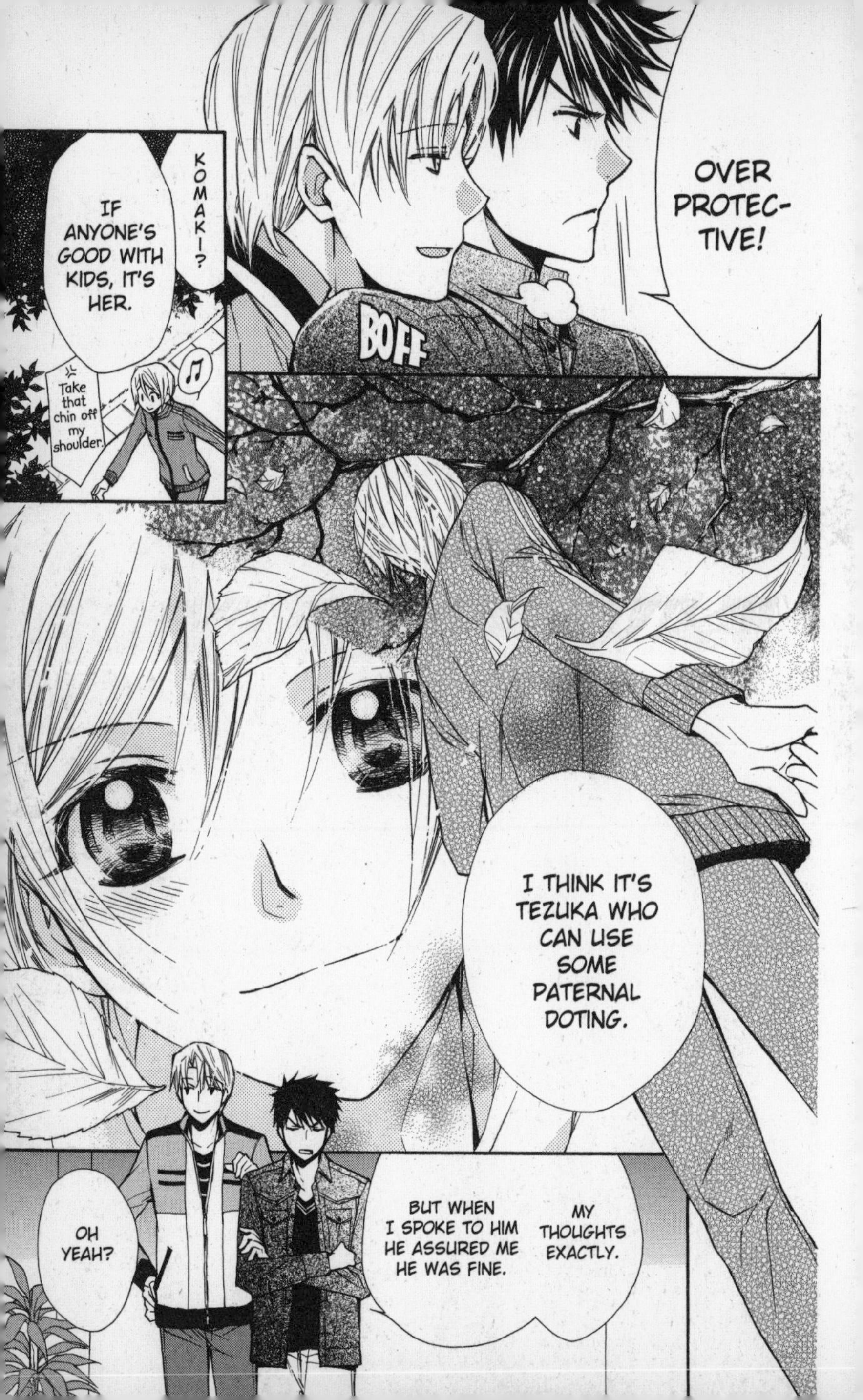
OVER PROTECTIVE!
BOFF
KOMAKI?
IF ANYONE'S GOOD WITH KIDS, IT'S HER.
Take that chin off my shoulder.
I THINK IT'S TEZUKA WHO CAN USE SOME PATERNAL DOTING.
MY THOUGHTS EXACTLY.
BUT WHEN I SPOKE TO HIM HE ASSURED ME HE WAS FINE.
OH YEAH?

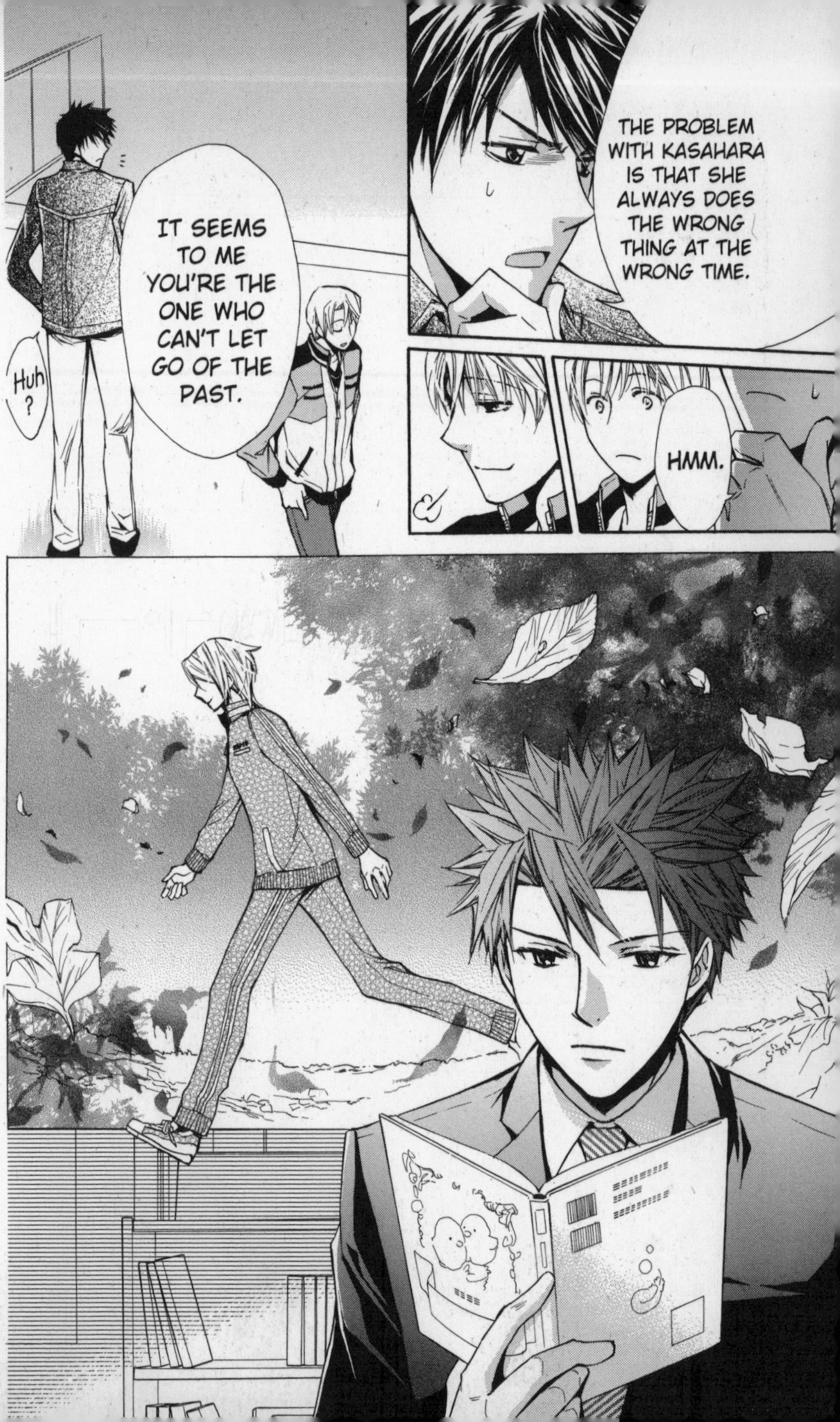
THE PROBLEM WITH KASAHARA IS THAT SHE ALWAYS DOES THE WRONG THING AT THE WRONG TIME.
HMM.
IT SEEMS TO ME YOU'RE THE ONE WHO CAN'T LET GO OF THE PAST.
Huh?

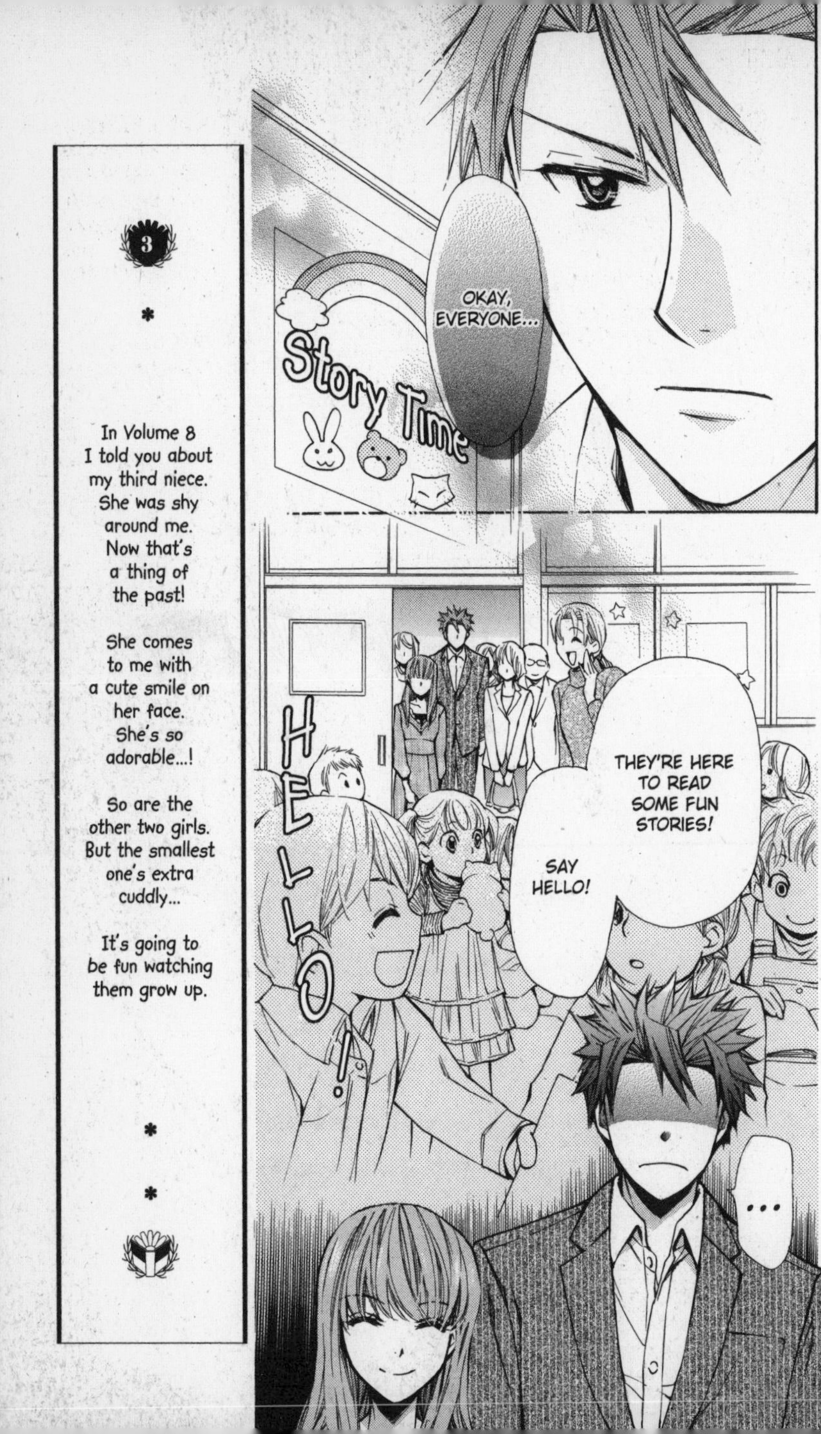
OKAY, EVERYONE...
Story Time
THEY'RE HERE TO READ SOME FUN STORIES!
SAY HELLO!
HELLO!
...

3

*

In Volume 8 I told you about my third niece. She was shy around me. Now that's a thing of the past!

She comes to me with a cute smile on her face. She's so adorable...!

So are the other two girls. But the smallest one's extra cuddly...

It's going to be fun watching them grow up.

*

*

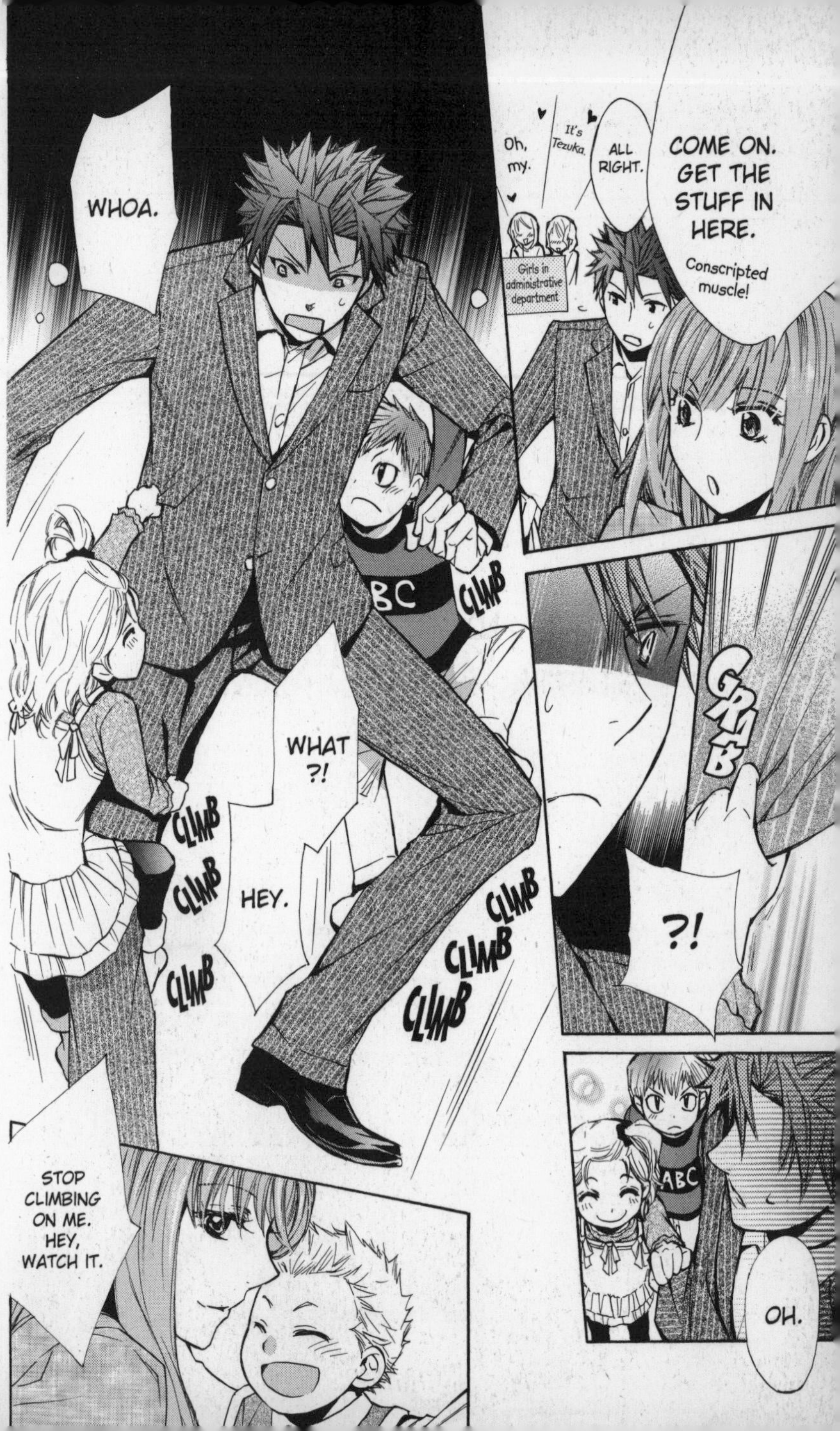
COME ON. GET THE STUFF IN HERE.
Conscripted muscle!
ALL RIGHT.
It's Tezuka.
Oh, my.
Girls in administrative department
GRAB
?!
OH.
WHOA.
CLIMB
WHAT ?!
CLIMB
CLIMB
HEY.
CLIMB
CLIMB
CLIMB
CLIMB
STOP CLIMBING ON ME. HEY, WATCH IT.

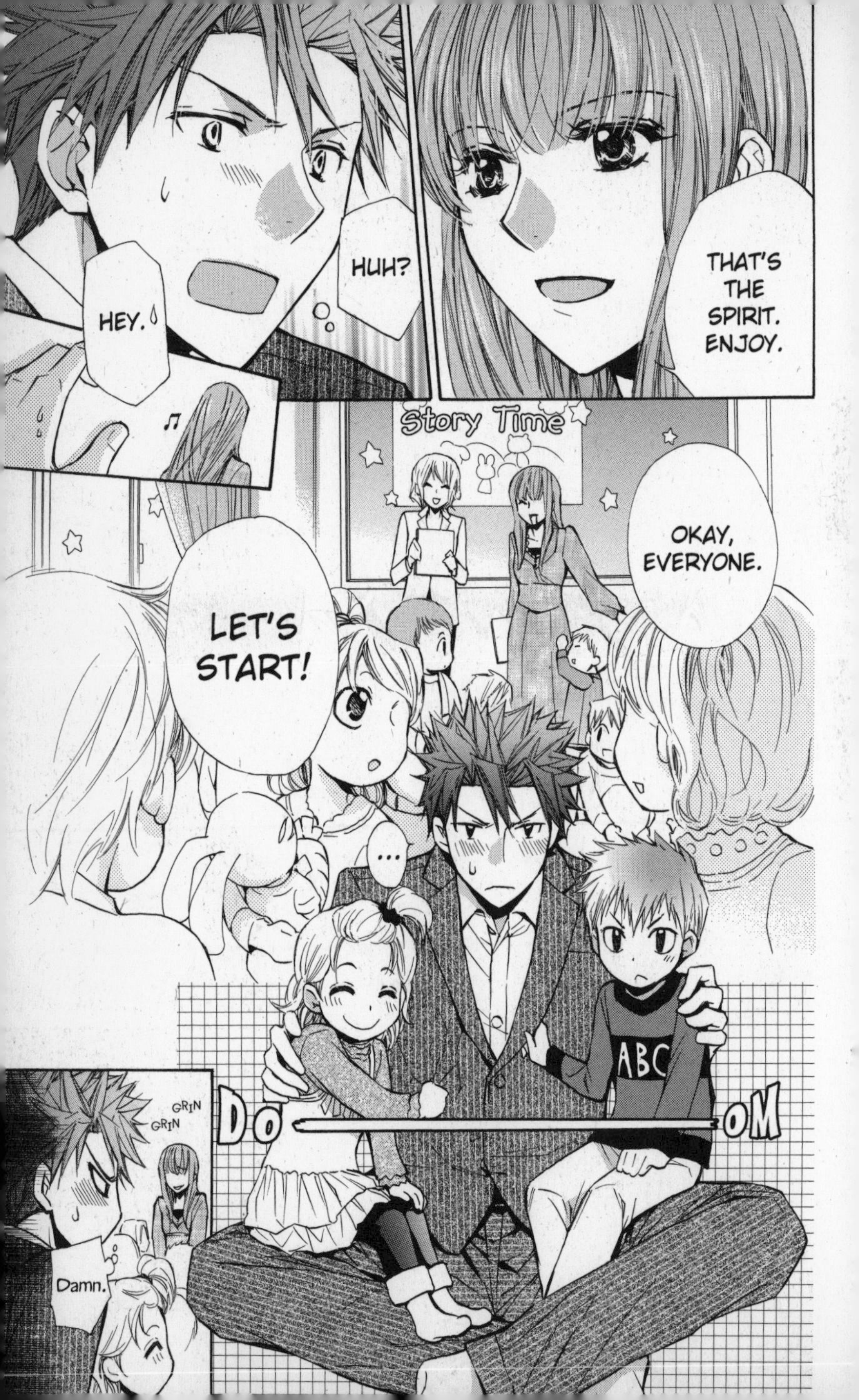
THAT'S THE SPIRIT. ENJOY.
HUH?
HEY.
Story Time
OKAY, EVERYONE.
LET'S START!
...
DOOM
GRIN GRIN
Damn.

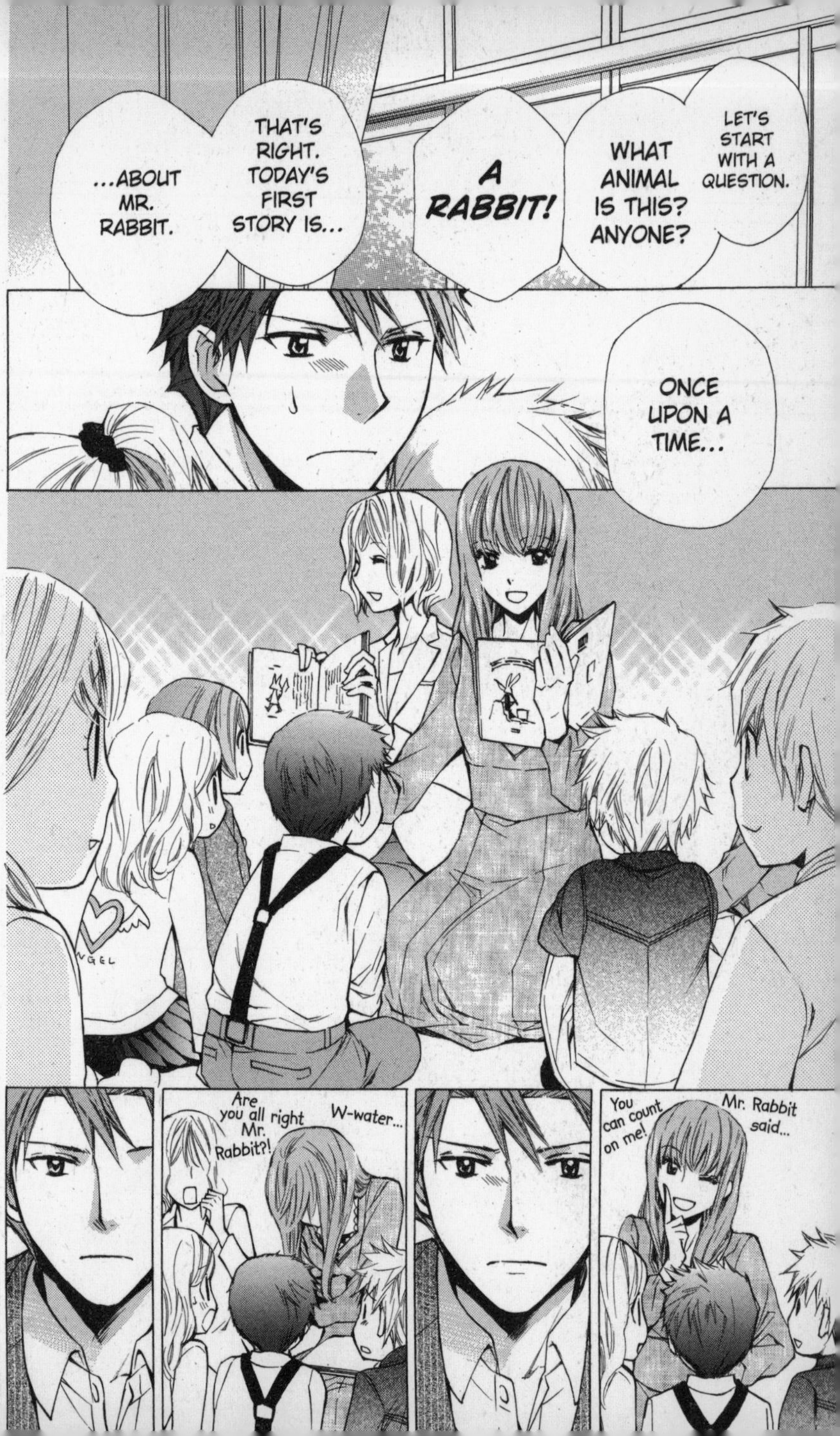
LET'S START WITH A QUESTION.
WHAT ANIMAL IS THIS? ANYONE?
A RABBIT!
THAT'S RIGHT. TODAY'S FIRST STORY IS...
...ABOUT MR. RABBIT.
ONCE UPON A TIME...
Mr. Rabbit said...
You can count on me!
W-water...
Are you all right Mr. Rabbit?!

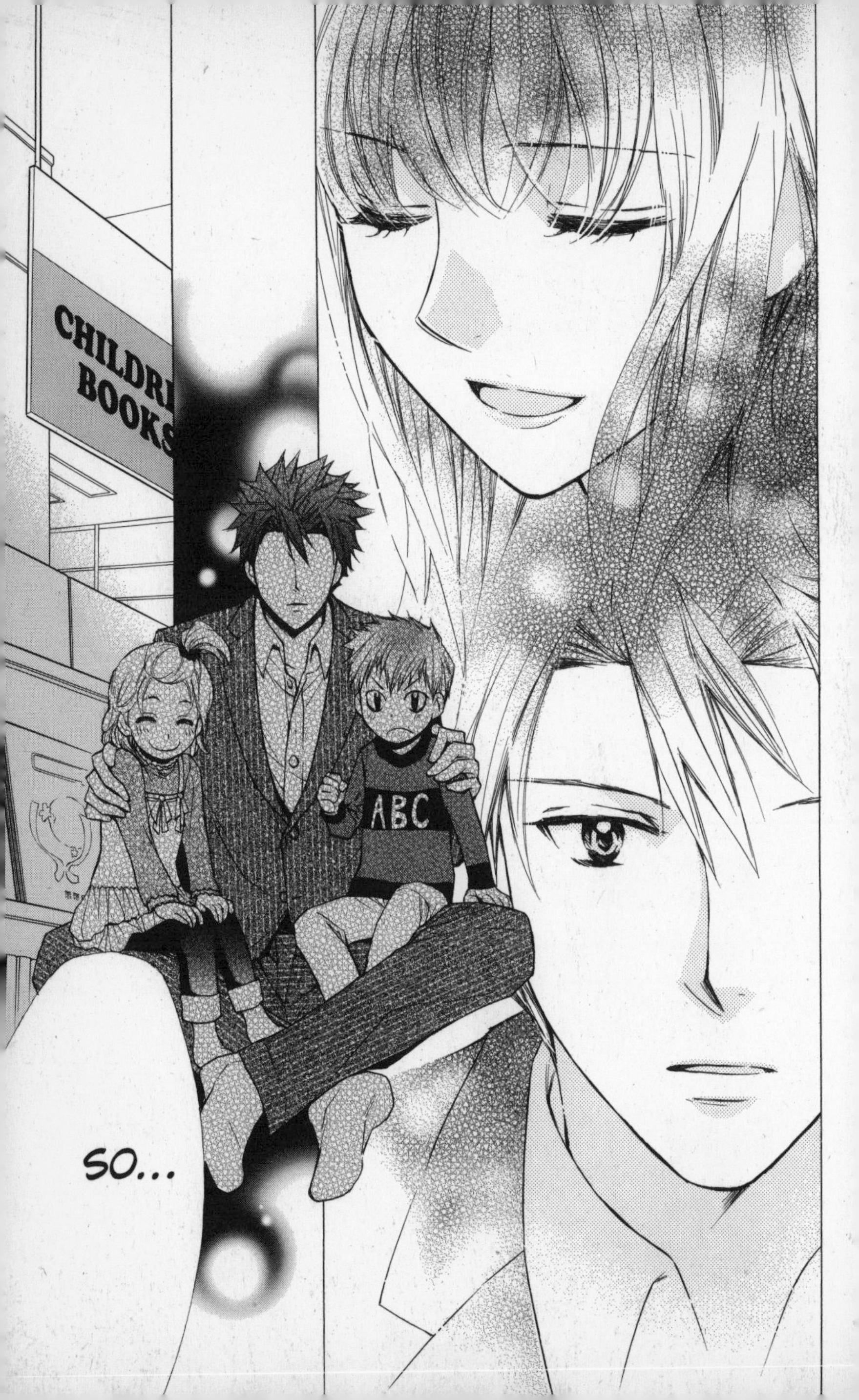
SO...
ABC
CHILDR
BOOKS

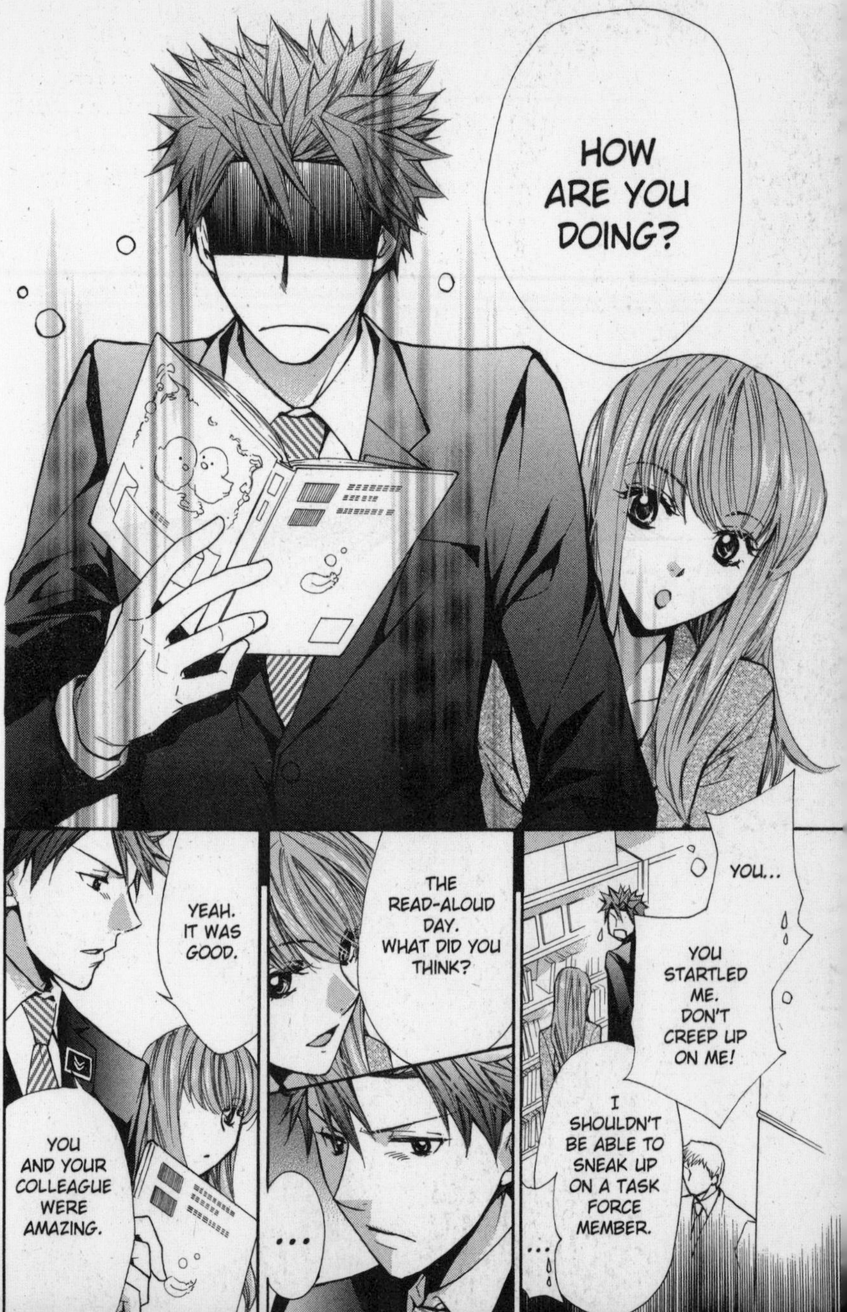

HOW ARE YOU DOING?
YOU...
YOU STARTLED ME. DON'T CREEP UP ON ME!
I SHOULDN'T BE ABLE TO SNEAK UP ON A TASK FORCE MEMBER.
...
THE READ-ALOUD DAY. WHAT DID YOU THINK?
...
YEAH. IT WAS GOOD.
YOU AND YOUR COLLEAGUE WERE AMAZING.

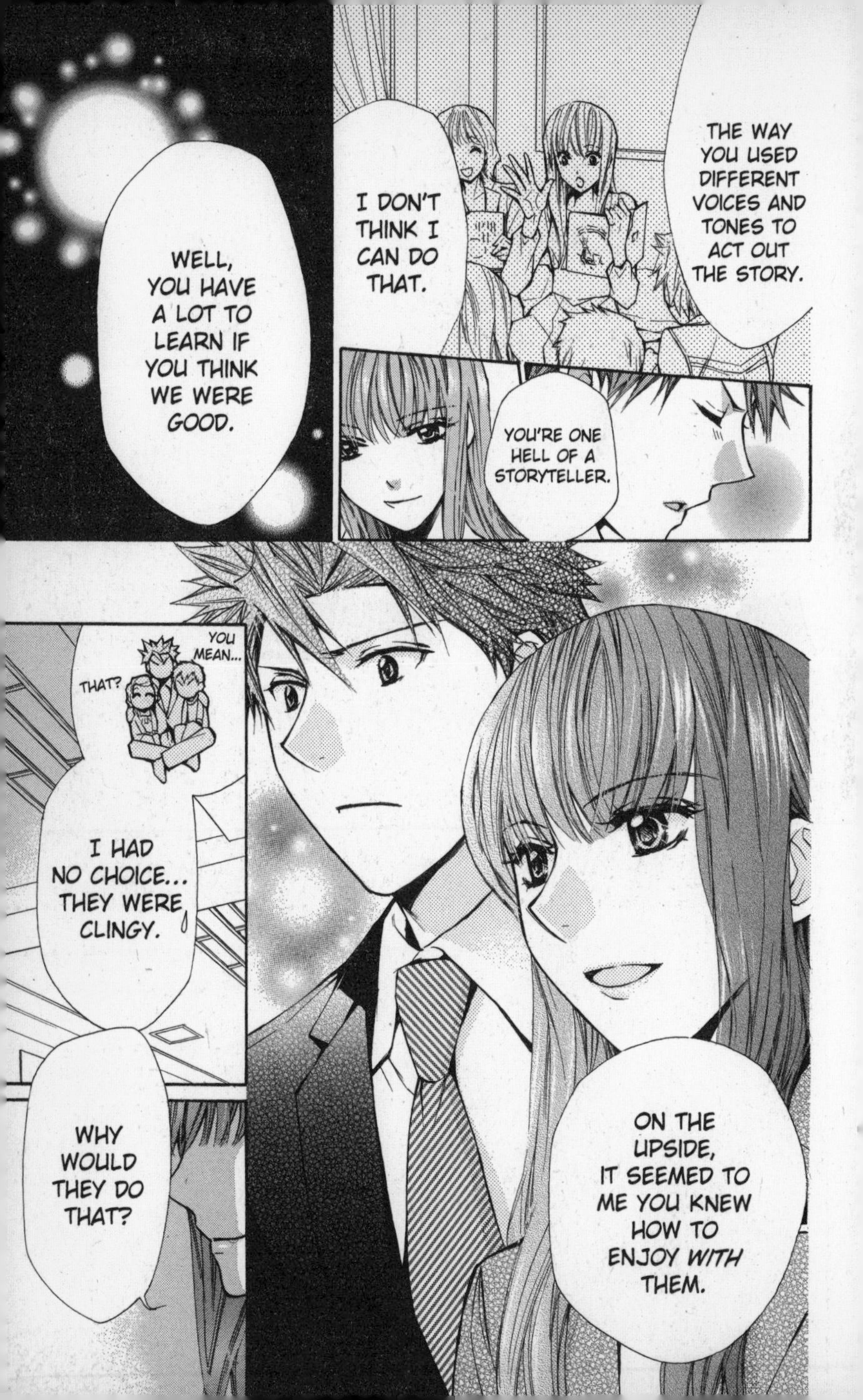
THE WAY YOU USED DIFFERENT VOICES AND TONES TO ACT OUT THE STORY.
I DON'T THINK I CAN DO THAT.
YOU'RE ONE HELL OF A STORYTELLER.
WELL, YOU HAVE A LOT TO LEARN IF YOU THINK WE WERE GOOD.
ON THE UPSIDE, IT SEEMED TO ME YOU KNEW HOW TO ENJOY *WITH* THEM.
YOU MEAN...
THAT?
I HAD NO CHOICE... THEY WERE CLINGY.
WHY WOULD THEY DO THAT?

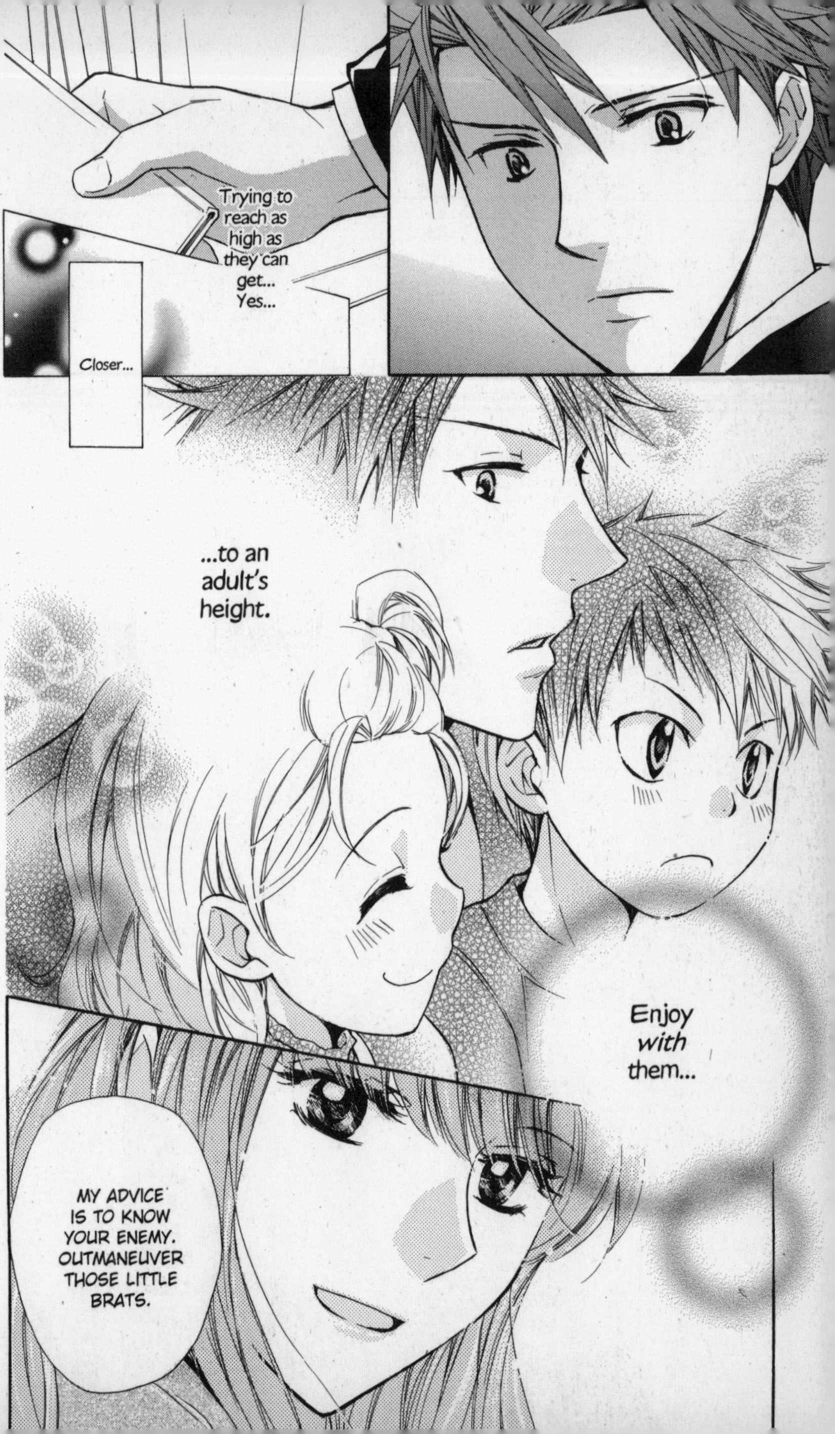
Trying to reach as high as they can get... Yes...
Closer...
...to an adult's height.
Enjoy *with* them...
MY ADVICE IS TO KNOW YOUR ENEMY. OUTMANEUVER THOSE LITTLE BRATS.

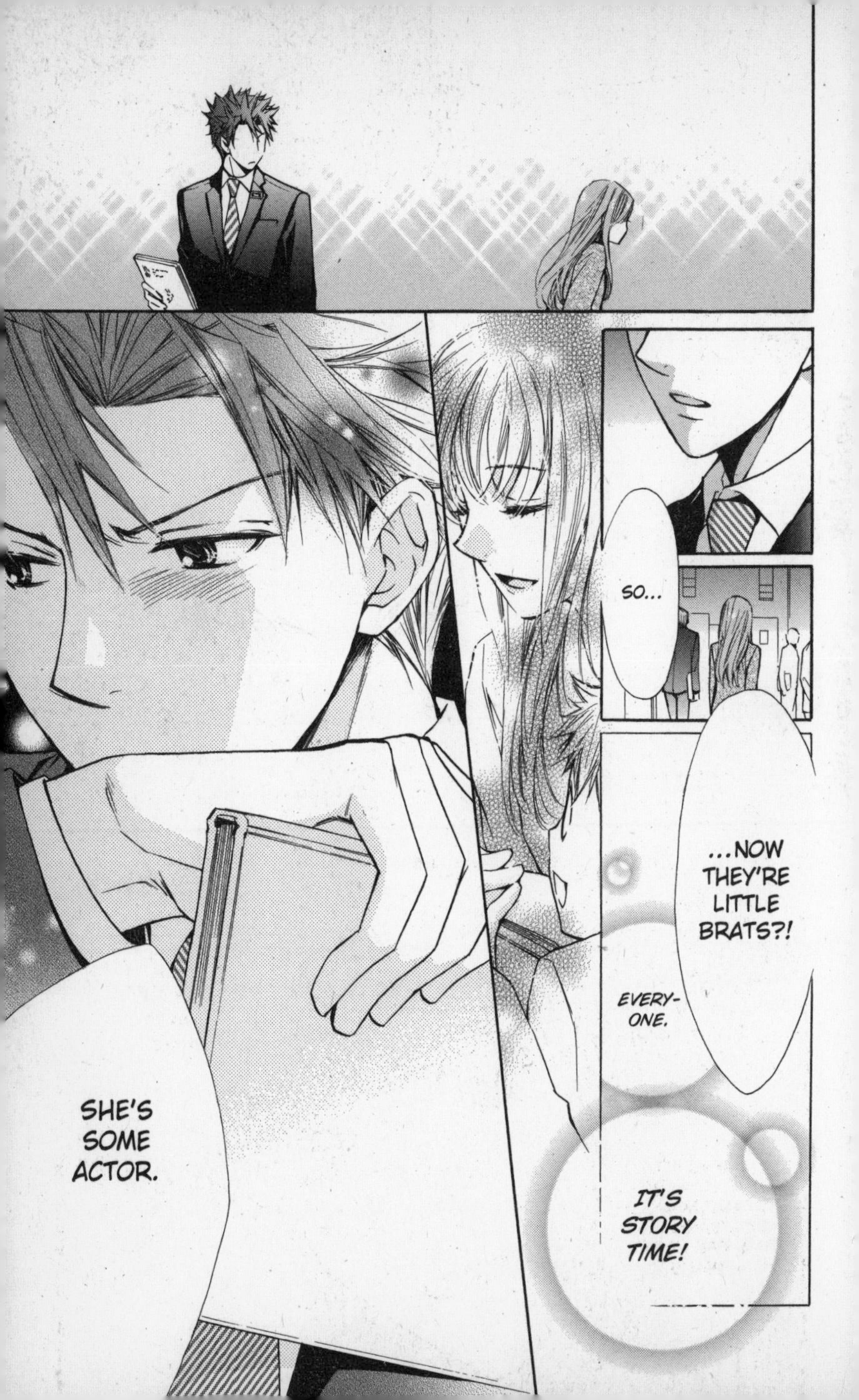
SO...
...NOW THEY'RE LITTLE BRATS?!
EVERY-ONE.
IT'S STORY TIME!
SHE'S SOME ACTOR.

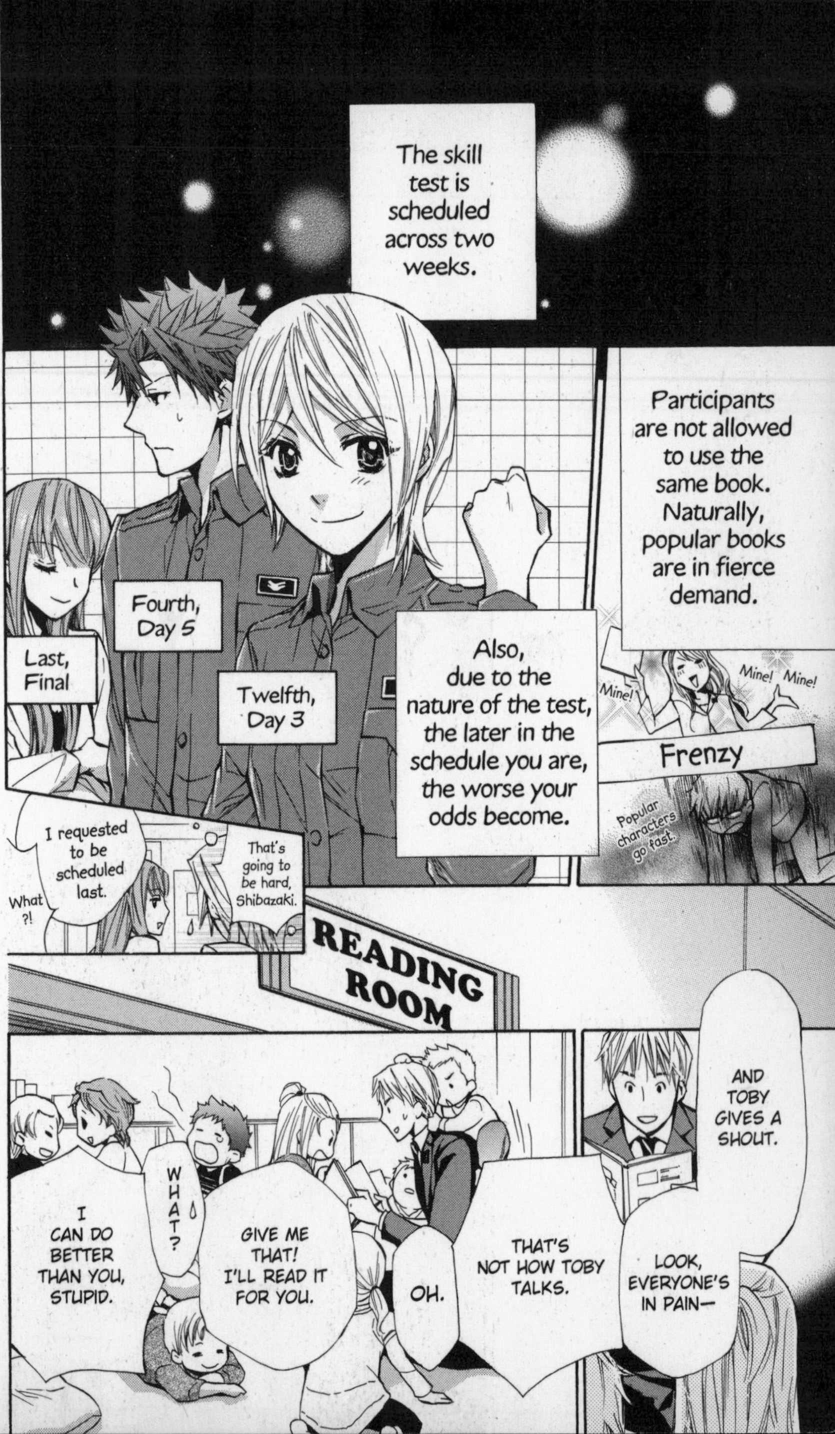

The skill test is scheduled across two weeks.
Twelfth, Day 3
Fourth, Day 5
Last, Final
Participants are not allowed to use the same book. Naturally, popular books are in fierce demand.
Mine! Mine! Mine!
Frenzy
Popular characters go fast.
Also, due to the nature of the test, the later in the schedule you are, the worse your odds become.
That's going to be hard, Shibazaki.
I requested to be scheduled last.
What ?!
READING ROOM
AND TOBY GIVES A SHOUT.
LOOK, EVERYONE'S IN PAIN—
THAT'S NOT HOW TOBY TALKS.
OH.
GIVE ME THAT! I'LL READ IT FOR YOU.
WHAT?
I CAN DO BETTER THAN YOU, STUPID.

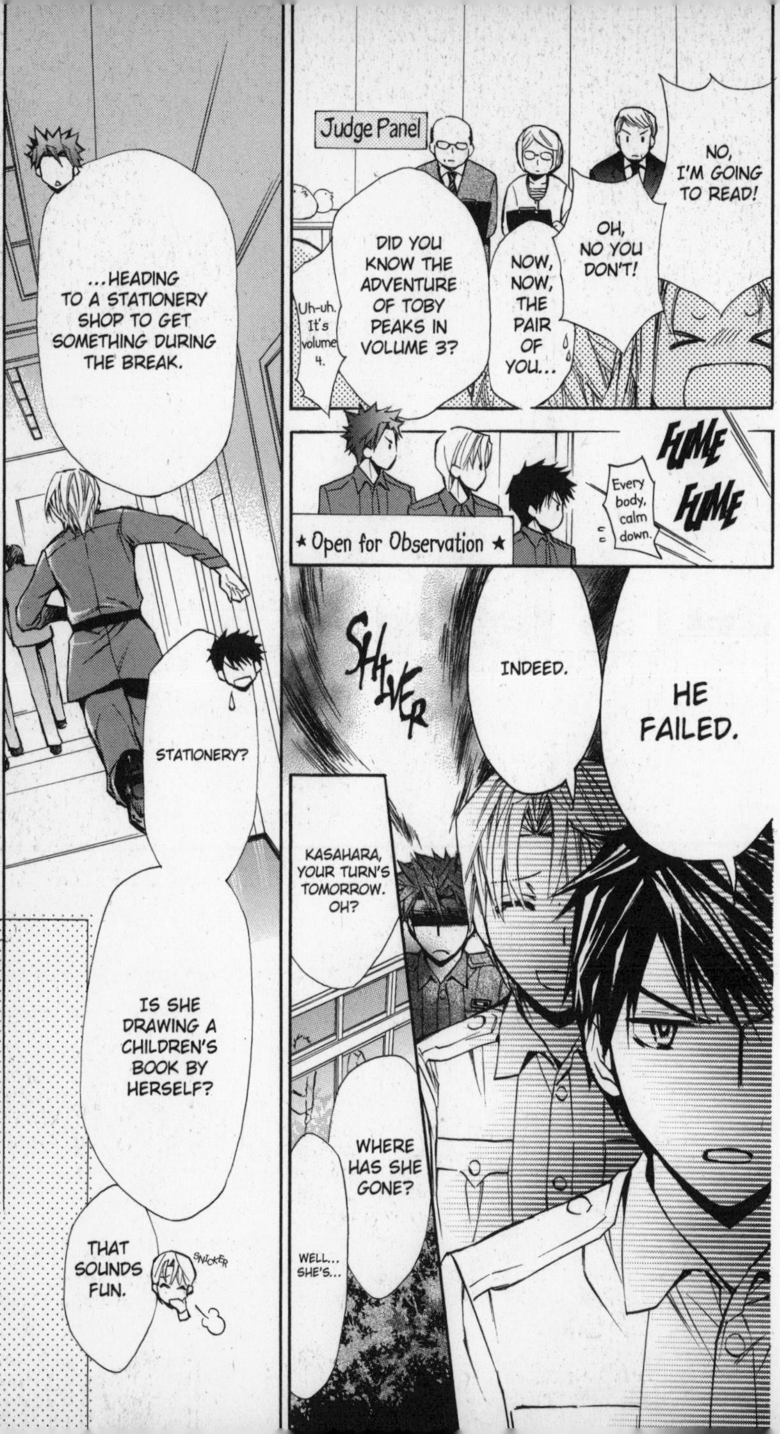
NO, I'M GOING TO READ!
OH, NO YOU DON'T!
Judge Panel
NOW, NOW, THE PAIR OF YOU...
DID YOU KNOW THE ADVENTURE OF TOBY PEAKS IN VOLUME 3?
Uh-uh. It's volume 4.
FUME FUME
Every body, calm down.
★ Open for Observation ★
HE FAILED.
INDEED.
SHIVER
KASAHARA, YOUR TURN'S TOMORROW. OH?
WHERE HAS SHE GONE?
WELL... SHE'S...
...HEADING TO A STATIONERY SHOP TO GET SOMETHING DURING THE BREAK.
STATIONERY?
IS SHE DRAWING A CHILDREN'S BOOK BY HERSELF?
THAT SOUNDS FUN.
SNICKER

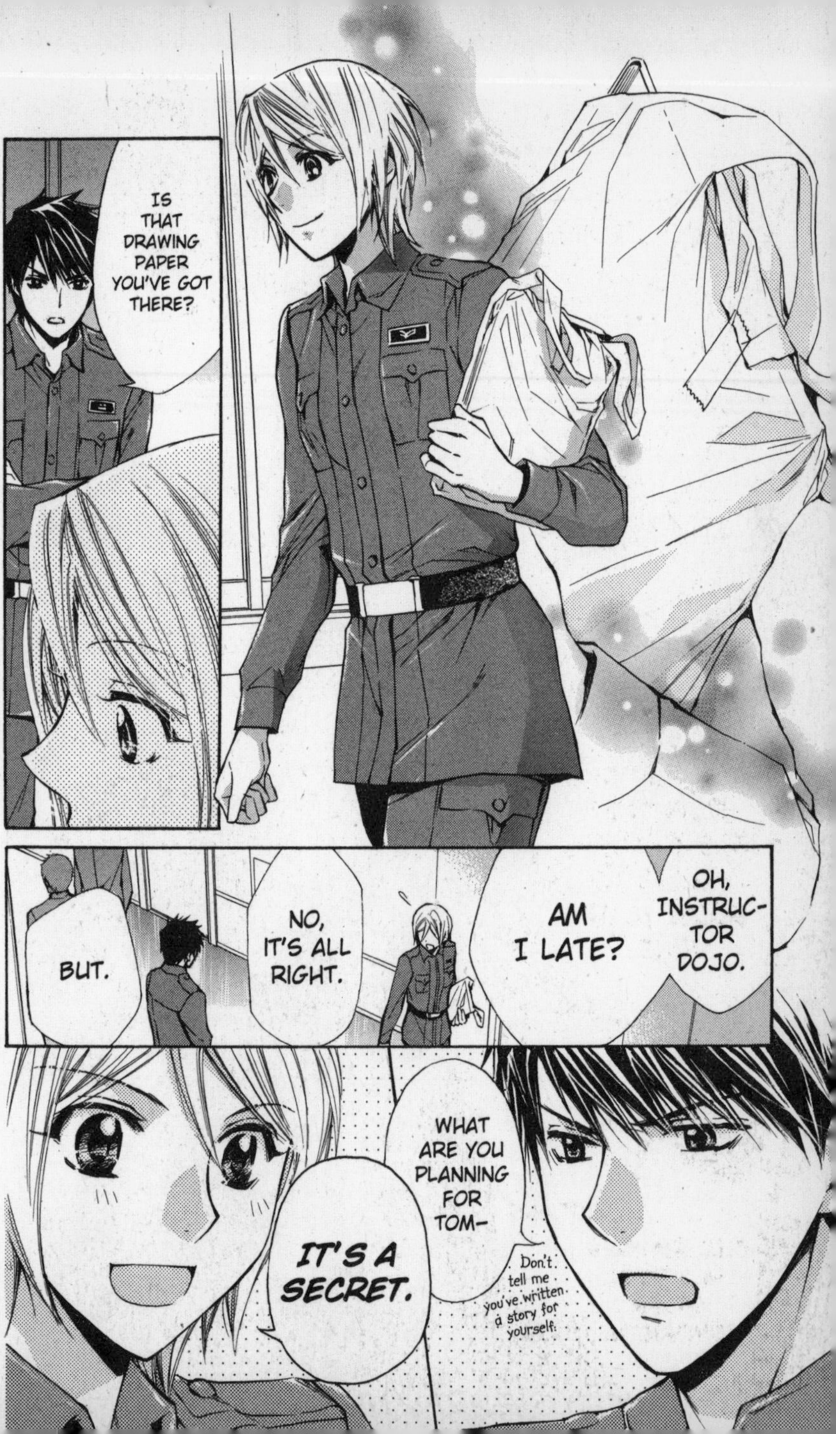
IS THAT DRAWING PAPER YOU'VE GOT THERE?
OH, INSTRUCTOR DOJO.
AM I LATE?
NO, IT'S ALL RIGHT.
BUT.
WHAT ARE YOU PLANNING FOR TOM-
IT'S A SECRET.
Don't tell me you've written a story for yourself.

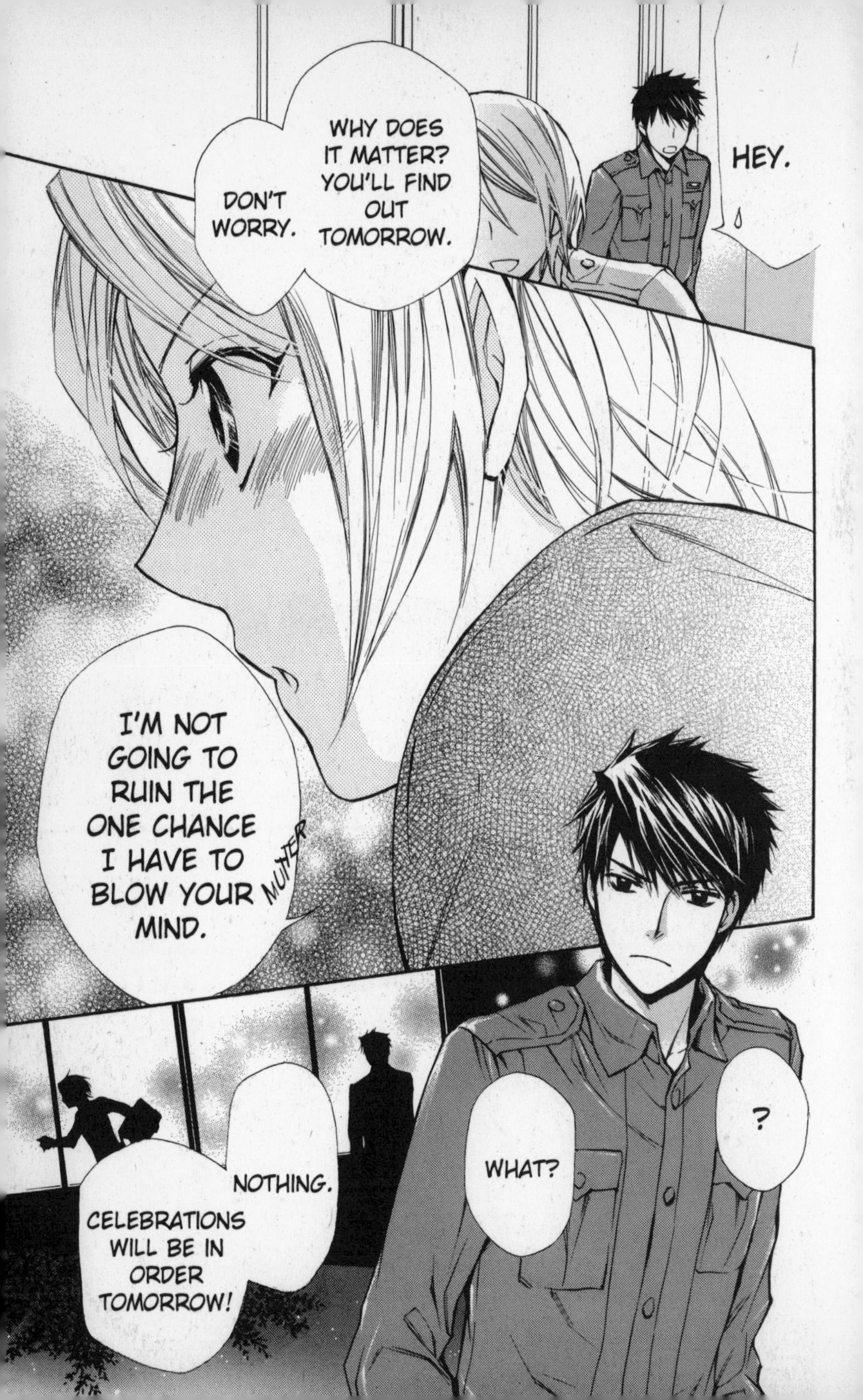
HEY.
WHY DOES IT MATTER? YOU'LL FIND OUT TOMORROW.
DON'T WORRY.
I'M NOT GOING TO RUIN THE ONE CHANCE I HAVE TO BLOW YOUR MIND.
MUTTER
?
WHAT?
NOTHING.
CELEBRATIONS WILL BE IN ORDER TOMORROW!

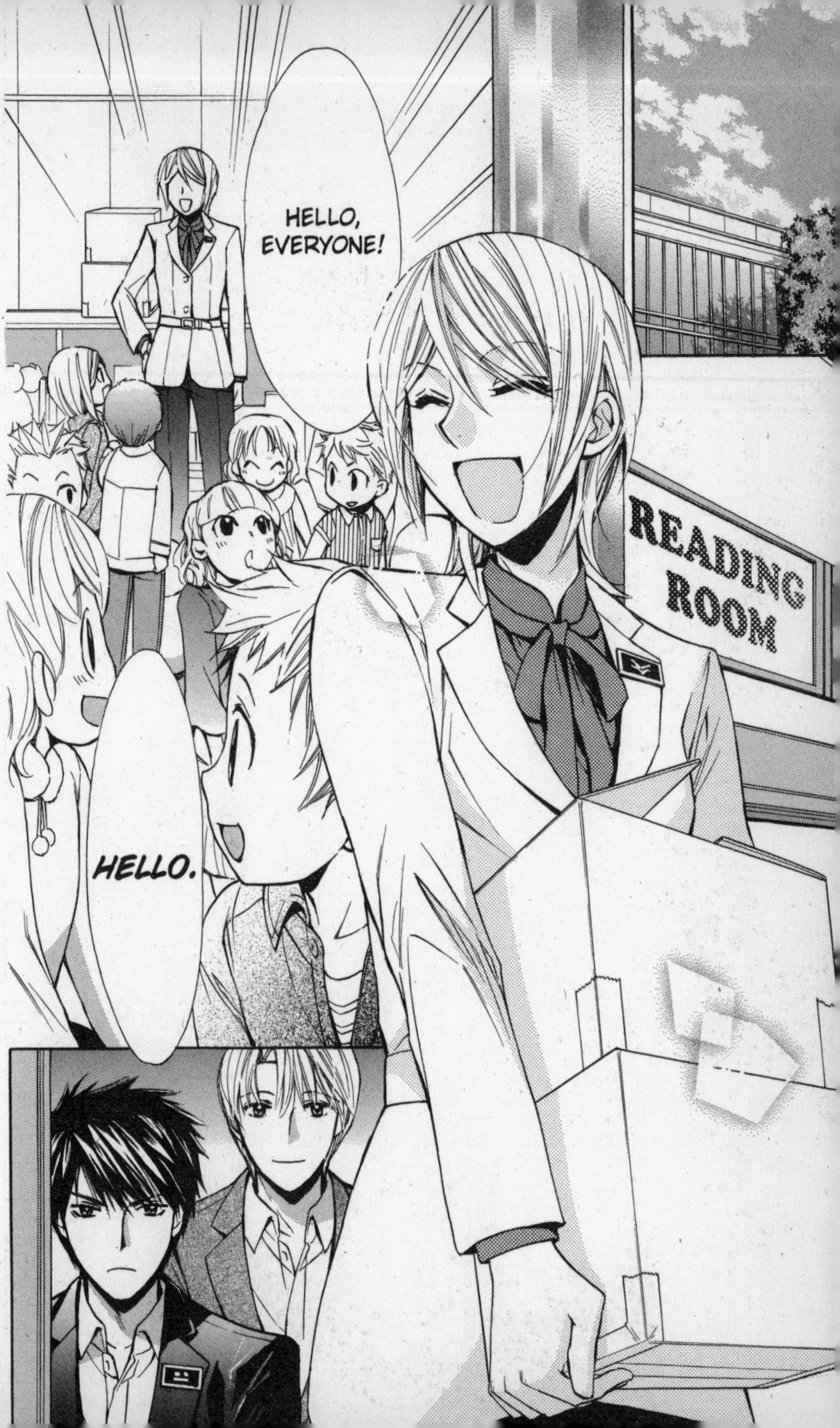
HELLO, EVERYONE!
READING ROOM
HELLO.

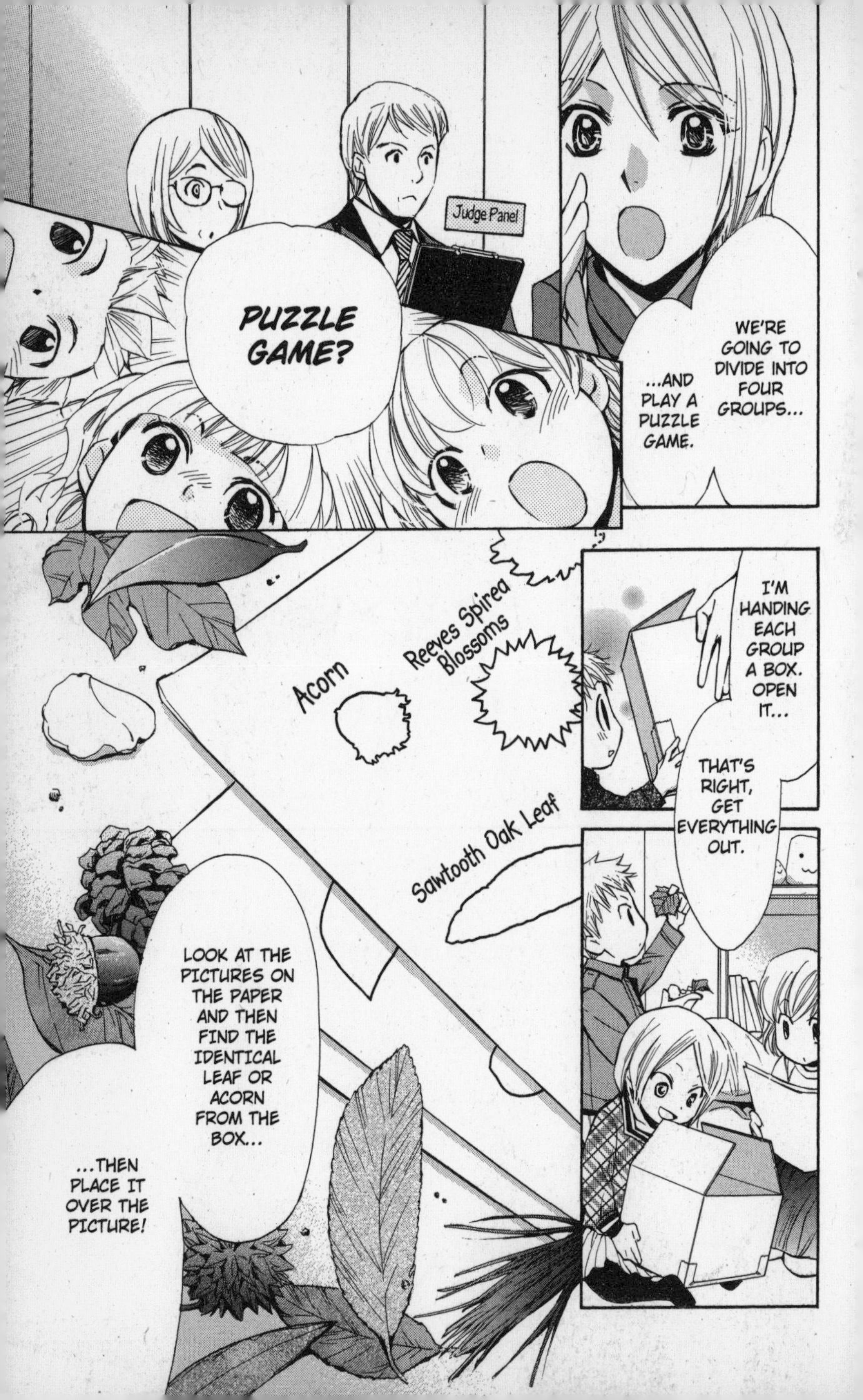
WE'RE GOING TO DIVIDE INTO FOUR GROUPS...
...AND PLAY A PUZZLE GAME.
Judge Panel
PUZZLE GAME?
I'M HANDING EACH GROUP A BOX. OPEN IT...
THAT'S RIGHT, GET EVERYTHING OUT.
Reeves Spirea Blossoms
Acorn
Sawtooth Oak Leaf
LOOK AT THE PICTURES ON THE PAPER AND THEN FIND THE IDENTICAL LEAF OR ACORN FROM THE BOX...
...THEN PLACE IT OVER THE PICTURE!

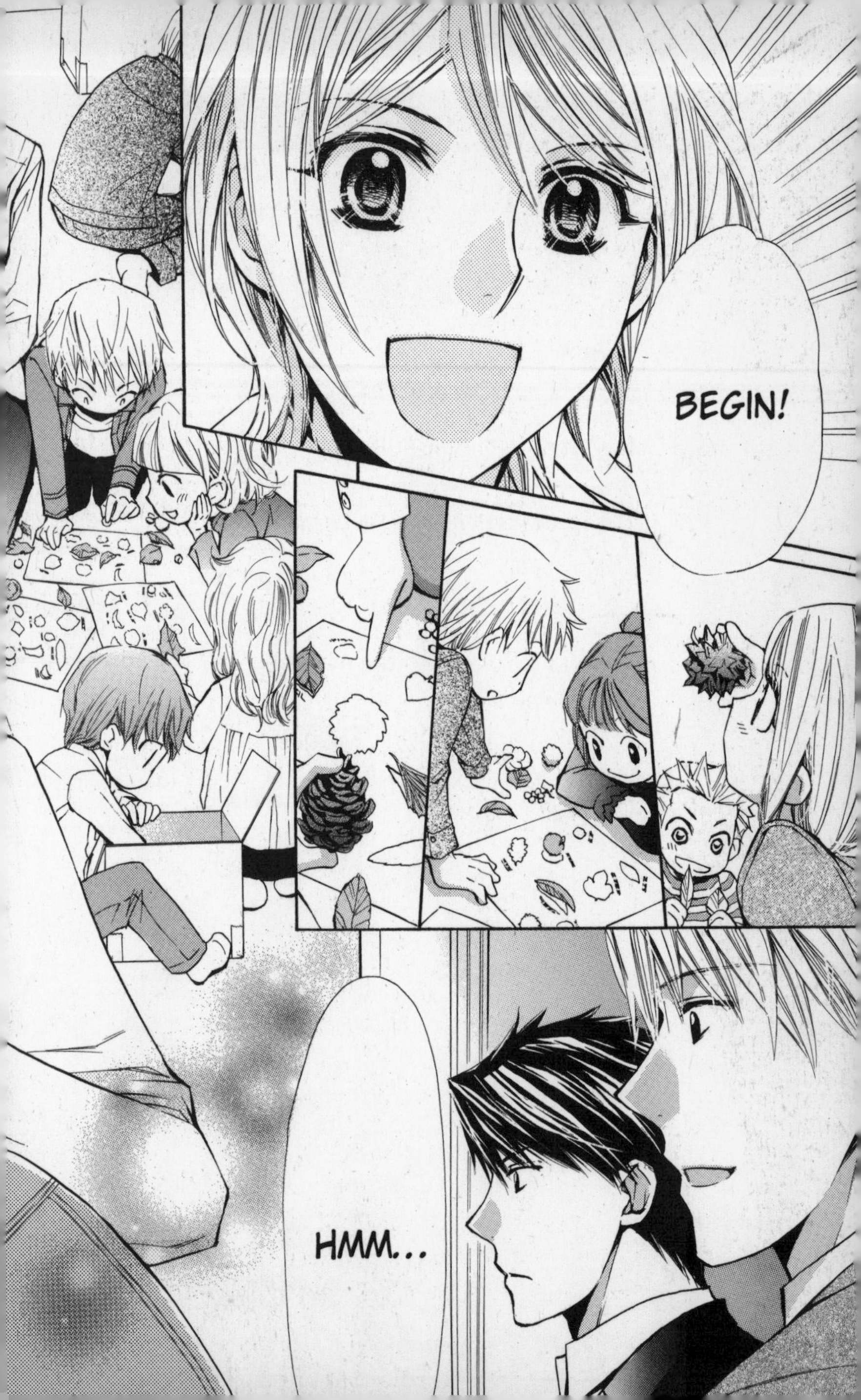
BEGIN!
HMM...

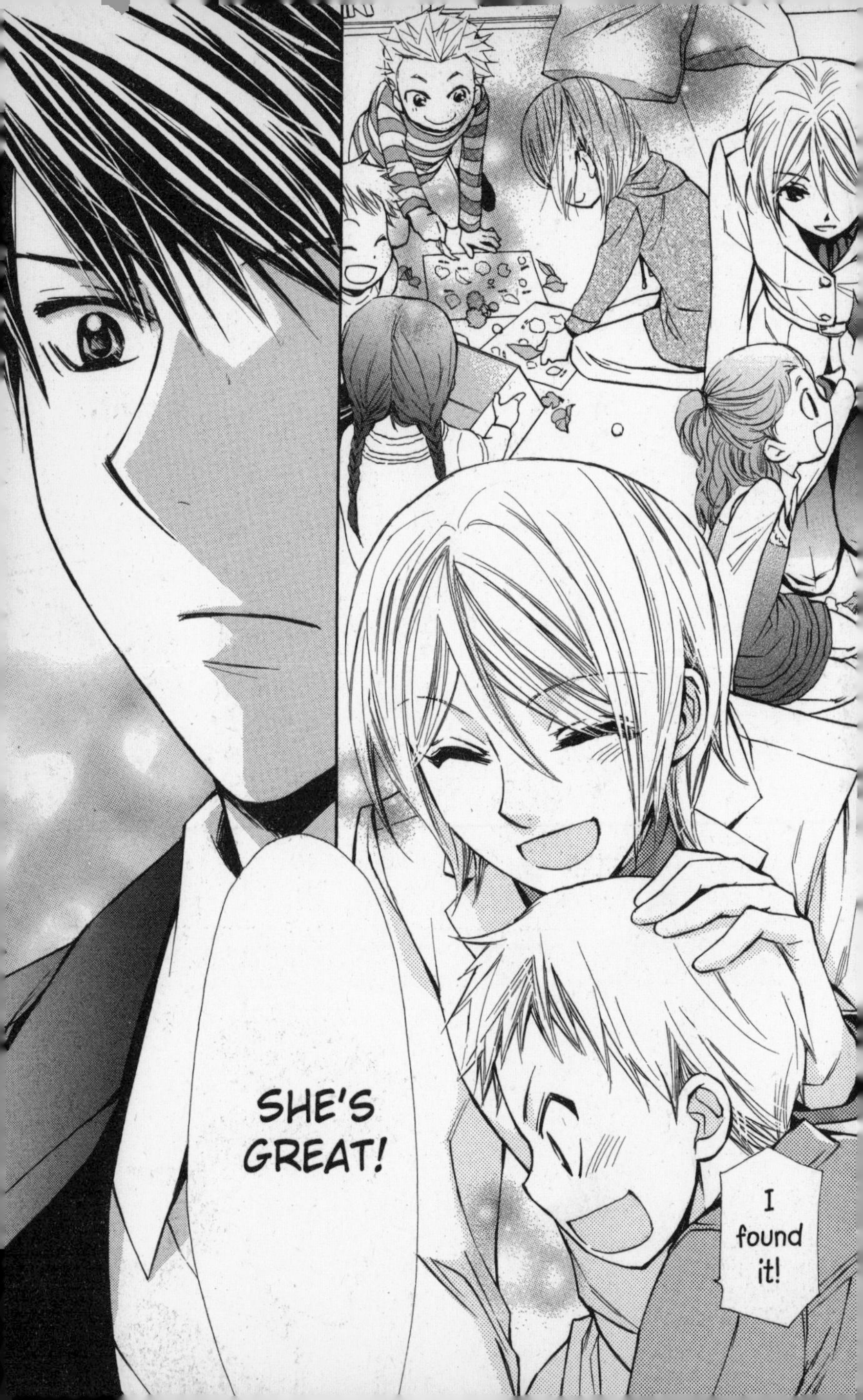
I found it!
SHE'S GREAT!

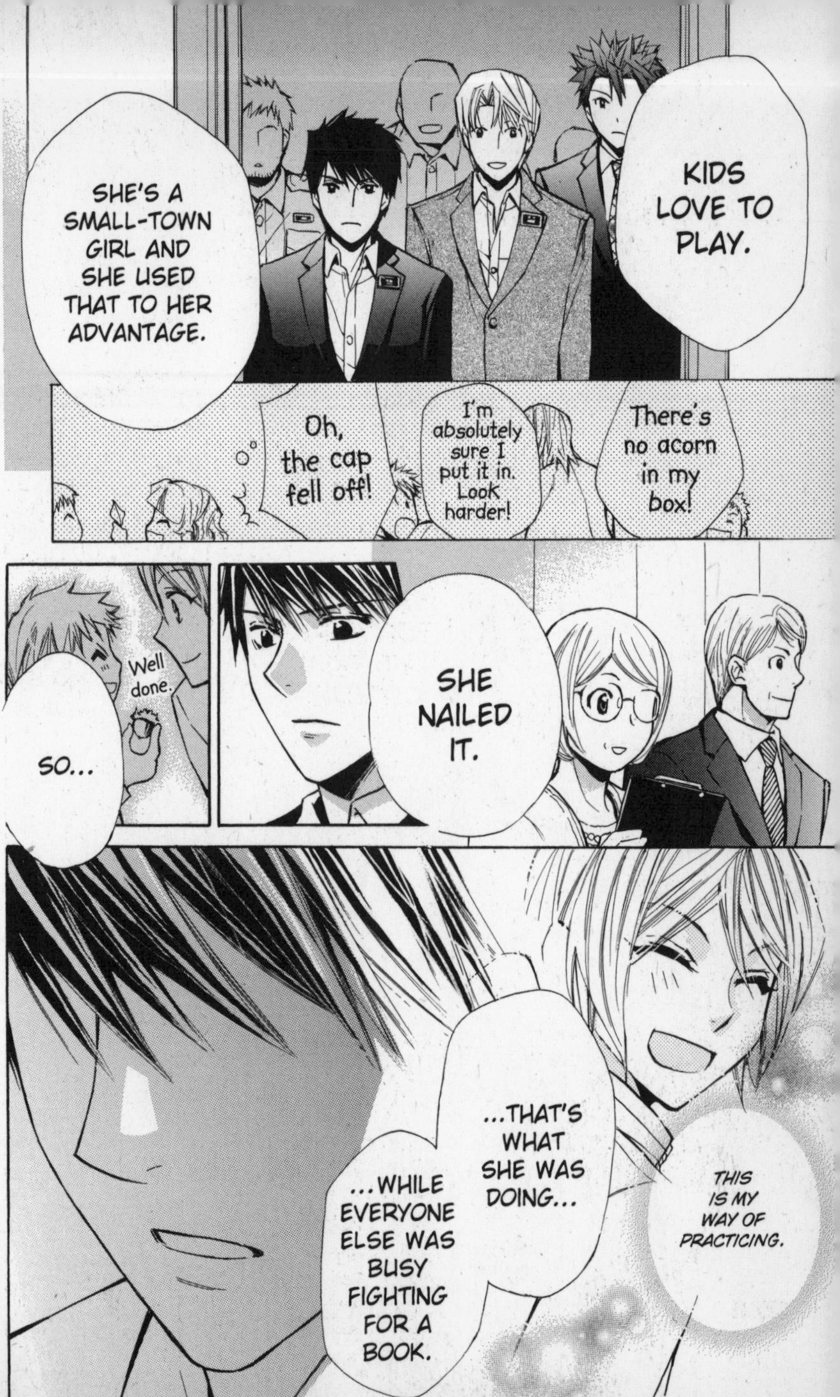
KIDS LOVE TO PLAY.
SHE'S A SMALL-TOWN GIRL AND SHE USED THAT TO HER ADVANTAGE.
There's no acorn in my box!
I'm absolutely sure I put it in. Look harder!
Oh, the cap fell off!
SHE NAILED IT.
Well done.
SO...
THIS IS MY WAY OF PRACTICING.
...THAT'S WHAT SHE WAS DOING...
...WHILE EVERYONE ELSE WAS BUSY FIGHTING FOR A BOOK.

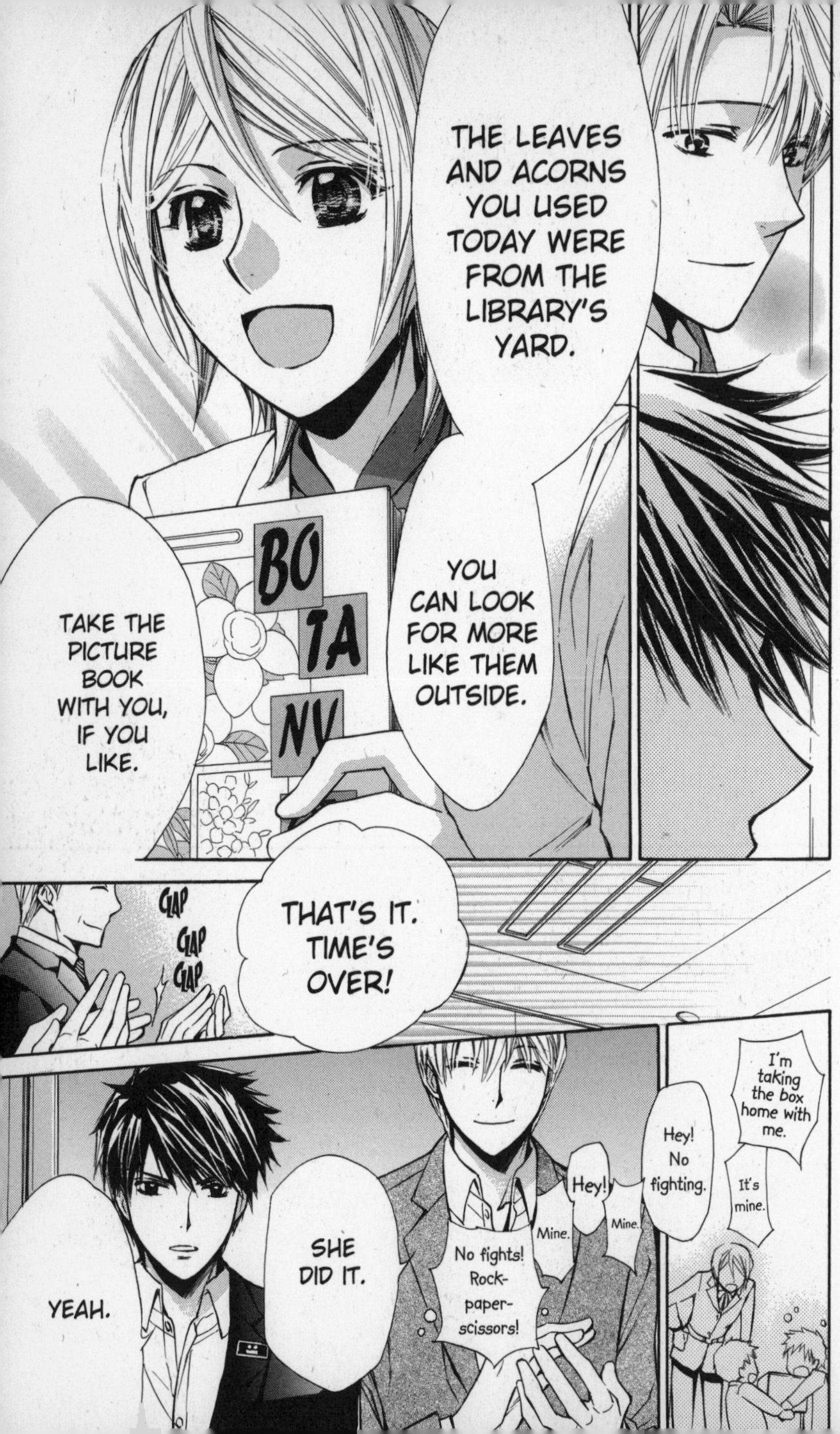
THE LEAVES AND ACORNS YOU USED TODAY WERE FROM THE LIBRARY'S YARD.
YOU CAN LOOK FOR MORE LIKE THEM OUTSIDE.
BO TA NY
TAKE THE PICTURE BOOK WITH YOU, IF YOU LIKE.
THAT'S IT. TIME'S OVER!
CLAP CLAP CLAP
I'm taking the box home with me.
It's mine.
Hey! No fighting.
Hey!
Mine.
Mine.
No fights! Rock-paper-scissors!
SHE DID IT.
YEAH.

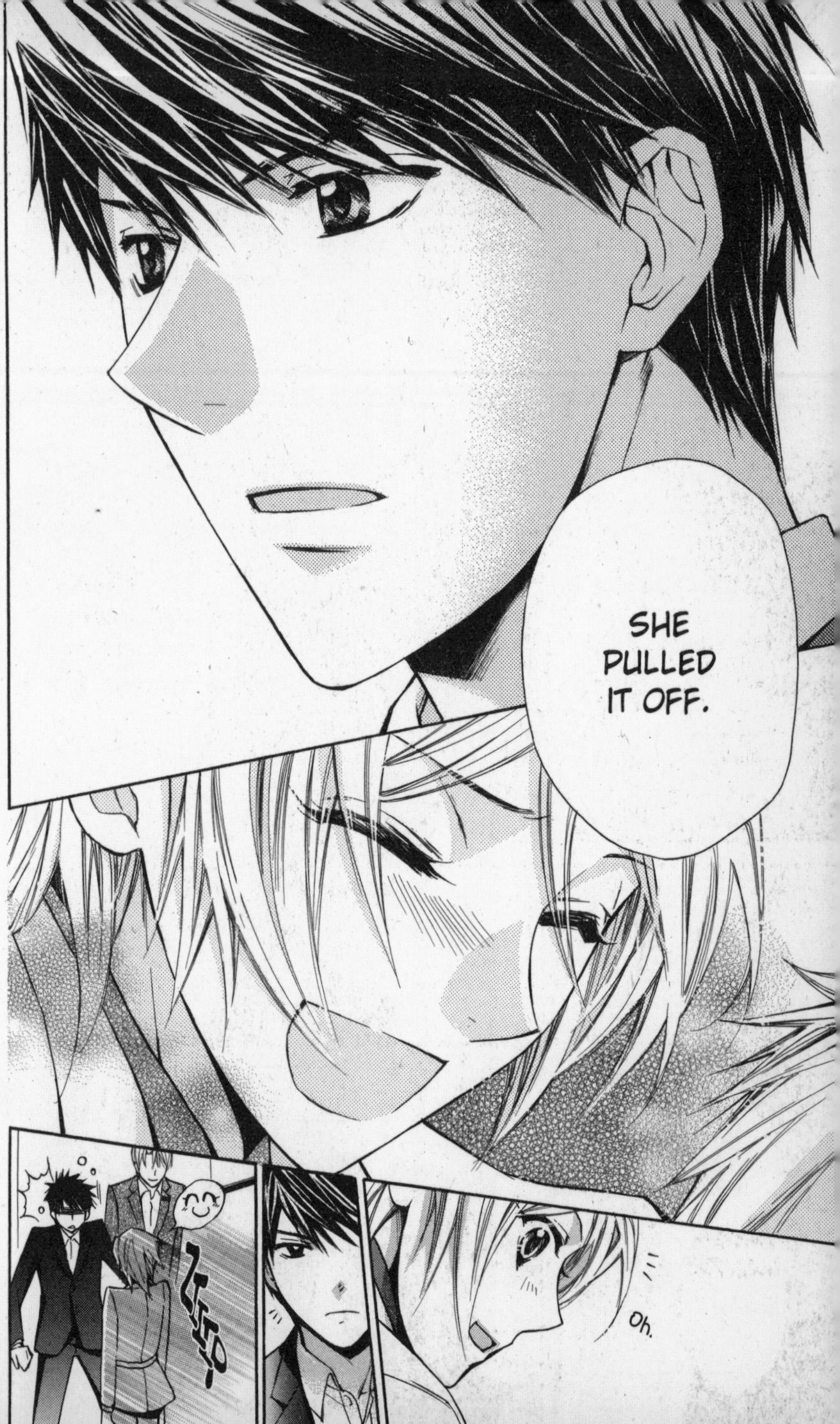
SHE PULLED IT OFF.
Oh.
ZIIP!

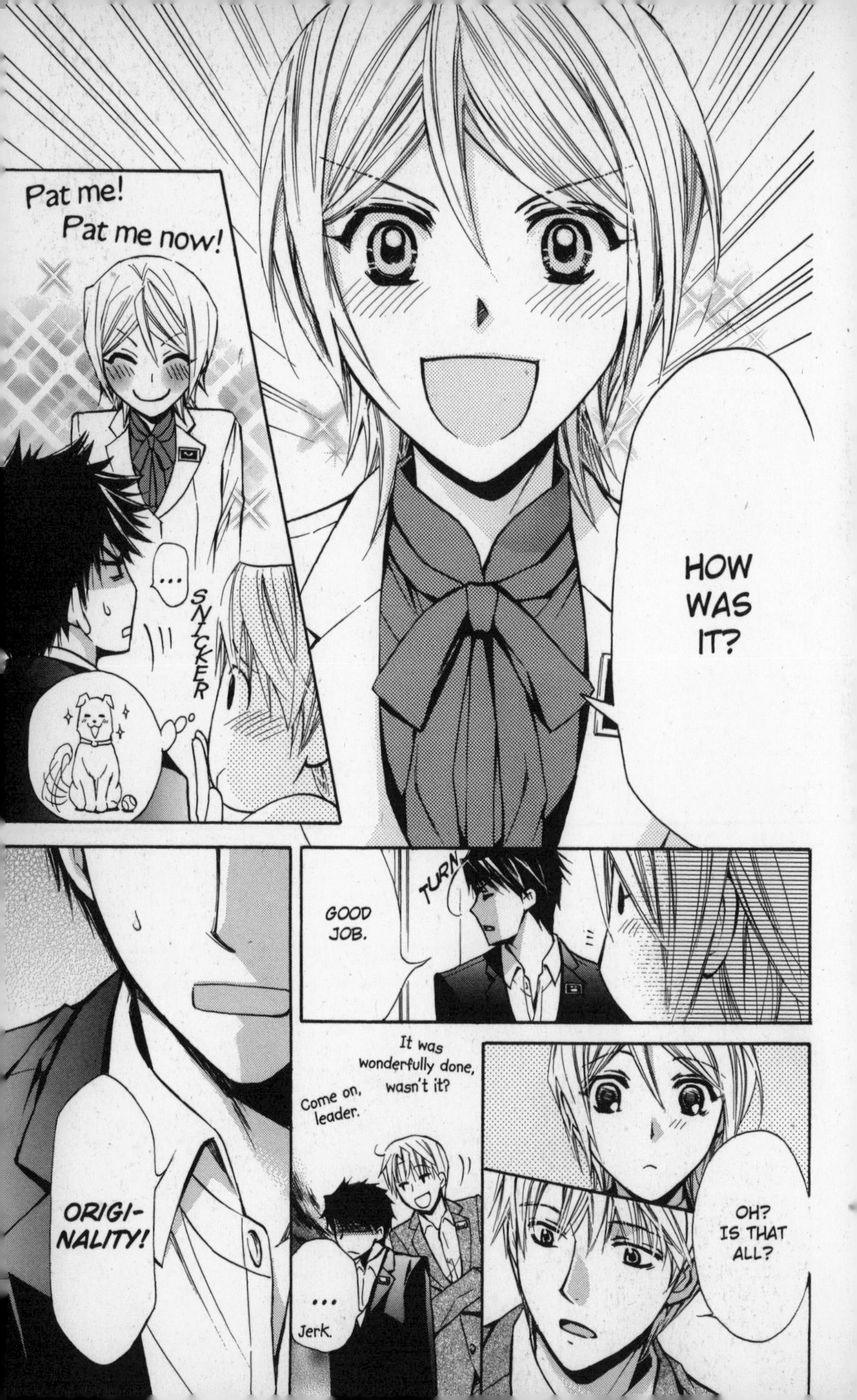
HOW WAS IT?
Pat me! Pat me now!
...
SNICKER
TURN
GOOD JOB.
OH? IS THAT ALL?
It was wonderfully done, wasn't it?
Come on, leader.
... Jerk.
ORIGI-NALITY!

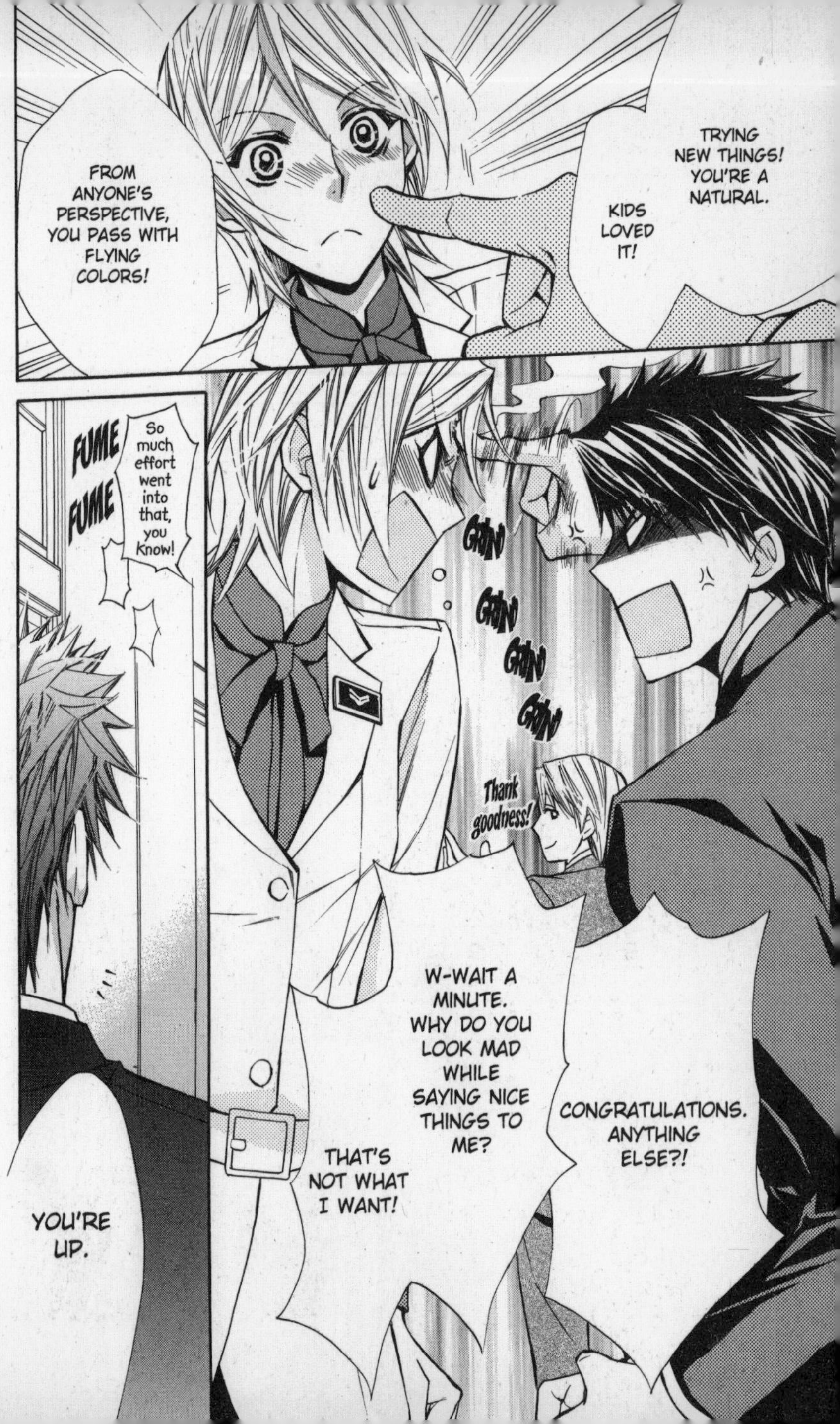
TRYING NEW THINGS! YOU'RE A NATURAL.
KIDS LOVED IT!
FROM ANYONE'S PERSPECTIVE, YOU PASS WITH FLYING COLORS!
GRIND GRIND GRIND GRIND
Thank goodness!
CONGRATULATIONS. ANYTHING ELSE?!
W-WAIT A MINUTE. WHY DO YOU LOOK MAD WHILE SAYING NICE THINGS TO ME?
THAT'S NOT WHAT I WANT!
FUME FUME
So much effort went into that, you know!
YOU'RE UP.

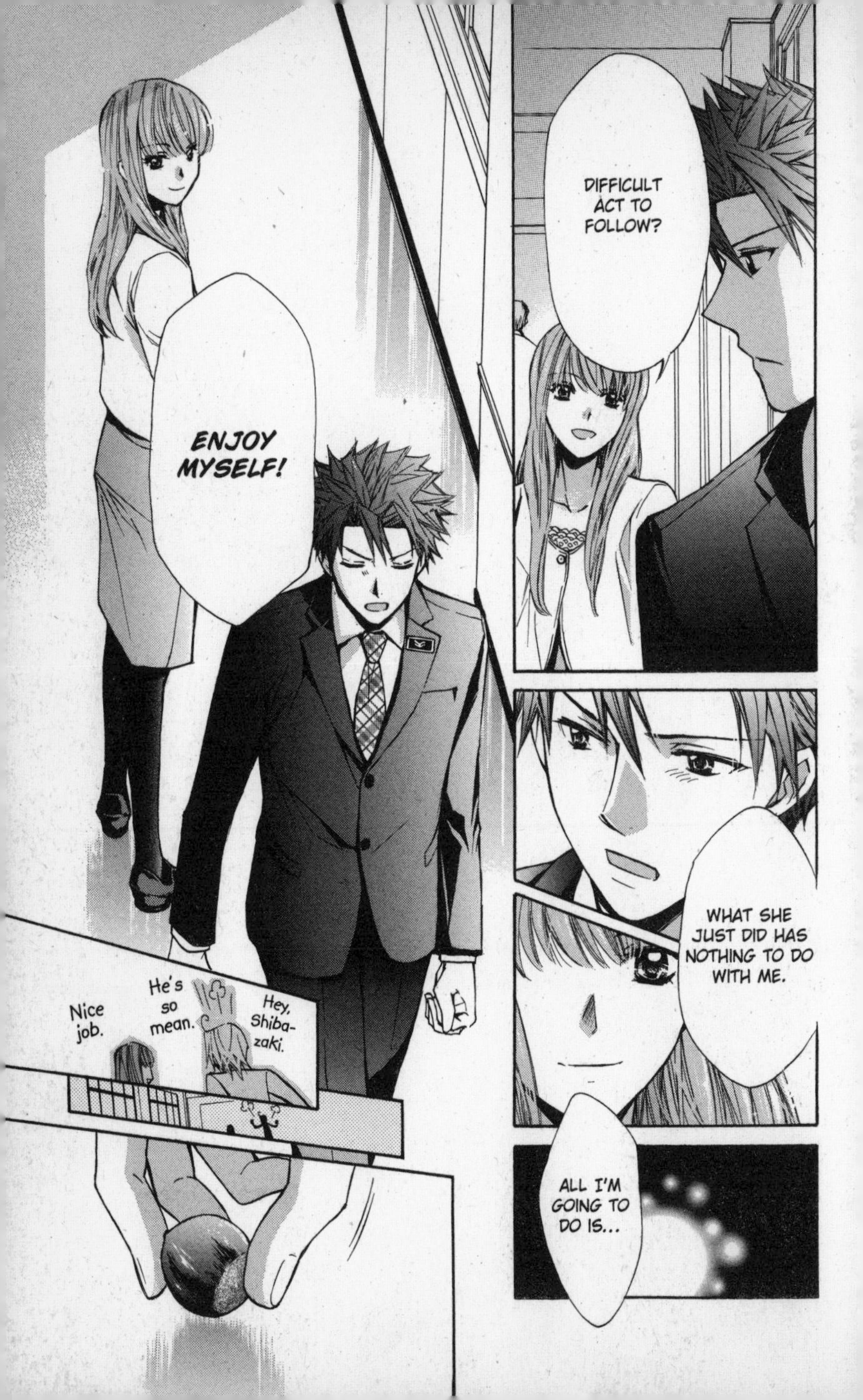
DIFFICULT ACT TO FOLLOW?
WHAT SHE JUST DID HAS NOTHING TO DO WITH ME.
ALL I'M GOING TO DO IS...
ENJOY MYSELF!
Hey, Shiba-zaki.
He's so mean.
Nice job.

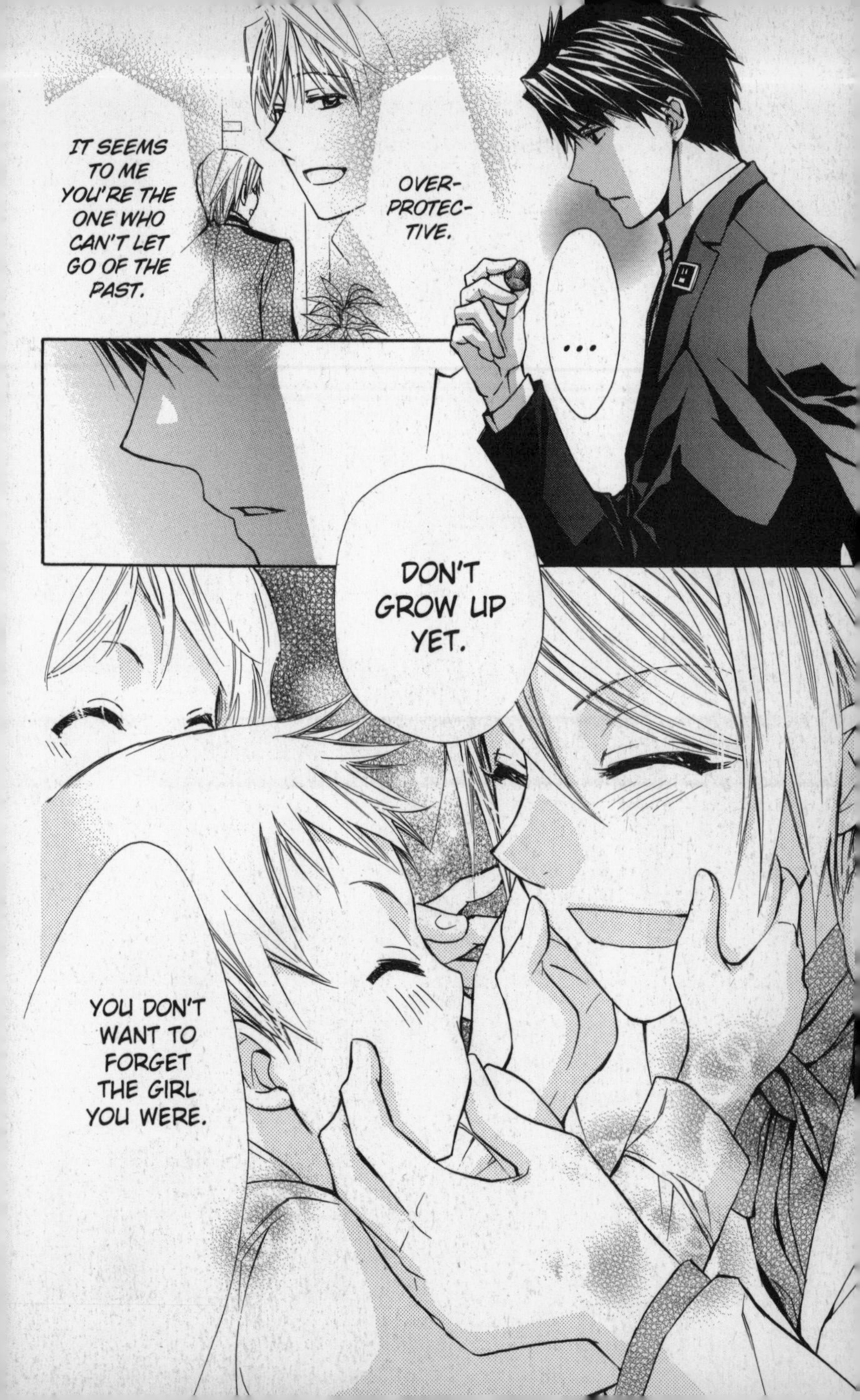
...
OVER-PROTECTIVE.
IT SEEMS TO ME YOU'RE THE ONE WHO CAN'T LET GO OF THE PAST.
DON'T GROW UP YET.
YOU DON'T WANT TO FORGET THE GIRL YOU WERE.

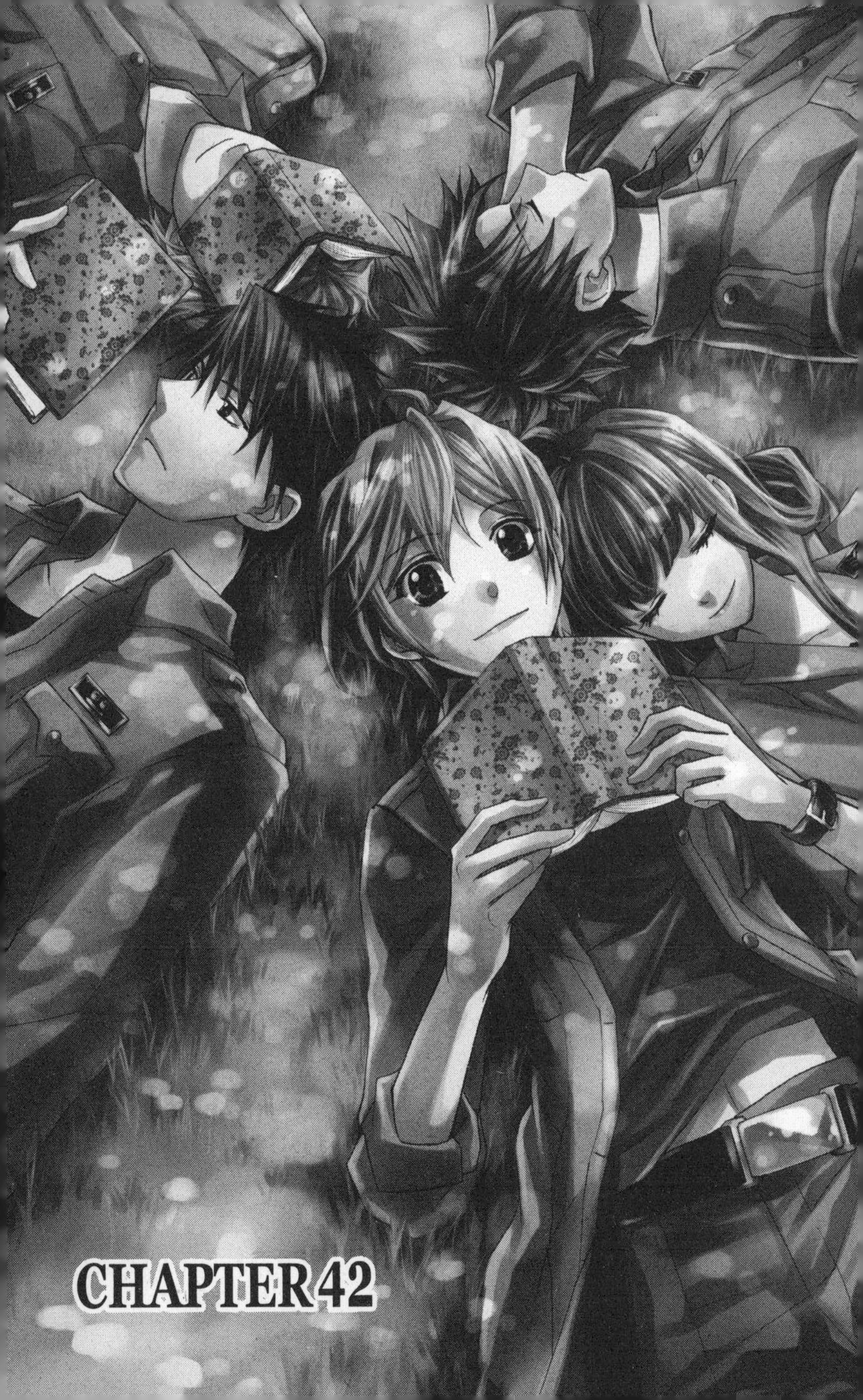
CHAPTER 42

Deep in Thought–One Winter Day

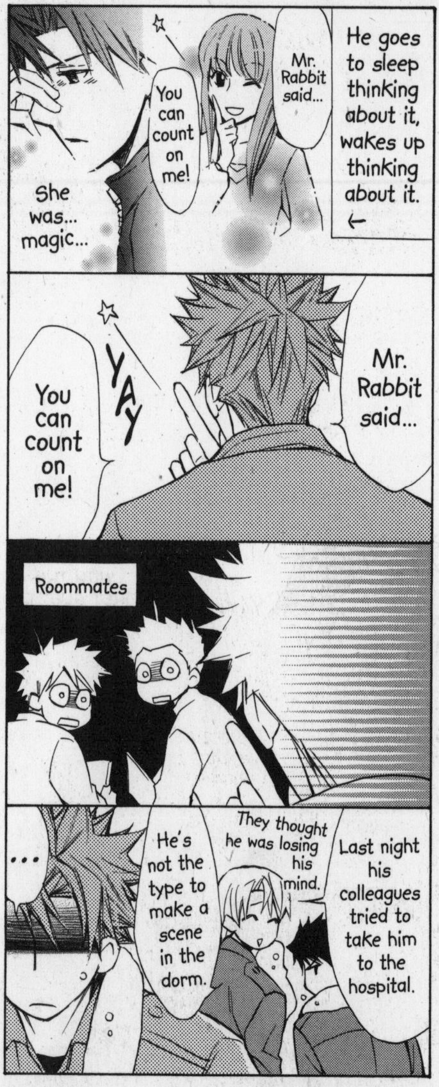
He goes to sleep thinking about it, wakes up thinking about it. ←
Mr. Rabbit said...
You can count on me!
She was... magic...
Mr. Rabbit said...
YAY
You can count on me!
Roommates
Last night his colleagues tried to take him to the hospital.
They thought he was losing his mind.
He's not the type to make a scene in the dorm.
...

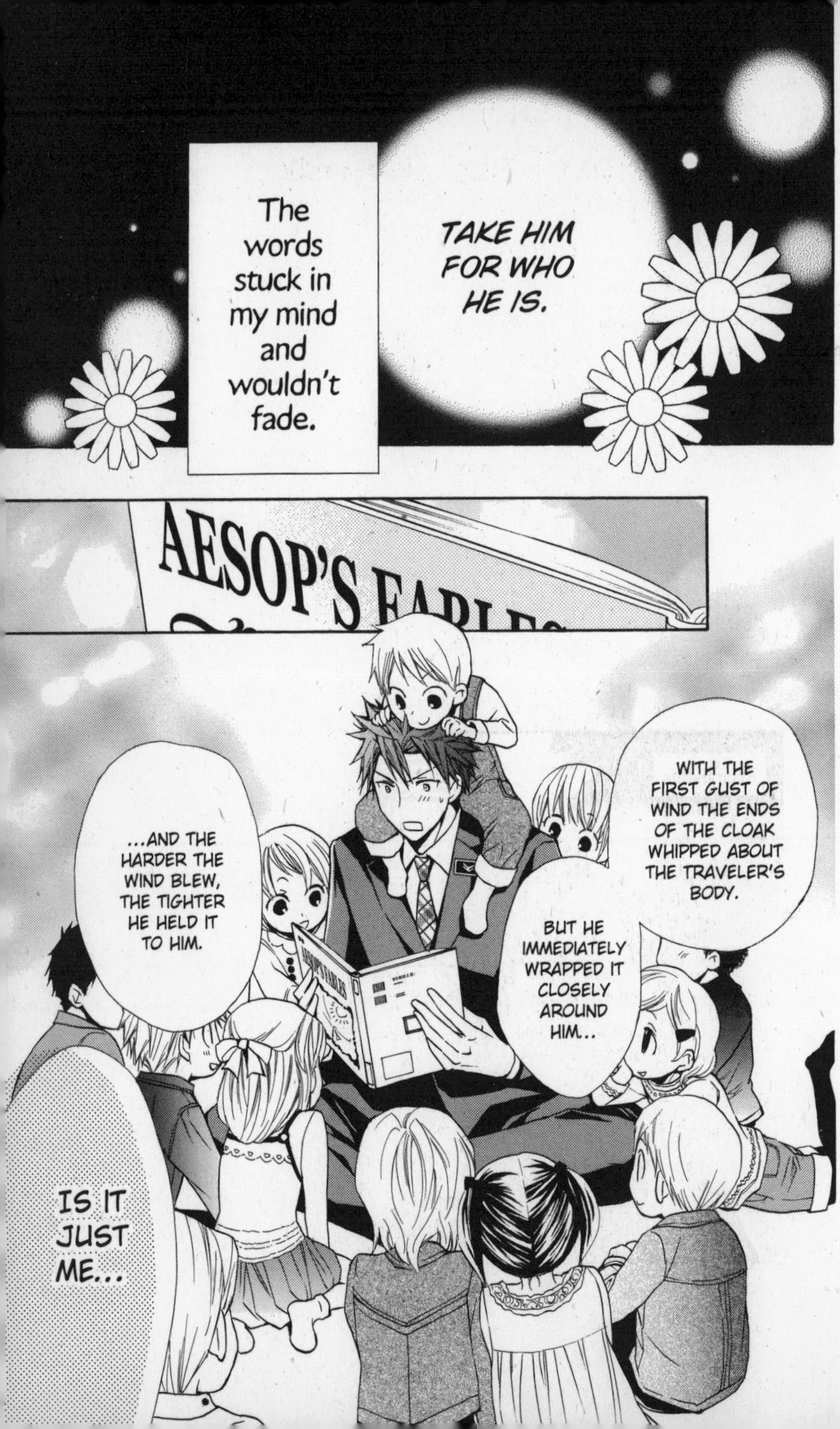
TAKE HIM FOR WHO HE IS.
The words stuck in my mind and wouldn't fade.
AESOP'S
WITH THE FIRST GUST OF WIND THE ENDS OF THE CLOAK WHIPPED ABOUT THE TRAVELER'S BODY.
BUT HE IMMEDIATELY WRAPPED IT CLOSELY AROUND HIM...
...AND THE HARDER THE WIND BLEW, THE TIGHTER HE HELD IT TO HIM.
IS IT JUST ME...

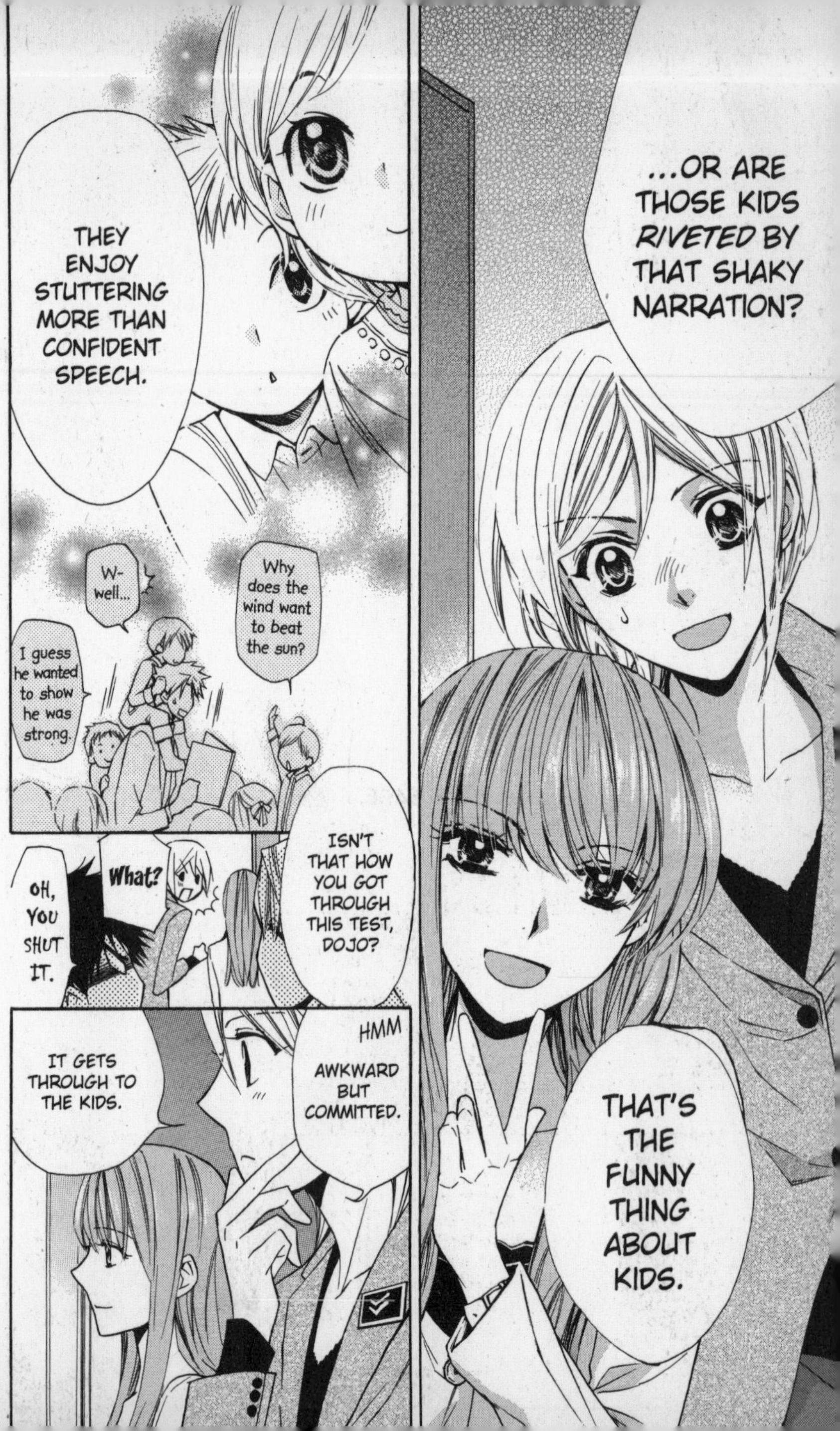
...OR ARE THOSE KIDS *RIVETED* BY THAT SHAKY NARRATION?
THAT'S THE FUNNY THING ABOUT KIDS.
THEY ENJOY STUTTERING MORE THAN CONFIDENT SPEECH.
Why does the wind want to beat the sun?
W-well...
I guess he wanted to show he was strong.
ISN'T THAT HOW YOU GOT THROUGH THIS TEST, DOJO?
What?
OH, YOU SHUT IT.
HMM
AWKWARD BUT COMMITTED.
IT GETS THROUGH TO THE KIDS.

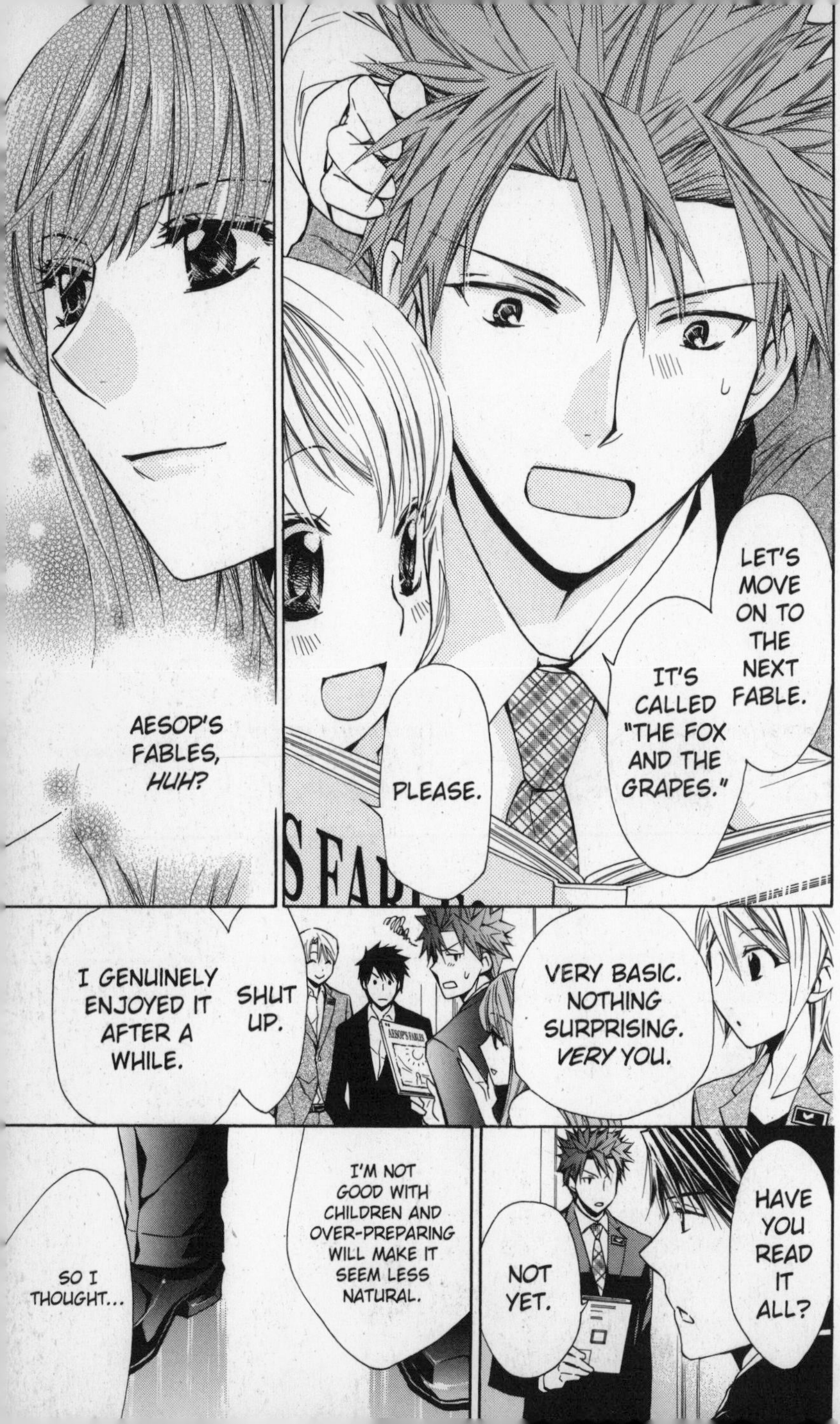
LET'S MOVE ON TO THE NEXT FABLE.
IT'S CALLED "THE FOX AND THE GRAPES."
PLEASE.
AESOP'S FABLES, *HUH?*
VERY BASIC. NOTHING SURPRISING. *VERY YOU.*
AESOP'S FABLES
SHUT UP.
I GENUINELY ENJOYED IT AFTER A WHILE.
HAVE YOU READ IT ALL?
NOT YET.
I'M NOT GOOD WITH CHILDREN AND OVER-PREPARING WILL MAKE IT SEEM LESS NATURAL.
SO I THOUGHT...

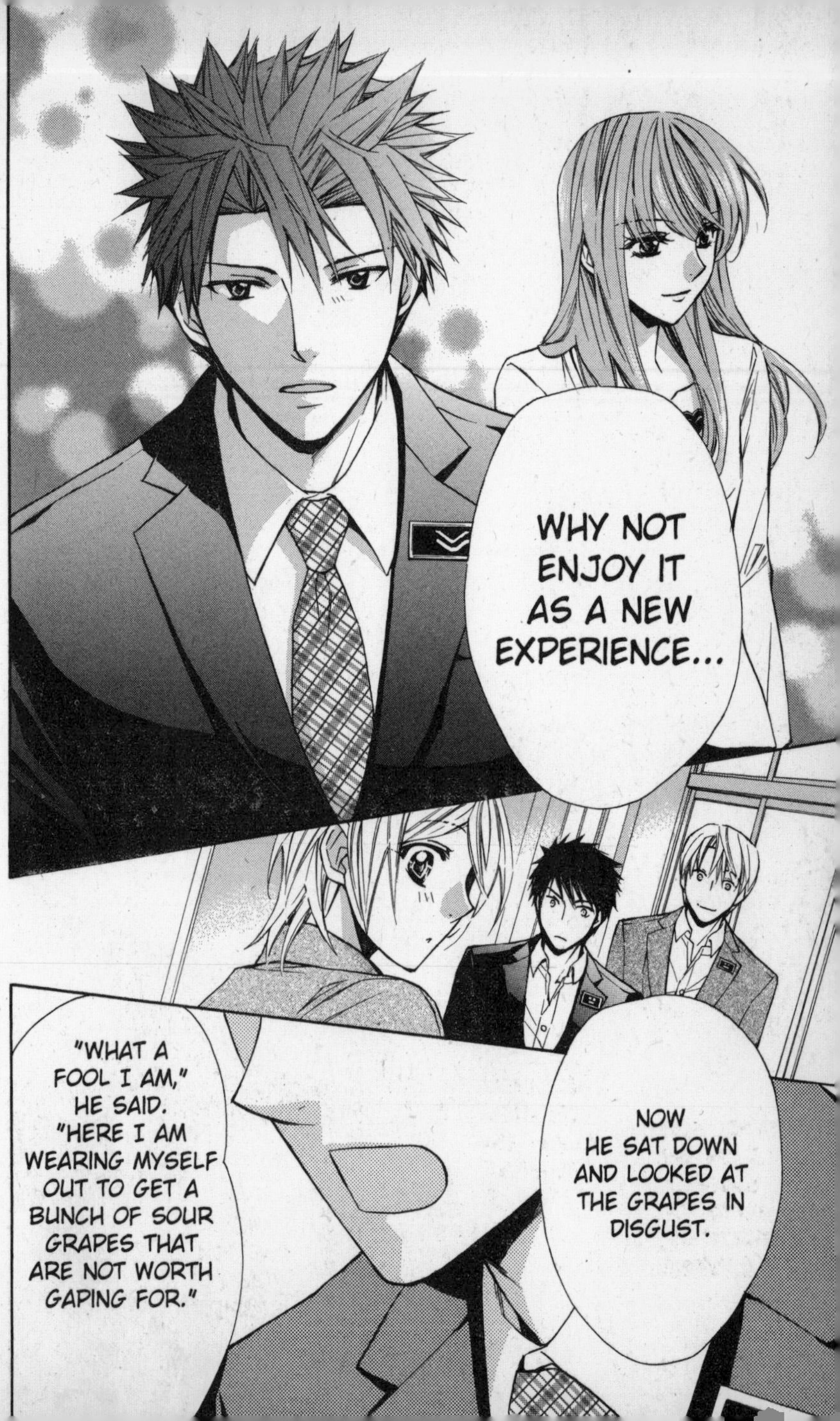
WHY NOT ENJOY IT AS A NEW EXPERIENCE...
NOW HE SAT DOWN AND LOOKED AT THE GRAPES IN DISGUST.
"WHAT A FOOL I AM," HE SAID. "HERE I AM WEARING MYSELF OUT TO GET A BUNCH OF SOUR GRAPES THAT ARE NOT WORTH GAPING FOR."

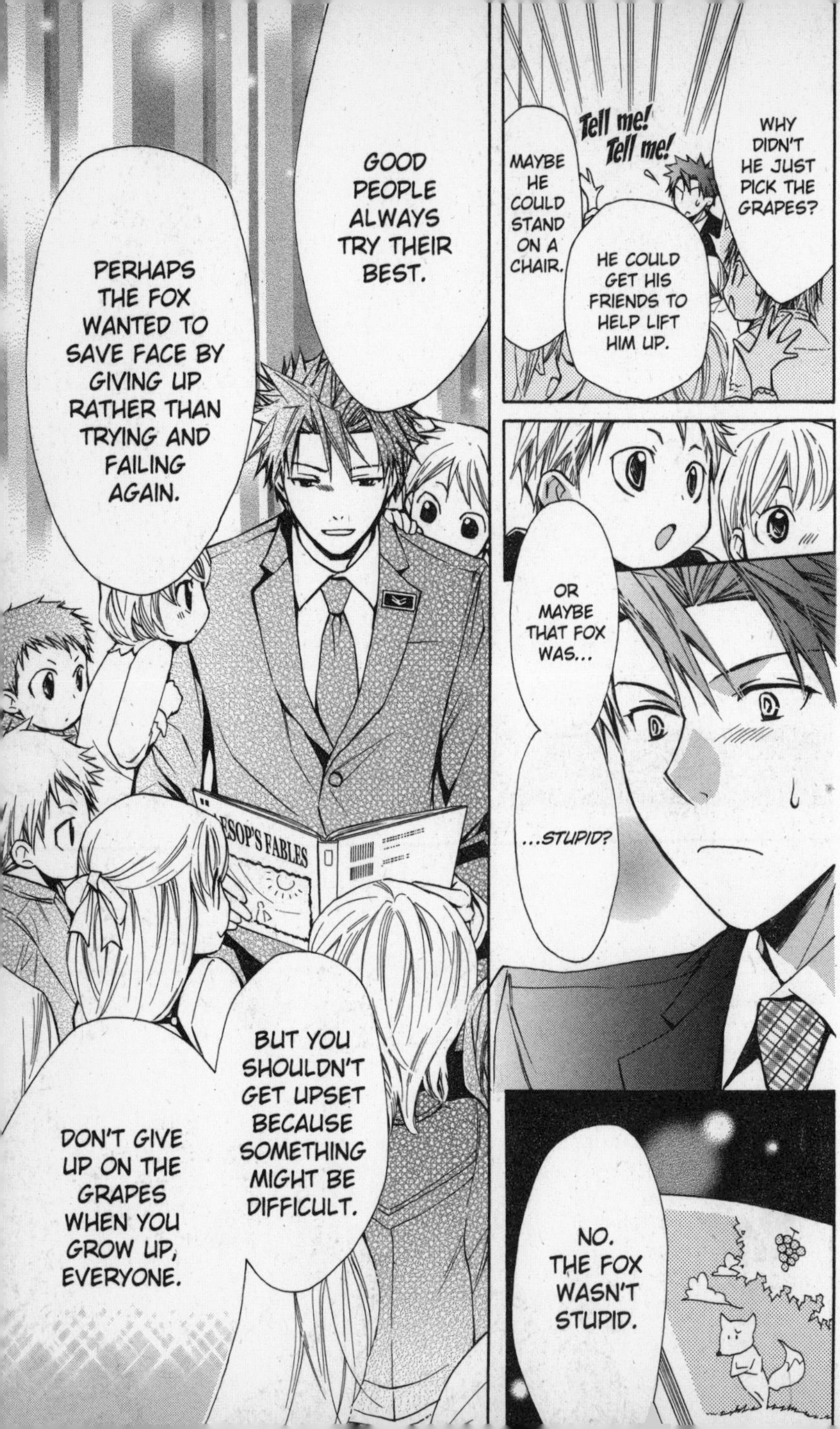
WHY DIDN'T HE JUST PICK THE GRAPES?
Tell me! Tell me!
MAYBE HE COULD STAND ON A CHAIR.
HE COULD GET HIS FRIENDS TO HELP LIFT HIM UP.
OR MAYBE THAT FOX WAS...
...STUPID?
NO. THE FOX WASN'T STUPID.
GOOD PEOPLE ALWAYS TRY THEIR BEST.
PERHAPS THE FOX WANTED TO SAVE FACE BY GIVING UP RATHER THAN TRYING AND FAILING AGAIN.
AESOP'S FABLES
BUT YOU SHOULDN'T GET UPSET BECAUSE SOMETHING MIGHT BE DIFFICULT.
DON'T GIVE UP ON THE GRAPES WHEN YOU GROW UP, EVERYONE.

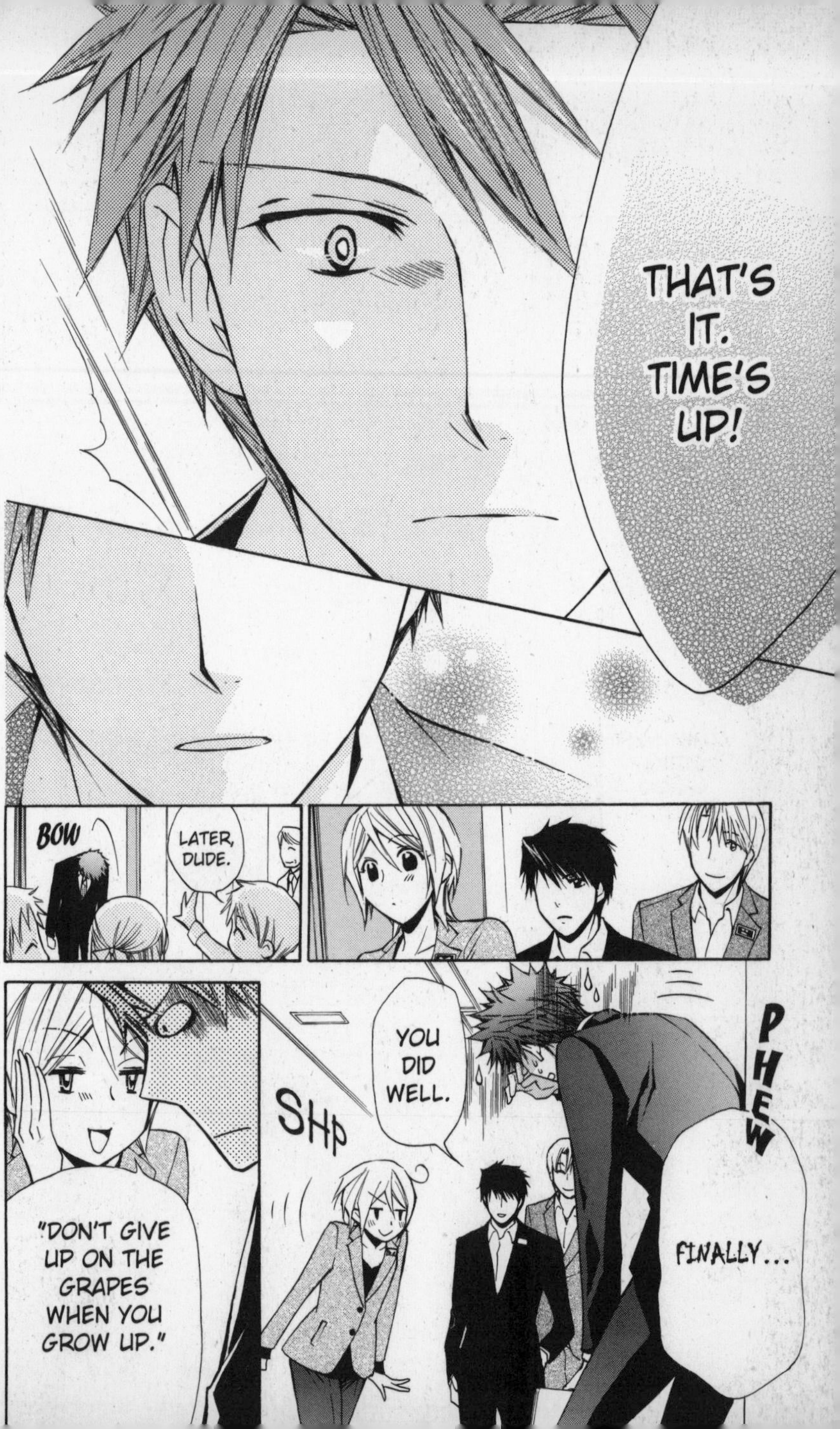
THAT'S IT. TIME'S UP!
BOW
LATER, DUDE.
PHEW
FINALLY...
YOU DID WELL.
SHp
"DON'T GIVE UP ON THE GRAPES WHEN YOU GROW UP."

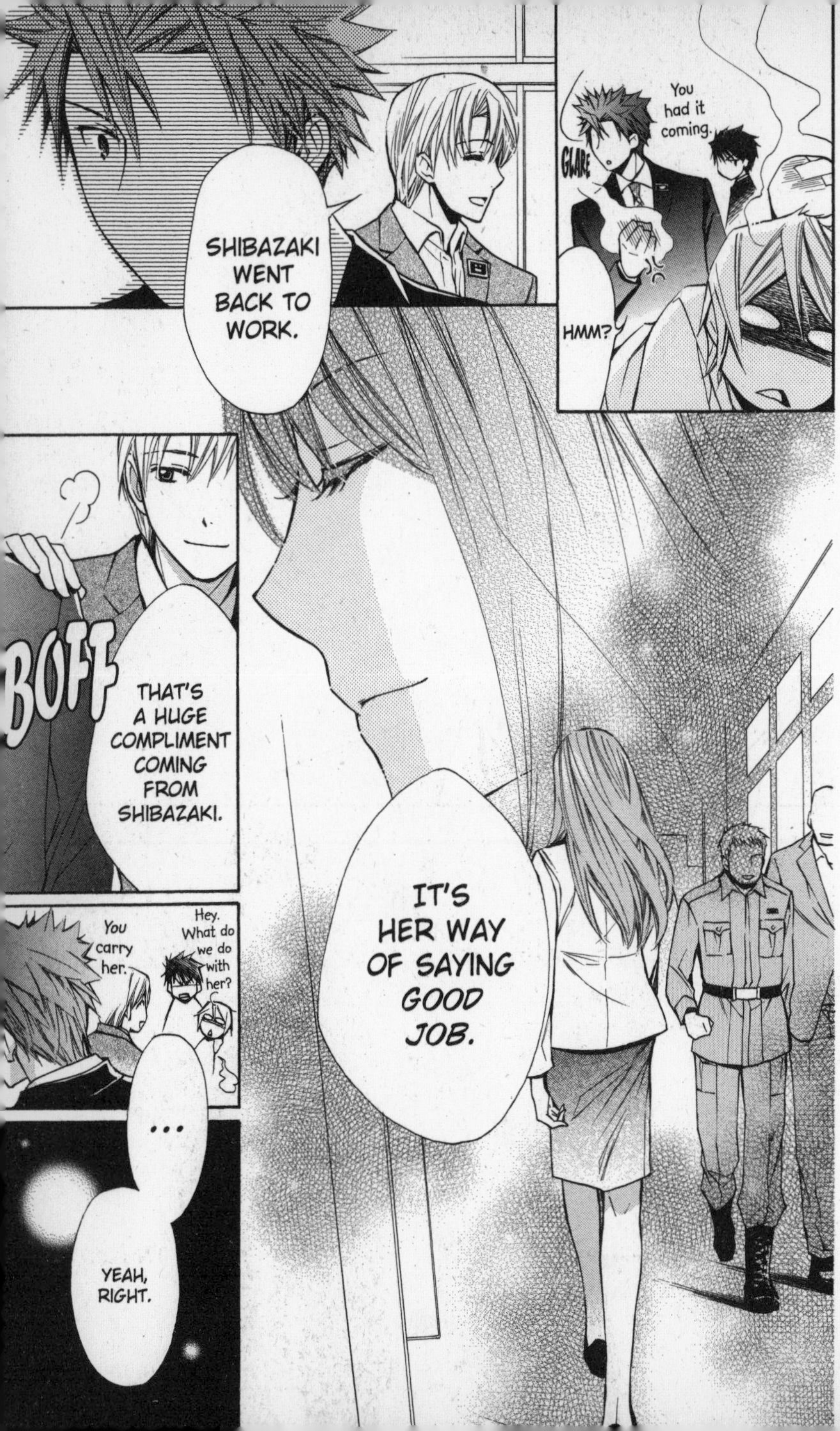
You had it coming.
GLARE
HMM?
SHIBAZAKI WENT BACK TO WORK.
IT'S HER WAY OF SAYING GOOD JOB.
BOFF
THAT'S A HUGE COMPLIMENT COMING FROM SHIBAZAKI.
Hey. What do we do with her?
You carry her.
...
YEAH, RIGHT.

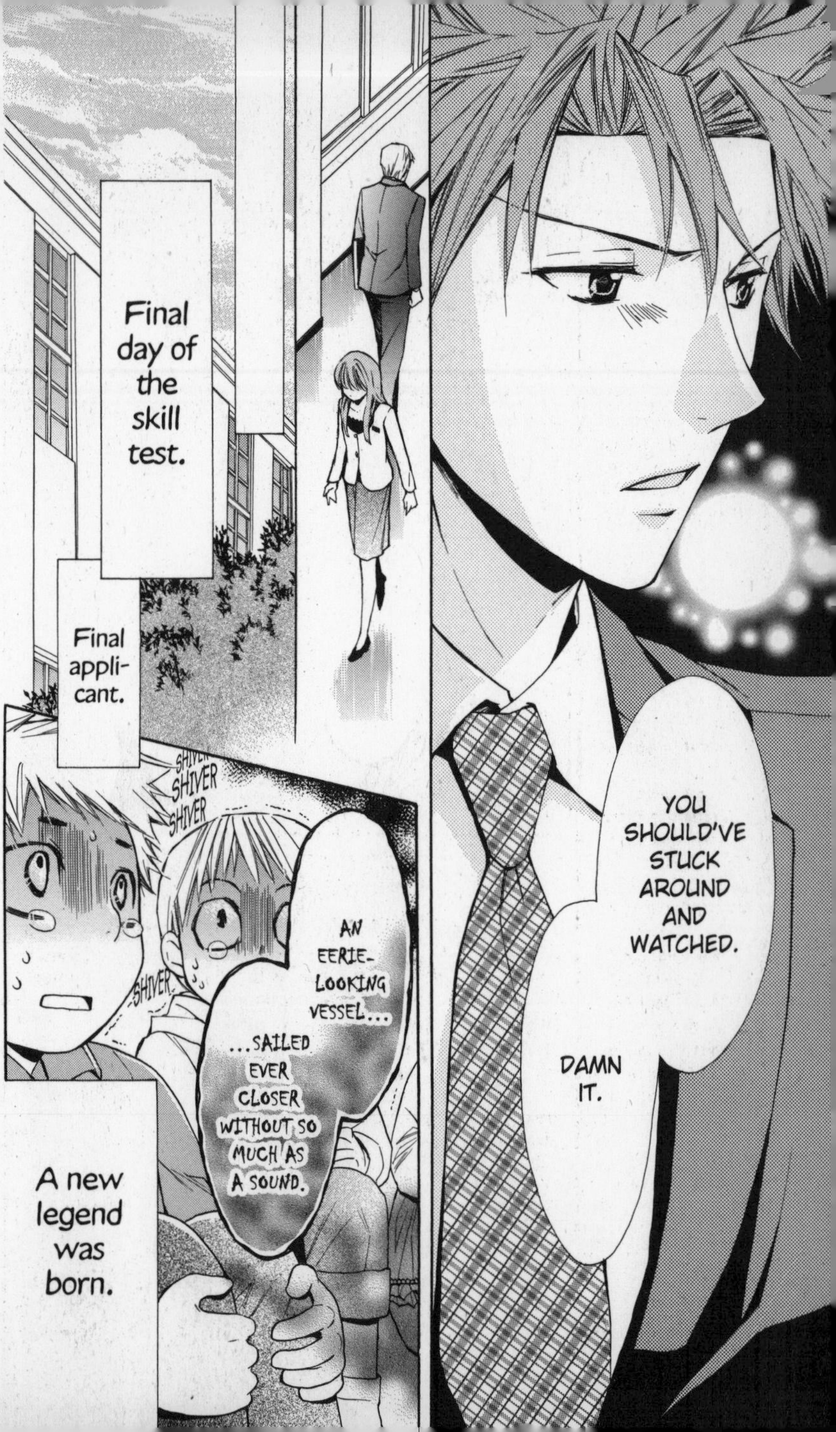
YOU SHOULD'VE STUCK AROUND AND WATCHED.
DAMN IT.
Final day of the skill test.
Final appli-cant.
SHIVER SHIVER SHIVER
AN EERIE-LOOKING VESSEL...
...SAILED EVER CLOSER WITHOUT SO MUCH AS A SOUND.
SHIVER
A new legend was born.

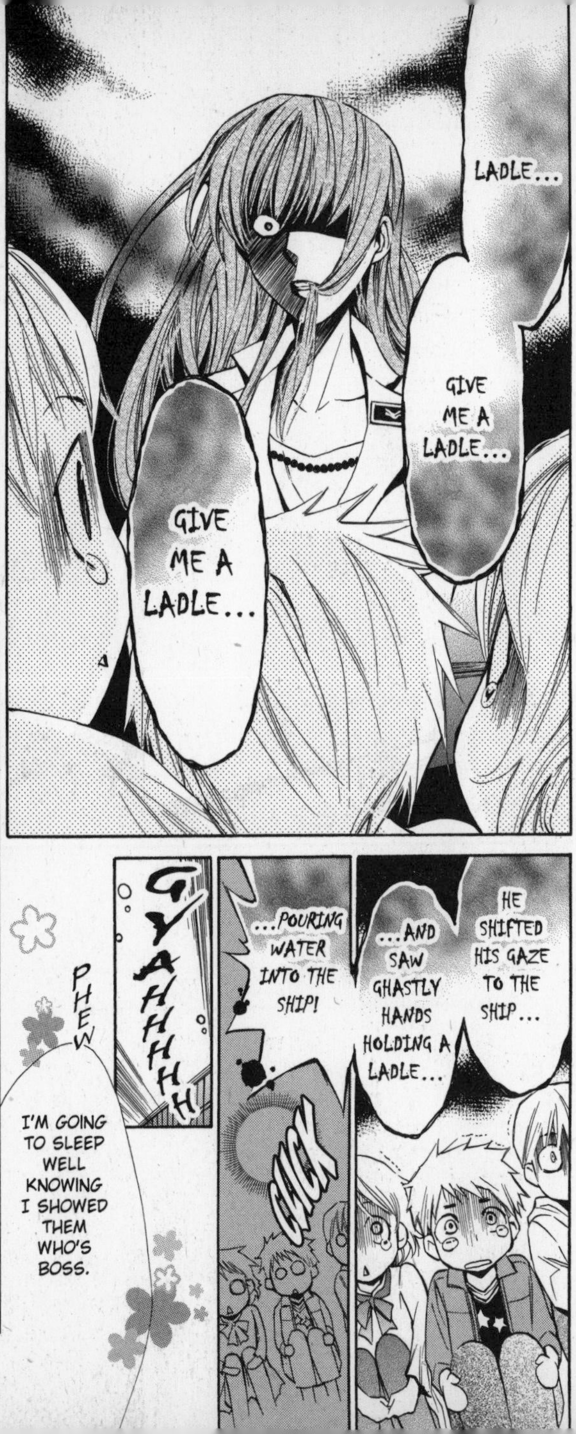
LADLE...
GIVE ME A LADLE...
GIVE ME A LADLE...
HE SHIFTED HIS GAZE TO THE SHIP...
...AND SAW GHASTLY HANDS HOLDING A LADLE...
...POURING WATER INTO THE SHIP!
CLICK
GYAHHHHH
PHEW
I'M GOING TO SLEEP WELL KNOWING I SHOWED THEM WHO'S BOSS.

4

*

I'm a hardcore gamer. I play many genres but a particular adventure game has been keeping my hands full.

It's a very famous one.

When I first started it I didn't have much experience as a player.

But once I got into it there was no going back... I can do it all day long!

My weapon is an ax. If you see me on that adventure game, feel free to join me!

*

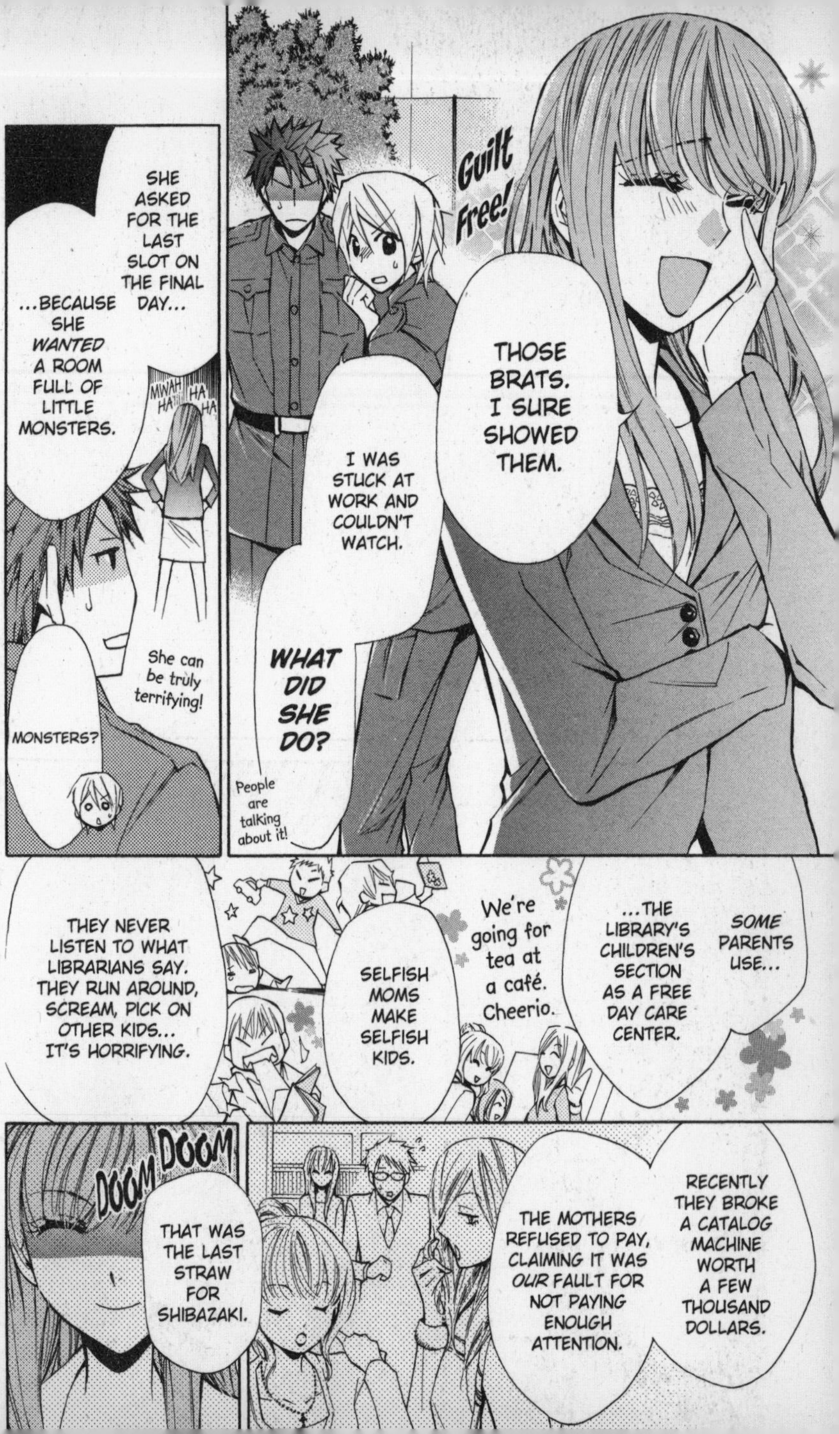
Guilt Free!
THOSE BRATS. I SURE SHOWED THEM.
I WAS STUCK AT WORK AND COULDN'T WATCH.
WHAT DID SHE DO?
People are talking about it!
SHE ASKED FOR THE LAST SLOT ON THE FINAL DAY...
...BECAUSE SHE WANTED A ROOM FULL OF LITTLE MONSTERS.
MWAH HA HA HA HA
She can be truly terrifying!
MONSTERS?
SOME PARENTS USE...
...THE LIBRARY'S CHILDREN'S SECTION AS A FREE DAY CARE CENTER.
We're going for tea at a café. Cheerio.
SELFISH MOMS MAKE SELFISH KIDS.
THEY NEVER LISTEN TO WHAT LIBRARIANS SAY. THEY RUN AROUND, SCREAM, PICK ON OTHER KIDS... IT'S HORRIFYING.
RECENTLY THEY BROKE A CATALOG MACHINE WORTH A FEW THOUSAND DOLLARS.
THE MOTHERS REFUSED TO PAY, CLAIMING IT WAS OUR FAULT FOR NOT PAYING ENOUGH ATTENTION.
DOOM DOOM
THAT WAS THE LAST STRAW FOR SHIBAZAKI.

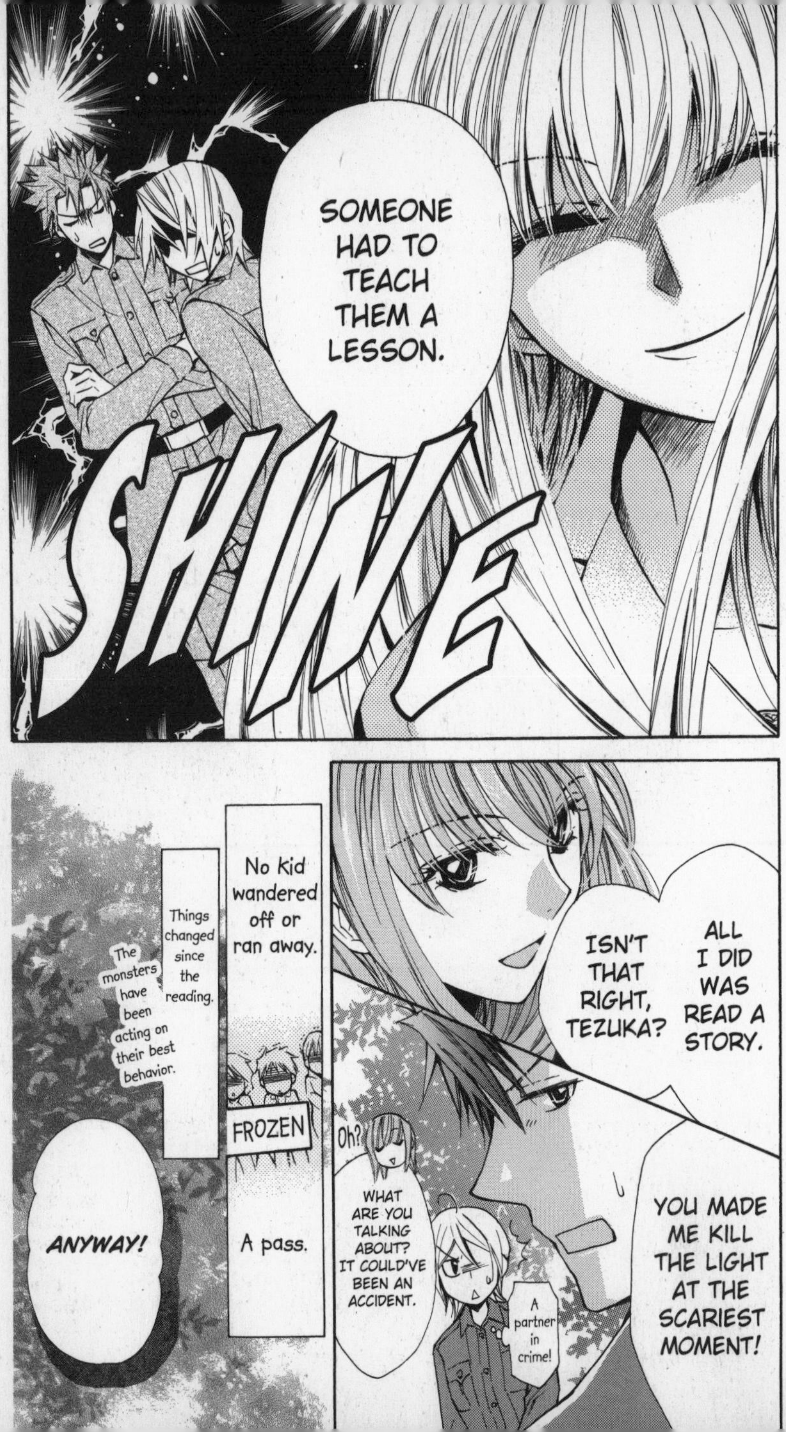
SOMEONE HAD TO TEACH THEM A LESSON.
SHINE
ALL I DID WAS READ A STORY.
ISN'T THAT RIGHT, TEZUKA?
YOU MADE ME KILL THE LIGHT AT THE SCARIEST MOMENT!
Oh?
WHAT ARE YOU TALKING ABOUT? IT COULD'VE BEEN AN ACCIDENT.
A partner in crime!
No kid wandered off or ran away.
FROZEN
A pass.
Things changed since the reading.
The monsters have been acting on their best behavior.
ANYWAY!

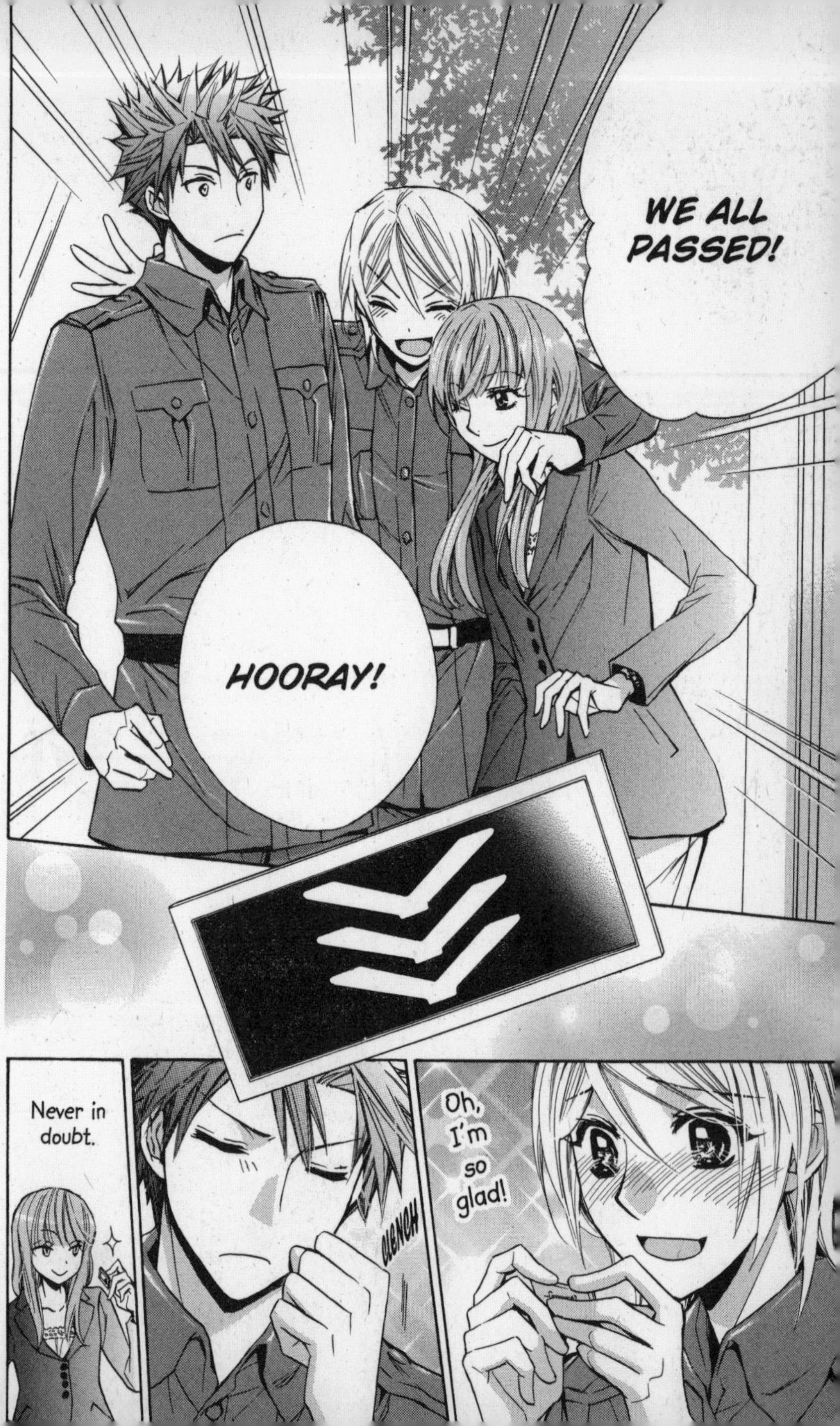
WE ALL PASSED!
HOORAY!
Oh, I'm so glad!
CLENCH
Never in doubt.

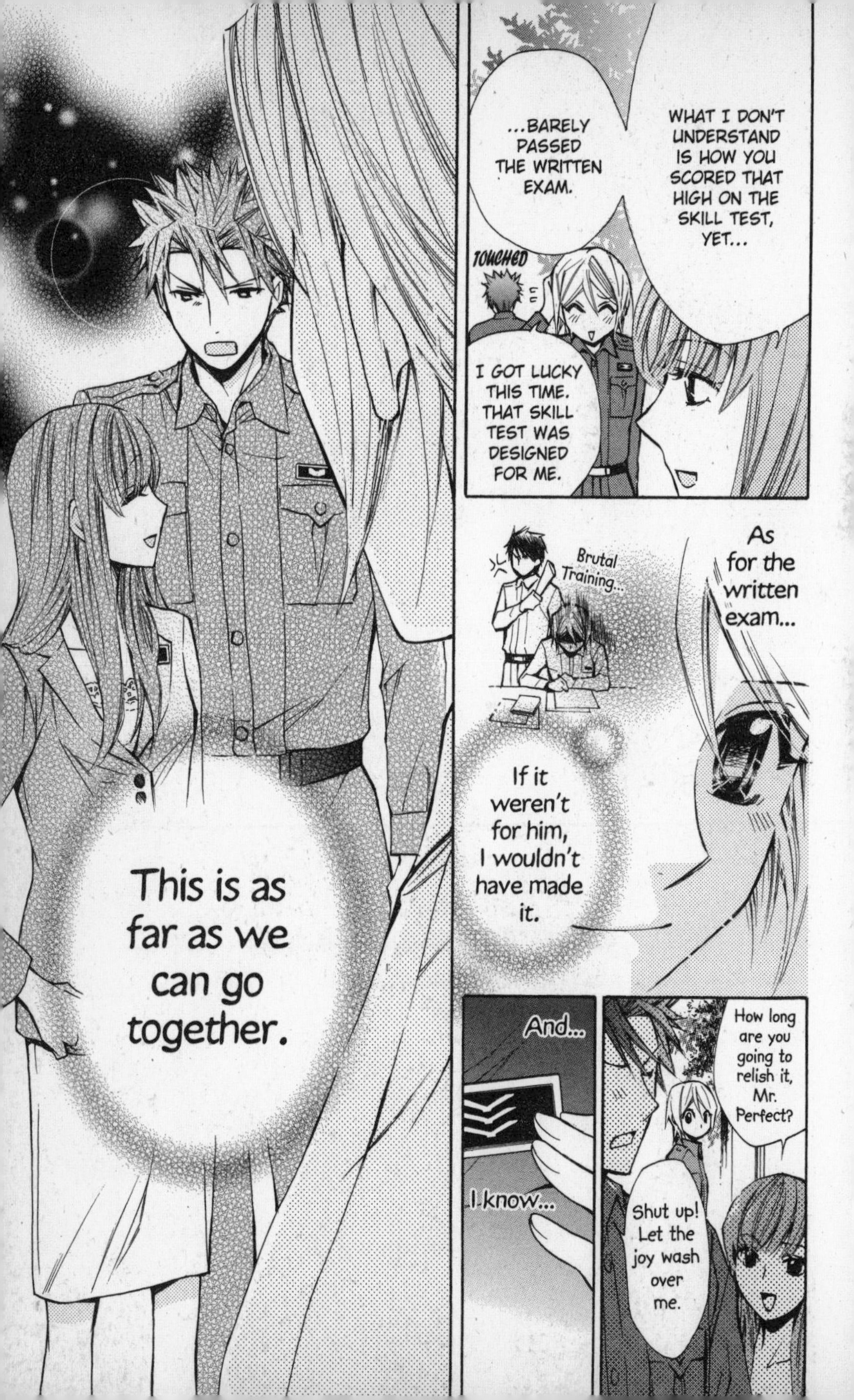
WHAT I DON'T UNDERSTAND IS HOW YOU SCORED THAT HIGH ON THE SKILL TEST, YET...
...BARELY PASSED THE WRITTEN EXAM.
TOUCHED
I GOT LUCKY THIS TIME. THAT SKILL TEST WAS DESIGNED FOR ME.
As for the written exam...
Brutal Training...
If it weren't for him, I wouldn't have made it.
How long are you going to relish it, Mr. Perfect?
Shut up! Let the joy wash over me.
And...
I know...
This is as far as we can go together.

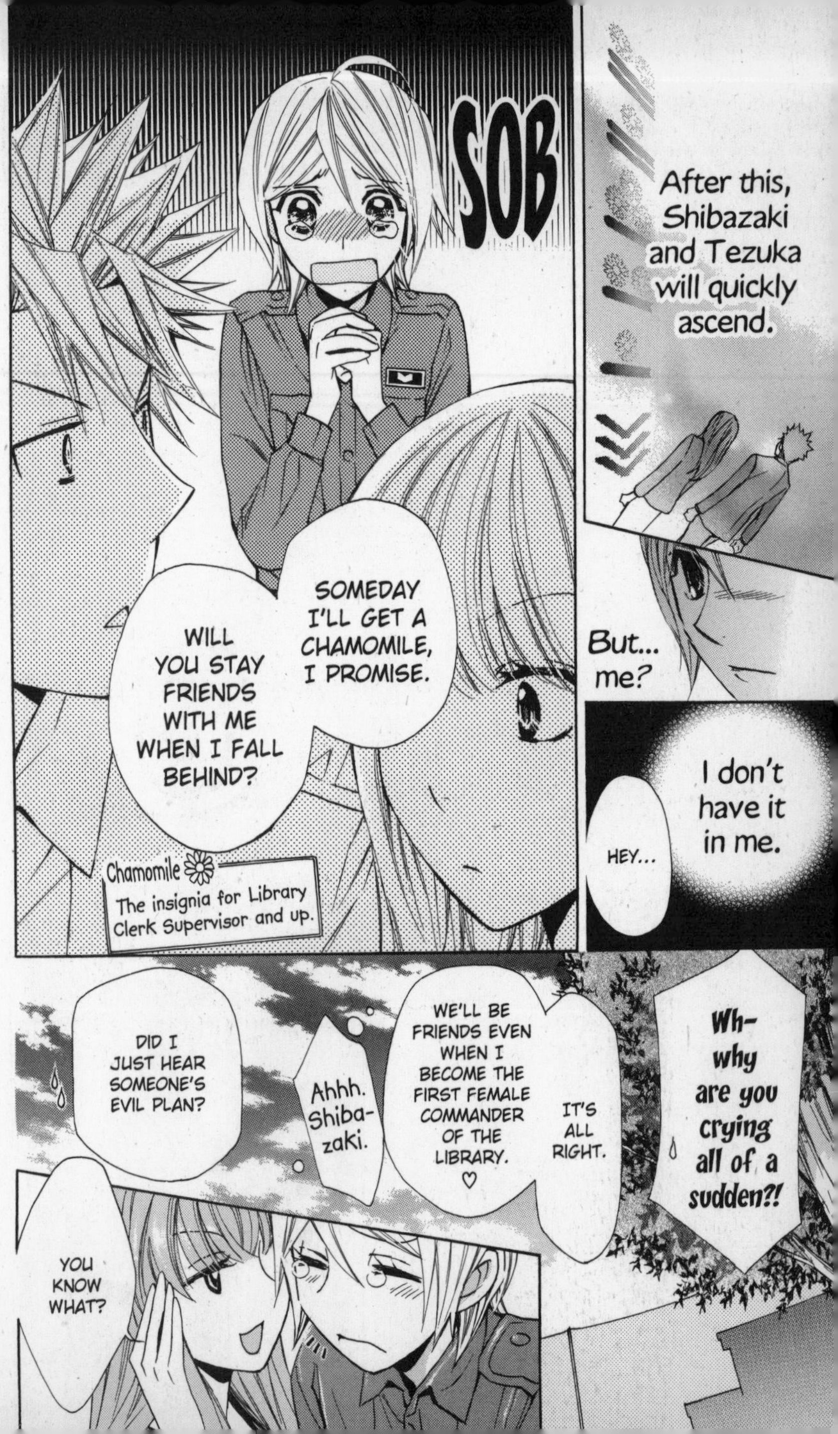
After this, Shibazaki and Tezuka will quickly ascend.
But... me?
I don't have it in me.
HEY...
SOB
SOMEDAY I'LL GET A CHAMOMILE, I PROMISE.
WILL YOU STAY FRIENDS WITH ME WHEN I FALL BEHIND?
Chamomile
The insignia for Library Clerk Supervisor and up.
Wh-why are you crying all of a sudden?!
IT'S ALL RIGHT.
WE'LL BE FRIENDS EVEN WHEN I BECOME THE FIRST FEMALE COMMANDER OF THE LIBRARY. ♡
Ahhh. Shibazaki.
DID I JUST HEAR SOMEONE'S EVIL PLAN?
YOU KNOW WHAT?

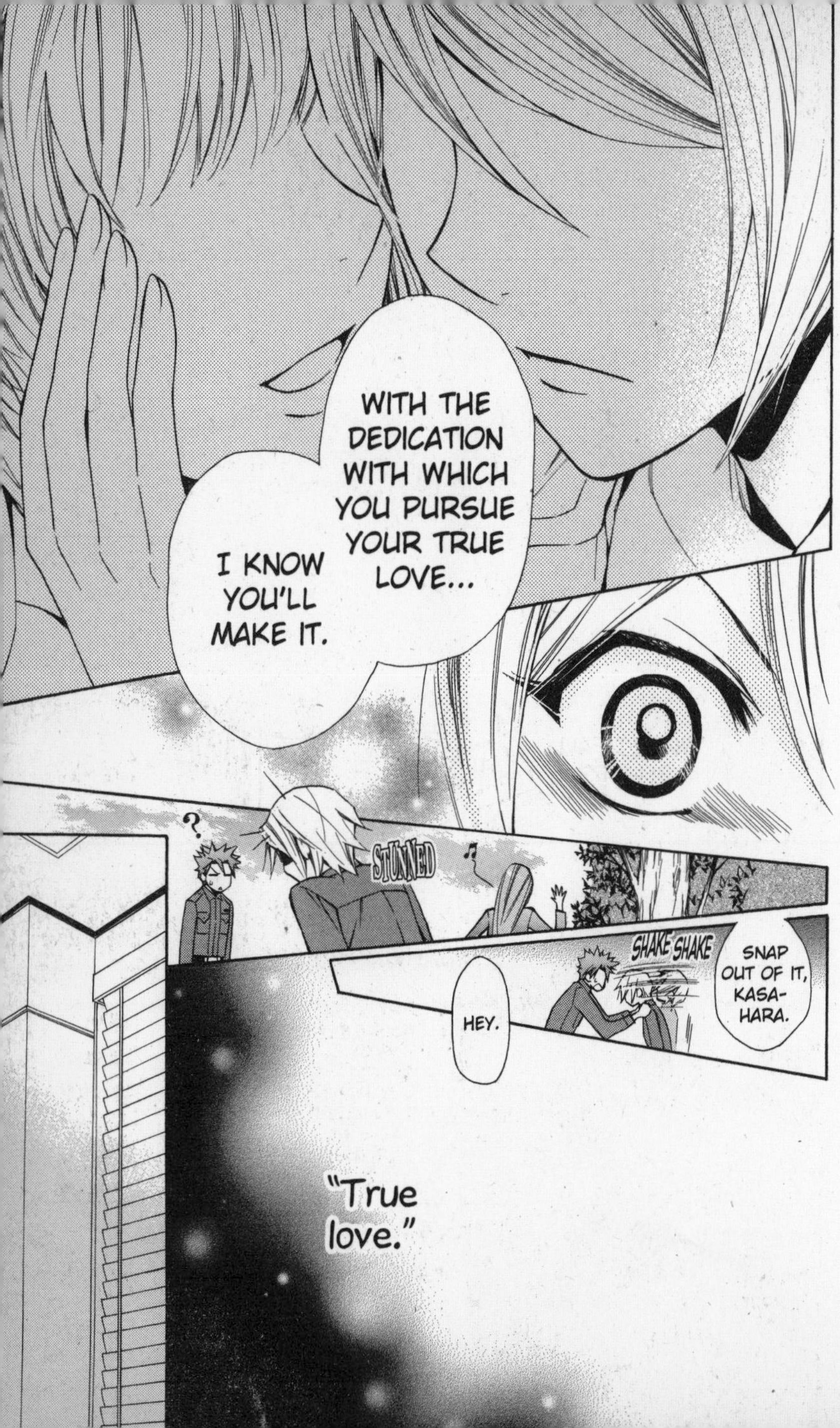
WITH THE DEDICATION WITH WHICH YOU PURSUE YOUR TRUE LOVE...
I KNOW YOU'LL MAKE IT.
STUNNED
?
SNAP OUT OF IT, KASA-HARA.
SHAKE SHAKE
HEY.
"True love."

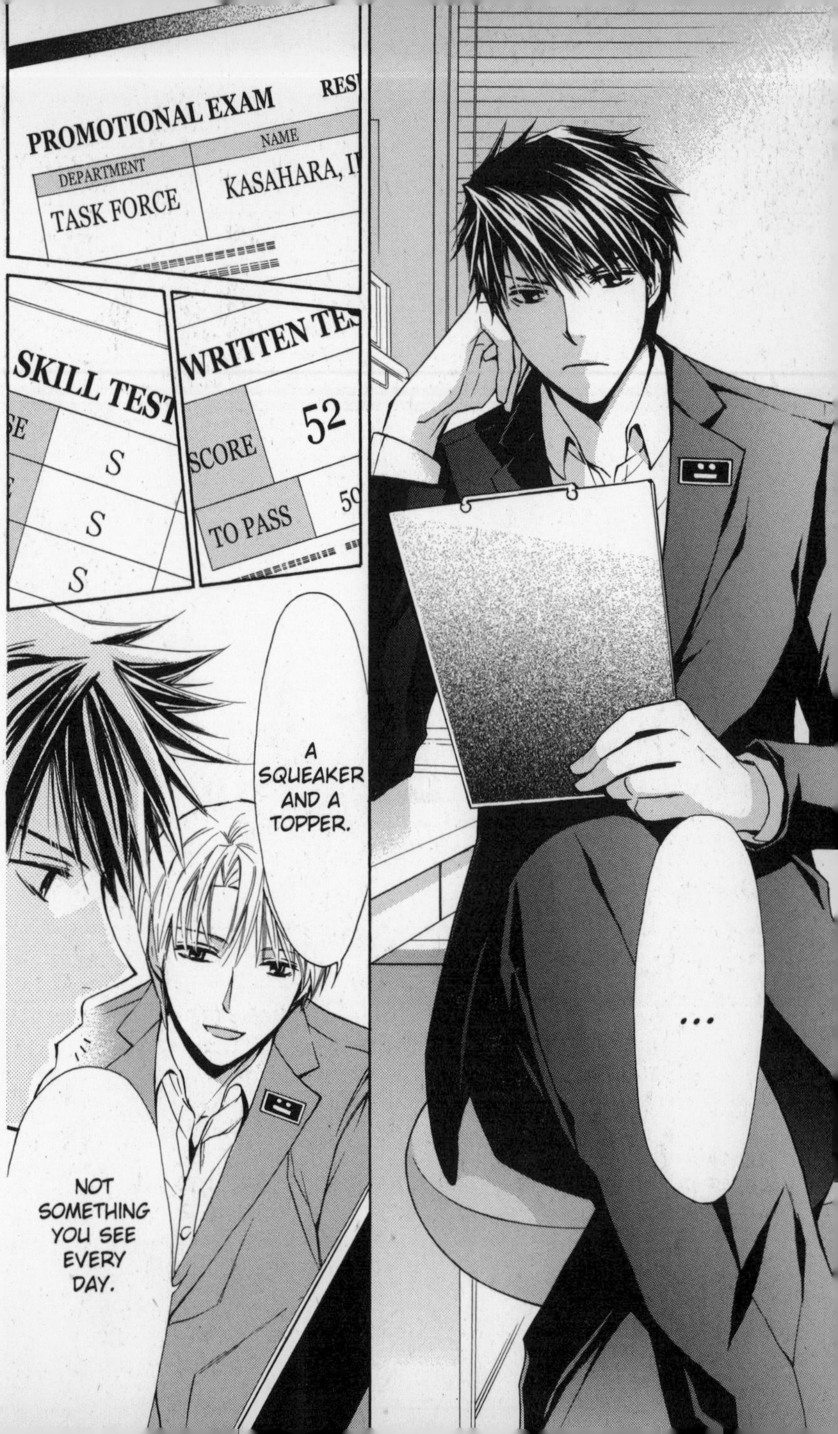
...
PROMOTIONAL EXAM
RES
DEPARTMENT
NAME
TASK FORCE
KASAHARA, I
SKILL TEST
S
S
S
WRITTEN TES
SCORE
52
TO PASS
50
A SQUEAKER AND A TOPPER.
NOT SOMETHING YOU SEE EVERY DAY.

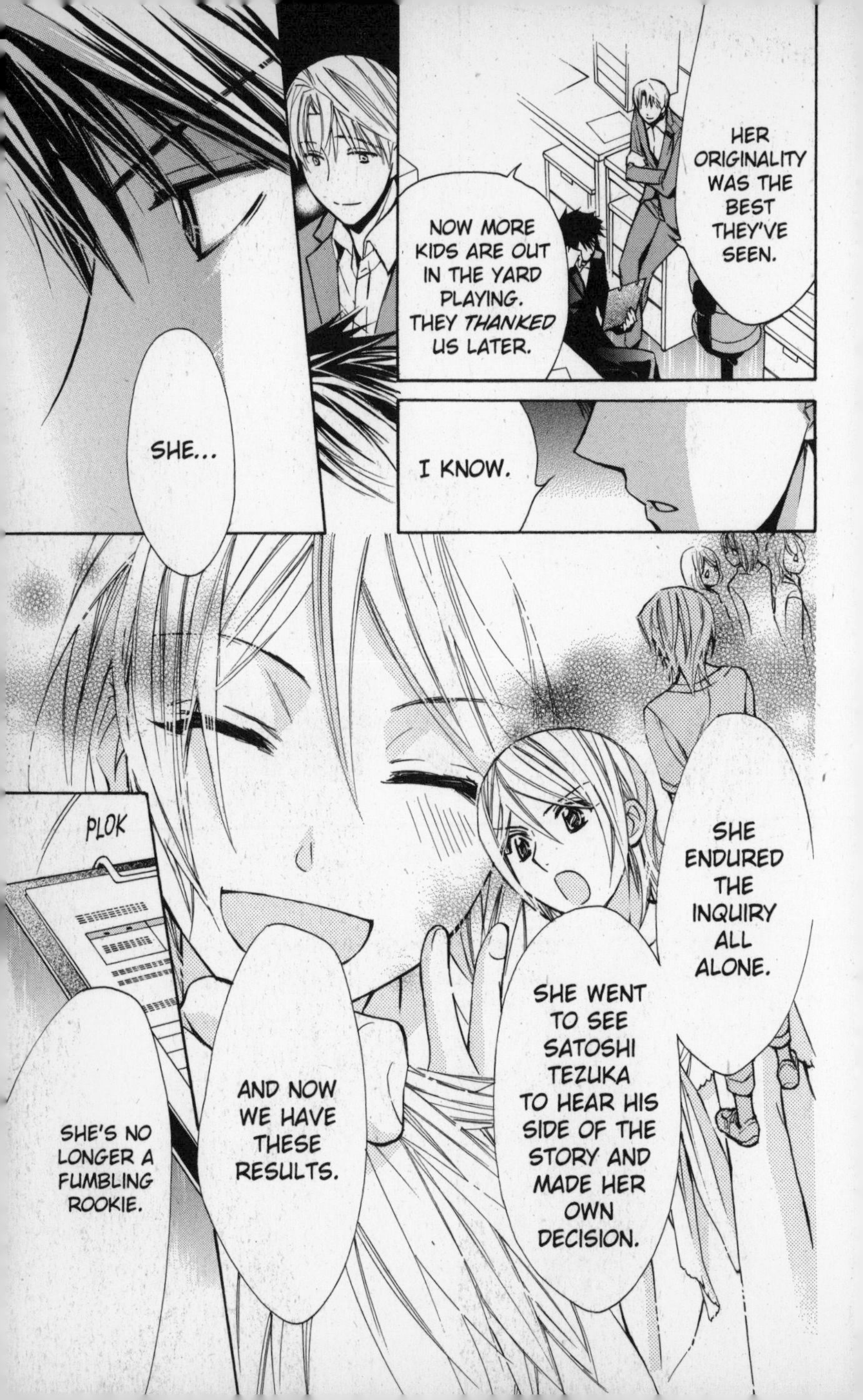
HER ORIGINALITY WAS THE BEST THEY'VE SEEN.
NOW MORE KIDS ARE OUT IN THE YARD PLAYING. THEY *THANKED* US LATER.
I KNOW.
SHE...
SHE ENDURED THE INQUIRY ALL ALONE.
SHE WENT TO SEE SATOSHI TEZUKA TO HEAR HIS SIDE OF THE STORY AND MADE HER OWN DECISION.
PLOK
AND NOW WE HAVE THESE RESULTS.
SHE'S NO LONGER A FUMBLING ROOKIE.

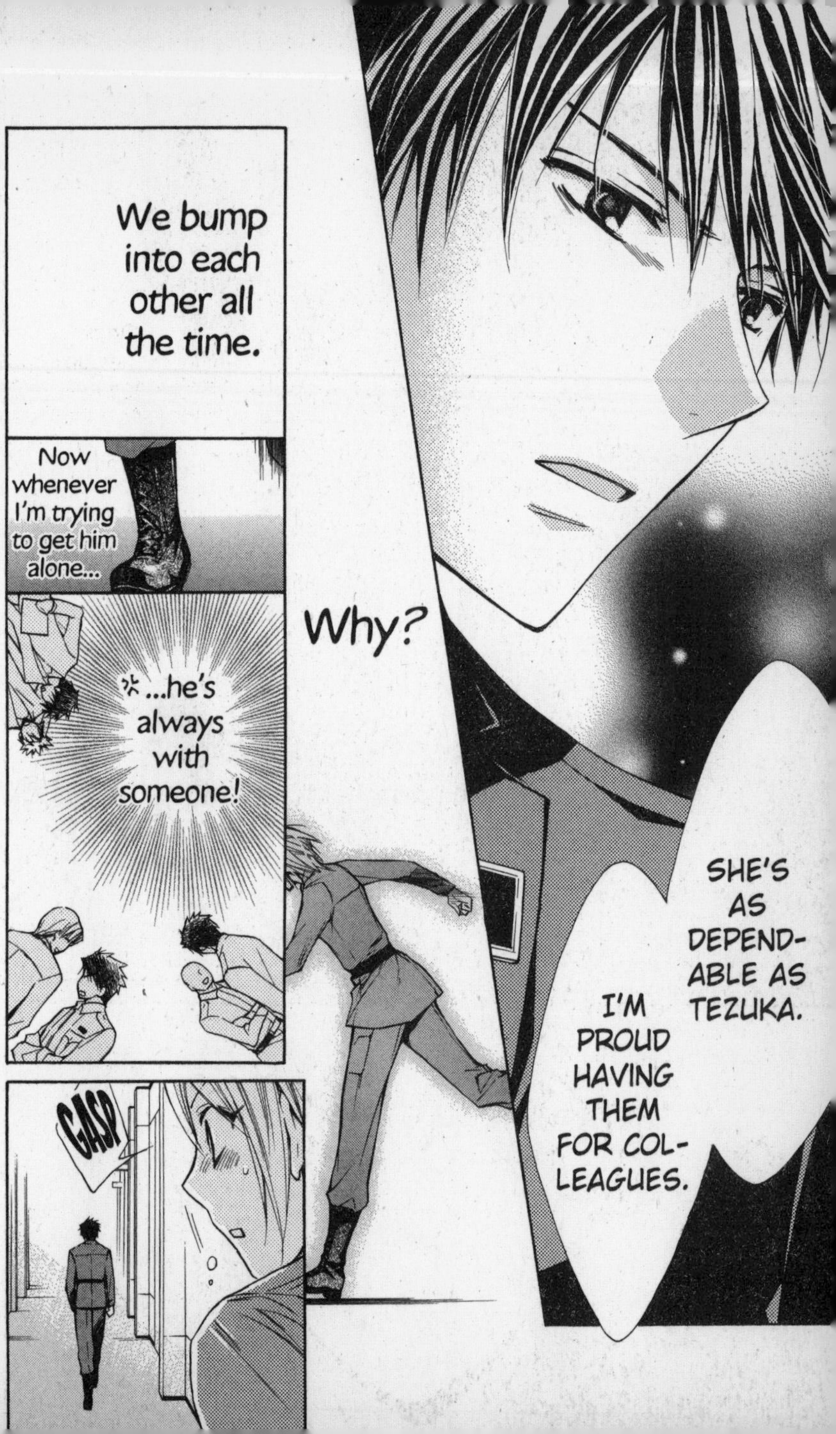
SHE'S AS DEPEND-ABLE AS TEZUKA.
I'M PROUD HAVING THEM FOR COL-LEAGUES.
Why?
We bump into each other all the time.
Now whenever I'm trying to get him alone...
...he's always with someone!
GASP

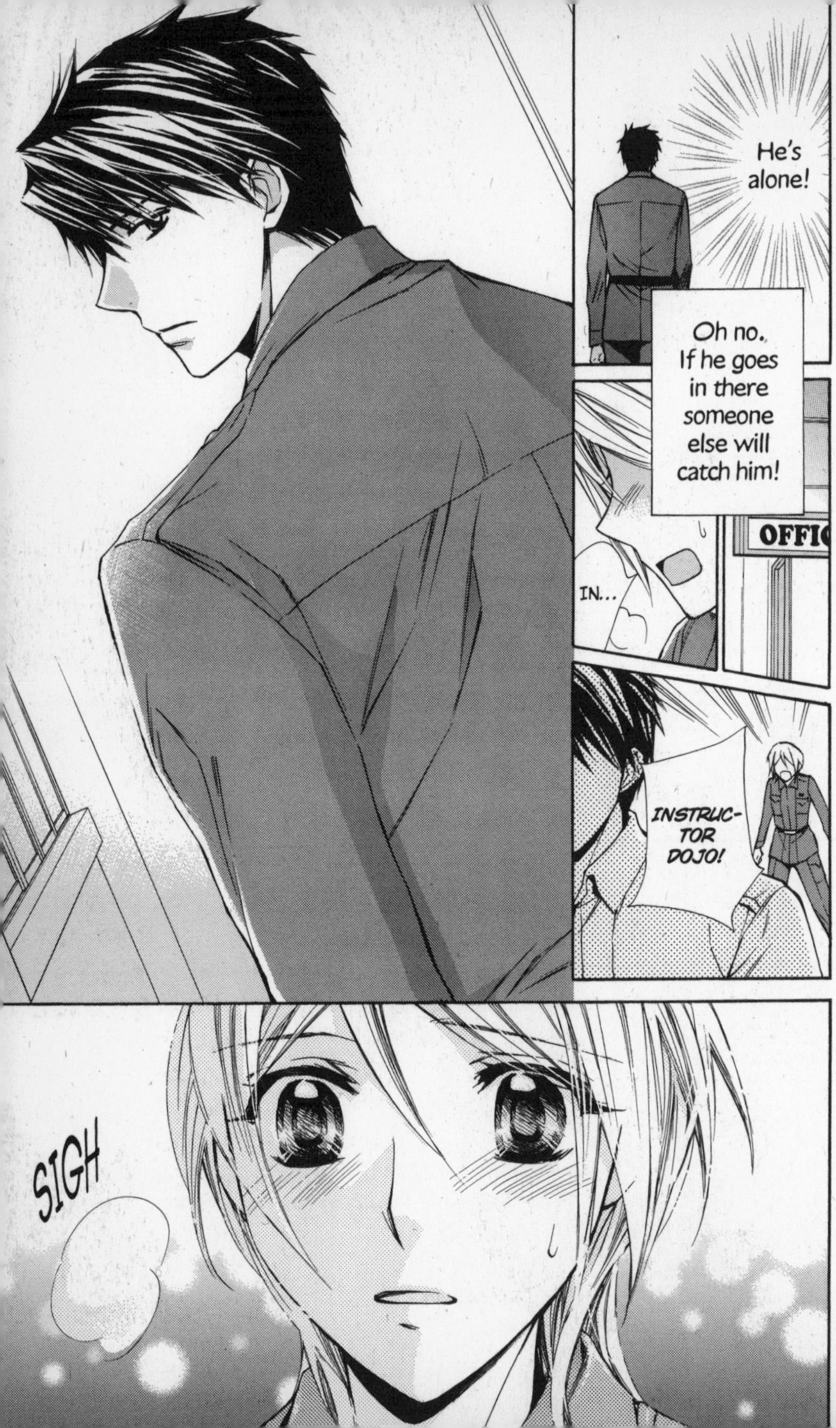
He's alone!
Oh no. If he goes in there someone else will catch him!
IN...
INSTRUC-TOR DOJO!
SIGH

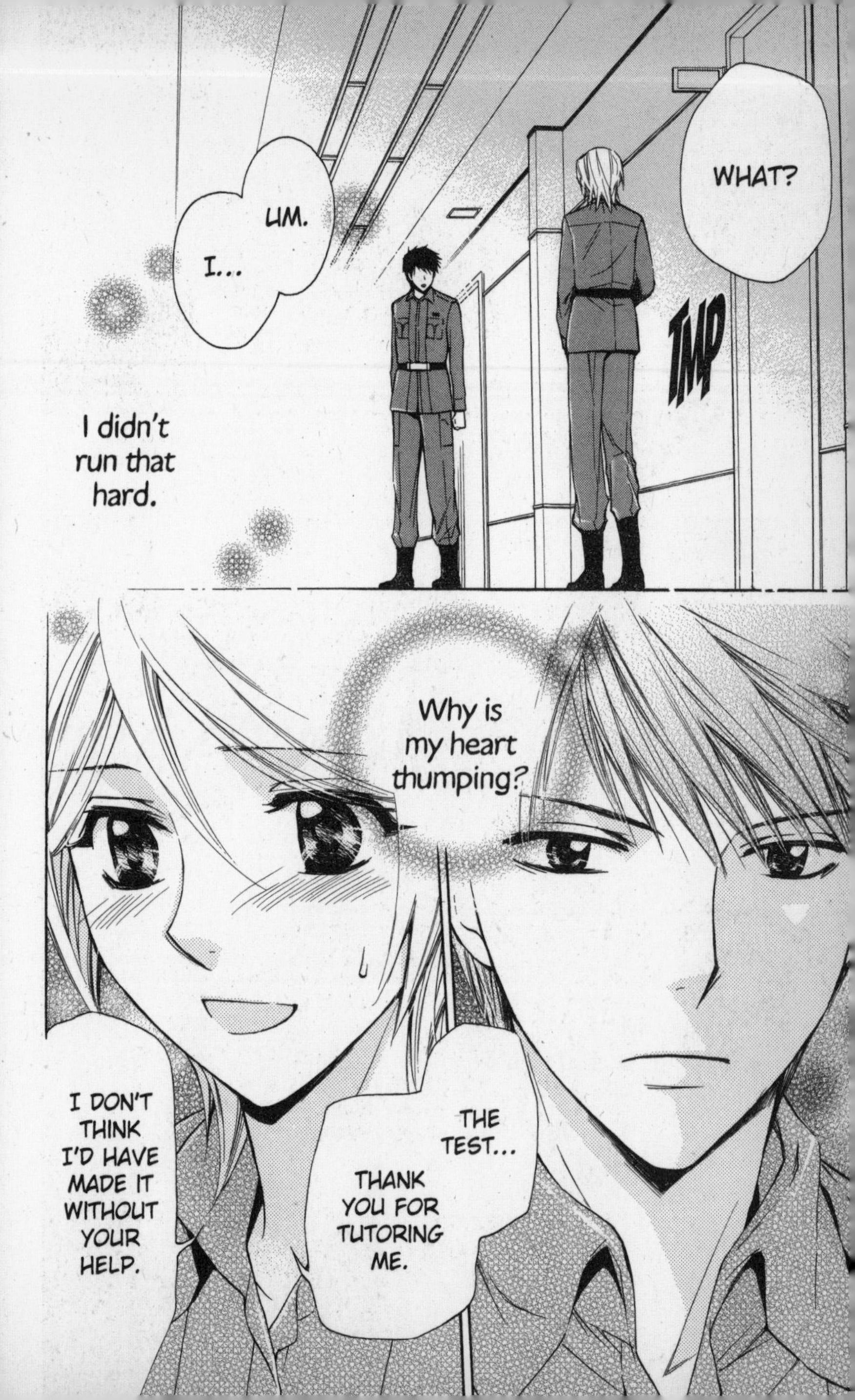
WHAT?
TMP
UM.
I...
I didn't run that hard.
Why is my heart thumping?
THE TEST...
THANK YOU FOR TUTORING ME.
I DON'T THINK I'D HAVE MADE IT WITHOUT YOUR HELP.

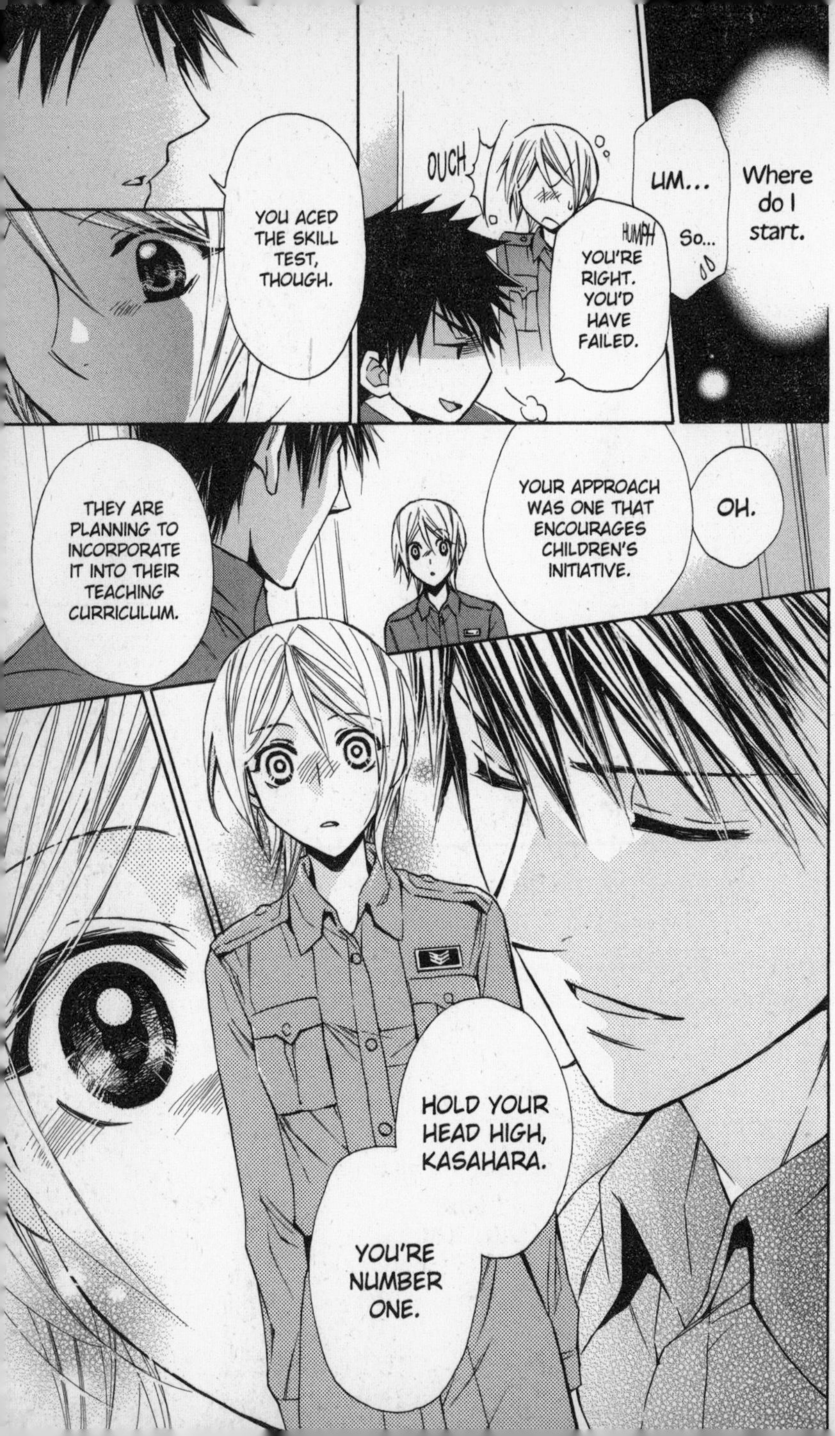
UM...
So...
Where do I start.
OUCH
HUMPH
YOU'RE RIGHT. YOU'D HAVE FAILED.
YOU ACED THE SKILL TEST, THOUGH.
OH.
YOUR APPROACH WAS ONE THAT ENCOURAGES CHILDREN'S INITIATIVE.
THEY ARE PLANNING TO INCORPORATE IT INTO THEIR TEACHING CURRICULUM.
HOLD YOUR HEAD HIGH, KASAHARA.
YOU'RE NUMBER ONE.

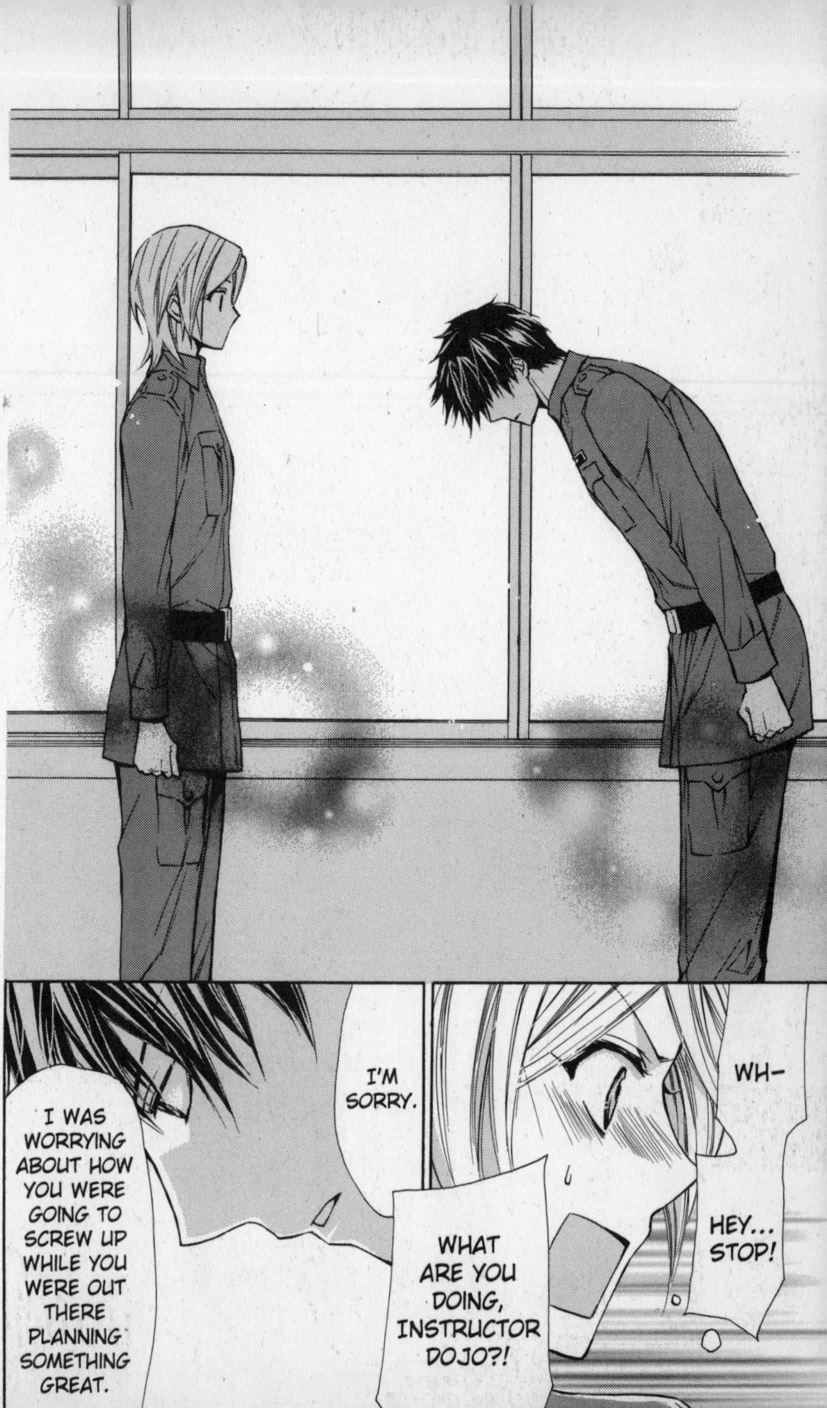
WH-
HEY... STOP!
WHAT ARE YOU DOING, INSTRUCTOR DOJO?!
I'M SORRY.
I WAS WORRYING ABOUT HOW YOU WERE GOING TO SCREW UP WHILE YOU WERE OUT THERE PLANNING SOMETHING GREAT.

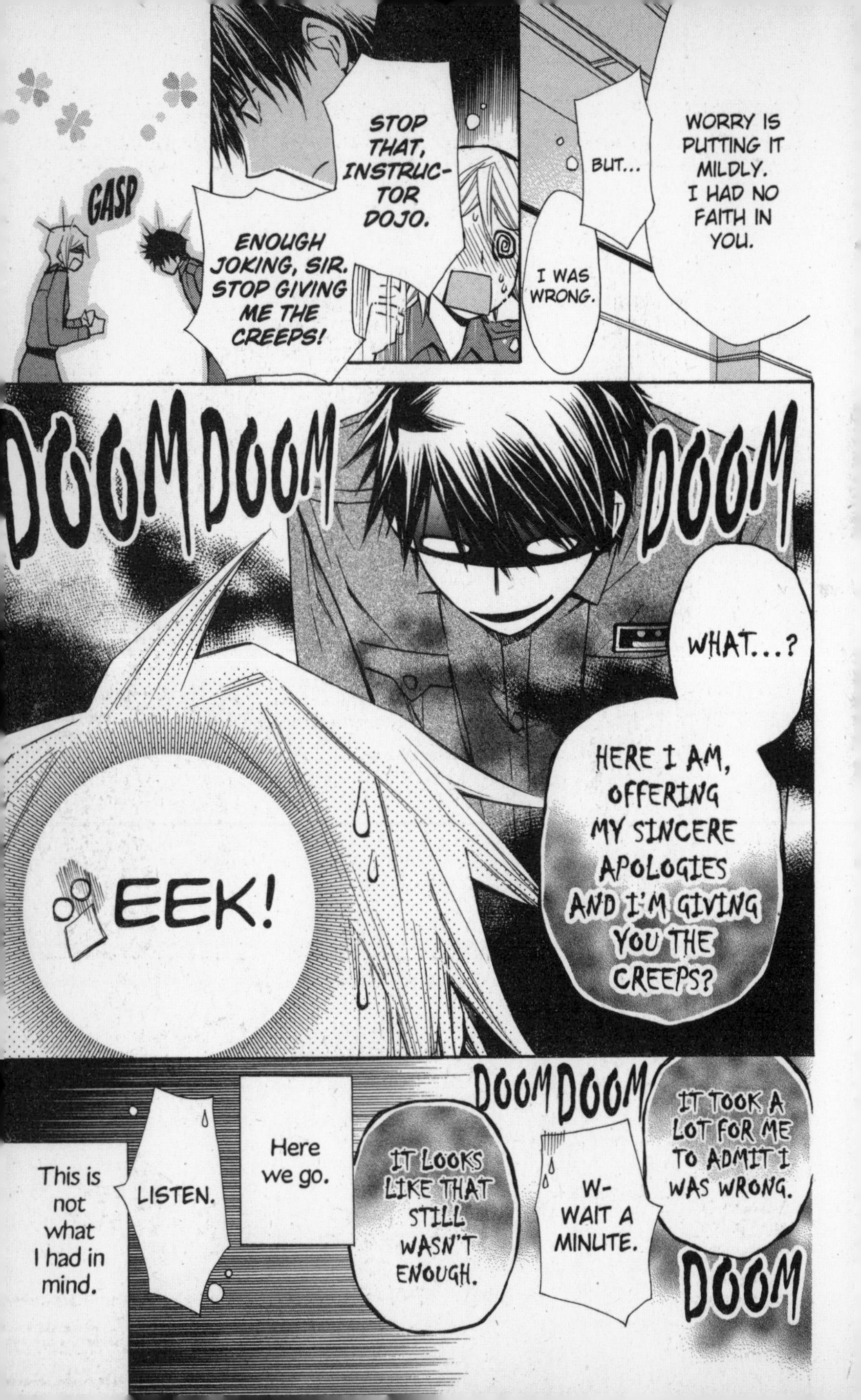
WORRY IS PUTTING IT MILDLY. I HAD NO FAITH IN YOU.
BUT...
I WAS WRONG.
STOP THAT, INSTRUCTOR DOJO.
ENOUGH JOKING, SIR. STOP GIVING ME THE CREEPS!
GASP
DOOM
DOOMDOOM
WHAT...?
HERE I AM, OFFERING MY SINCERE APOLOGIES AND I'M GIVING YOU THE CREEPS?
EEK!
DOOMDOOM
IT TOOK A LOT FOR ME TO ADMIT I WAS WRONG.
DOOM
W-WAIT A MINUTE.
IT LOOKS LIKE THAT STILL WASN'T ENOUGH.
Here we go.
LISTEN.
This is not what I had in mind.

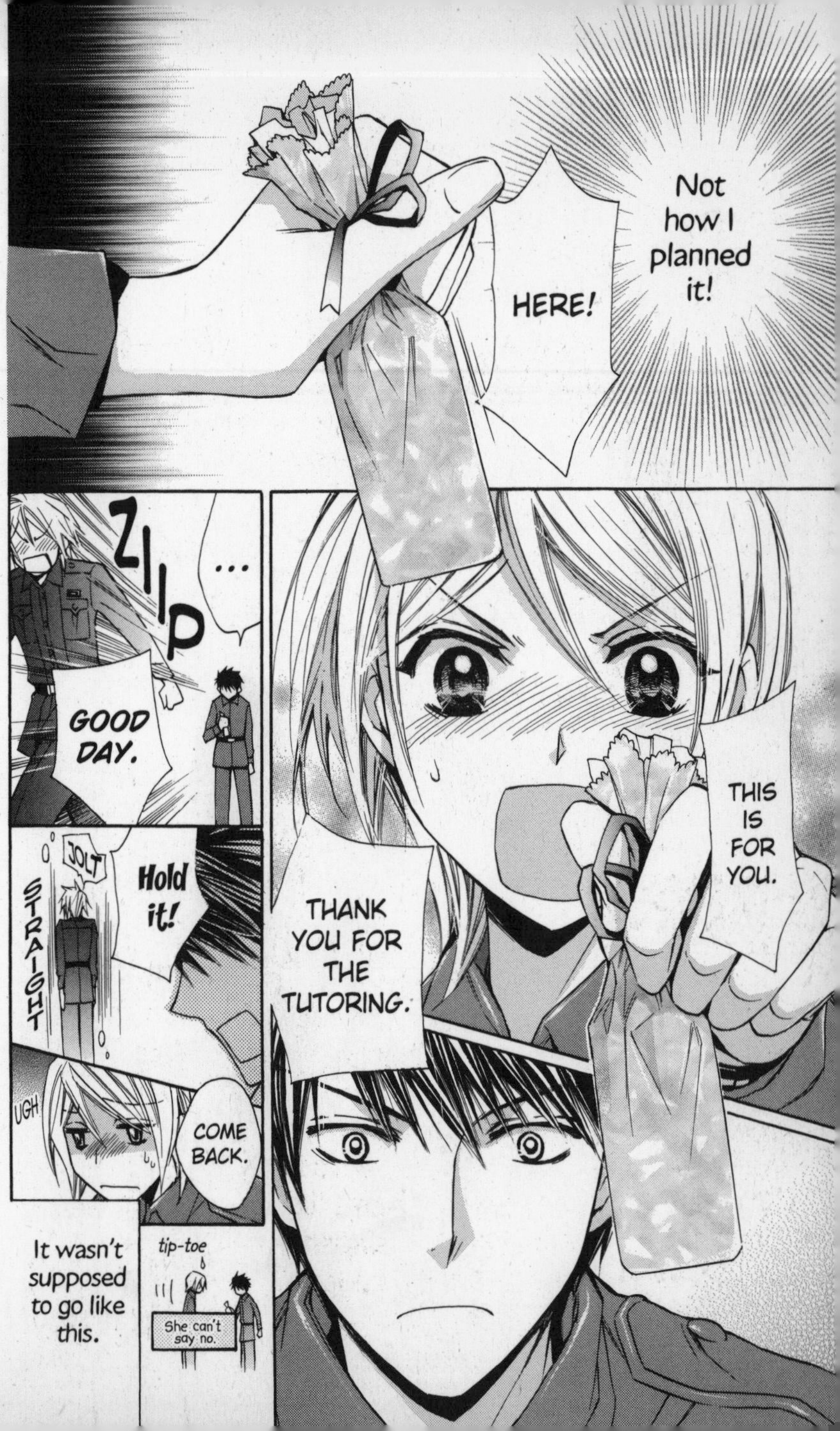
Not how I planned it!
HERE!
THIS IS FOR YOU.
THANK YOU FOR THE TUTORING.
...
ZIIP
GOOD DAY.
Hold it!
JOLT
STRAIGHT
COME BACK.
UGH
tip-toe
She can't say no.
It wasn't supposed to go like this.

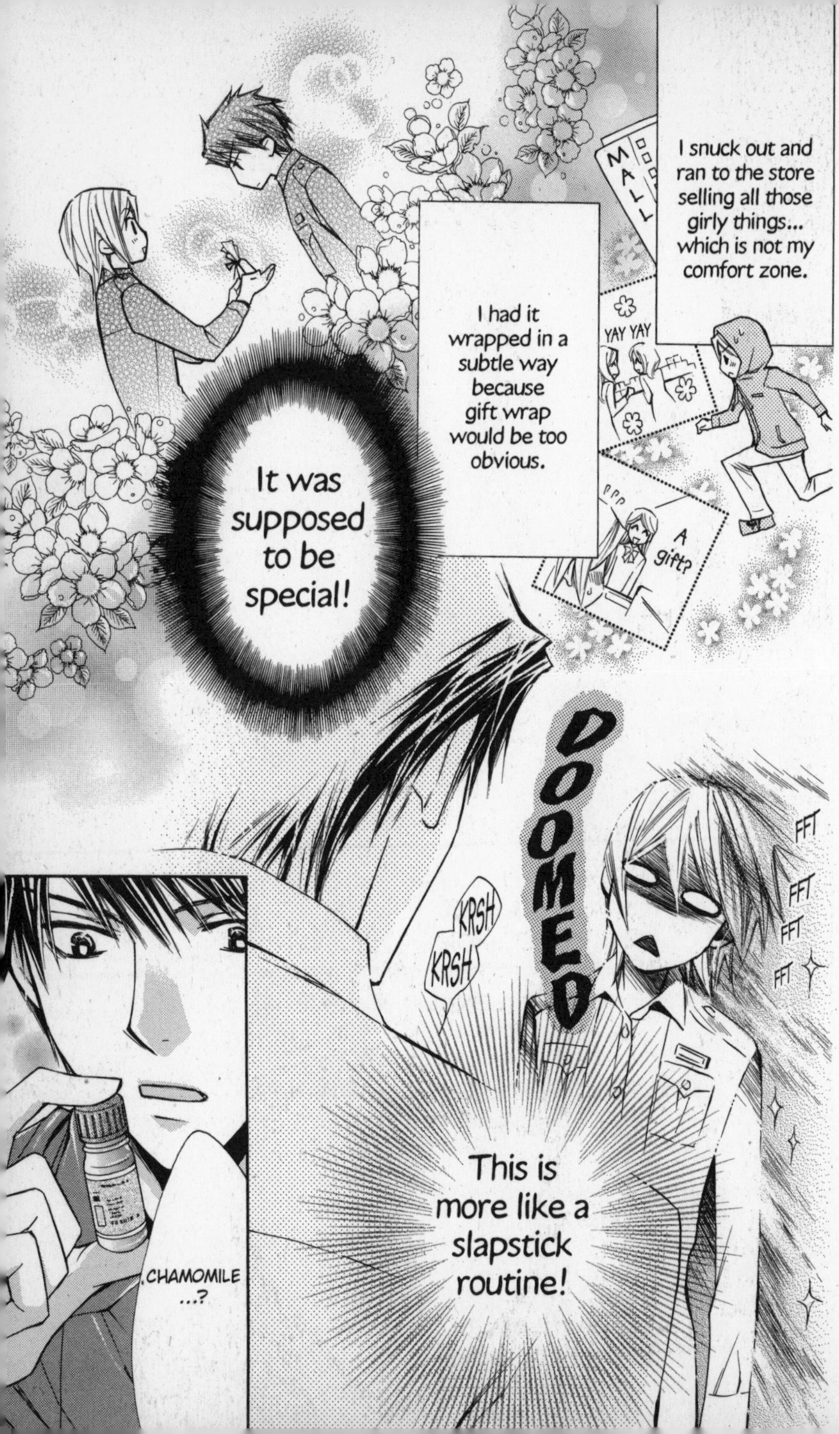
I snuck out and ran to the store selling all those girly things... which is not my comfort zone.
MALL
YAY YAY
A gift?
I had it wrapped in a subtle way because gift wrap would be too obvious.
It was supposed to be special!
DOOOMED
FFT
FFT
FFT
FFT
KRSH
KRSH
This is more like a slapstick routine!
CHAMOMILE ...?

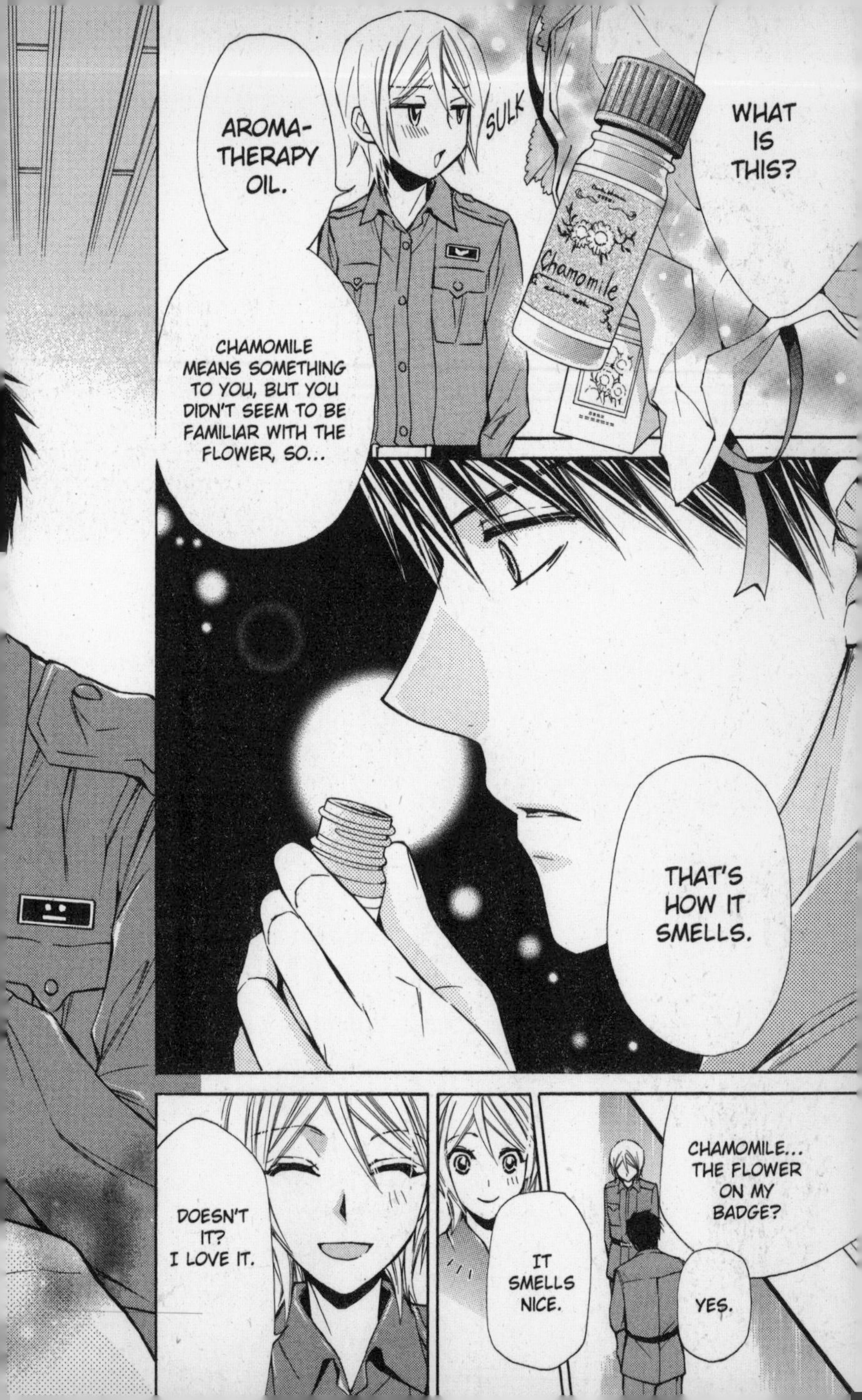
WHAT IS THIS?
SULK
Chamomile
AROMA-THERAPY OIL.
CHAMOMILE MEANS SOMETHING TO YOU, BUT YOU DIDN'T SEEM TO BE FAMILIAR WITH THE FLOWER, SO...
THAT'S HOW IT SMELLS.
CHAMOMILE... THE FLOWER ON MY BADGE?
YES.
IT SMELLS NICE.
DOESN'T IT? I LOVE IT.

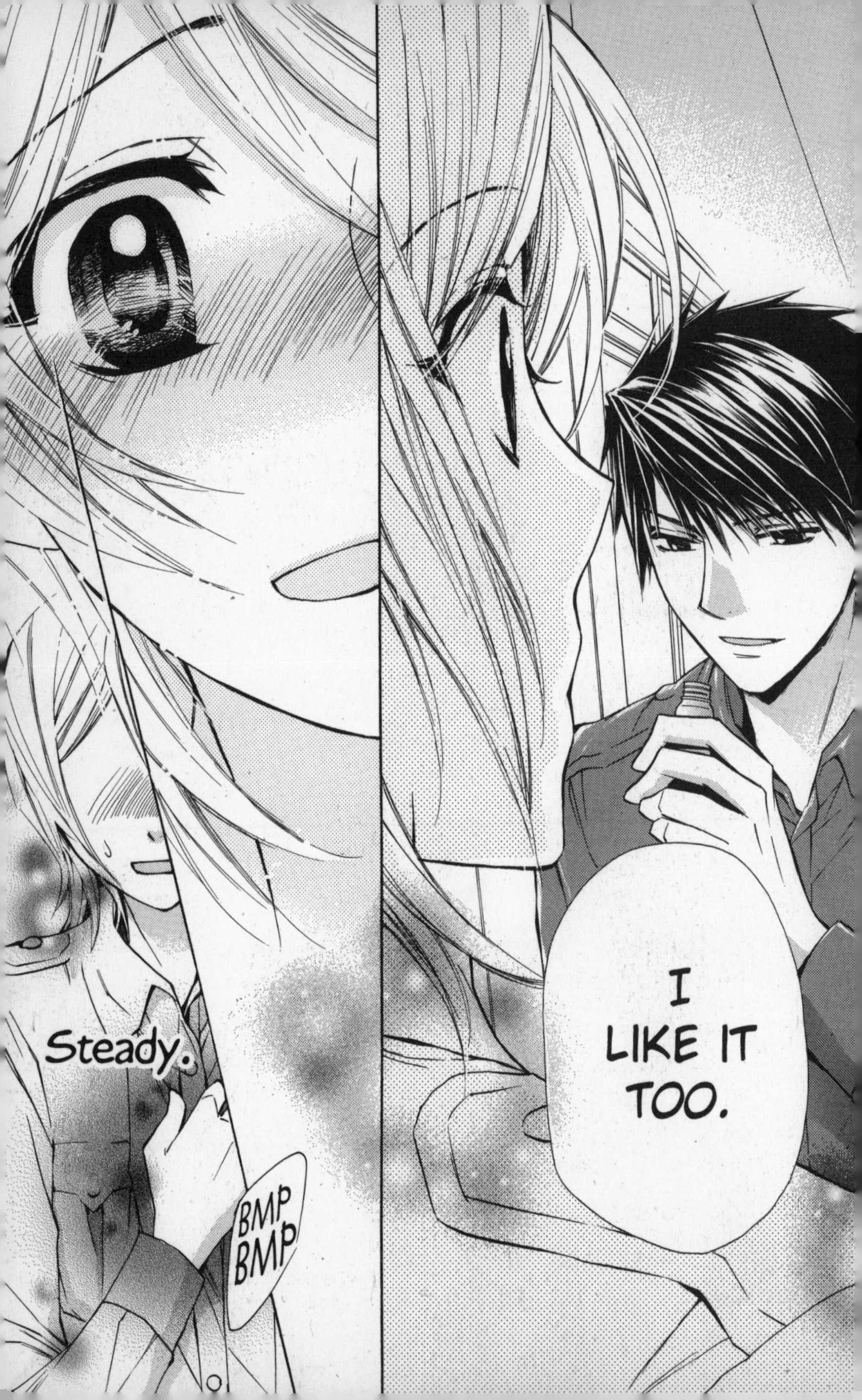
I LIKE IT TOO.
Steady.
BMP BMP

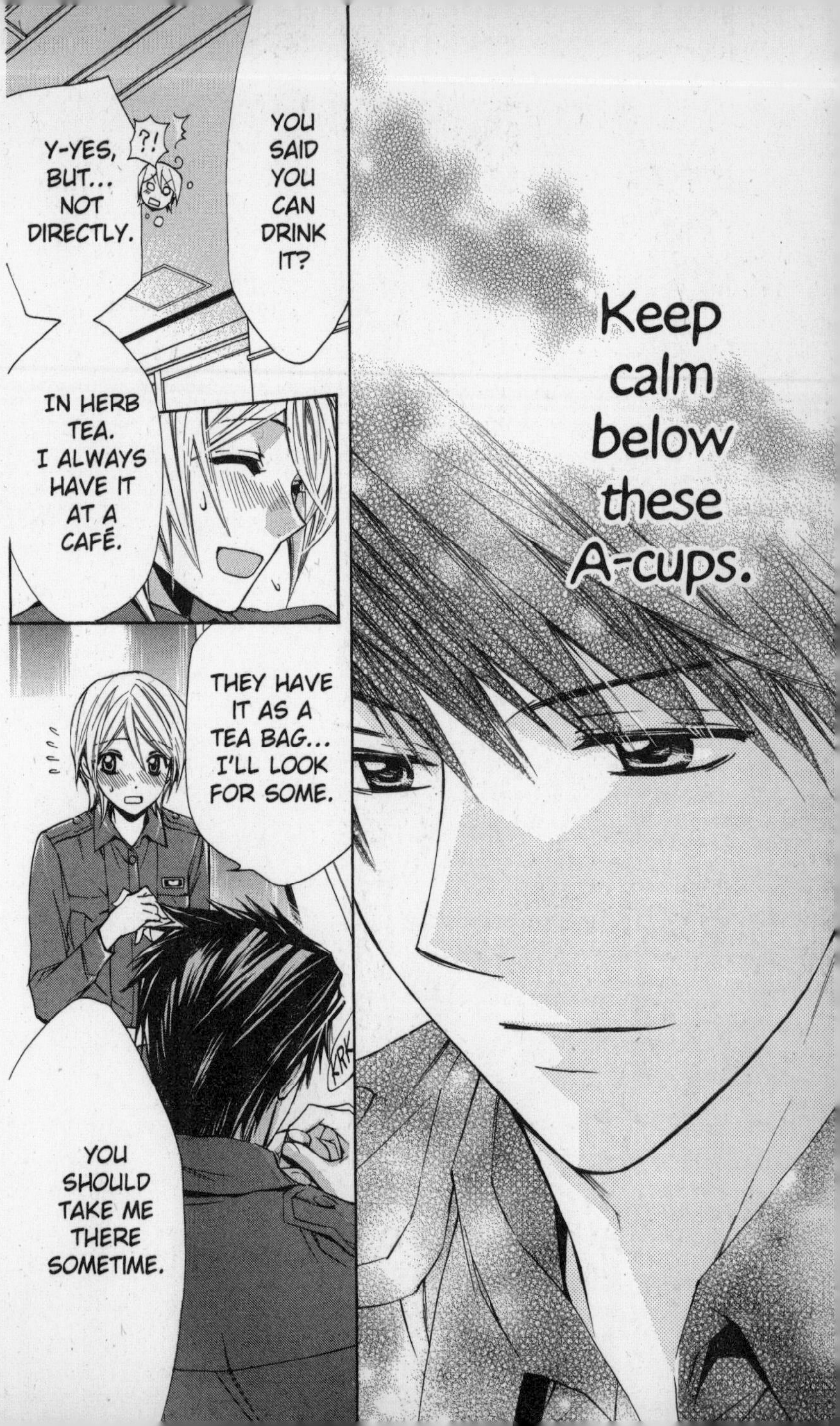
Keep calm below these A-cups.
YOU SAID YOU CAN DRINK IT?
?!
Y-YES, BUT... NOT DIRECTLY.
IN HERB TEA. I ALWAYS HAVE IT AT A CAFÉ.
THEY HAVE IT AS A TEA BAG... I'LL LOOK FOR SOME.
KRK
YOU SHOULD TAKE ME THERE SOMETIME.

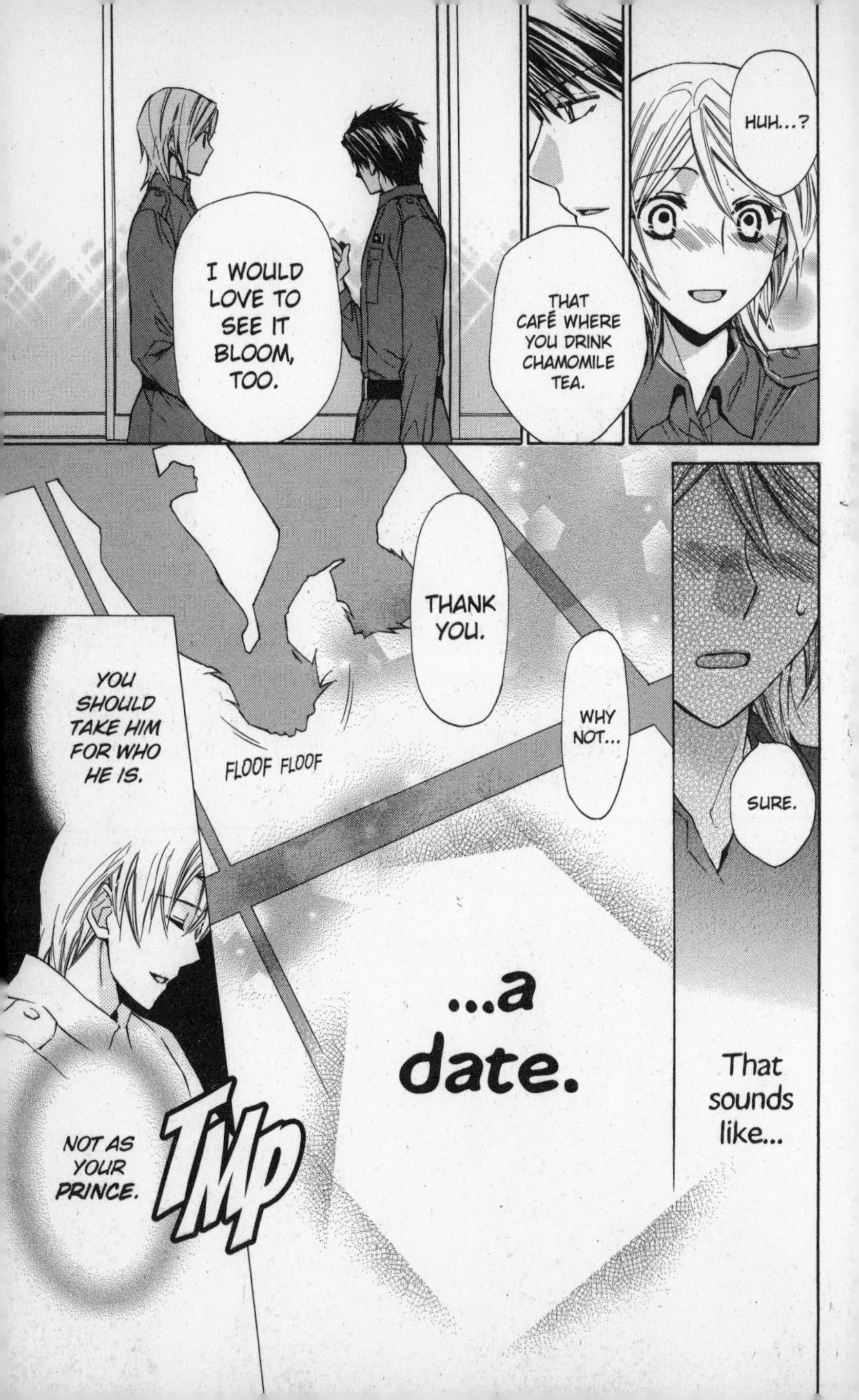
HUH...?
THAT CAFÉ WHERE YOU DRINK CHAMOMILE TEA.
I WOULD LOVE TO SEE IT BLOOM, TOO.
THANK YOU.
WHY NOT...
SURE.
That sounds like...
...a date.
FLOOF FLOOF
YOU SHOULD TAKE HIM FOR WHO HE IS.
TMP
NOT AS YOUR PRINCE.

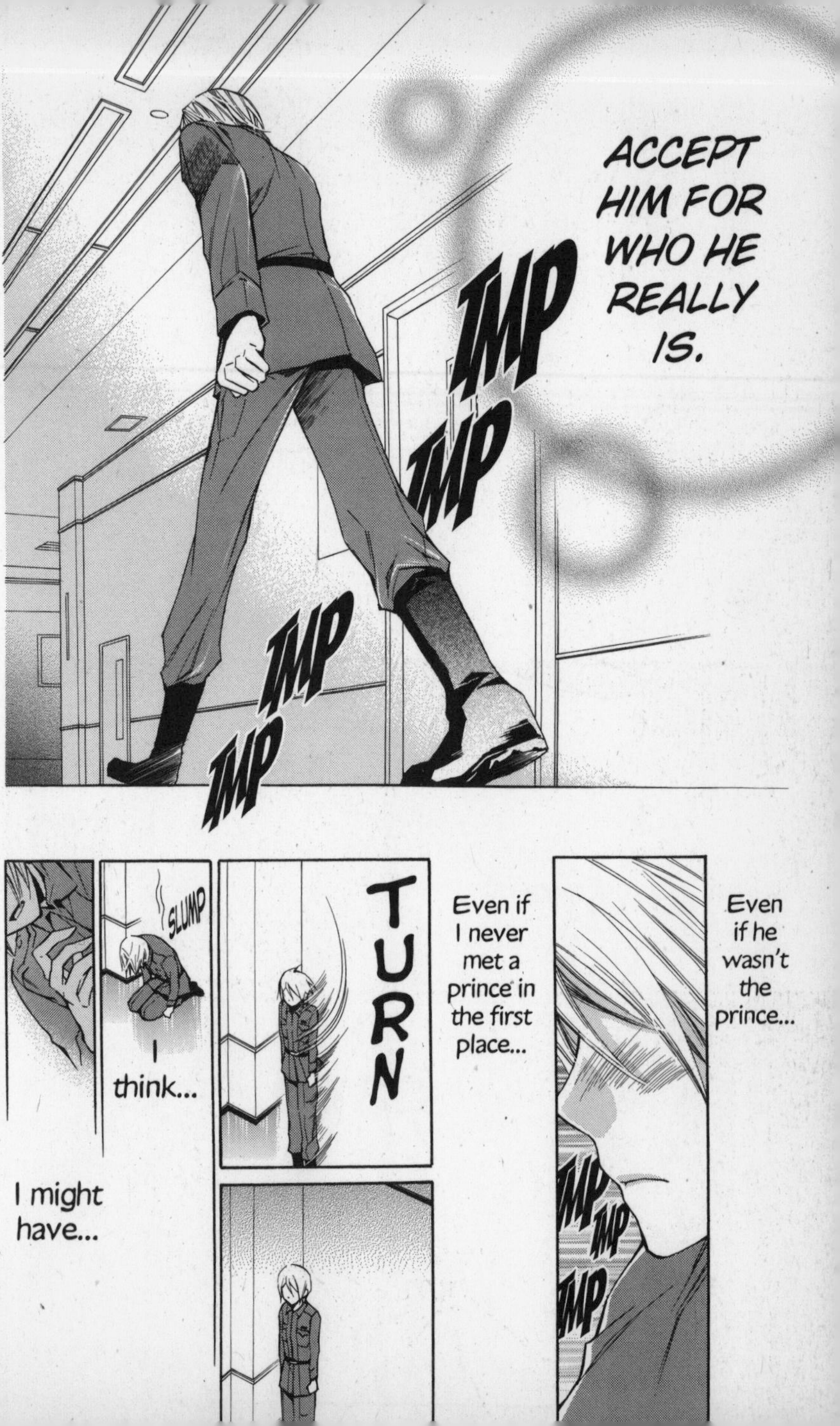
ACCEPT HIM FOR WHO HE REALLY IS.
TMP TMP
TMP TMP
Even if he wasn't the prince...
TMP TMP TMP
Even if I never met a prince in the first place...
TURN
SLUMP
I think...
I might have...

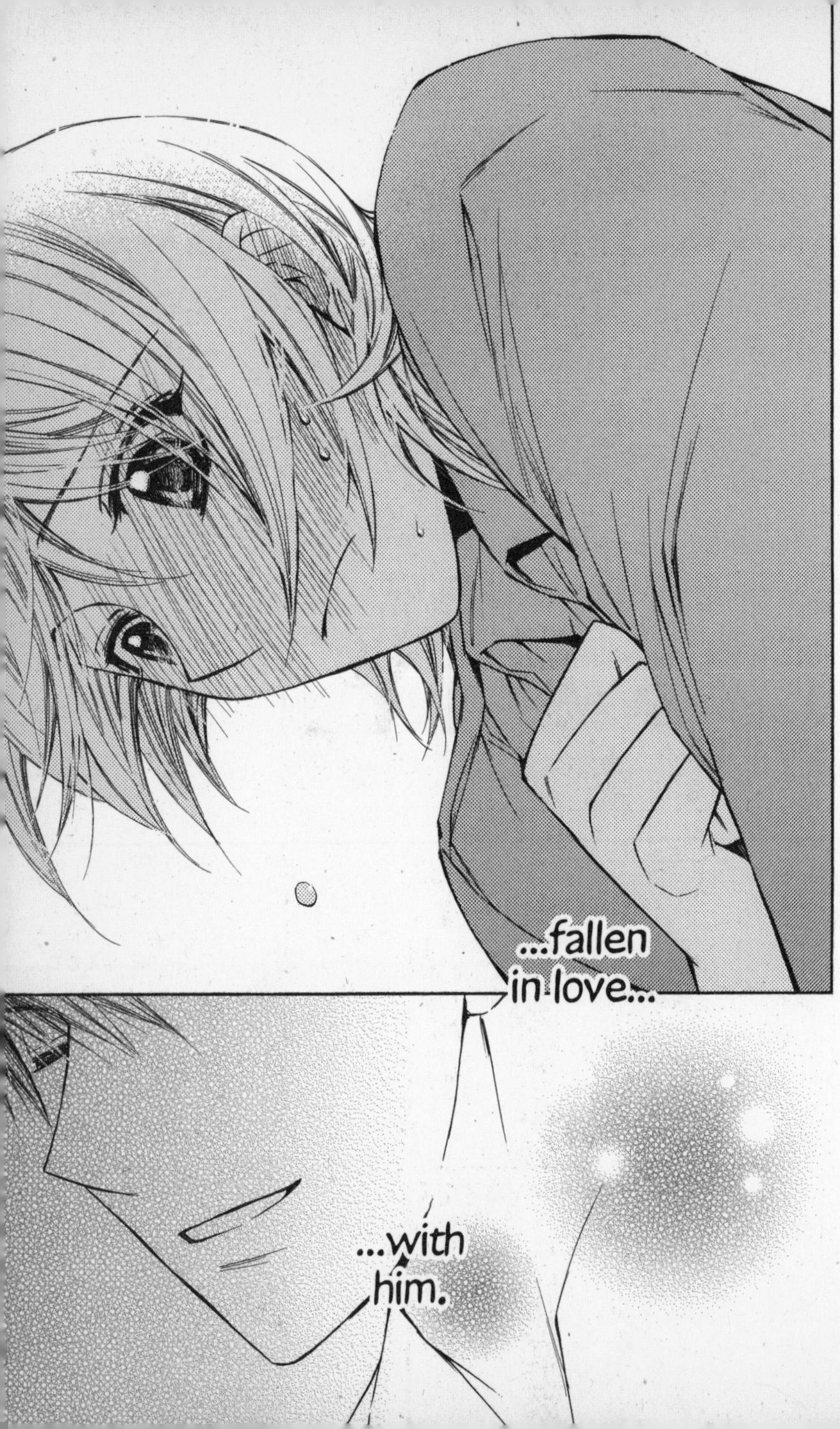
...fallen in love...
...with him.

Secret Admirer part 8

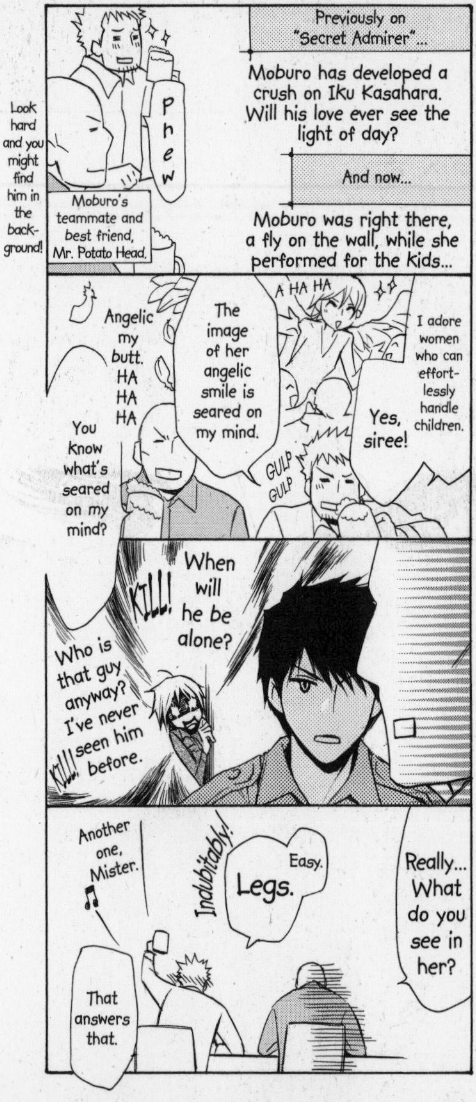
Previously on "Secret Admirer"...
Moburo has developed a crush on Iku Kasahara. Will his love ever see the light of day?
And now...
Moburo was right there, a fly on the wall, while she performed for the kids...
Phew
Moburo's teammate and best friend, Mr. Potato Head.
Look hard and you might find him in the back-ground!
I adore women who can effort-lessly handle children.
A HA HA
Yes, siree!
The image of her angelic smile is seared on my mind.
GULP GULP
Angelic my butt. HA HA HA
You know what's seared on my mind?
When will he be alone?
KILL!
Who is that guy anyway? I've never seen him before.
KILL!
Really... What do you see in her?
Easy.
Legs.
Indubitably!
Another one, Mister.
That answers that.

"I give up," by Mr. Potato Head.

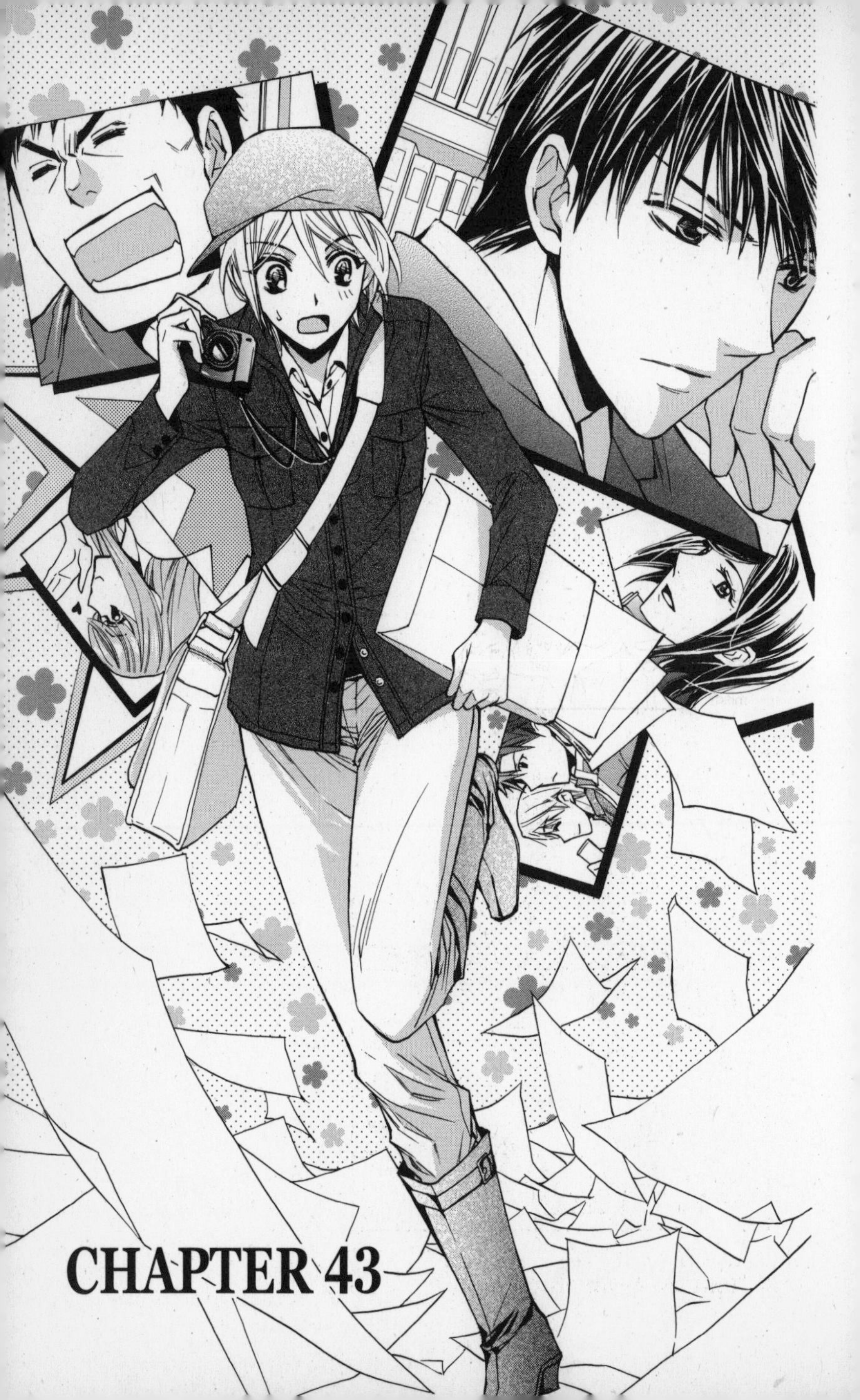
CHAPTER 43

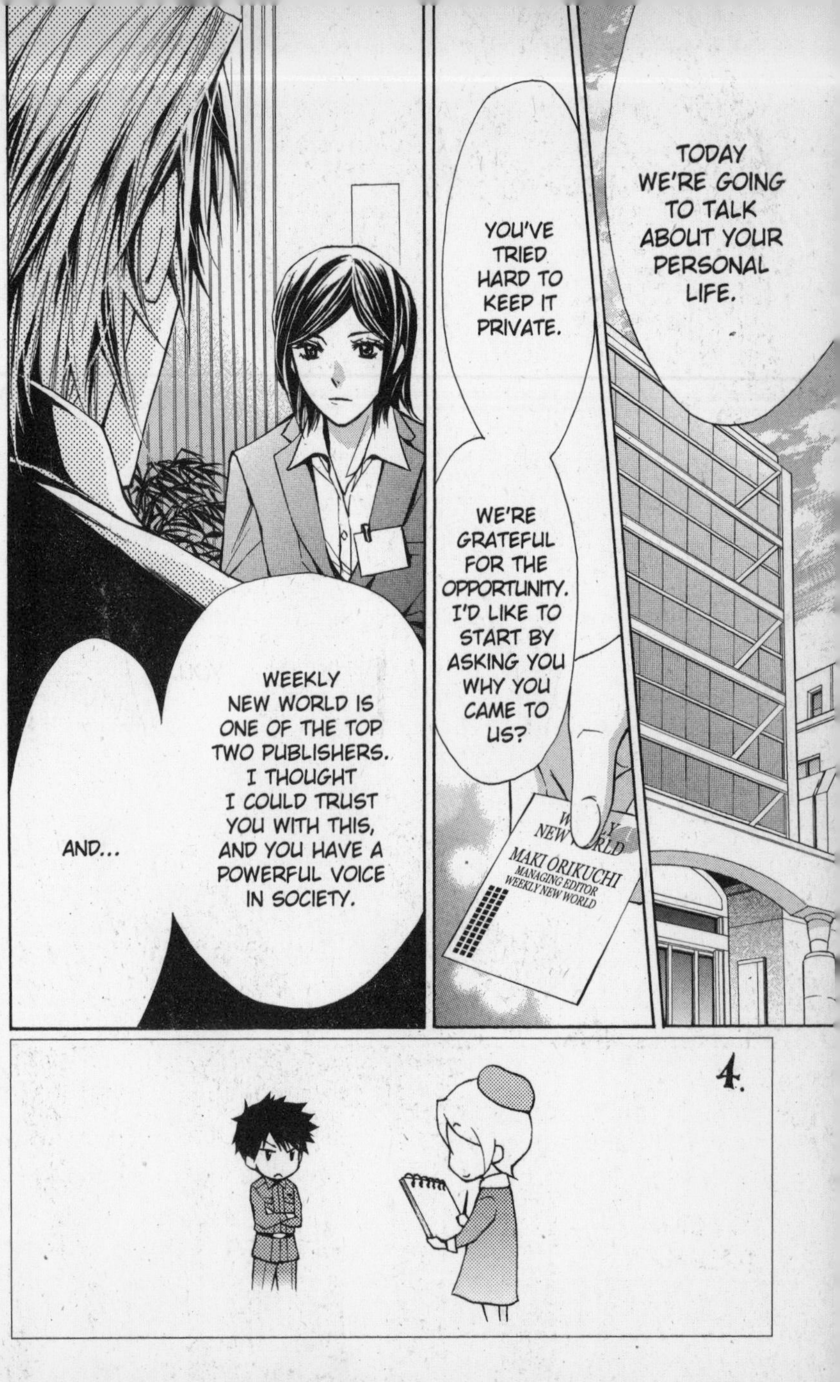
TODAY WE'RE GOING TO TALK ABOUT YOUR PERSONAL LIFE.
YOU'VE TRIED HARD TO KEEP IT PRIVATE.
WE'RE GRATEFUL FOR THE OPPORTUNITY. I'D LIKE TO START BY ASKING YOU WHY YOU CAME TO US?
MAKI ORIKUCHI
MANAGING EDITOR
WEEKLY NEW WORLD
WEEKLY NEW WORLD IS ONE OF THE TOP TWO PUBLISHERS. I THOUGHT I COULD TRUST YOU WITH THIS, AND YOU HAVE A POWERFUL VOICE IN SOCIETY.
AND...
4.

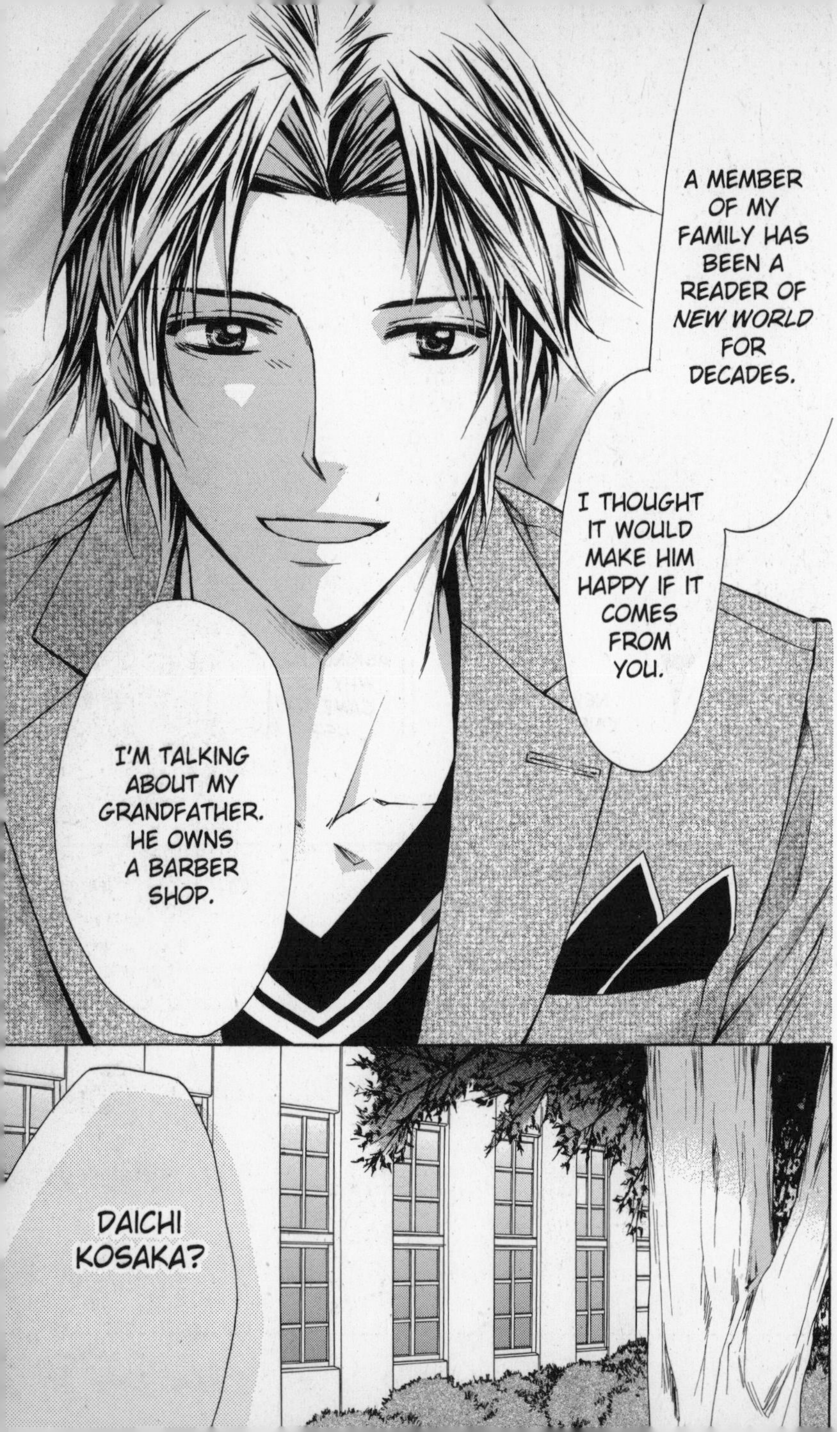
A MEMBER OF MY FAMILY HAS BEEN A READER OF *NEW WORLD* FOR DECADES.
I THOUGHT IT WOULD MAKE HIM HAPPY IF IT COMES FROM YOU.
I'M TALKING ABOUT MY GRANDFATHER. HE OWNS A BARBER SHOP.
DAICHI KOSAKA?

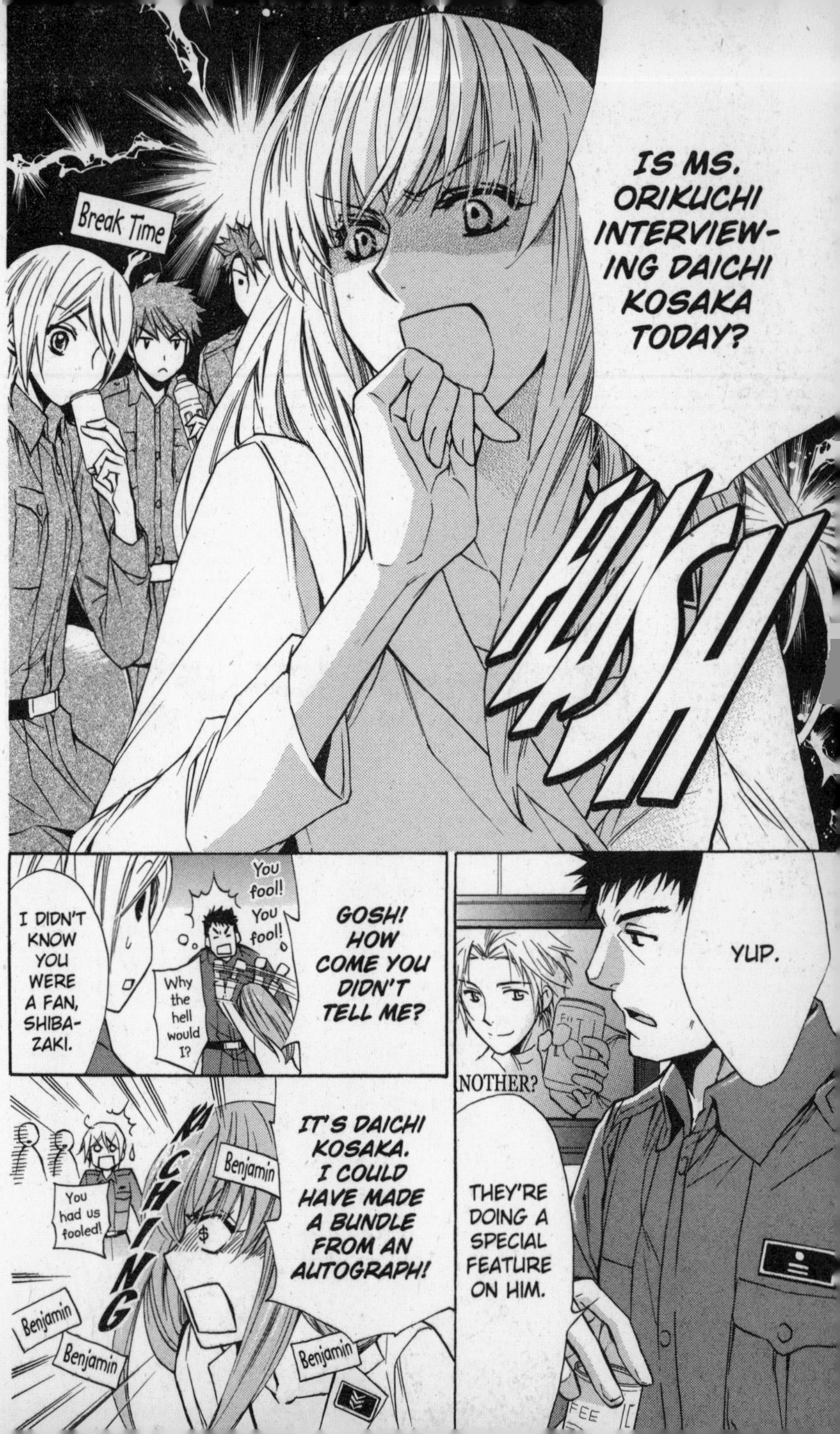
IS MS. ORIKUCHI INTERVIEWING DAICHI KOSAKA TODAY?
Break Time
YUP.
NOTHER?
THEY'RE DOING A SPECIAL FEATURE ON HIM.
GOSH! HOW COME YOU DIDN'T TELL ME?
You fool! You fool!
Why the hell would I?
I DIDN'T KNOW YOU WERE A FAN, SHIBAZAKI.
IT'S DAICHI KOSAKA. I COULD HAVE MADE A BUNDLE FROM AN AUTOGRAPH!
Benjamin
KACHING
You had us fooled!
Benjamin
Benjamin
Benjamin

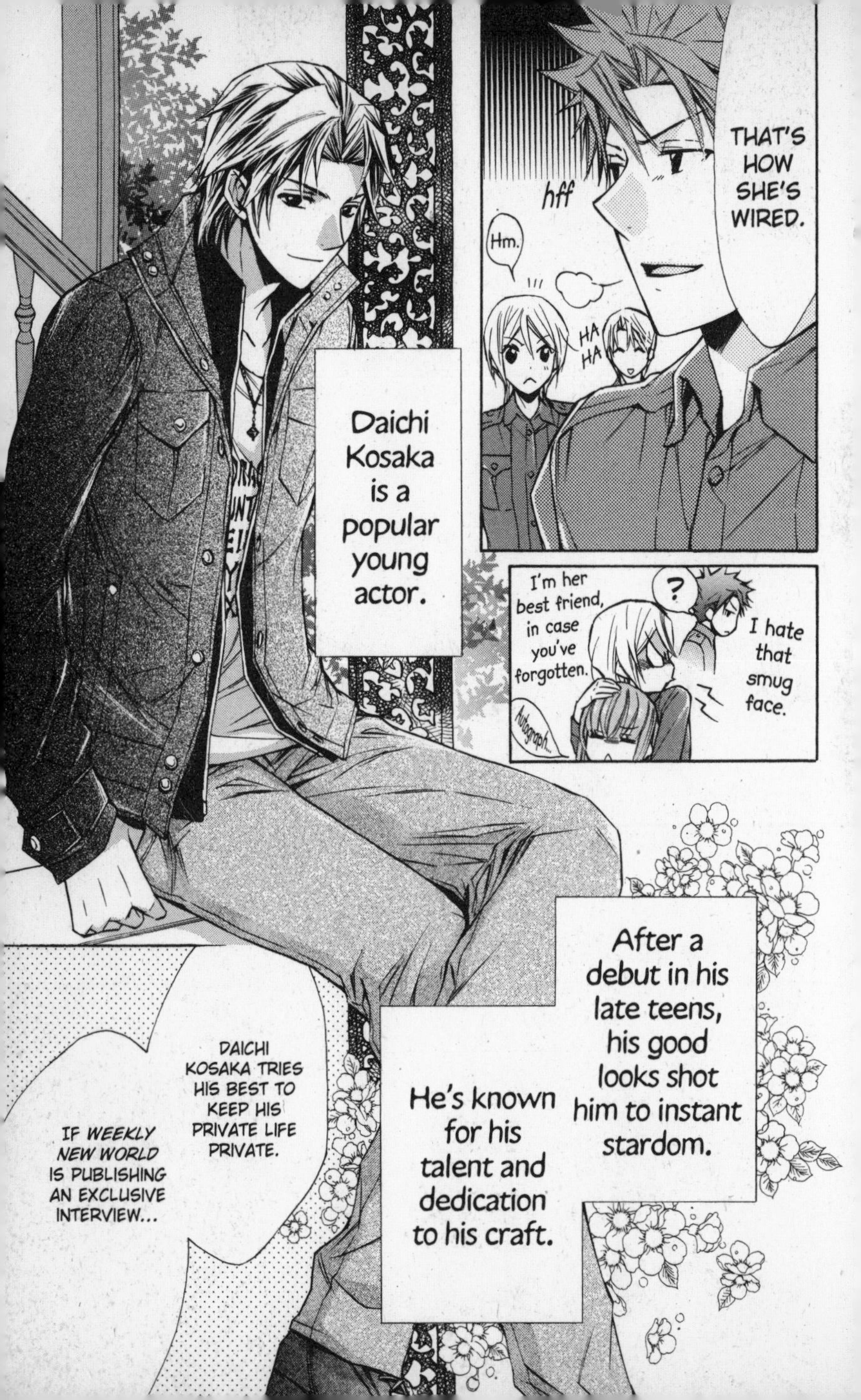
THAT'S HOW SHE'S WIRED.
hff
Hm.
HA HA
?
I hate that smug face.
I'm her best friend, in case you've forgotten.
Autograph...
Daichi Kosaka is a popular young actor.
After a debut in his late teens, his good looks shot him to instant stardom.
He's known for his talent and dedication to his craft.
DAICHI KOSAKA TRIES HIS BEST TO KEEP HIS PRIVATE LIFE PRIVATE.
IF *WEEKLY NEW WORLD* IS PUBLISHING AN EXCLUSIVE INTERVIEW...

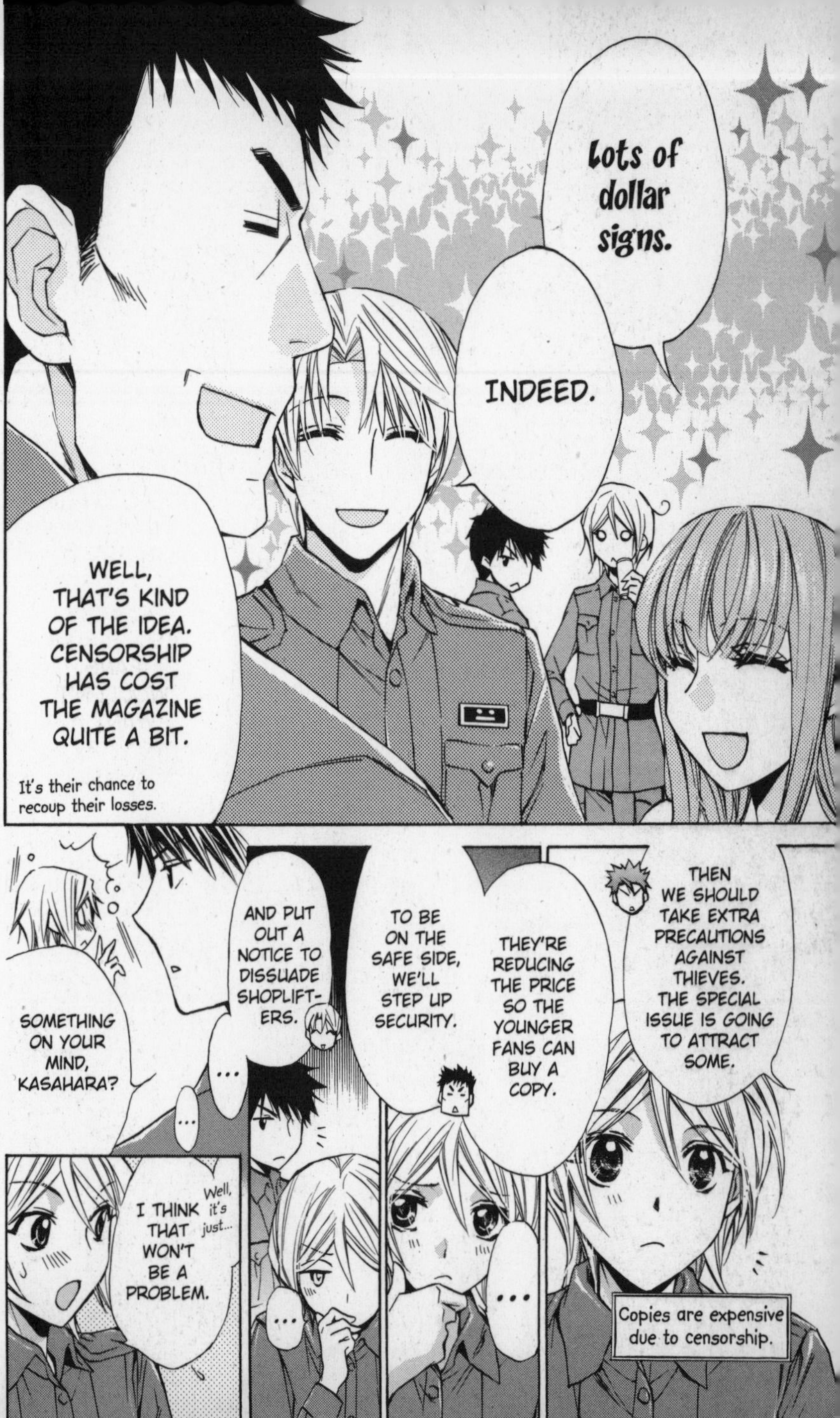
Lots of dollar signs.
INDEED.
WELL, THAT'S KIND OF THE IDEA. CENSORSHIP HAS COST THE MAGAZINE QUITE A BIT.
It's their chance to recoup their losses.
THEN WE SHOULD TAKE EXTRA PRECAUTIONS AGAINST THIEVES. THE SPECIAL ISSUE IS GOING TO ATTRACT SOME.
Copies are expensive due to censorship.
THEY'RE REDUCING THE PRICE SO THE YOUNGER FANS CAN BUY A COPY.
...
TO BE ON THE SAFE SIDE, WE'LL STEP UP SECURITY.
AND PUT OUT A NOTICE TO DISSUADE SHOPLIFTERS.
...
...
...
SOMETHING ON YOUR MIND, KASAHARA?
Well, it's just...
I THINK THAT WON'T BE A PROBLEM.

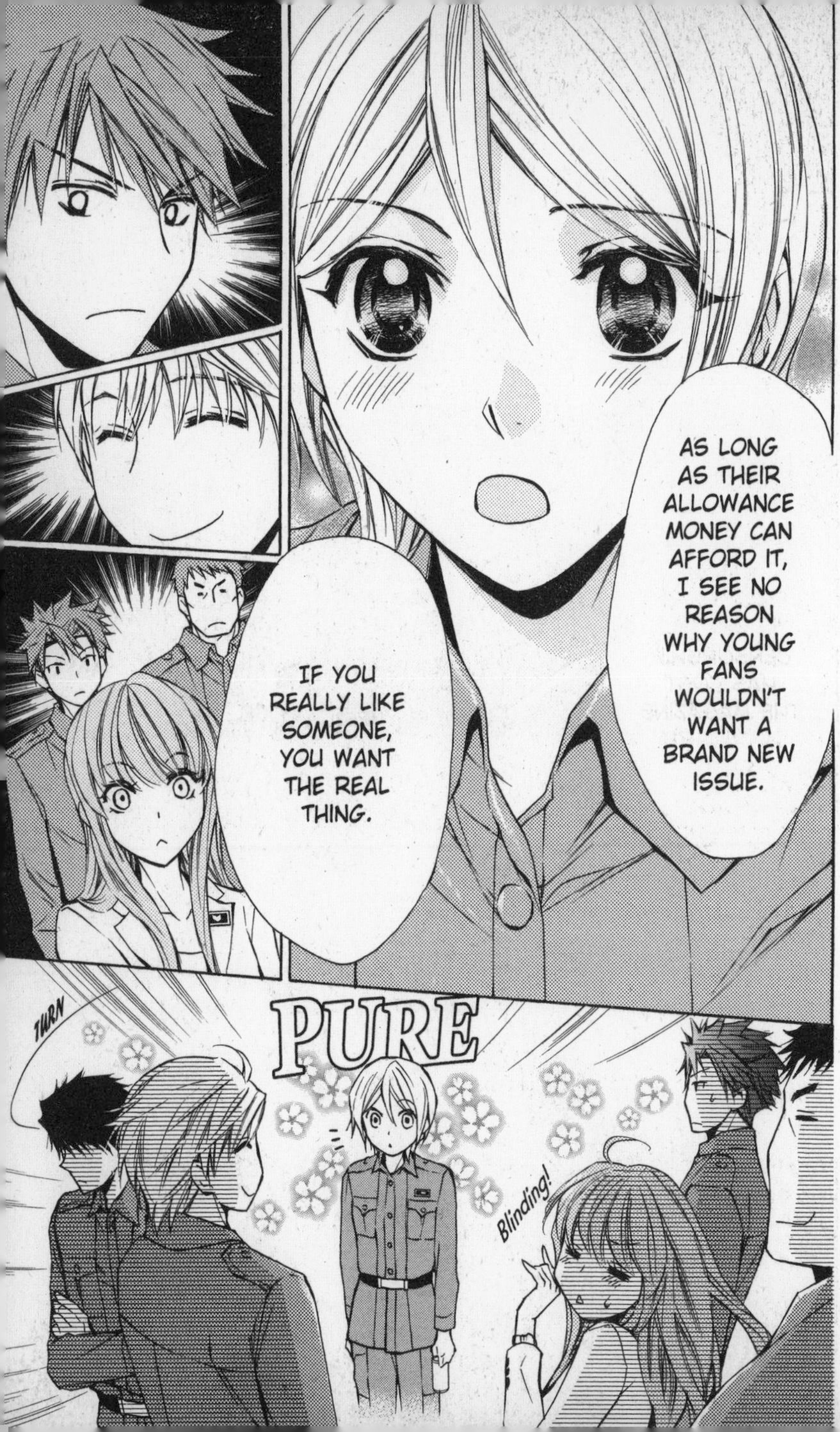
AS LONG AS THEIR ALLOWANCE MONEY CAN AFFORD IT, I SEE NO REASON WHY YOUNG FANS WOULDN'T WANT A BRAND NEW ISSUE.
IF YOU REALLY LIKE SOMEONE, YOU WANT THE REAL THING.
PURE
Blinding!
TURN

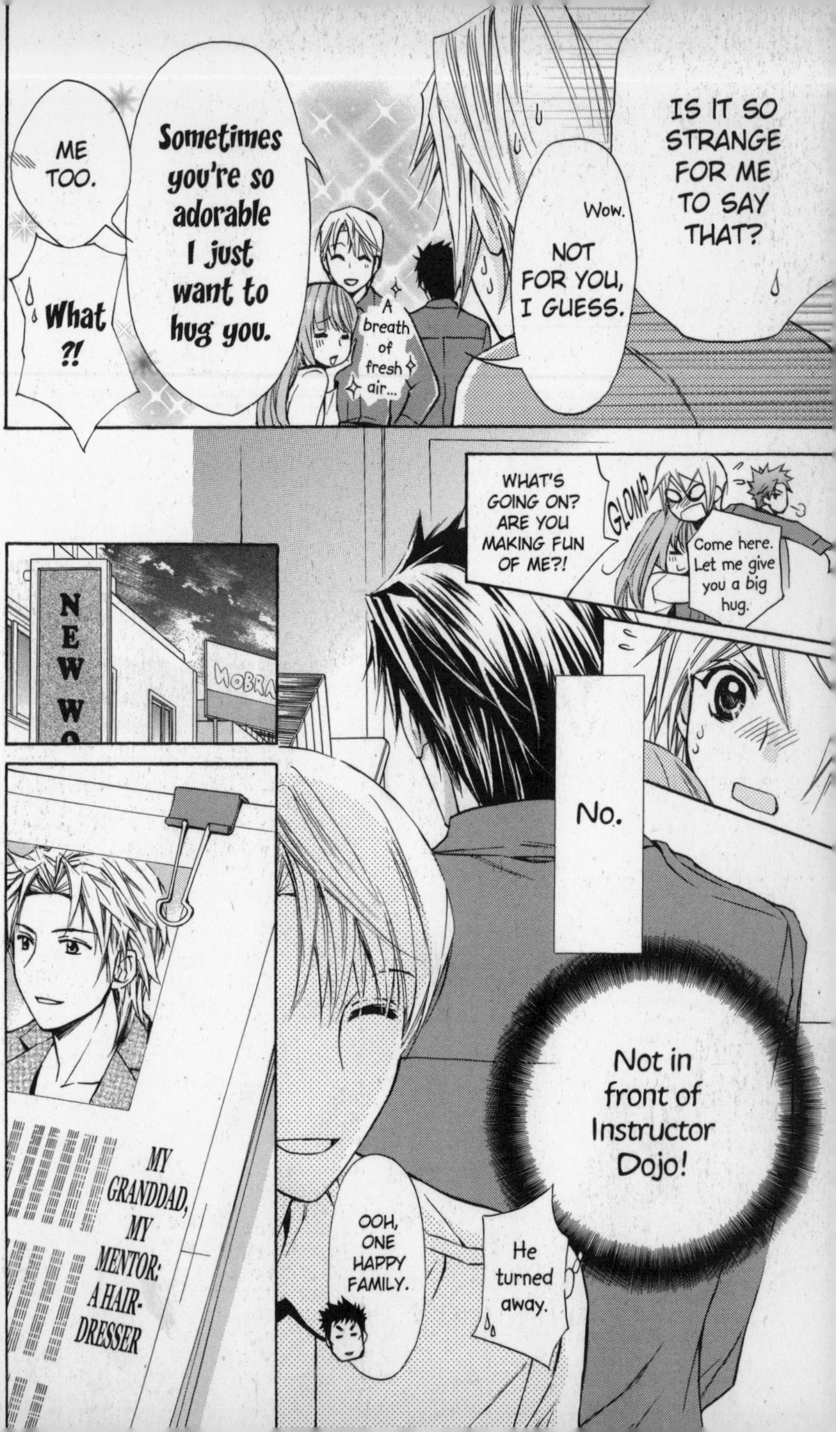
IS IT SO STRANGE FOR ME TO SAY THAT?
Wow.
NOT FOR YOU, I GUESS.
A breath of fresh air...
Sometimes you're so adorable I just want to hug you.
ME TOO.
What?!
Come here. Let me give you a big hug.
GLOMP
WHAT'S GOING ON? ARE YOU MAKING FUN OF ME?!
No.
Not in front of Instructor Dojo!
He turned away.
OOH, ONE HAPPY FAMILY.
NEW WO
MOBRA
MY GRANDDAD, MY MENTOR: A HAIR-DRESSER

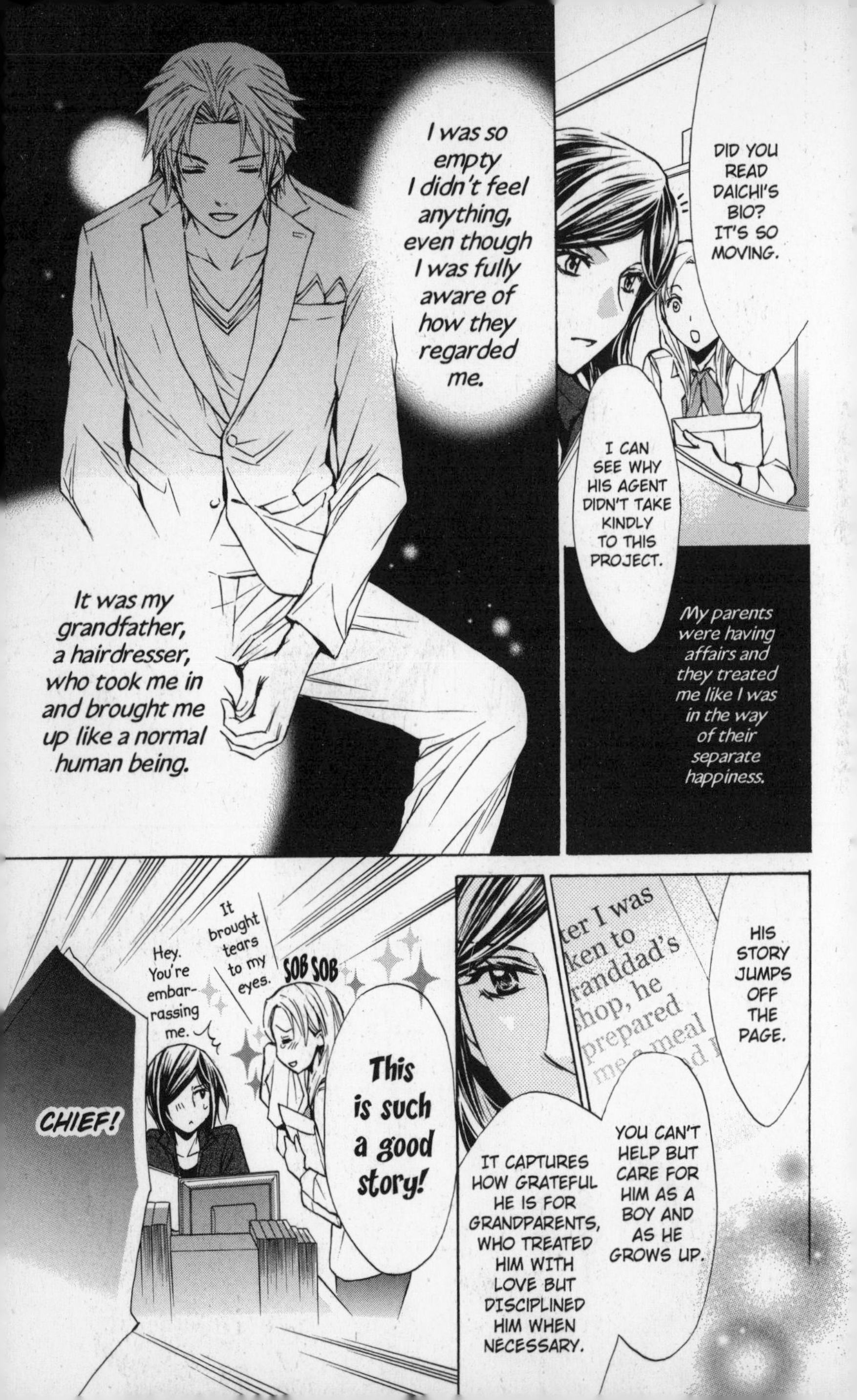

DID YOU READ DAICHI'S BIO? IT'S SO MOVING.
I CAN SEE WHY HIS AGENT DIDN'T TAKE KINDLY TO THIS PROJECT.
My parents were having affairs and they treated me like I was in the way of their separate happiness.
I was so empty I didn't feel anything, even though I was fully aware of how they regarded me.
It was my grandfather, a hairdresser, who took me in and brought me up like a normal human being.
ter I was
ken to
randdad's
shop, he
prepared
HIS STORY JUMPS OFF THE PAGE.
YOU CAN'T HELP BUT CARE FOR HIM AS A BOY AND AS HE GROWS UP.
IT CAPTURES HOW GRATEFUL HE IS FOR GRANDPARENTS, WHO TREATED HIM WITH LOVE BUT DISCIPLINED HIM WHEN NECESSARY.
This is such a good story!
SOB SOB
It brought tears to my eyes.
Hey. You're embar-rassing me.
CHIEF!

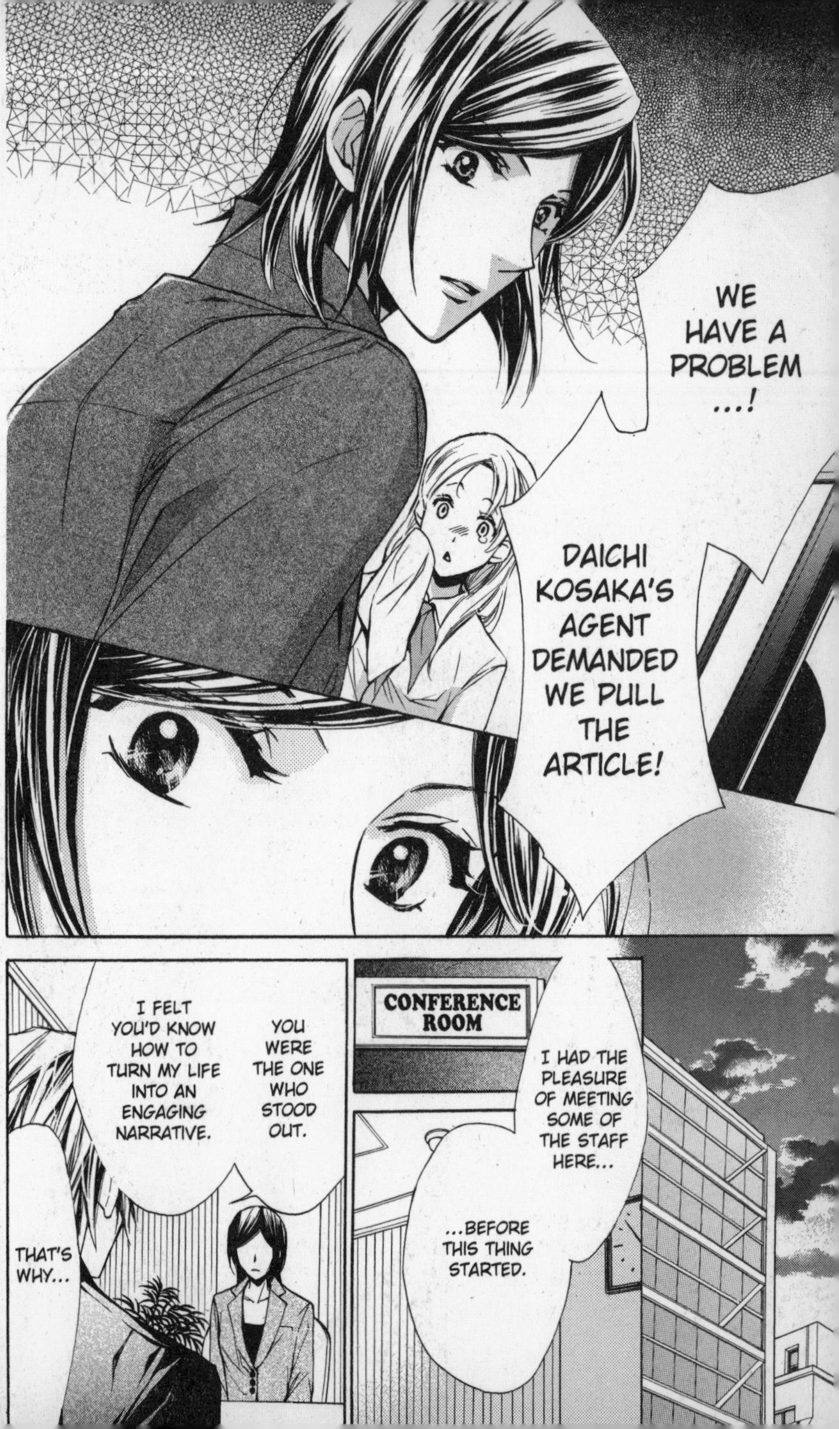
WE HAVE A PROBLEM ...!
DAICHI KOSAKA'S AGENT DEMANDED WE PULL THE ARTICLE!
CONFERENCE ROOM
I HAD THE PLEASURE OF MEETING SOME OF THE STAFF HERE...
...BEFORE THIS THING STARTED.
YOU WERE THE ONE WHO STOOD OUT.
I FELT YOU'D KNOW HOW TO TURN MY LIFE INTO AN ENGAGING NARRATIVE.
THAT'S WHY...

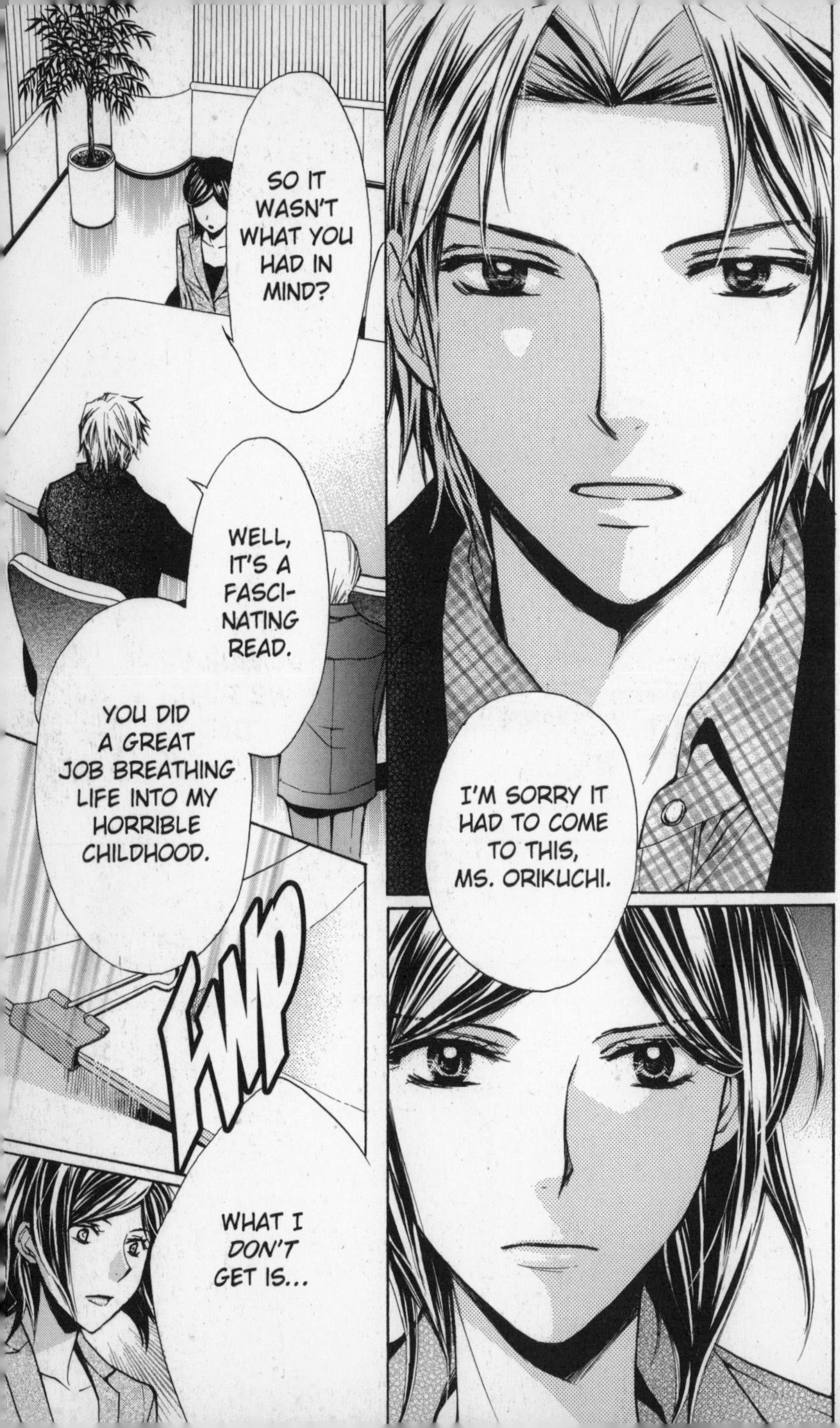

I'M SORRY IT HAD TO COME TO THIS, MS. ORIKUCHI.
SO IT WASN'T WHAT YOU HAD IN MIND?
WELL, IT'S A FASCINATING READ.
YOU DID A GREAT JOB BREATHING LIFE INTO MY HORRIBLE CHILDHOOD.
WHAT I DON'T GET IS...

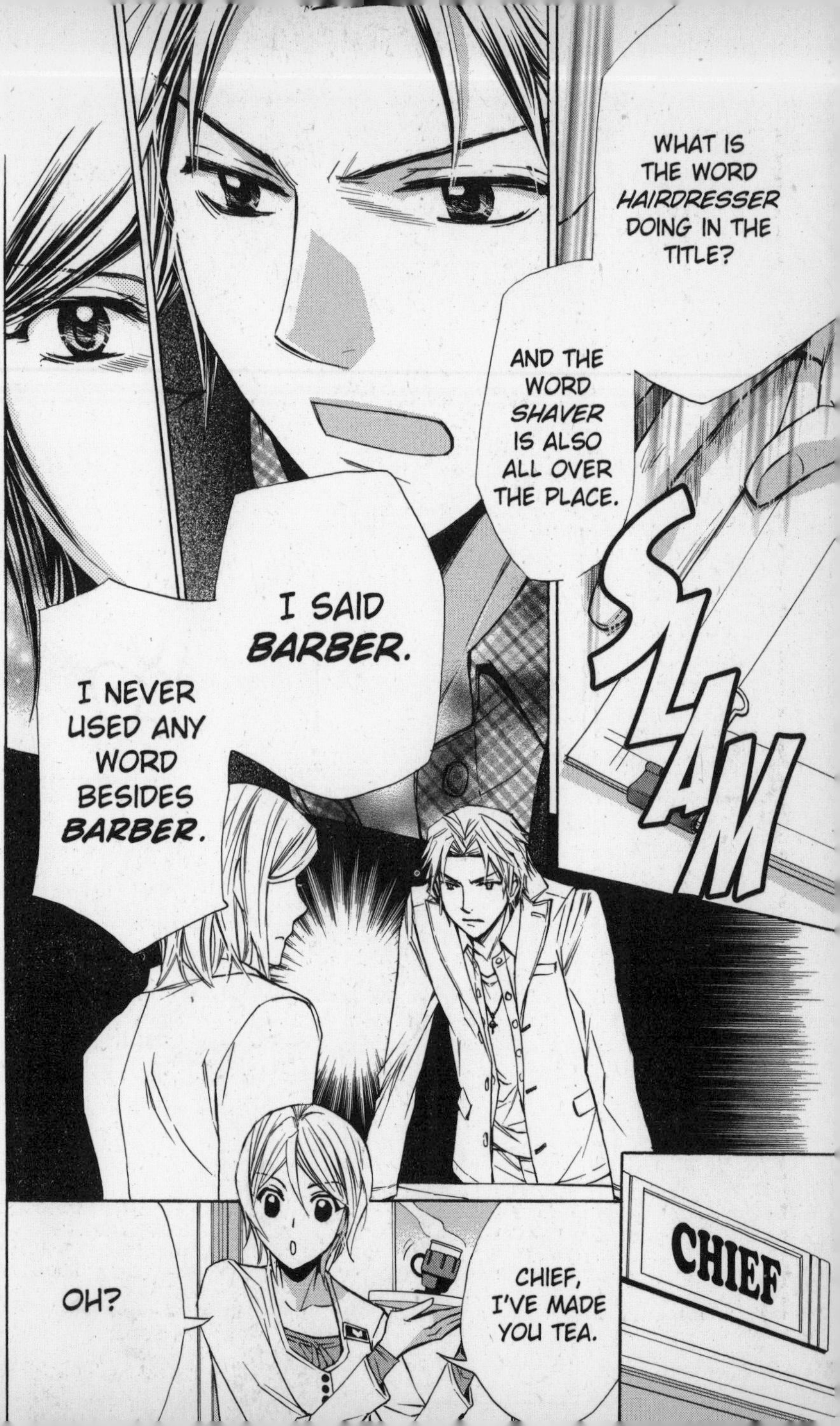
WHAT IS THE WORD HAIRDRESSER DOING IN THE TITLE?
AND THE WORD SHAVER IS ALSO ALL OVER THE PLACE.
SLAM
I SAID BARBER.
I NEVER USED ANY WORD BESIDES BARBER.
CHIEF
CHIEF, I'VE MADE YOU TEA.
OH?

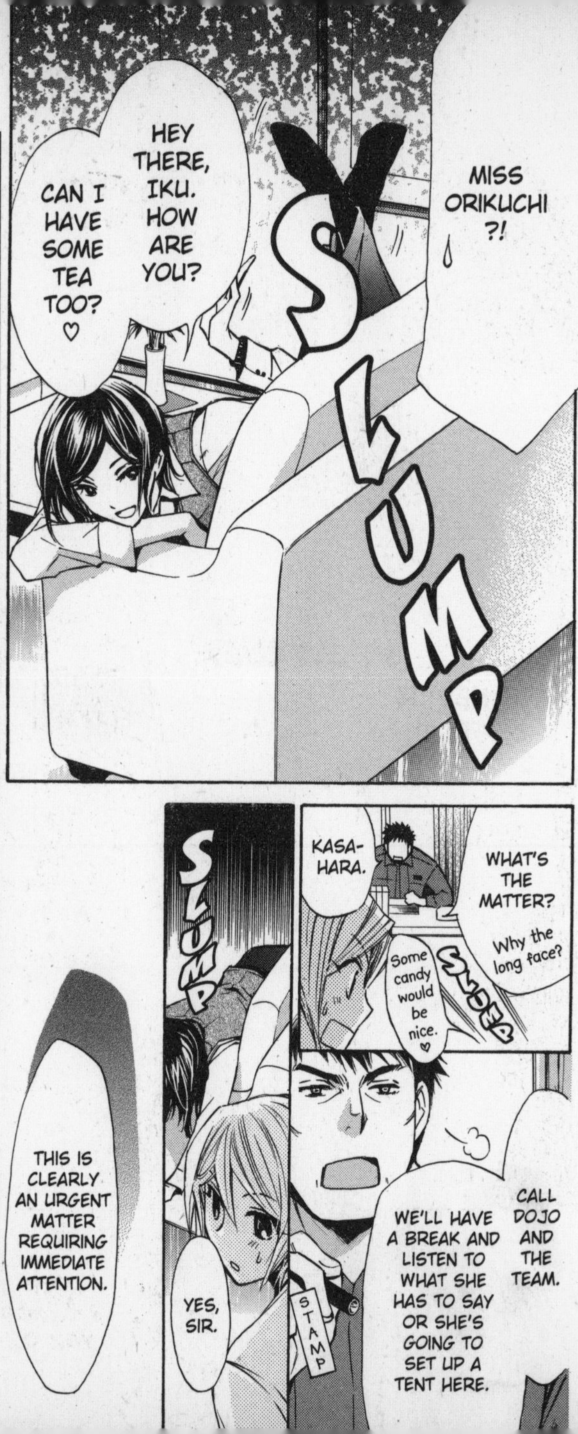
MISS ORIKUCHI ?!
HEY THERE, IKU. HOW ARE YOU?
CAN I HAVE SOME TEA TOO? ♡
SLUMP
WHAT'S THE MATTER?
Why the long face?
KASA-HARA.
SLUMP
Some candy would be nice. ♡
SLUMP
CALL DOJO AND THE TEAM.
WE'LL HAVE A BREAK AND LISTEN TO WHAT SHE HAS TO SAY OR SHE'S GOING TO SET UP A TENT HERE.
STAMP
YES, SIR.
THIS IS CLEARLY AN URGENT MATTER REQUIRING IMMEDIATE ATTENTION.

5

*

This is the final sidebar for this volume. Thank you so much for reading this far! Whenever I'm clutching a pen, scribbling, I feel like the luckiest person in the world.

Hope I can keep entertaining you.

See you soon.

Special thanks are at the end of the book.

Kiiro Yumi
弓きいろ

*

*

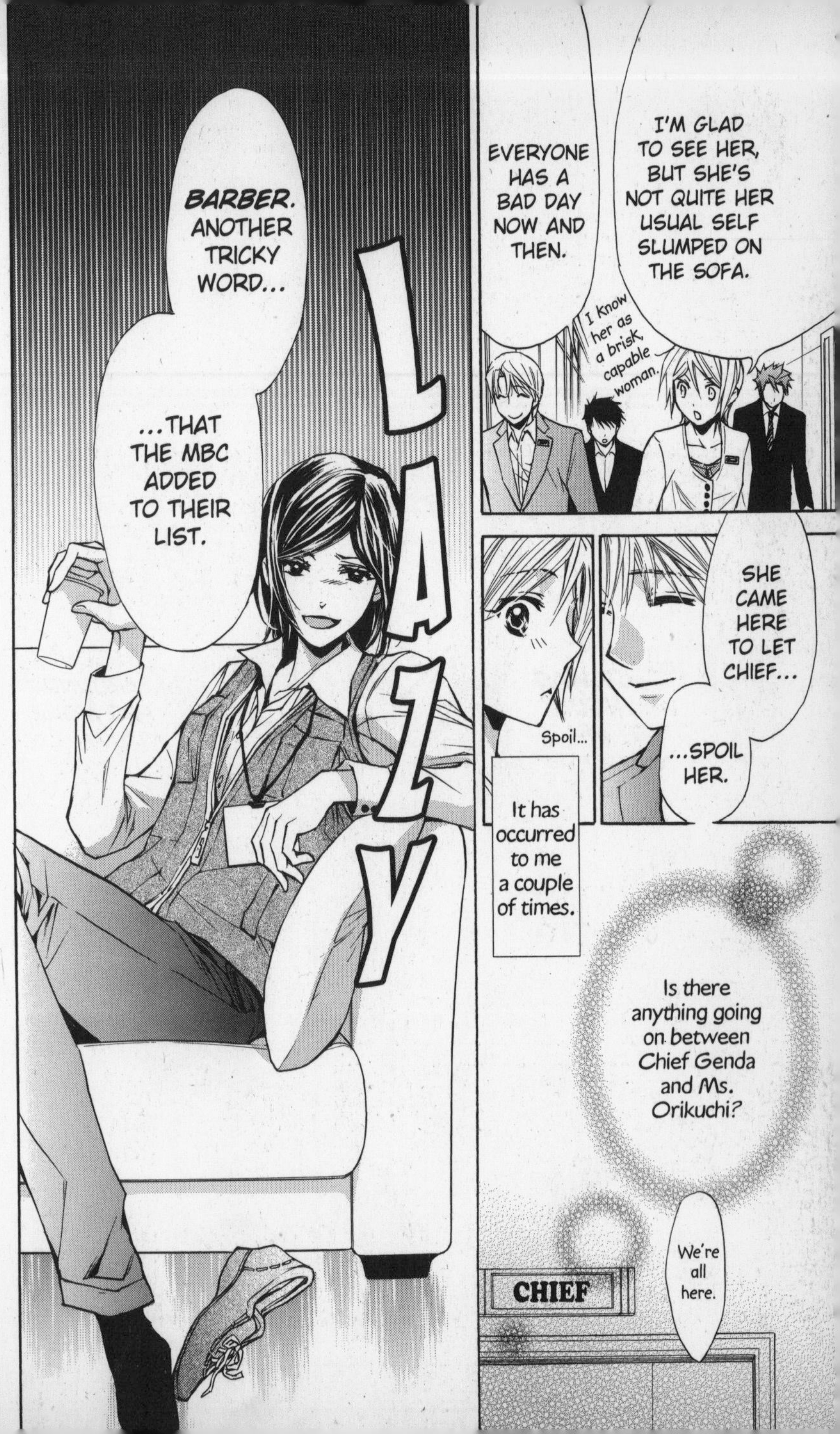
I'M GLAD TO SEE HER, BUT SHE'S NOT QUITE HER USUAL SELF SLUMPED ON THE SOFA.
EVERYONE HAS A BAD DAY NOW AND THEN.
I know her as a brisk, capable woman.
SHE CAME HERE TO LET CHIEF...
...SPOIL HER.
Spoil...
It has occurred to me a couple of times.
Is there anything going on between Chief Genda and Ms. Orikuchi?
We're all here.
CHIEF
BARBER. ANOTHER TRICKY WORD...
...THAT THE MBC ADDED TO THEIR LIST.
LAZY

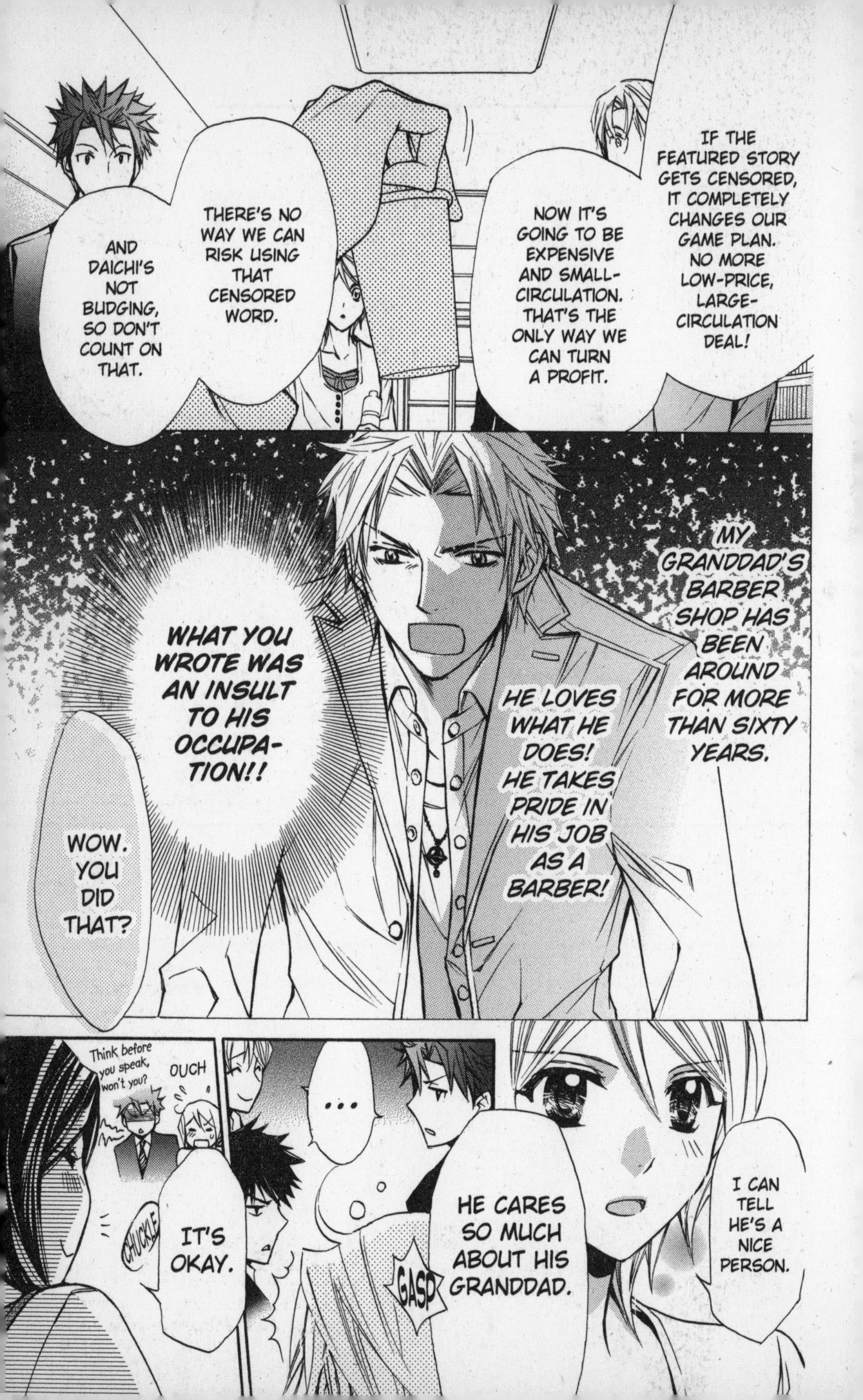
IF THE FEATURED STORY GETS CENSORED, IT COMPLETELY CHANGES OUR GAME PLAN. NO MORE LOW-PRICE, LARGE-CIRCULATION DEAL!
NOW IT'S GOING TO BE EXPENSIVE AND SMALL-CIRCULATION. THAT'S THE ONLY WAY WE CAN TURN A PROFIT.
THERE'S NO WAY WE CAN RISK USING THAT CENSORED WORD.
AND DAICHI'S NOT BUDGING, SO DON'T COUNT ON THAT.
MY GRANDDAD'S BARBER SHOP HAS BEEN AROUND FOR MORE THAN SIXTY YEARS.
HE LOVES WHAT HE DOES! HE TAKES PRIDE IN HIS JOB AS A BARBER!
WHAT YOU WROTE WAS AN INSULT TO HIS OCCUPATION!!
WOW. YOU DID THAT?
I CAN TELL HE'S A NICE PERSON.
HE CARES SO MUCH ABOUT HIS GRANDDAD.
GASP
...
IT'S OKAY.
CHUCKLE
Think before you speak, won't you?
OUCH

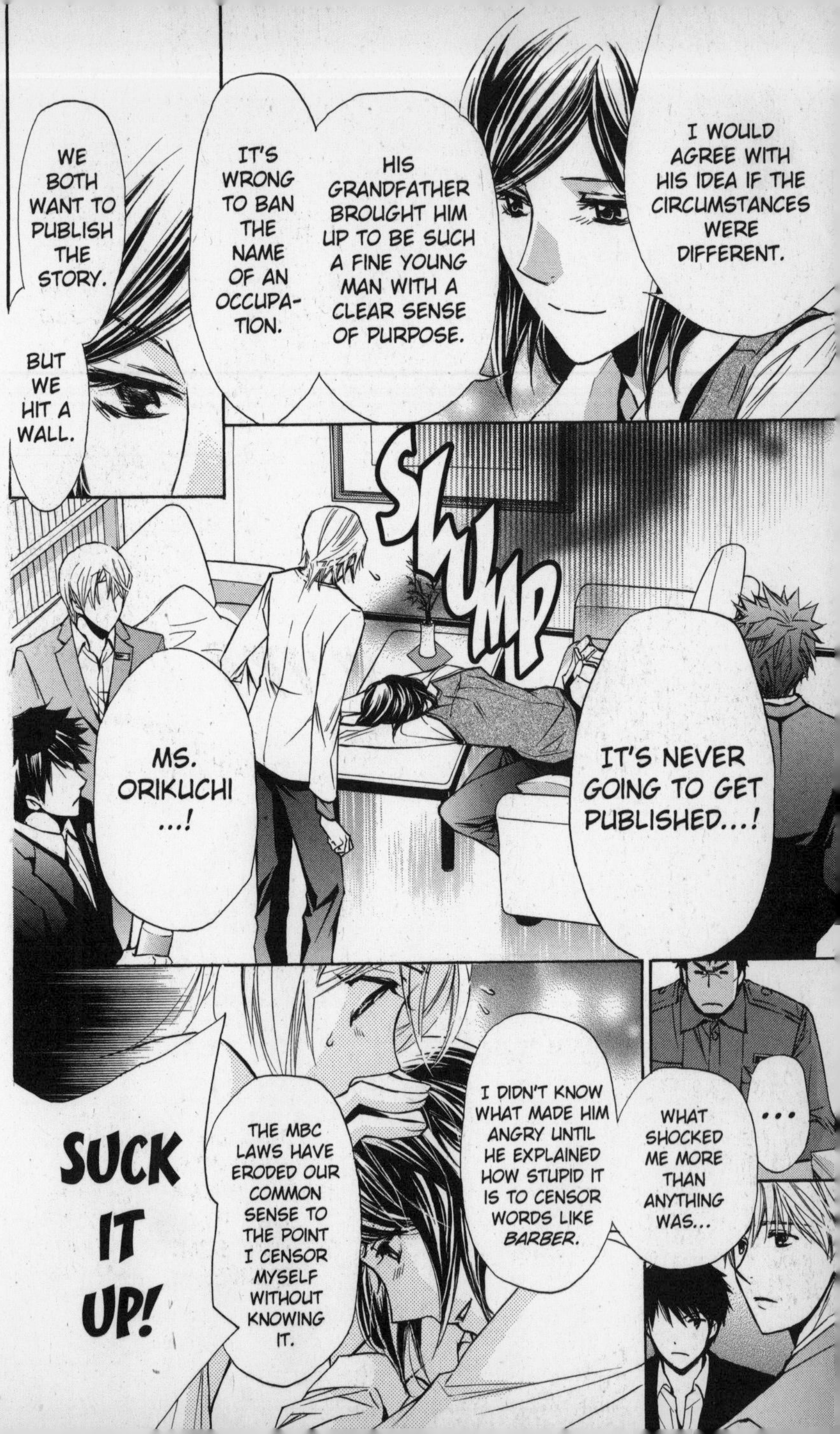
I WOULD AGREE WITH HIS IDEA IF THE CIRCUMSTANCES WERE DIFFERENT.
HIS GRANDFATHER BROUGHT HIM UP TO BE SUCH A FINE YOUNG MAN WITH A CLEAR SENSE OF PURPOSE.
IT'S WRONG TO BAN THE NAME OF AN OCCUPATION.
WE BOTH WANT TO PUBLISH THE STORY.
BUT WE HIT A WALL.
SLUMP
IT'S NEVER GOING TO GET PUBLISHED...!
MS. ORIKUCHI...!
...
WHAT SHOCKED ME MORE THAN ANYTHING WAS...
I DIDN'T KNOW WHAT MADE HIM ANGRY UNTIL HE EXPLAINED HOW STUPID IT IS TO CENSOR WORDS LIKE *BARBER*.
THE MBC LAWS HAVE ERODED OUR COMMON SENSE TO THE POINT I CENSOR MYSELF WITHOUT KNOWING IT.
SUCK IT UP!

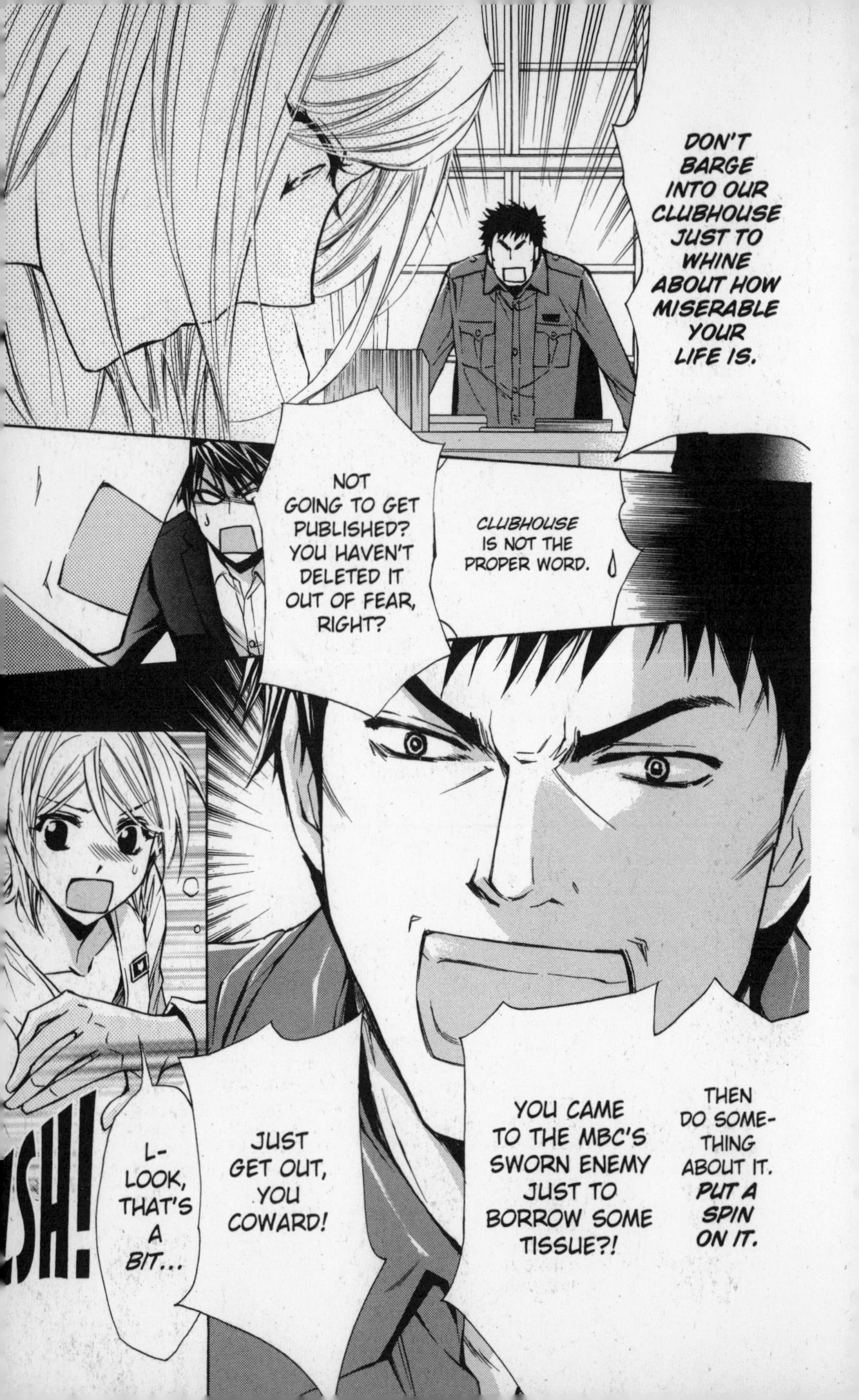

DON'T BARGE INTO OUR CLUBHOUSE JUST TO WHINE ABOUT HOW MISERABLE YOUR LIFE IS.
CLUBHOUSE IS NOT THE PROPER WORD.
NOT GOING TO GET PUBLISHED? YOU HAVEN'T DELETED IT OUT OF FEAR, RIGHT?
THEN DO SOME-THING ABOUT IT. PUT A SPIN ON IT.
YOU CAME TO THE MBC'S SWORN ENEMY JUST TO BORROW SOME TISSUE?!
JUST GET OUT, YOU COWARD!
L-LOOK, THAT'S A BIT...
SH!

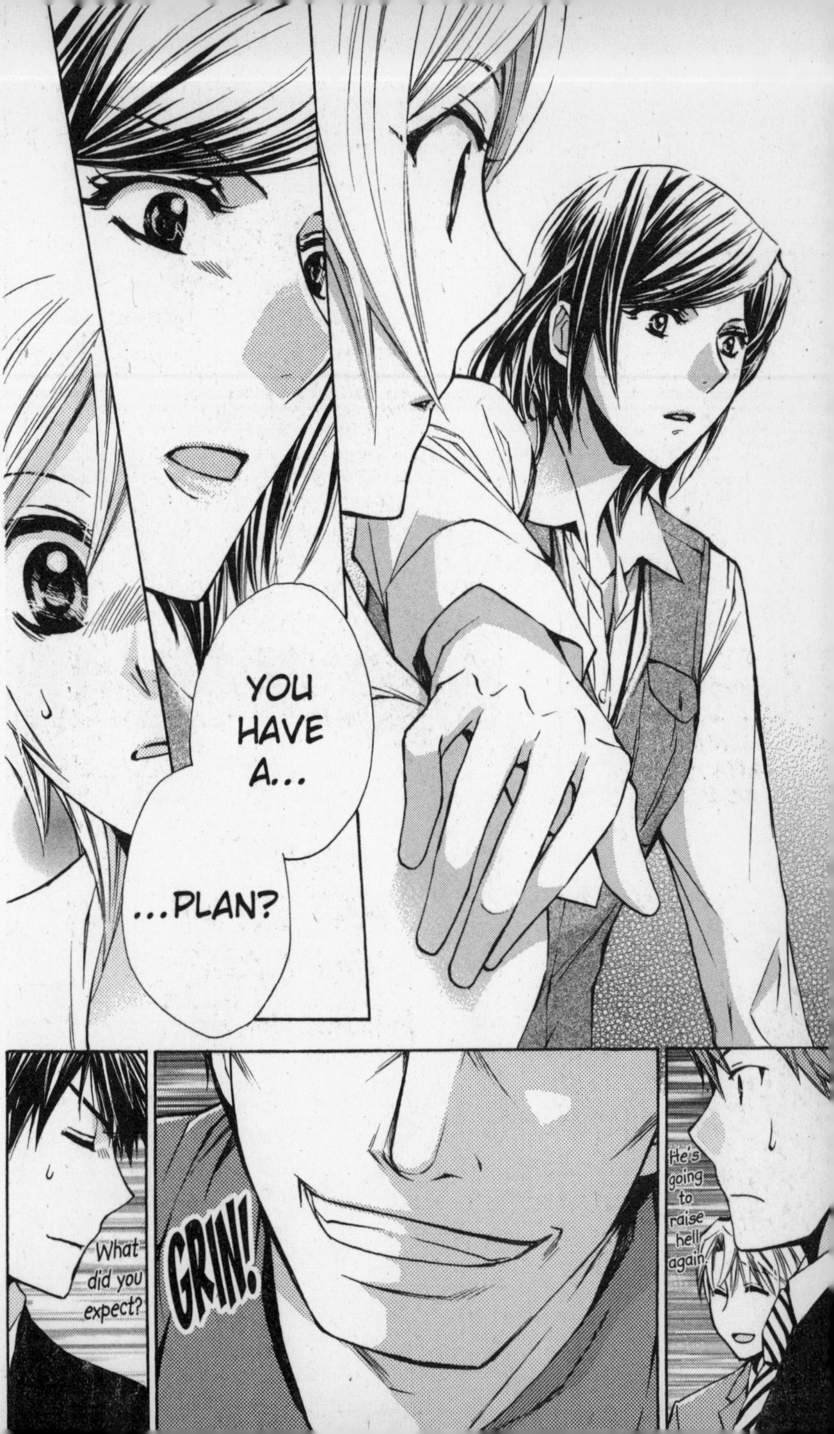
YOU HAVE A...
...PLAN?
He's going to raise hell again.
GRIN!
What did you expect?

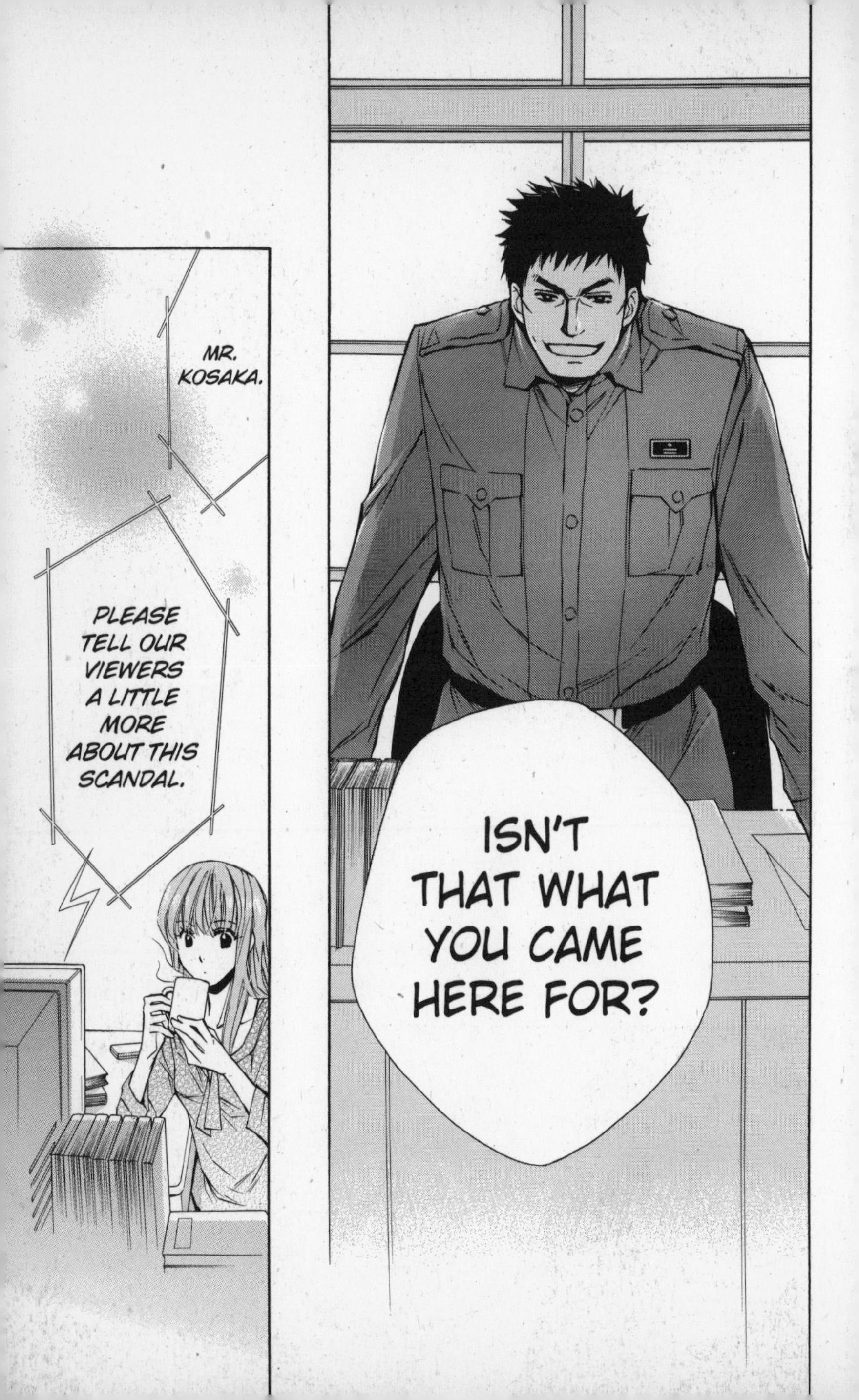
ISN'T THAT WHAT YOU CAME HERE FOR?
MR. KOSAKA.
PLEASE TELL OUR VIEWERS A LITTLE MORE ABOUT THIS SCANDAL.

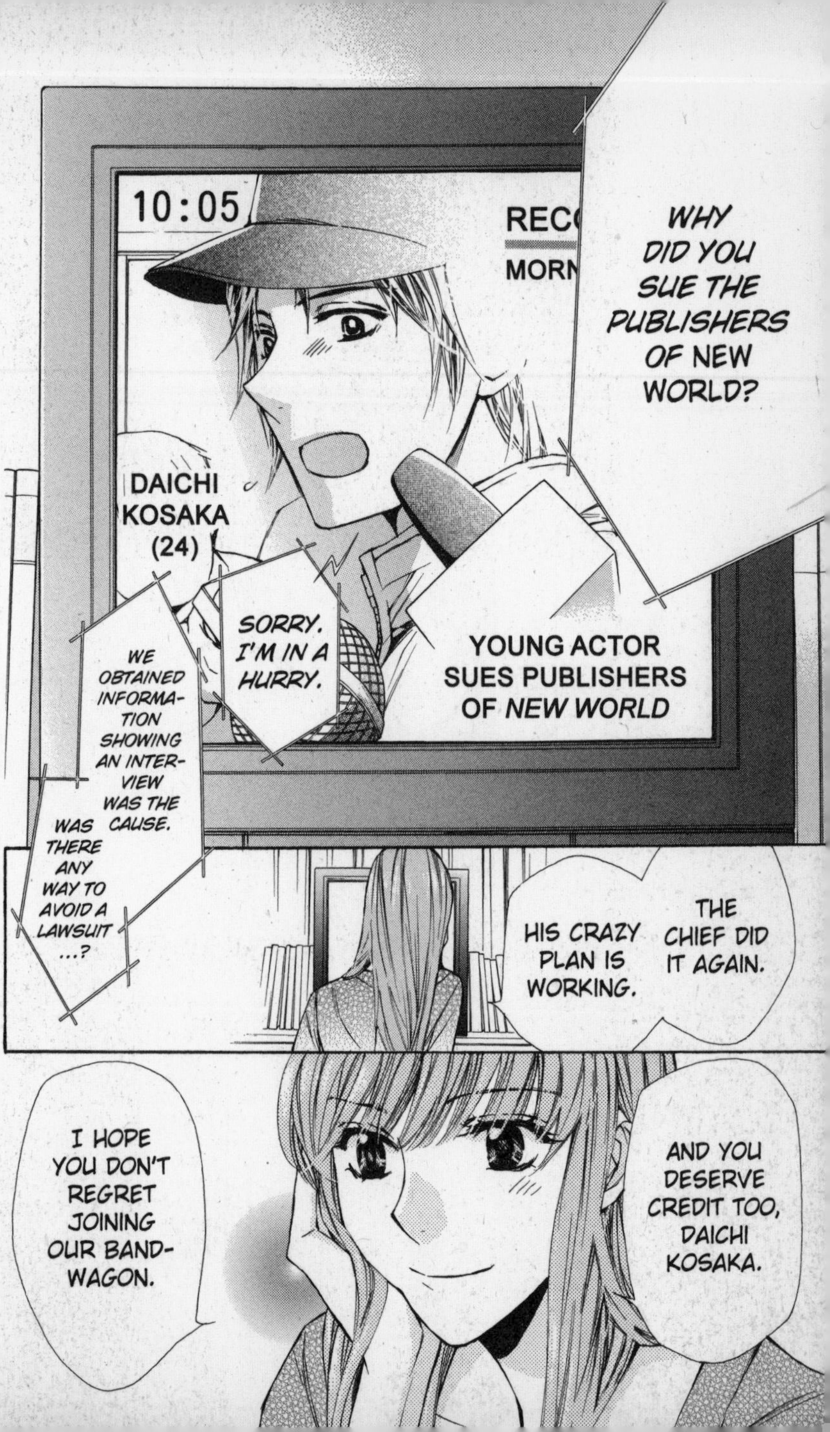
WHY DID YOU SUE THE PUBLISHERS OF NEW WORLD?
10:05
RECO
MORN
YOUNG ACTOR SUES PUBLISHERS OF *NEW WORLD*
DAICHI KOSAKA (24)
SORRY. I'M IN A HURRY.
WE OBTAINED INFORMATION SHOWING AN INTERVIEW WAS THE CAUSE.
WAS THERE ANY WAY TO AVOID A LAWSUIT...?
THE CHIEF DID IT AGAIN.
HIS CRAZY PLAN IS WORKING.
AND YOU DESERVE CREDIT TOO, DAICHI KOSAKA.
I HOPE YOU DON'T REGRET JOINING OUR BANDWAGON.

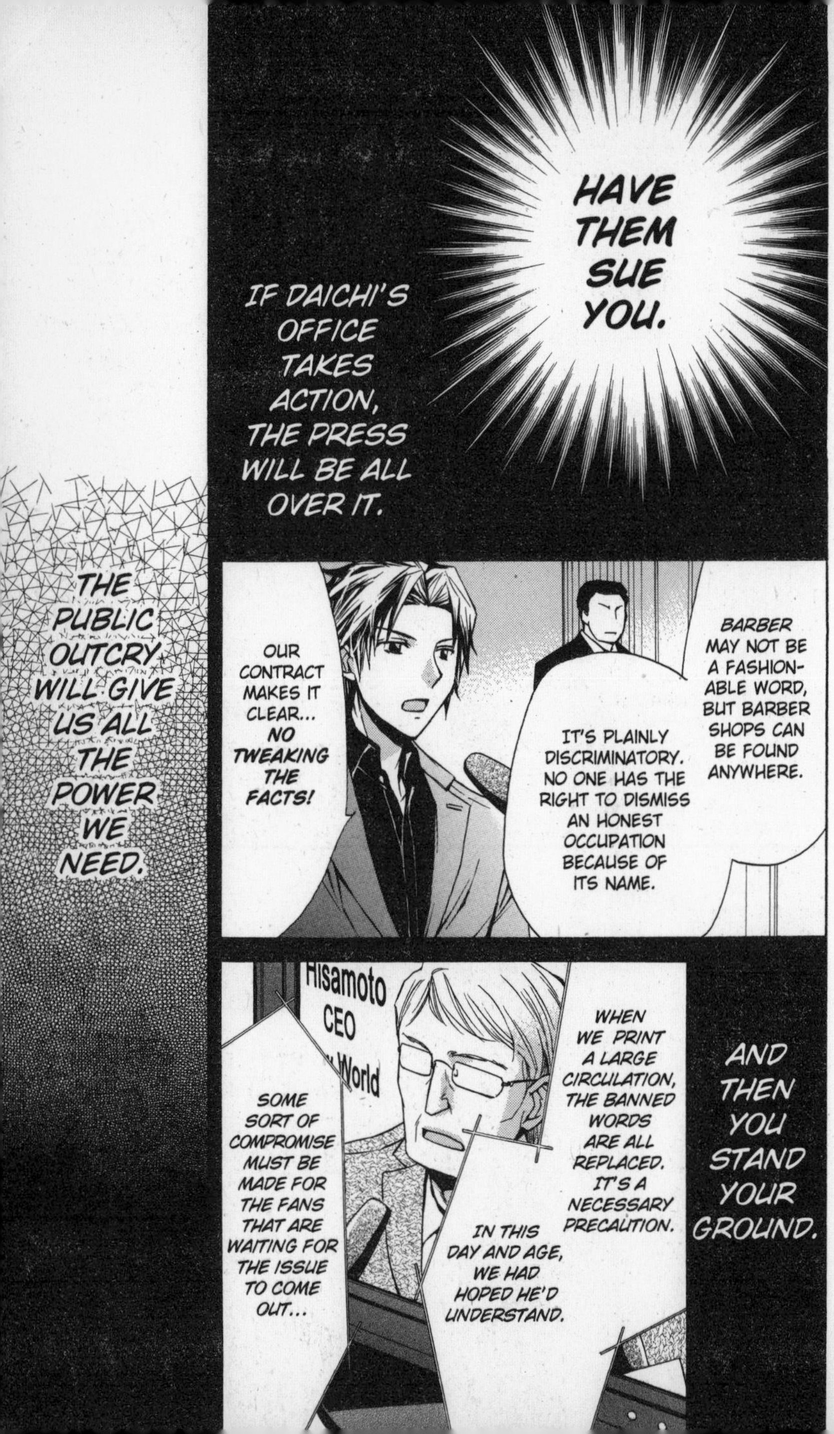
HAVE THEM SUE YOU.
IF DAICHI'S OFFICE TAKES ACTION, THE PRESS WILL BE ALL OVER IT.
THE PUBLIC OUTCRY WILL GIVE US ALL THE POWER WE NEED.
BARBER MAY NOT BE A FASHION-ABLE WORD, BUT BARBER SHOPS CAN BE FOUND ANYWHERE.
IT'S PLAINLY DISCRIMINATORY. NO ONE HAS THE RIGHT TO DISMISS AN HONEST OCCUPATION BECAUSE OF ITS NAME.
OUR CONTRACT MAKES IT CLEAR... NO TWEAKING THE FACTS!
AND THEN YOU STAND YOUR GROUND.
WHEN WE PRINT A LARGE CIRCULATION, THE BANNED WORDS ARE ALL REPLACED. IT'S A NECESSARY PRECAUTION.
IN THIS DAY AND AGE, WE HAD HOPED HE'D UNDERSTAND.
SOME SORT OF COMPROMISE MUST BE MADE FOR THE FANS THAT ARE WAITING FOR THE ISSUE TO COME OUT...
Hisamoto CEO
World

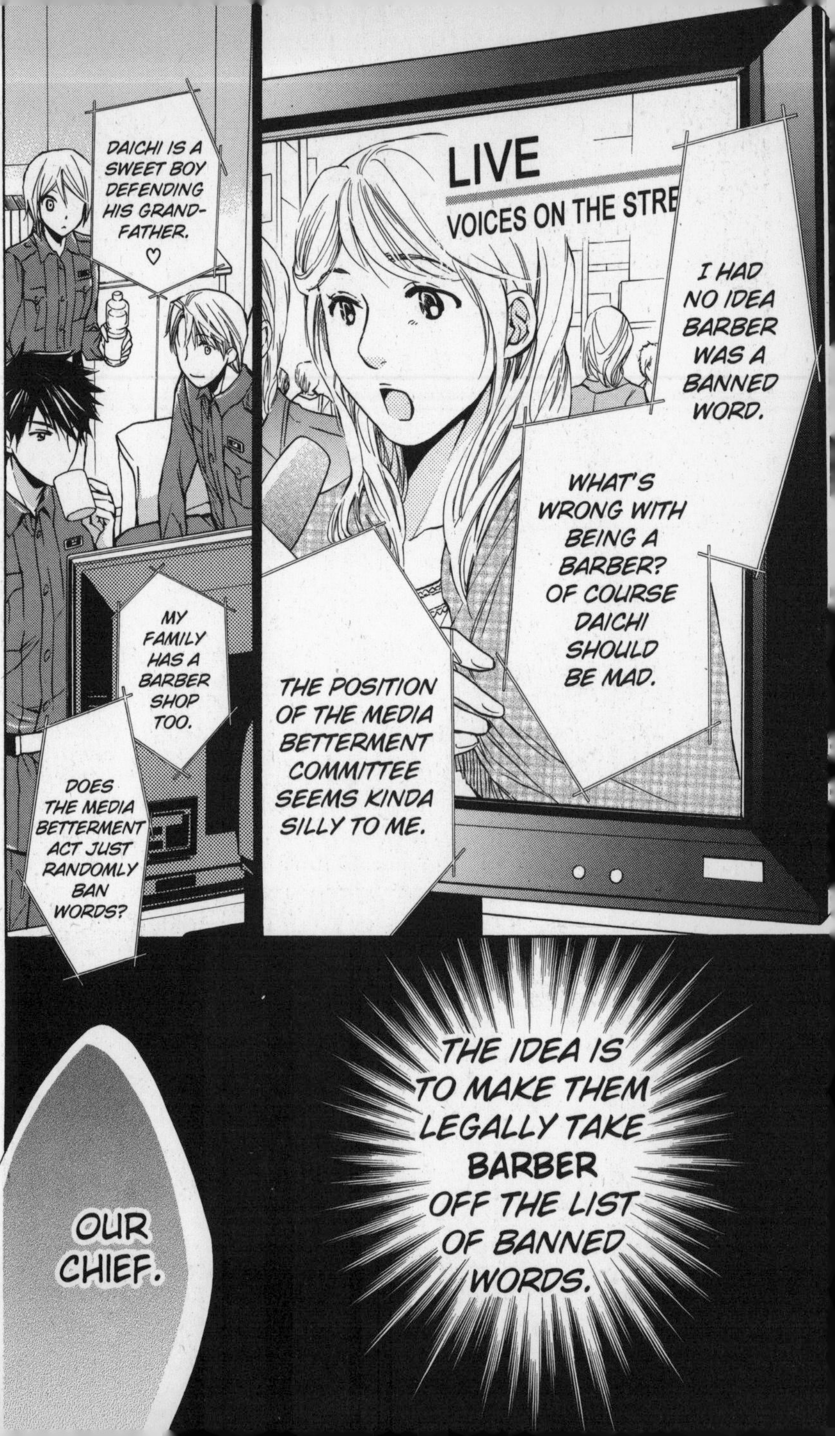
LIVE
VOICES ON THE STRE
I HAD NO IDEA BARBER WAS A BANNED WORD.
WHAT'S WRONG WITH BEING A BARBER? OF COURSE DAICHI SHOULD BE MAD.
THE POSITION OF THE MEDIA BETTERMENT COMMITTEE SEEMS KINDA SILLY TO ME.
DAICHI IS A SWEET BOY DEFENDING HIS GRAND-FATHER. ♡
MY FAMILY HAS A BARBER SHOP TOO.
DOES THE MEDIA BETTERMENT ACT JUST RANDOMLY BAN WORDS?
THE IDEA IS TO MAKE THEM LEGALLY TAKE BARBER OFF THE LIST OF BANNED WORDS.
OUR CHIEF.

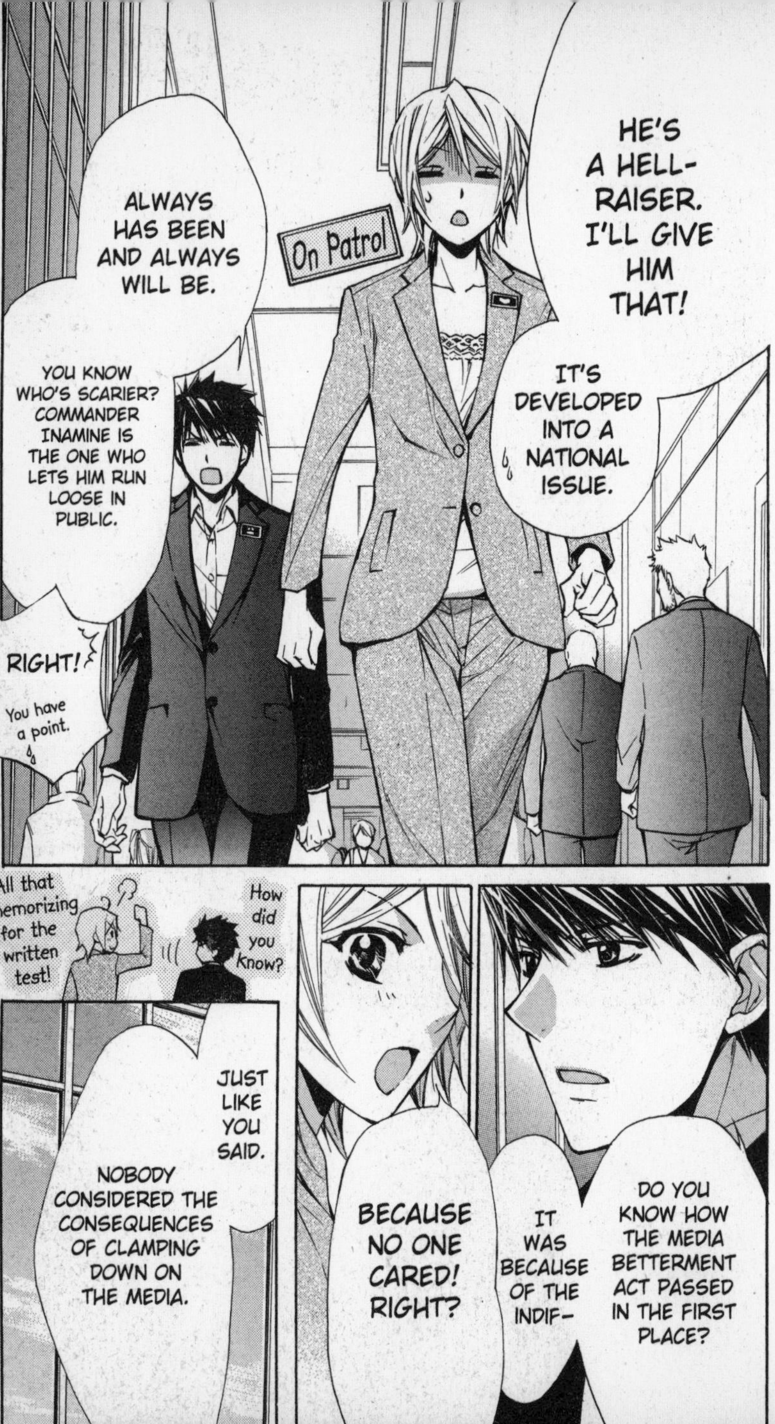
HE'S A HELL-RAISER. I'LL GIVE HIM THAT!
ALWAYS HAS BEEN AND ALWAYS WILL BE.
On Patrol
IT'S DEVELOPED INTO A NATIONAL ISSUE.
YOU KNOW WHO'S SCARIER? COMMANDER INAMINE IS THE ONE WHO LETS HIM RUN LOOSE IN PUBLIC.
RIGHT!
You have a point.
DO YOU KNOW HOW THE MEDIA BETTERMENT ACT PASSED IN THE FIRST PLACE?
IT WAS BECAUSE OF THE INDIF-
BECAUSE NO ONE CARED! RIGHT?
How did you know?
All that memorizing for the written test!
JUST LIKE YOU SAID.
NOBODY CONSIDERED THE CONSEQUENCES OF CLAMPING DOWN ON THE MEDIA.

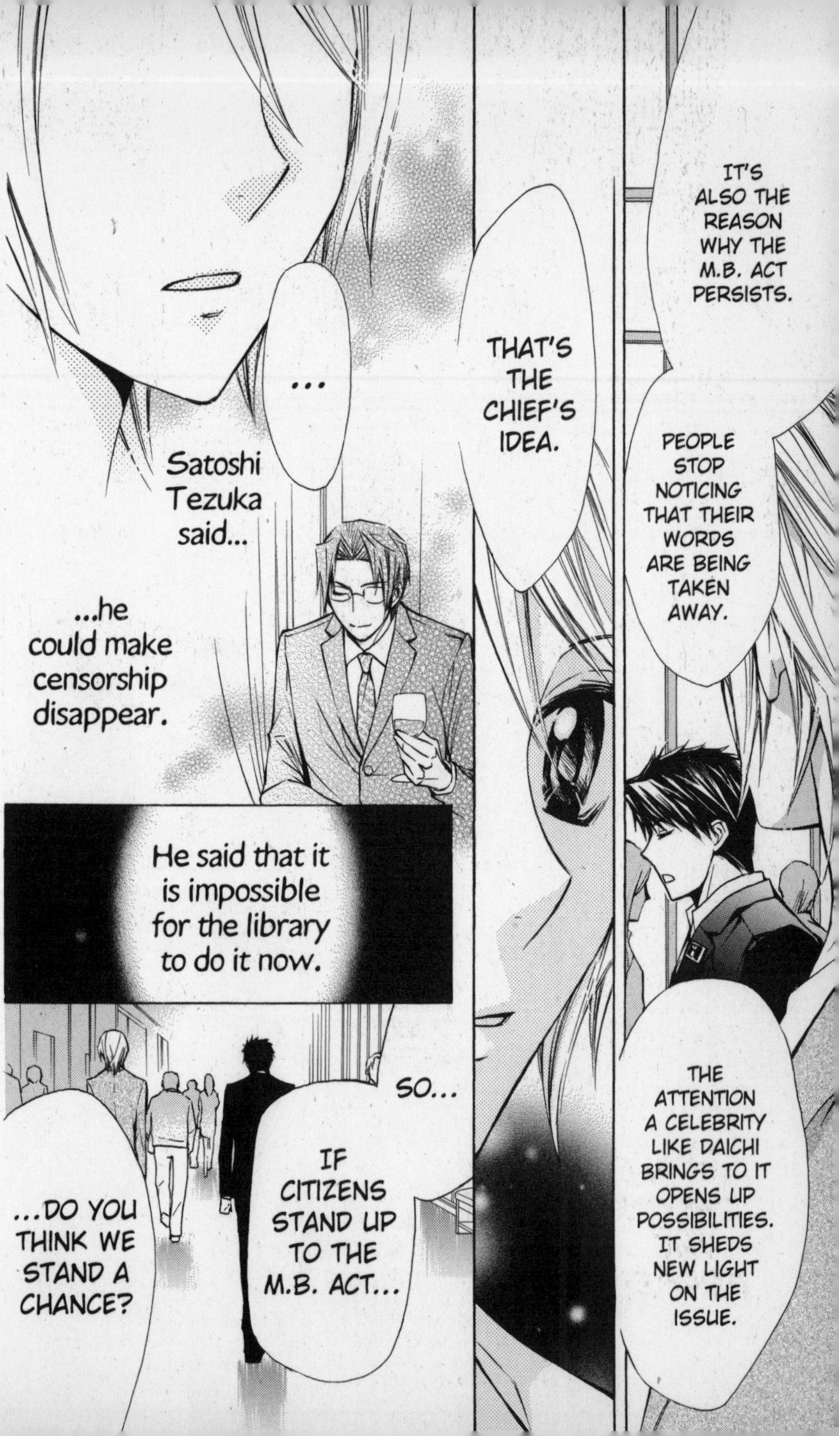
IT'S ALSO THE REASON WHY THE M.B. ACT PERSISTS.
PEOPLE STOP NOTICING THAT THEIR WORDS ARE BEING TAKEN AWAY.
THE ATTENTION A CELEBRITY LIKE DAICHI BRINGS TO IT OPENS UP POSSIBILITIES. IT SHEDS NEW LIGHT ON THE ISSUE.
THAT'S THE CHIEF'S IDEA.
...
Satoshi Tezuka said...
...he could make censorship disappear.
He said that it is impossible for the library to do it now.
SO...
IF CITIZENS STAND UP TO THE M.B. ACT...
...DO YOU THINK WE STAND A CHANCE?

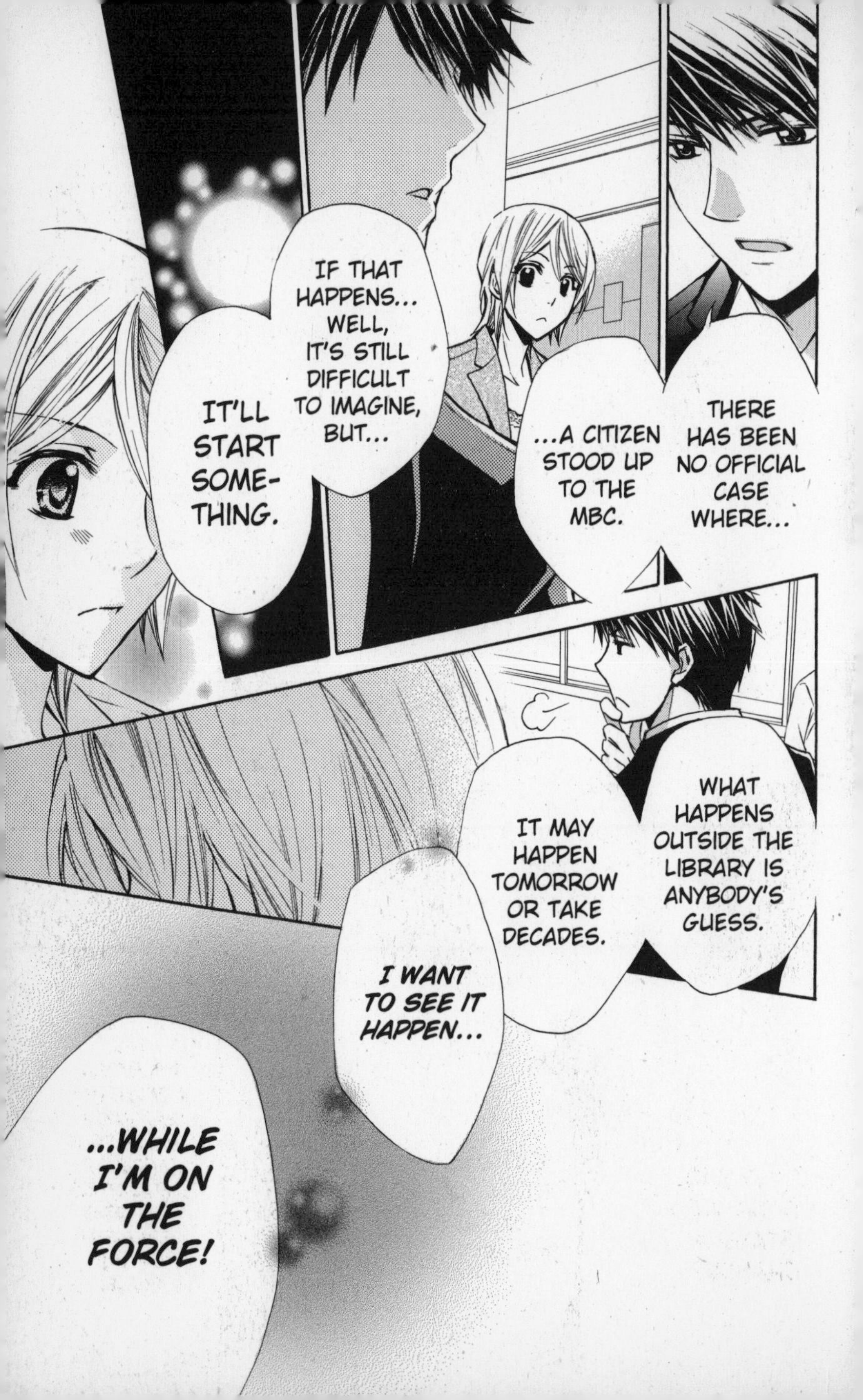
THERE HAS BEEN NO OFFICIAL CASE WHERE...
...A CITIZEN STOOD UP TO THE MBC.
IF THAT HAPPENS... WELL, IT'S STILL DIFFICULT TO IMAGINE, BUT...
IT'LL START SOME-THING.
WHAT HAPPENS OUTSIDE THE LIBRARY IS ANYBODY'S GUESS.
IT MAY HAPPEN TOMORROW OR TAKE DECADES.
I WANT TO SEE IT HAPPEN...
...WHILE I'M ON THE FORCE!

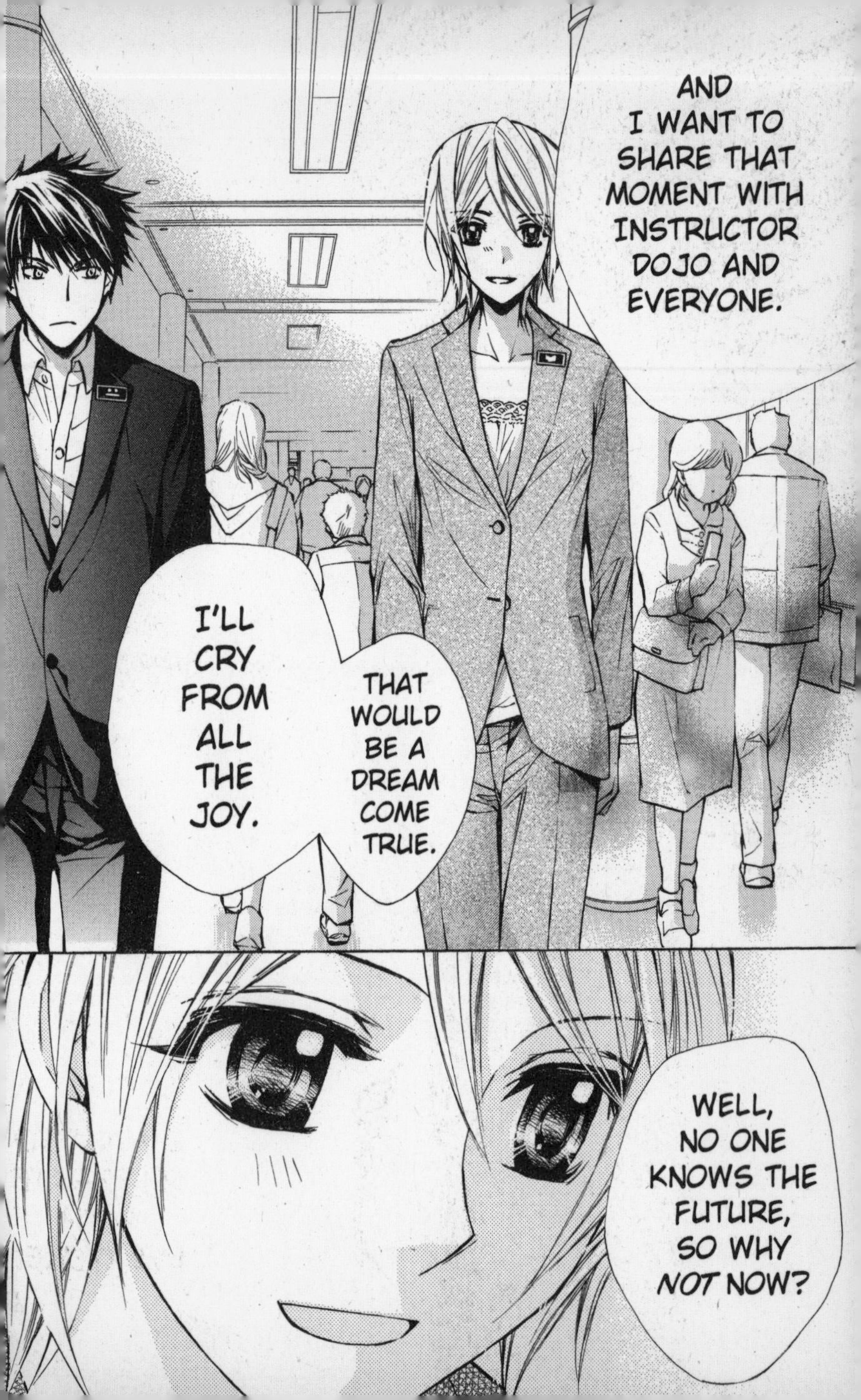
AND I WANT TO SHARE THAT MOMENT WITH INSTRUCTOR DOJO AND EVERYONE.
THAT WOULD BE A DREAM COME TRUE.
I'LL CRY FROM ALL THE JOY.
WELL, NO ONE KNOWS THE FUTURE, SO WHY *NOT* NOW?

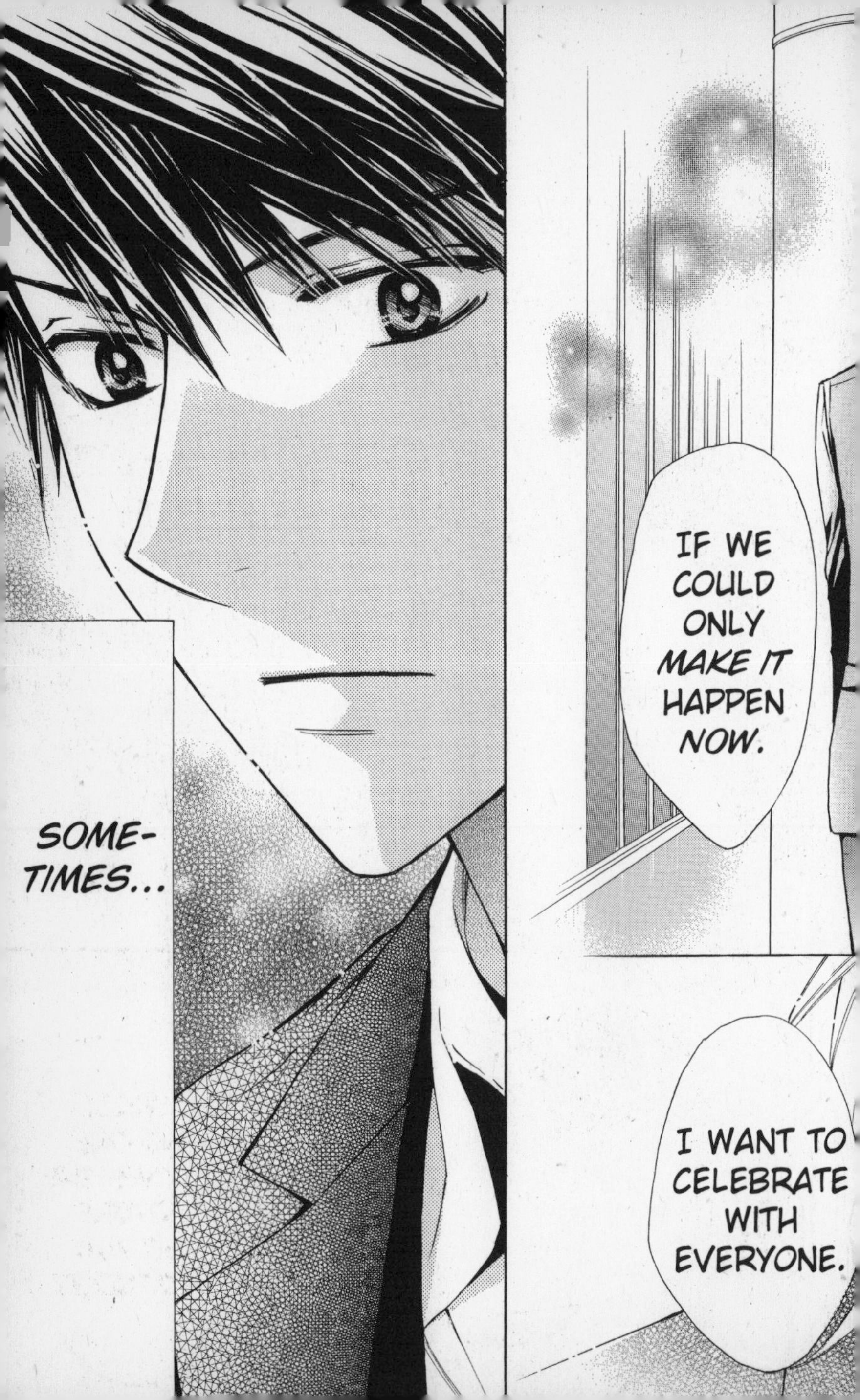
IF WE COULD ONLY *MAKE IT* HAPPEN *NOW*.
I WANT TO CELEBRATE WITH EVERYONE.
SOME-TIMES...

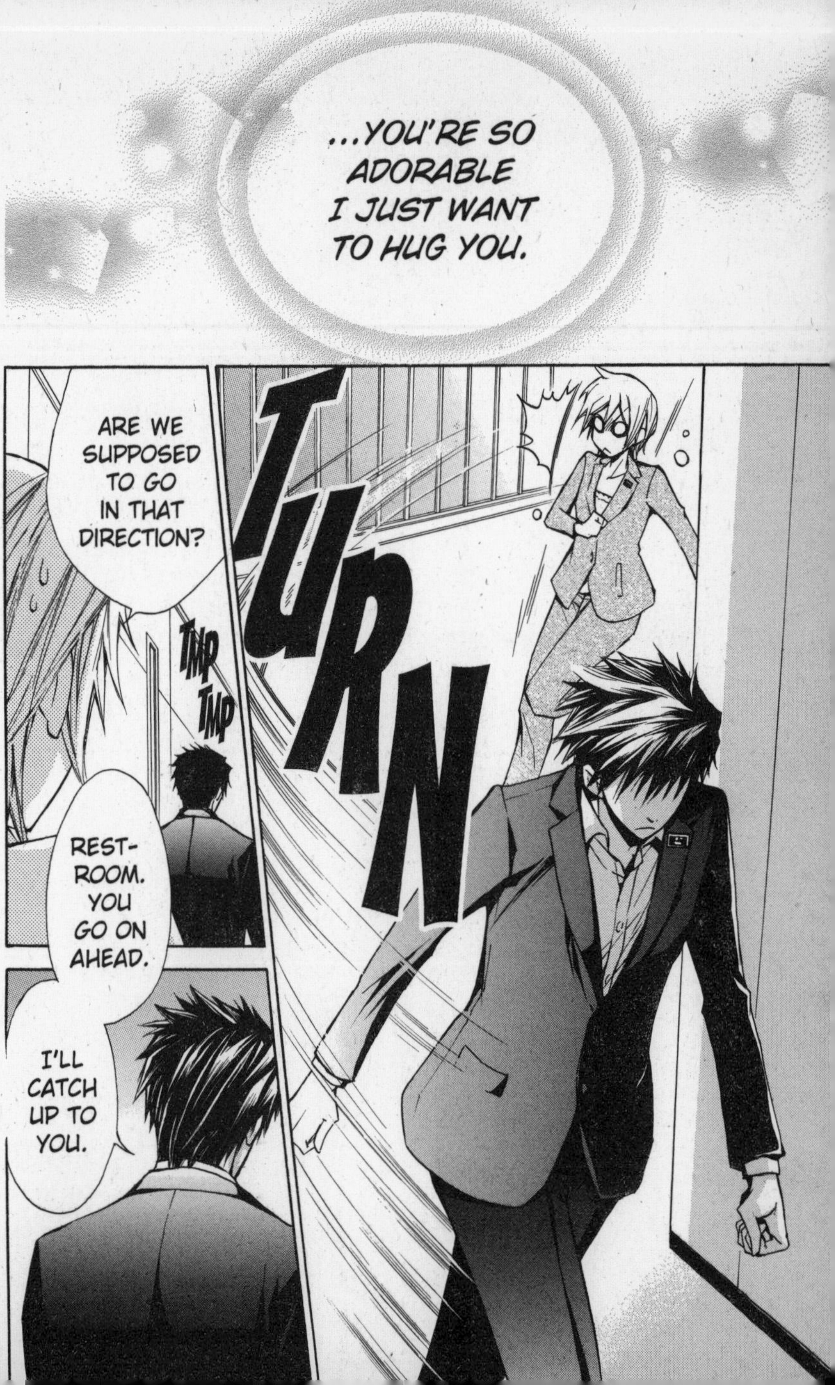
...YOU'RE SO ADORABLE I JUST WANT TO HUG YOU.
TURN
ARE WE SUPPOSED TO GO IN THAT DIRECTION?
TMP TMP
REST-ROOM. YOU GO ON AHEAD.
I'LL CATCH UP TO YOU.

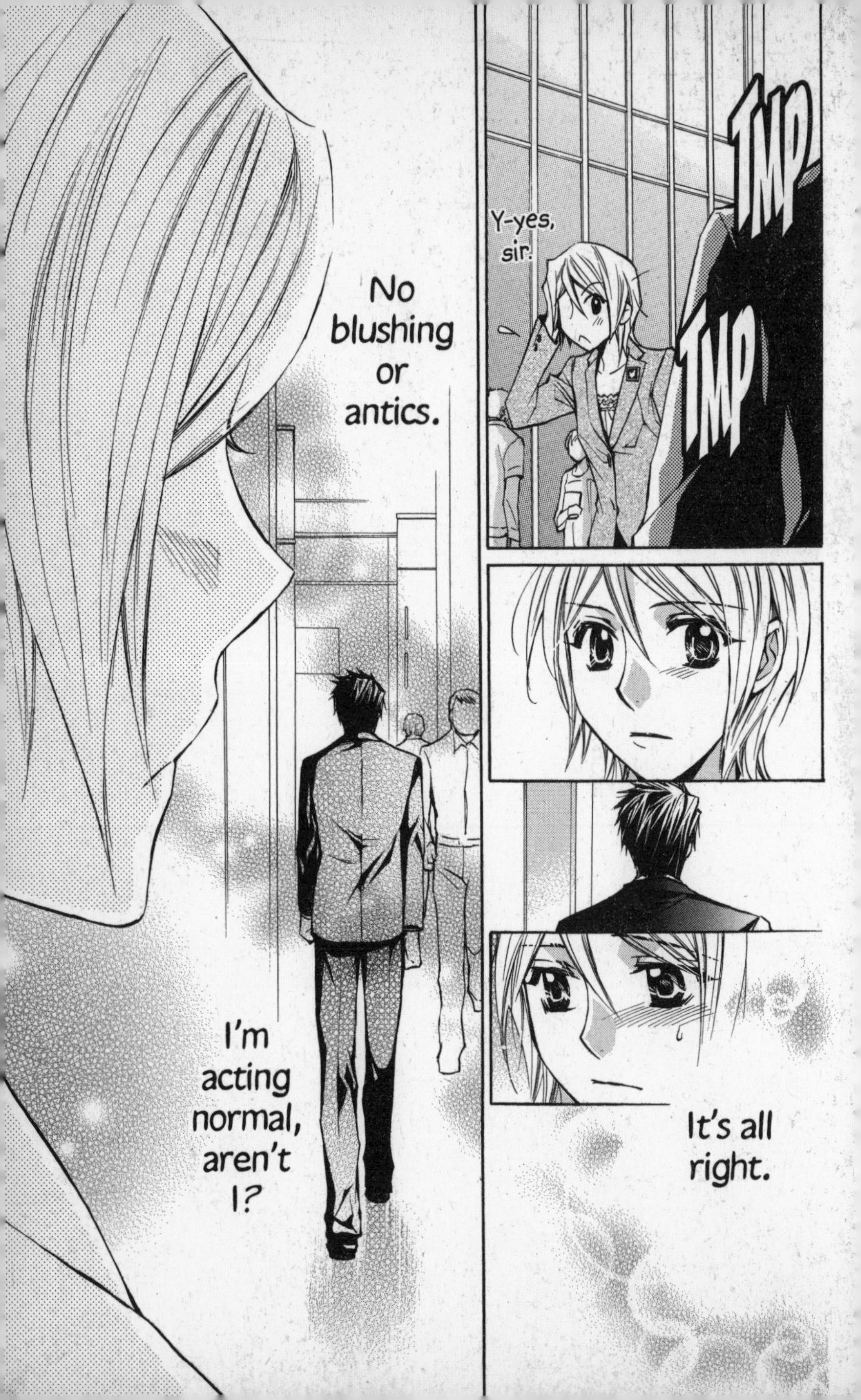
TMP
TMP
Y-yes, sir.
It's all right.
No blushing or antics.
I'm acting normal, aren't I?

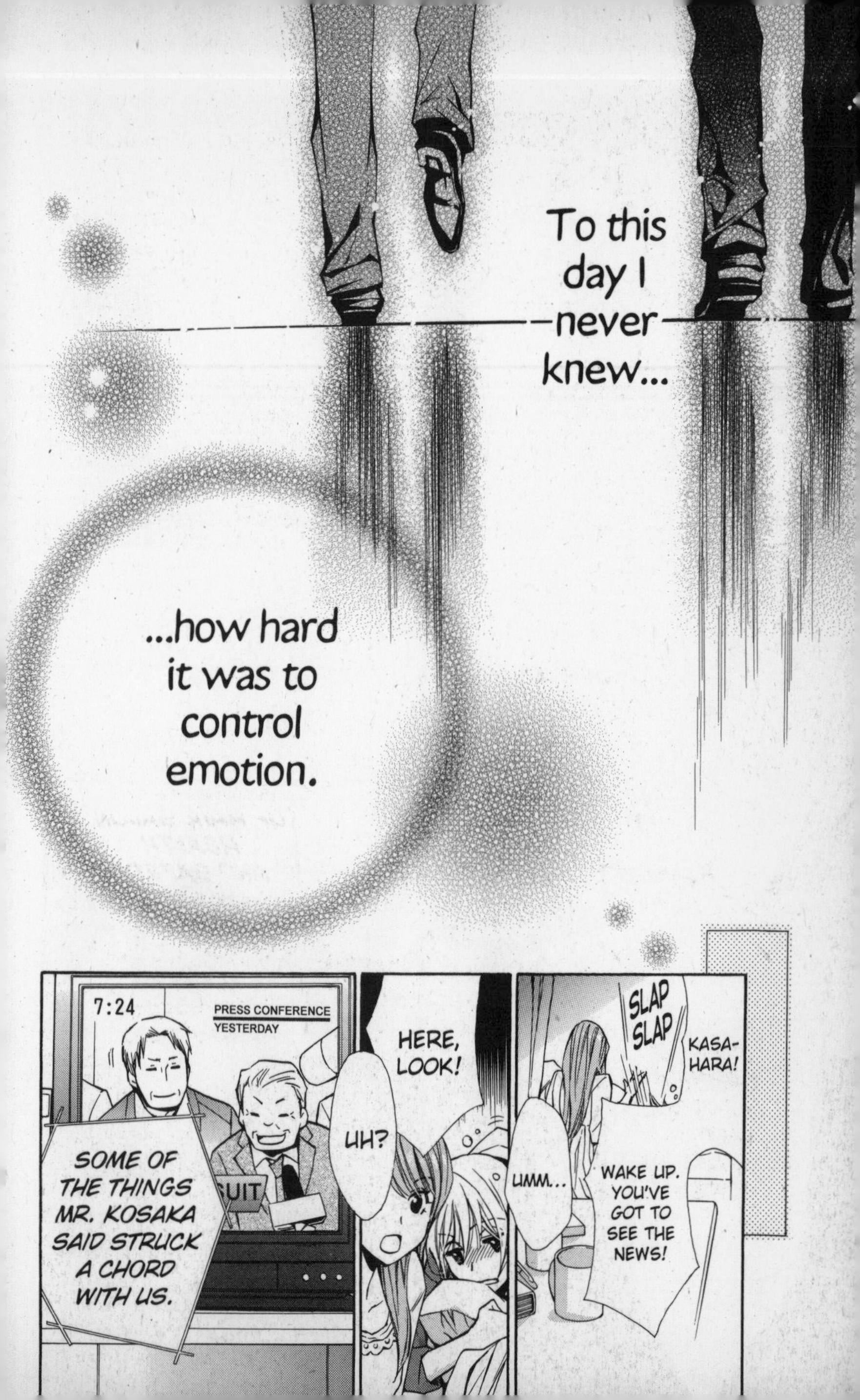
To this day I never knew...
...how hard it was to control emotion.
SLAP SLAP
KASA-HARA!
WAKE UP. YOU'VE GOT TO SEE THE NEWS!
UMM...
HERE, LOOK!
UH?
7:24
PRESS CONFERENCE
YESTERDAY
SOME OF THE THINGS MR. KOSAKA SAID STRUCK A CHORD WITH US.

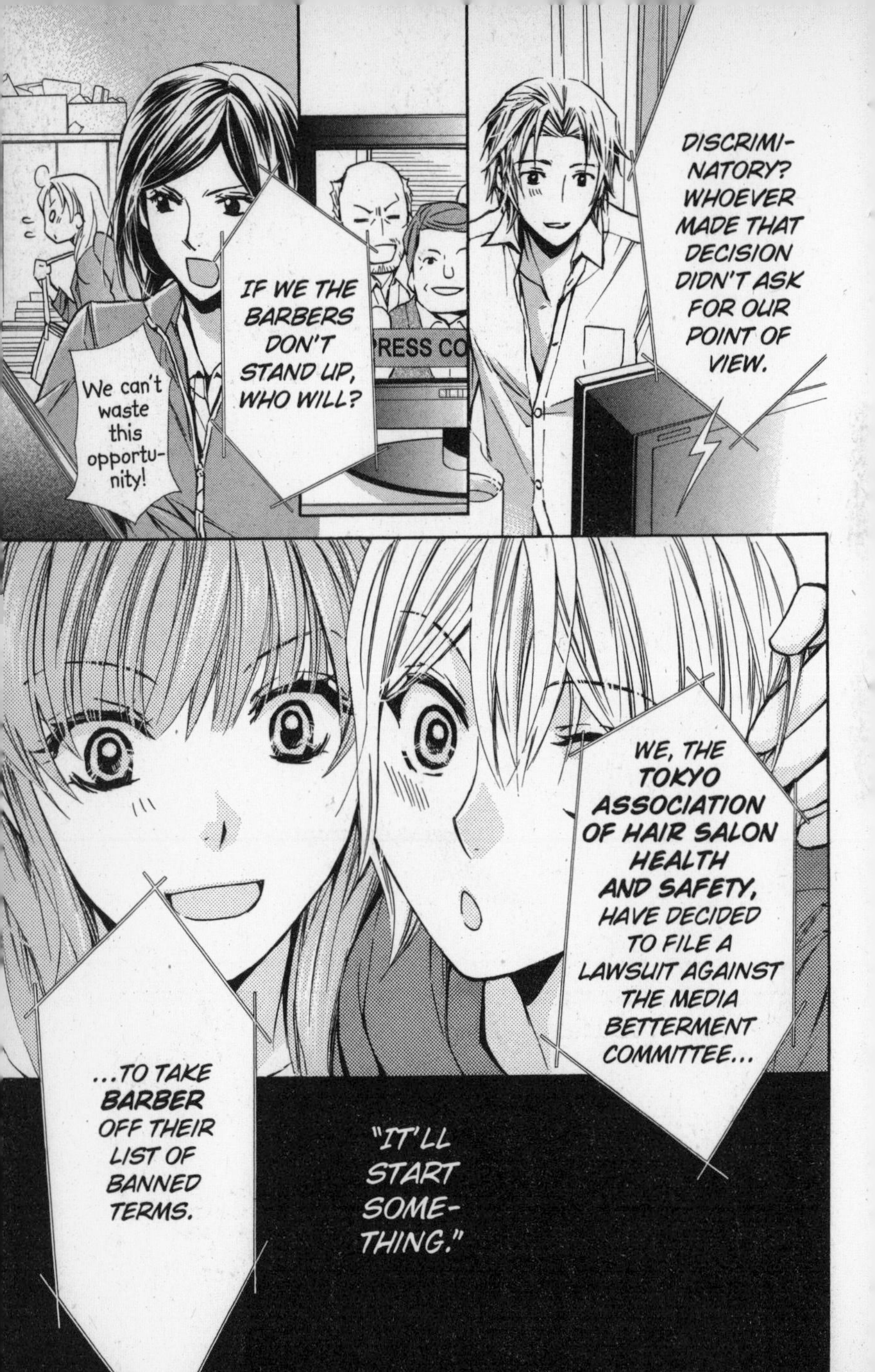
DISCRIMI-NATORY? WHOEVER MADE THAT DECISION DIDN'T ASK FOR OUR POINT OF VIEW.
IF WE THE BARBERS DON'T STAND UP, WHO WILL?
We can't waste this opportu-nity!
PRESS CO
WE, THE TOKYO ASSOCIATION OF HAIR SALON HEALTH AND SAFETY, HAVE DECIDED TO FILE A LAWSUIT AGAINST THE MEDIA BETTERMENT COMMITTEE...
...TO TAKE BARBER OFF THEIR LIST OF BANNED TERMS.
"IT'LL START SOME-THING."

LIBRARY WARS LOVE & WAR VOL 9/THE END

It's hard to control emotions.

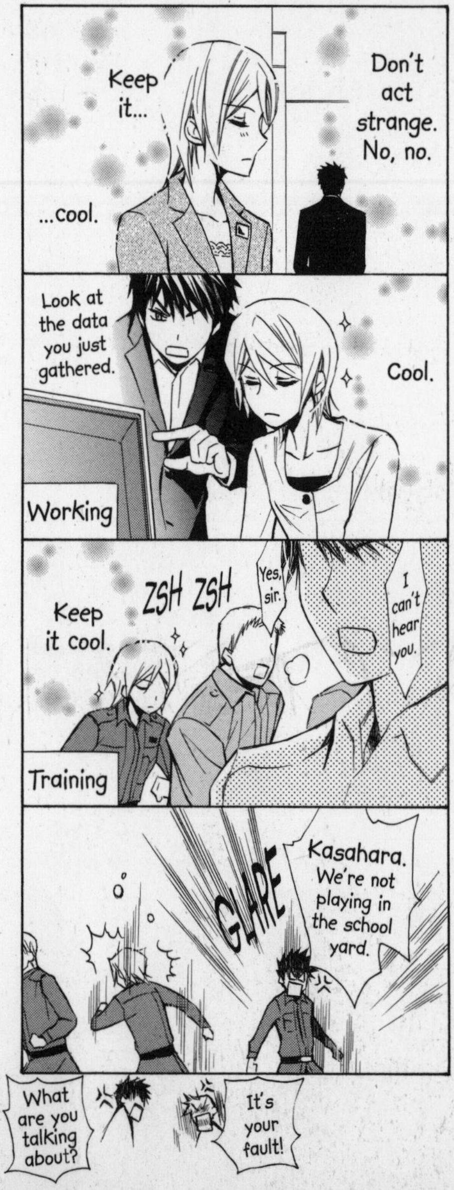

Don't act strange. No, no.
Keep it...
...cool.
Cool.
Look at the data you just gathered.
Working
I can't hear you.
Yes, sir.
ZSH ZSH
Keep it cool.
Training
Kasahara. We're not playing in the school yard.
GLARE
It's your fault!
What are you talking about?

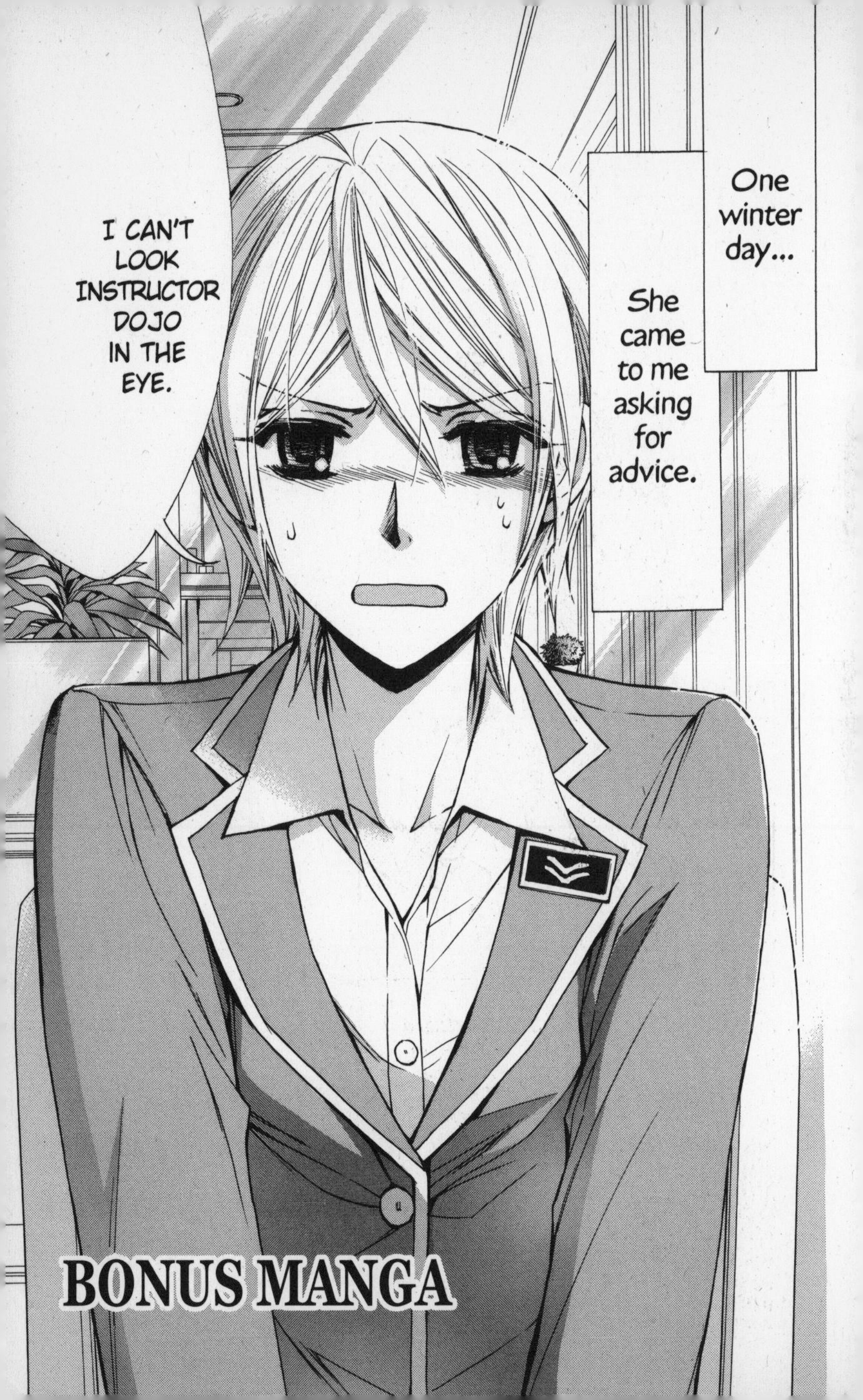
One winter day...
She came to me asking for advice.
I CAN'T LOOK INSTRUCTOR DOJO IN THE EYE.
BONUS MANGA

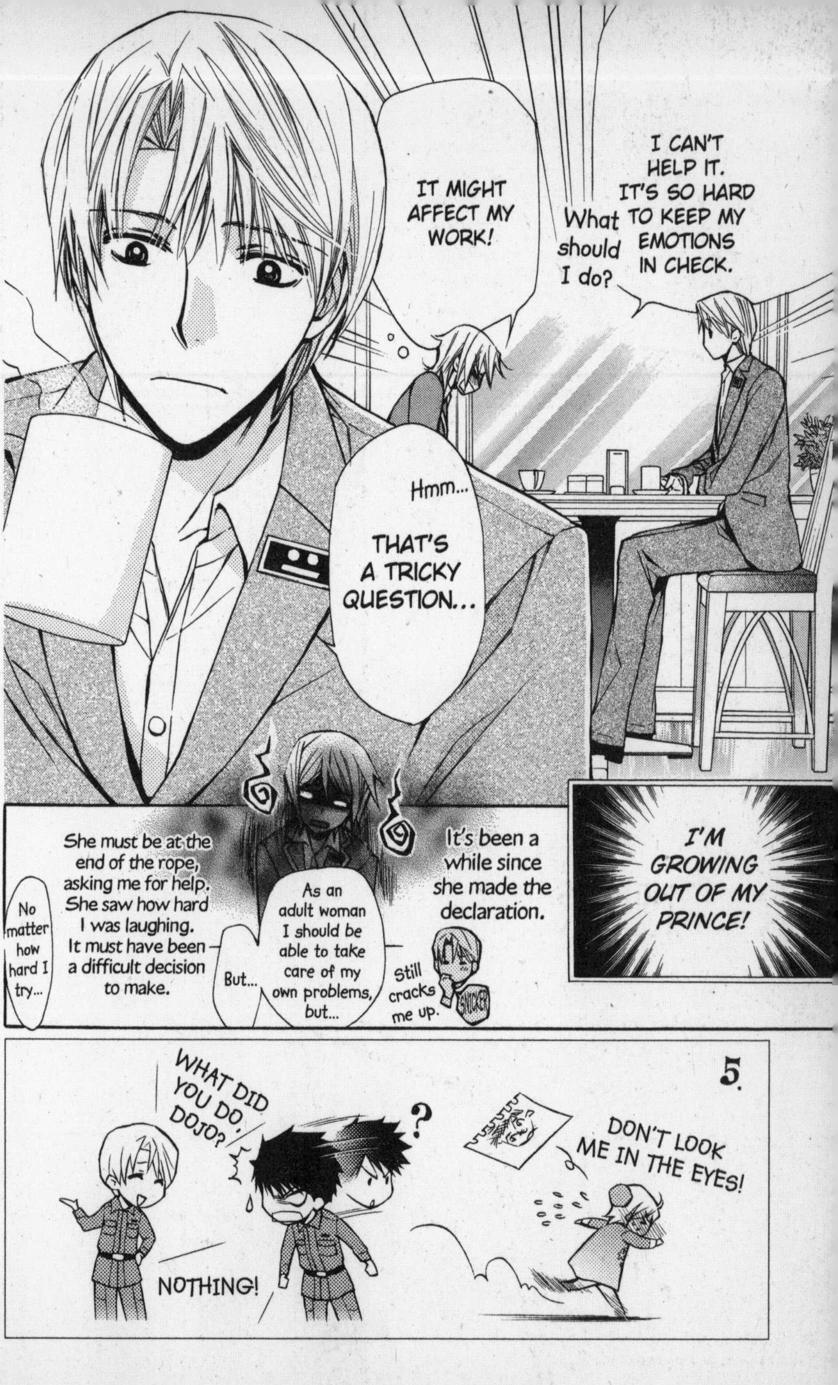
I CAN'T HELP IT. IT'S SO HARD TO KEEP MY EMOTIONS IN CHECK.
What should I do?
IT MIGHT AFFECT MY WORK!
Hmm...
THAT'S A TRICKY QUESTION...
I'M GROWING OUT OF MY PRINCE!
It's been a while since she made the declaration.
Still cracks me up.
SNICKER
As an adult woman I should be able to take care of my own problems, but...
But...
She must be at the end of the rope, asking me for help. She saw how hard I was laughing. It must have been a difficult decision to make.
No matter how hard I try...
5.
DON'T LOOK ME IN THE EYES!
?
WHAT DID YOU DO, DOJO?
NOTHING!

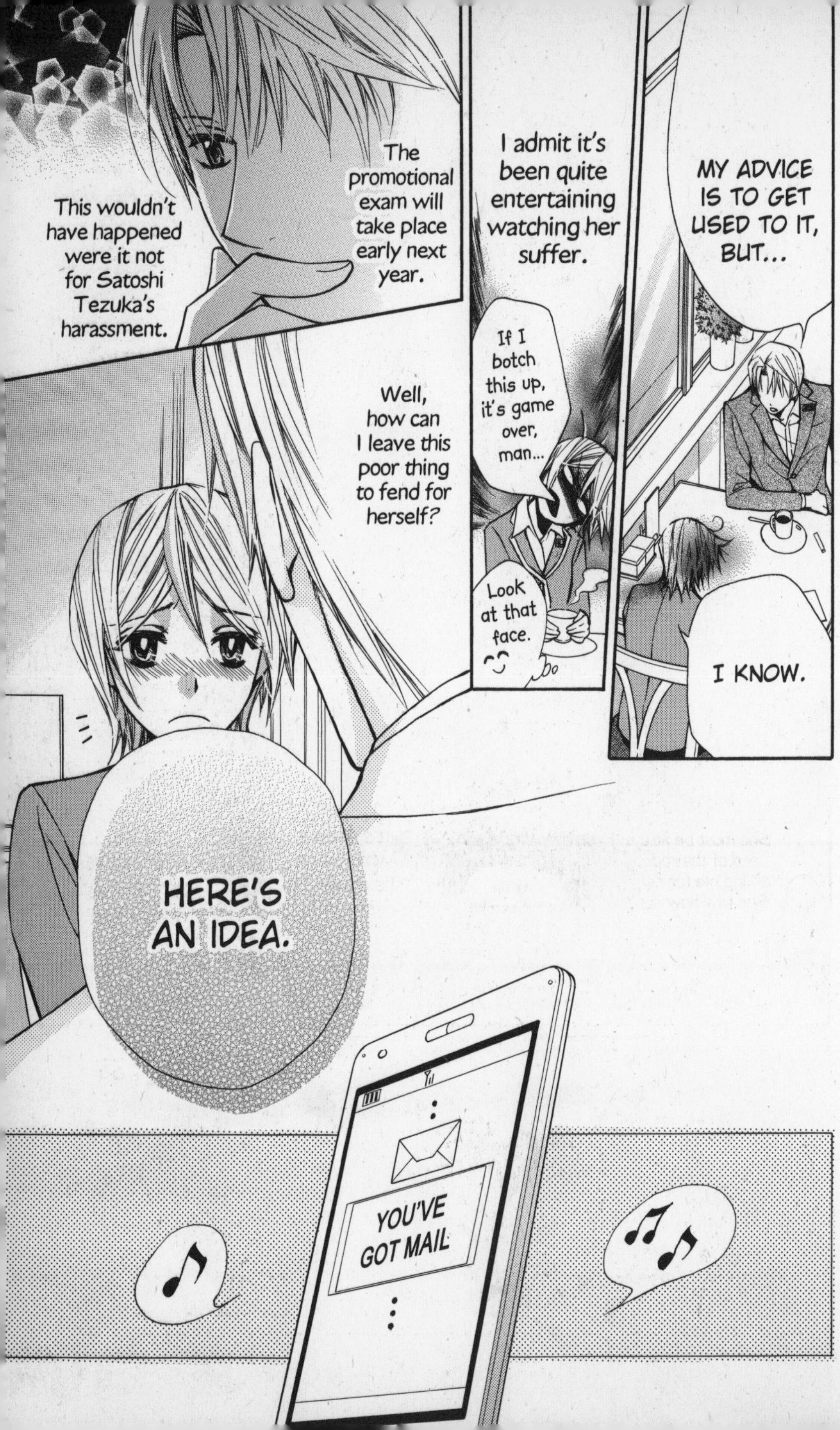
MY ADVICE IS TO GET USED TO IT, BUT...
I KNOW.
I admit it's been quite entertaining watching her suffer.
If I botch this up, it's game over, man...
Look at that face.
The promotional exam will take place early next year.
This wouldn't have happened were it not for Satoshi Tezuka's harassment.
Well, how can I leave this poor thing to fend for herself?
HERE'S AN IDEA.
YOU'VE GOT MAIL

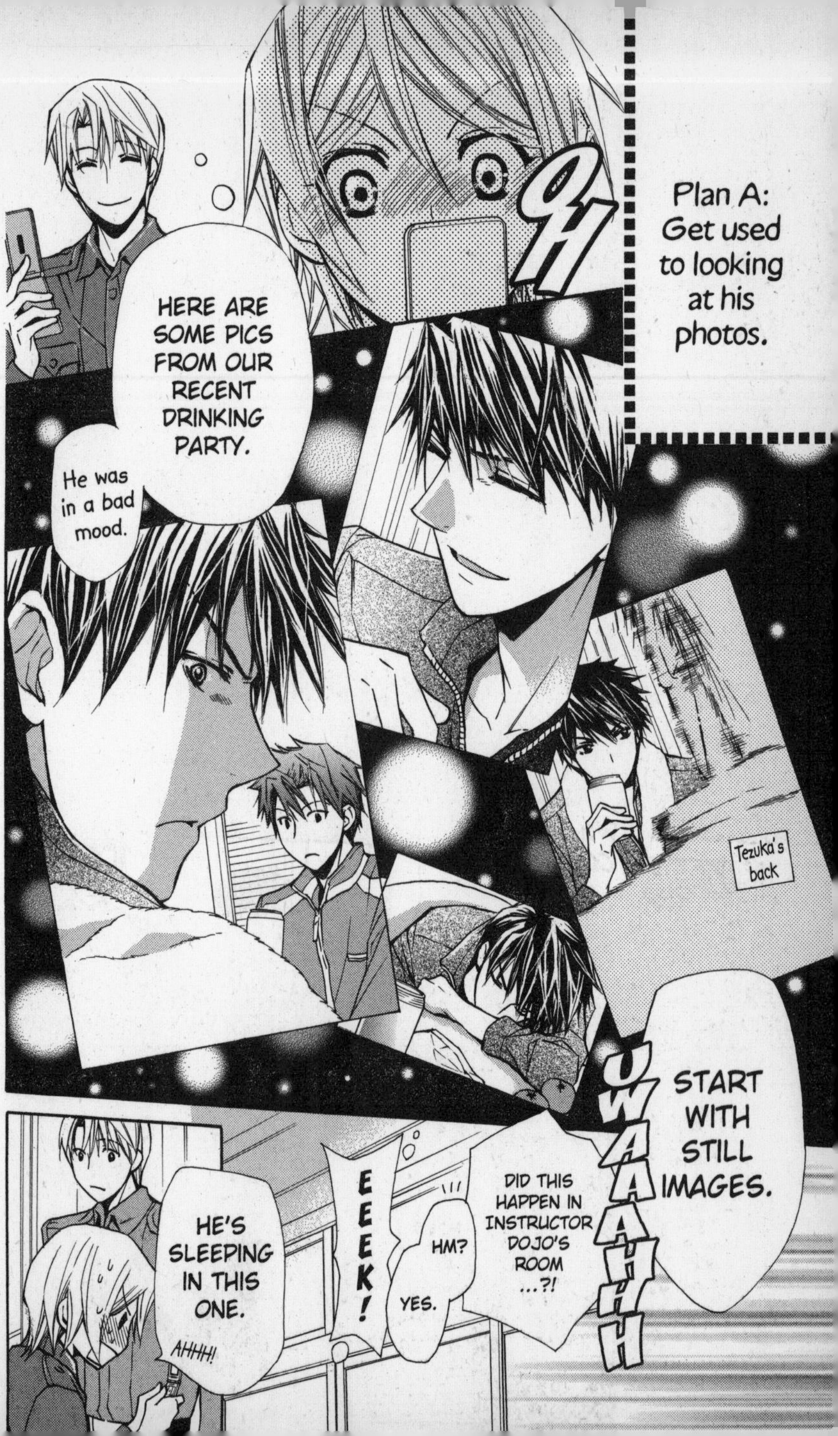
Plan A: Get used to looking at his photos.
OH
HERE ARE SOME PICS FROM OUR RECENT DRINKING PARTY.
He was in a bad mood.
Tezuka's back
START WITH STILL IMAGES.
UWAAAAHHHH
DID THIS HAPPEN IN INSTRUCTOR DOJO'S ROOM ...?!
HM?
YES.
EEEEK!
HE'S SLEEPING IN THIS ONE.
AHHH!

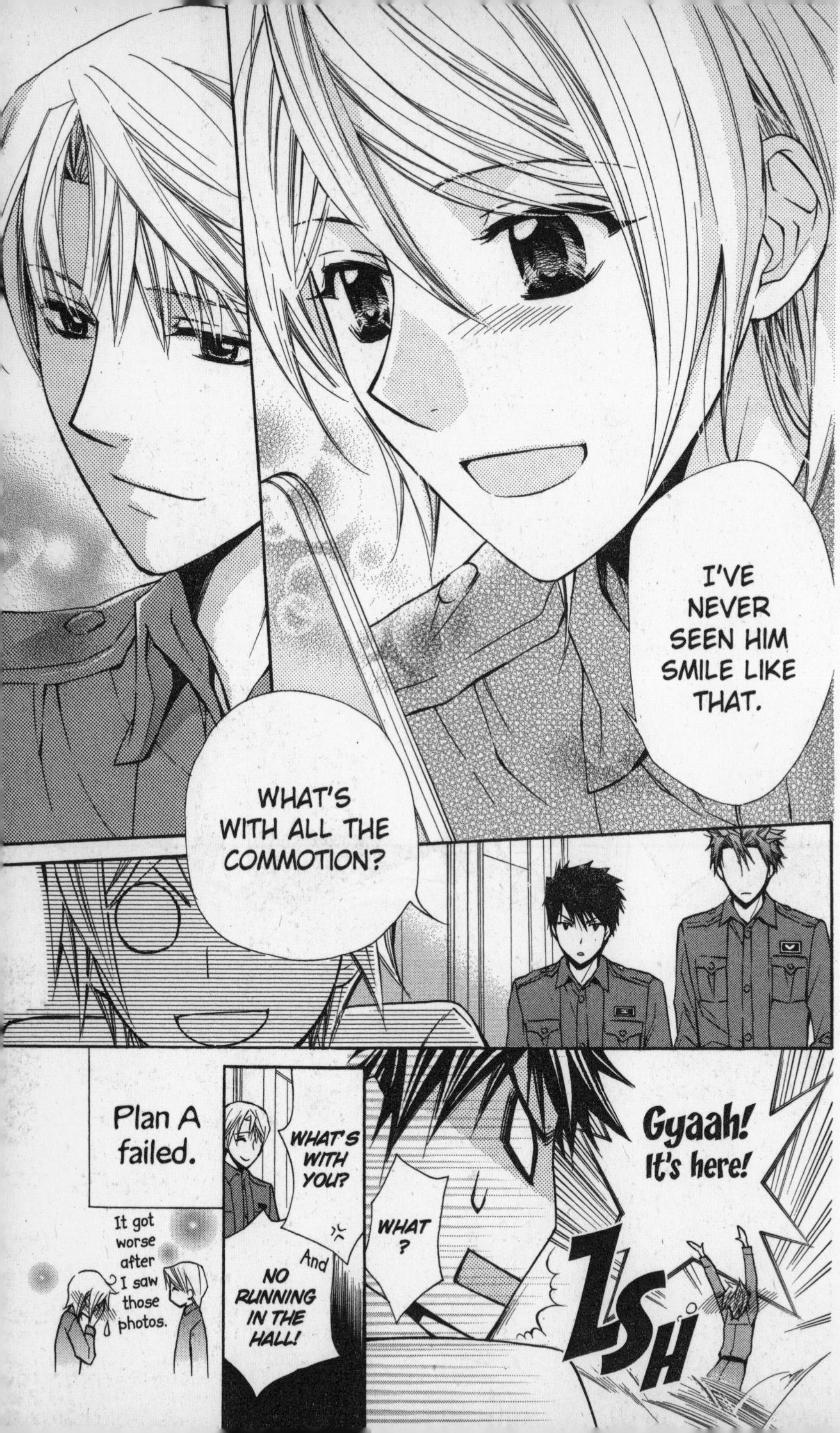
I'VE NEVER SEEN HIM SMILE LIKE THAT.
WHAT'S WITH ALL THE COMMOTION?
Gyaah! It's here!
ZSH
WHAT ?
WHAT'S WITH YOU?
And NO RUNNING IN THE HALL!
Plan A failed.
It got worse after I saw those photos.

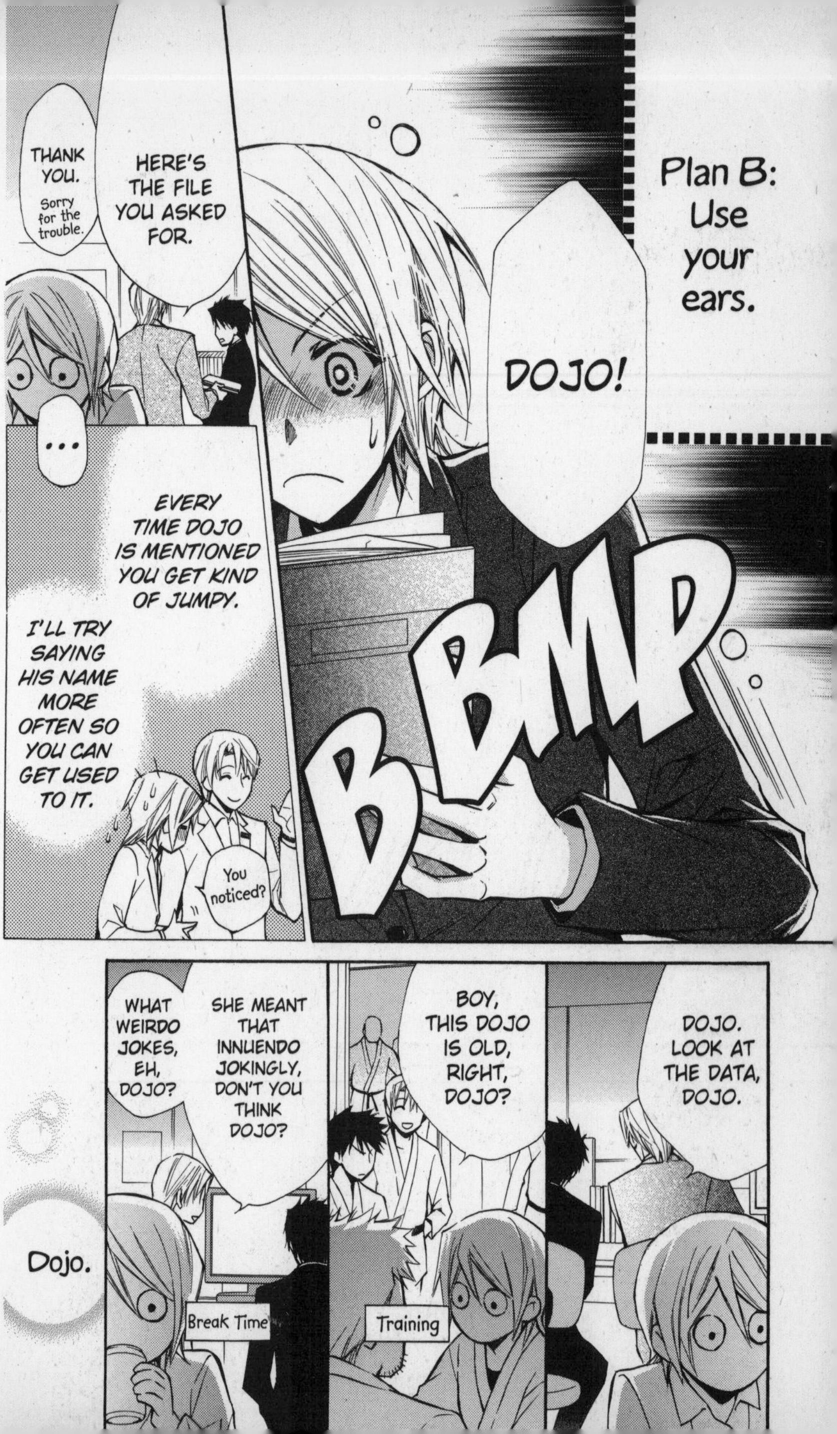
Plan B: Use your ears.
DOJO!
BMP
HERE'S THE FILE YOU ASKED FOR.
THANK YOU.
Sorry for the trouble.
...
EVERY TIME DOJO IS MENTIONED YOU GET KIND OF JUMPY.
I'LL TRY SAYING HIS NAME MORE OFTEN SO YOU CAN GET USED TO IT.
You noticed?
DOJO. LOOK AT THE DATA, DOJO.
BOY, THIS DOJO IS OLD, RIGHT, DOJO?
Training
SHE MEANT THAT INNUENDO JOKINGLY, DON'T YOU THINK DOJO?
WHAT WEIRDO JOKES, EH, DOJO?
Break Time
Dojo.

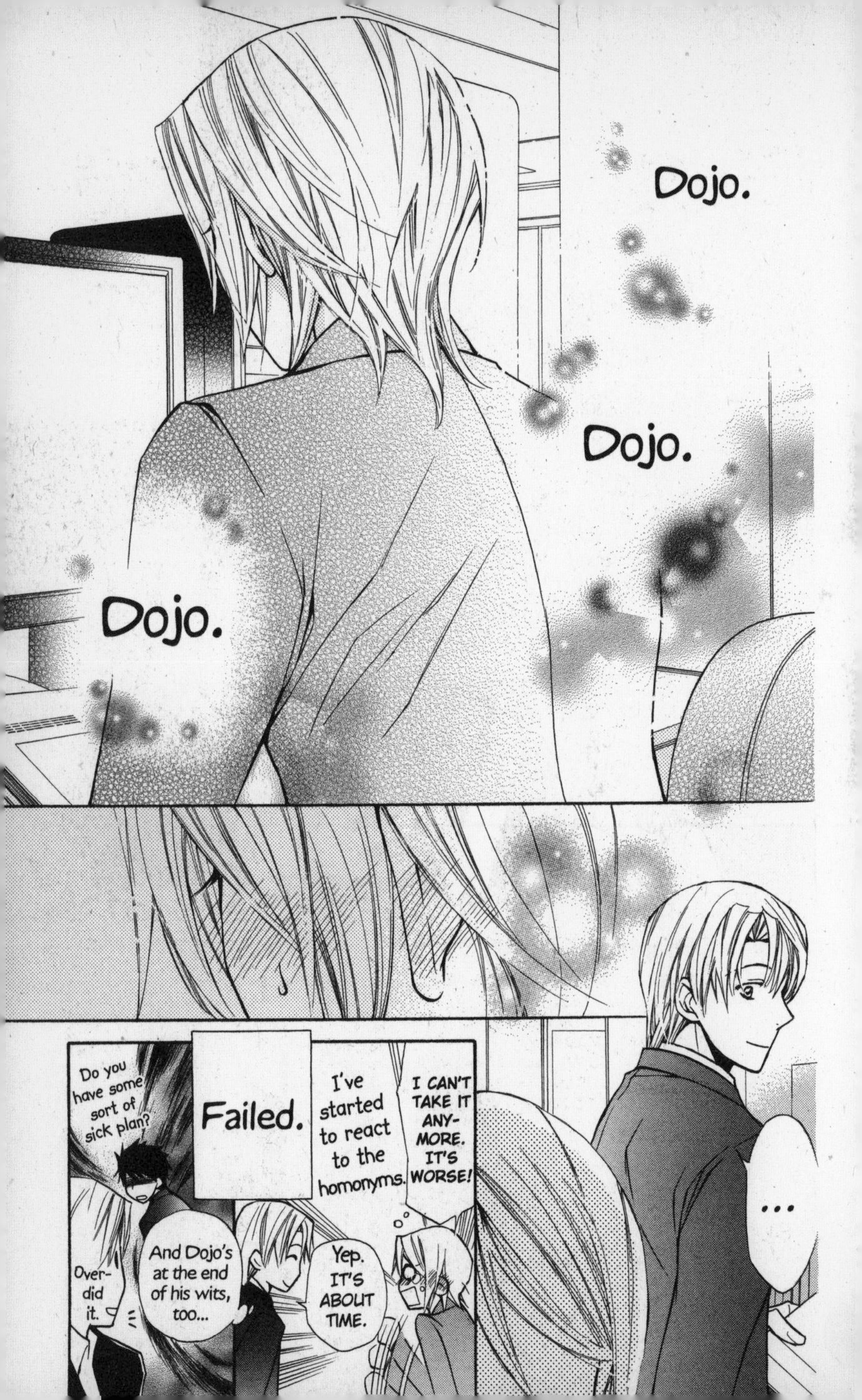
Dojo.
Dojo.
Dojo.
...
I CAN'T TAKE IT ANYMORE. IT'S WORSE!
I've started to react to the homonyms.
Failed.
Do you have some sort of sick plan?
Yep. IT'S ABOUT TIME.
And Dojo's at the end of his wits, too...
Over-did it.

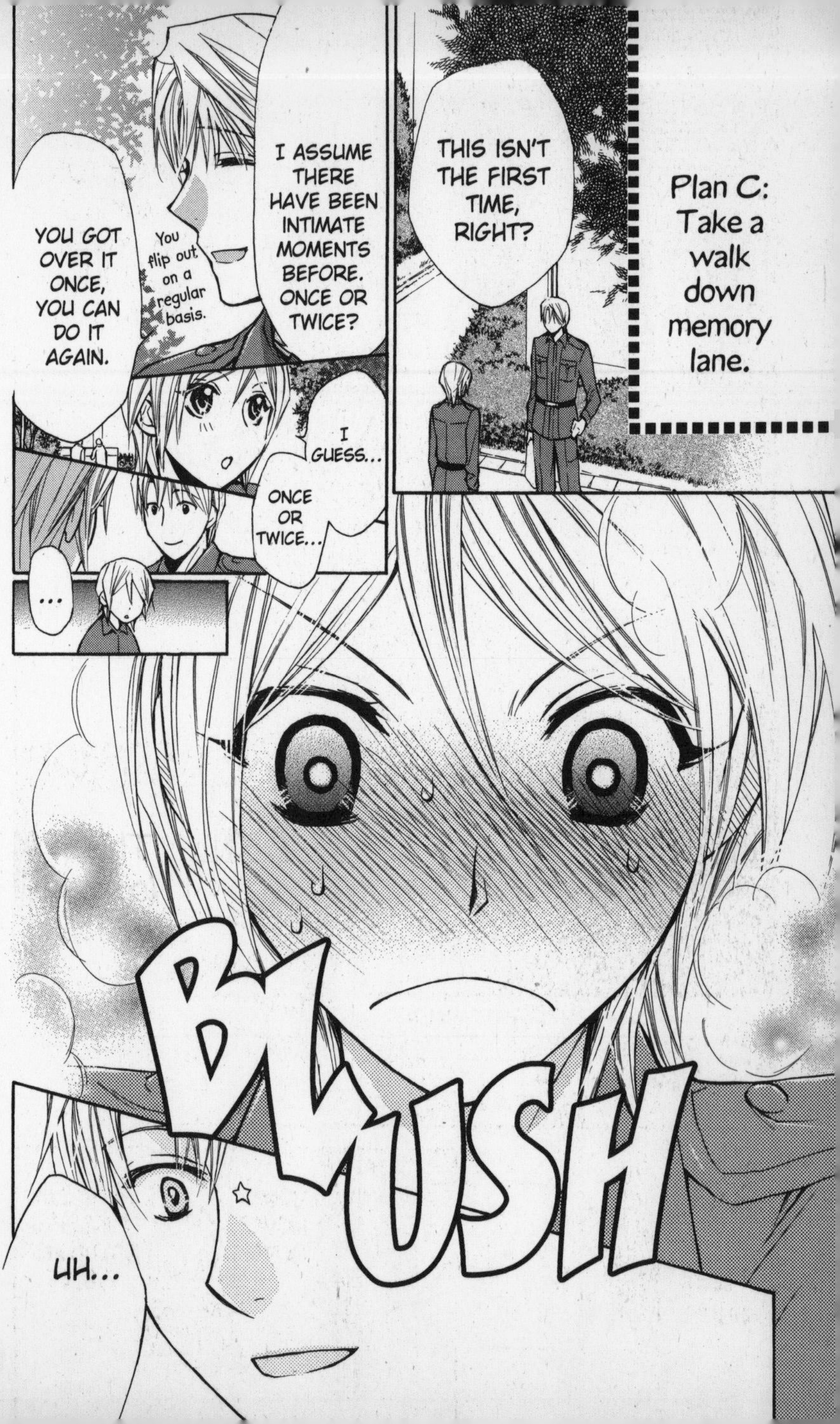
Plan C: Take a walk down memory lane.
THIS ISN'T THE FIRST TIME, RIGHT?
I ASSUME THERE HAVE BEEN INTIMATE MOMENTS BEFORE. ONCE OR TWICE?
You flip out on a regular basis.
YOU GOT OVER IT ONCE, YOU CAN DO IT AGAIN.
I GUESS...
ONCE OR TWICE...
...
BLUSH
UH...

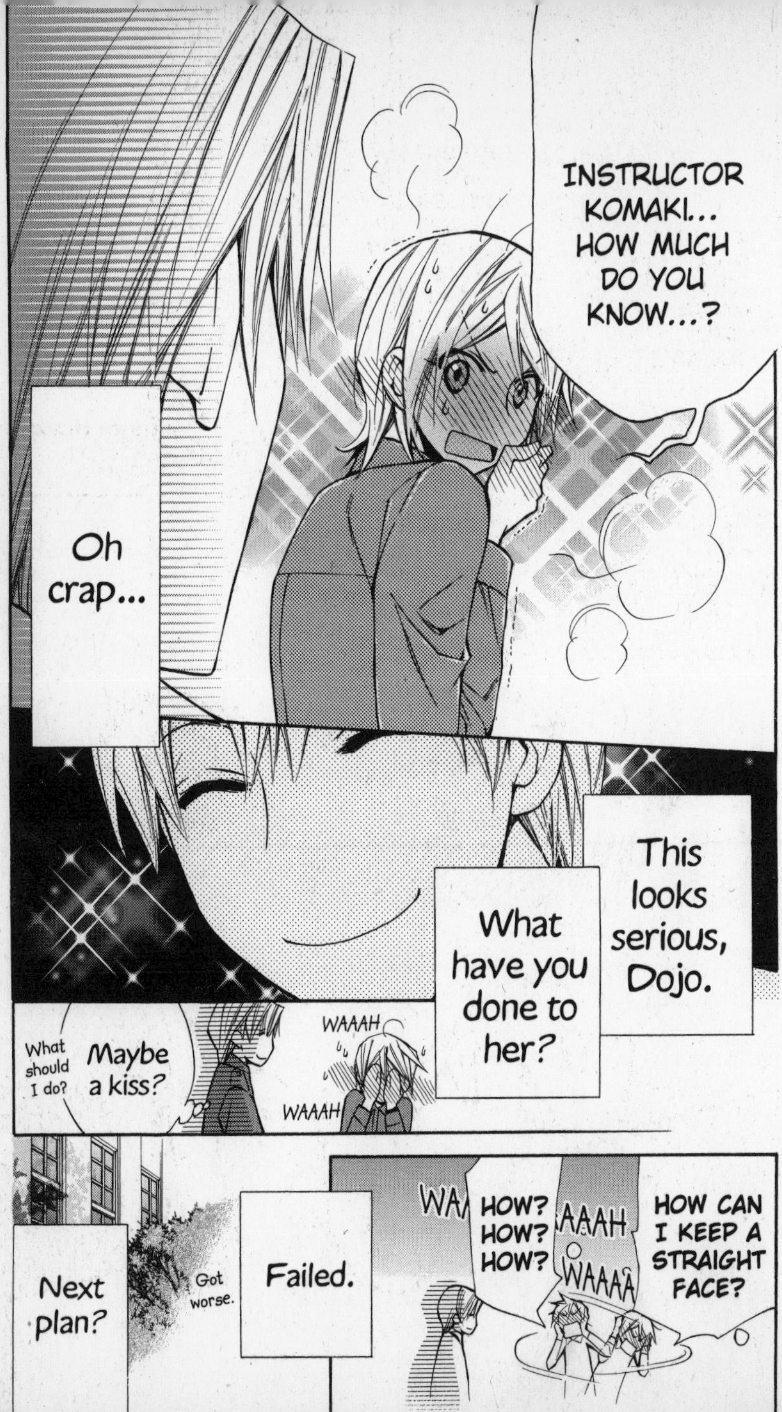

INSTRUCTOR KOMAKI... HOW MUCH DO YOU KNOW...?
Oh crap...
This looks serious, Dojo.
What have you done to her?
WAAAH
WAAAH
Maybe a kiss?
What should I do?
HOW CAN I KEEP A STRAIGHT FACE?
AAAH
WAAAA
HOW? HOW? HOW?
WA
Failed.
Got worse.
Next plan?

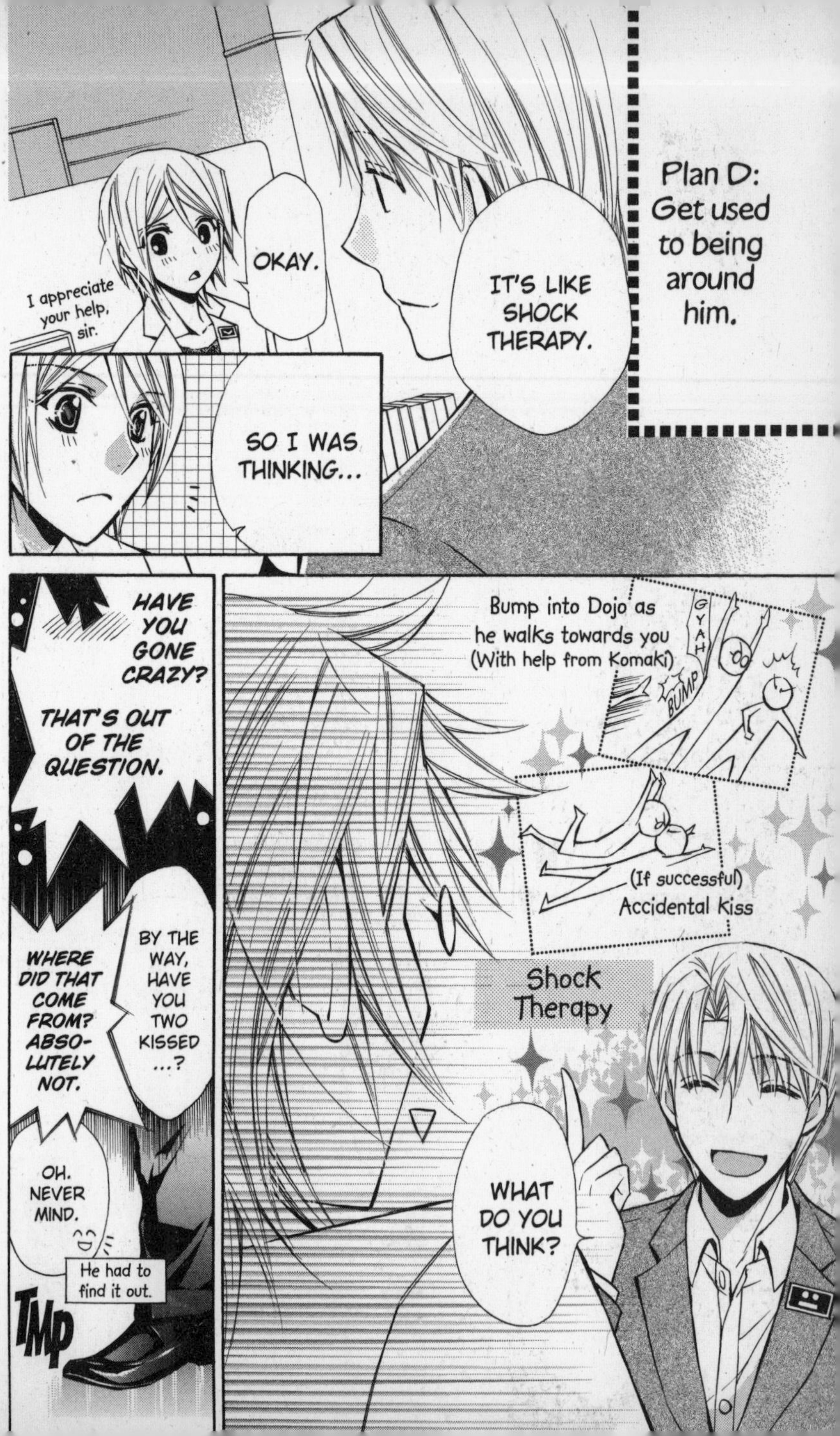
Plan D: Get used to being around him.
IT'S LIKE SHOCK THERAPY.
OKAY.
I appreciate your help, sir.
SO I WAS THINKING...
Bump into Dojo as he walks towards you (With help from Komaki)
GYAH
BUMP
(If successful) Accidental Kiss
Shock Therapy
WHAT DO YOU THINK?
HAVE YOU GONE CRAZY?
THAT'S OUT OF THE QUESTION.
BY THE WAY, HAVE YOU TWO KISSED ...?
WHERE DID THAT COME FROM? ABSOLUTELY NOT.
OH. NEVER MIND.
He had to find it out.
TMP

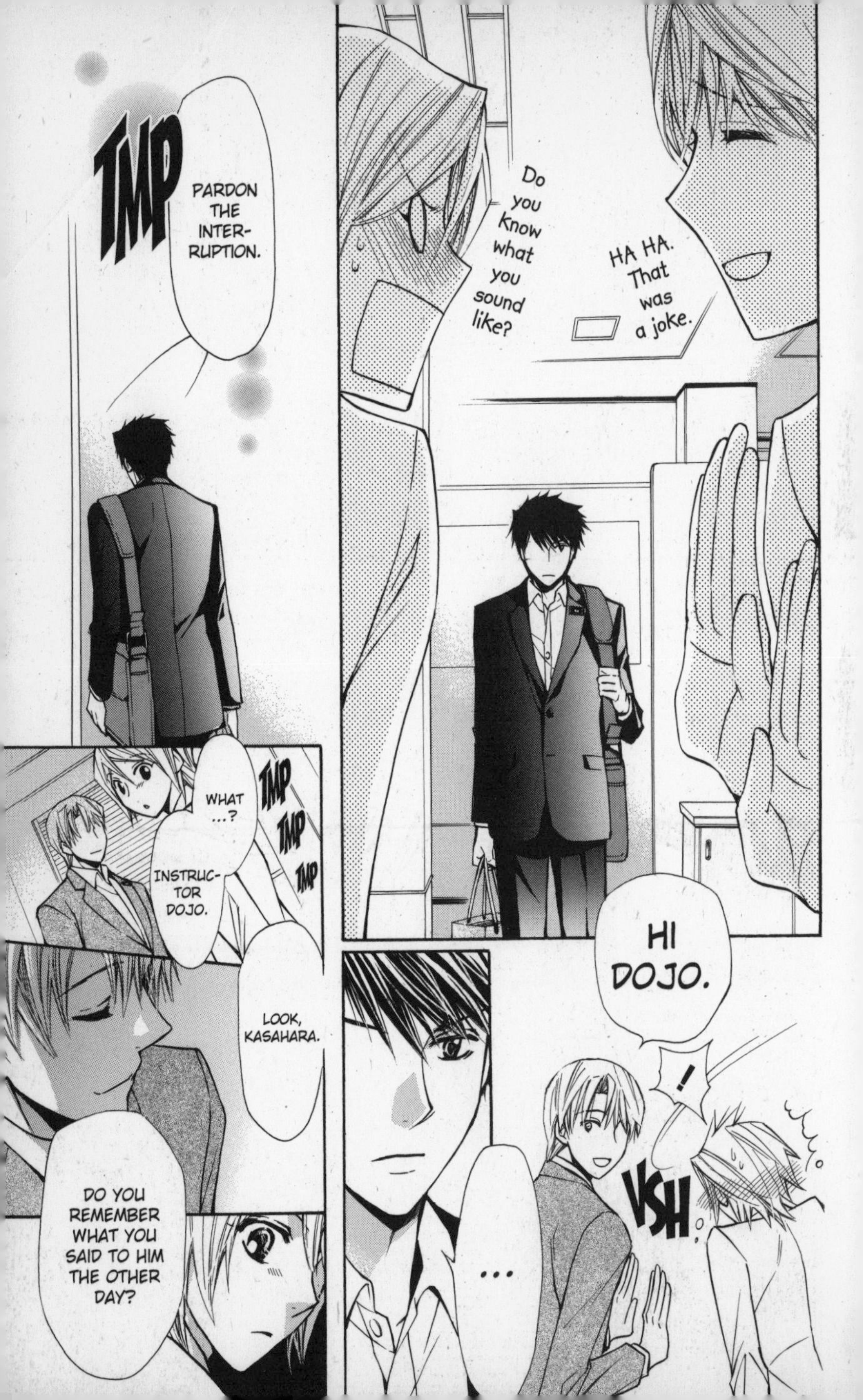
Do you know what you sound like?
HA HA. That was a joke.
HI DOJO.
!
VSH
...
TMP
PARDON THE INTER-RUPTION.
WHAT ...?
TMP TMP TMP
INSTRUC-TOR DOJO.
LOOK, KASAHARA.
DO YOU REMEMBER WHAT YOU SAID TO HIM THE OTHER DAY?

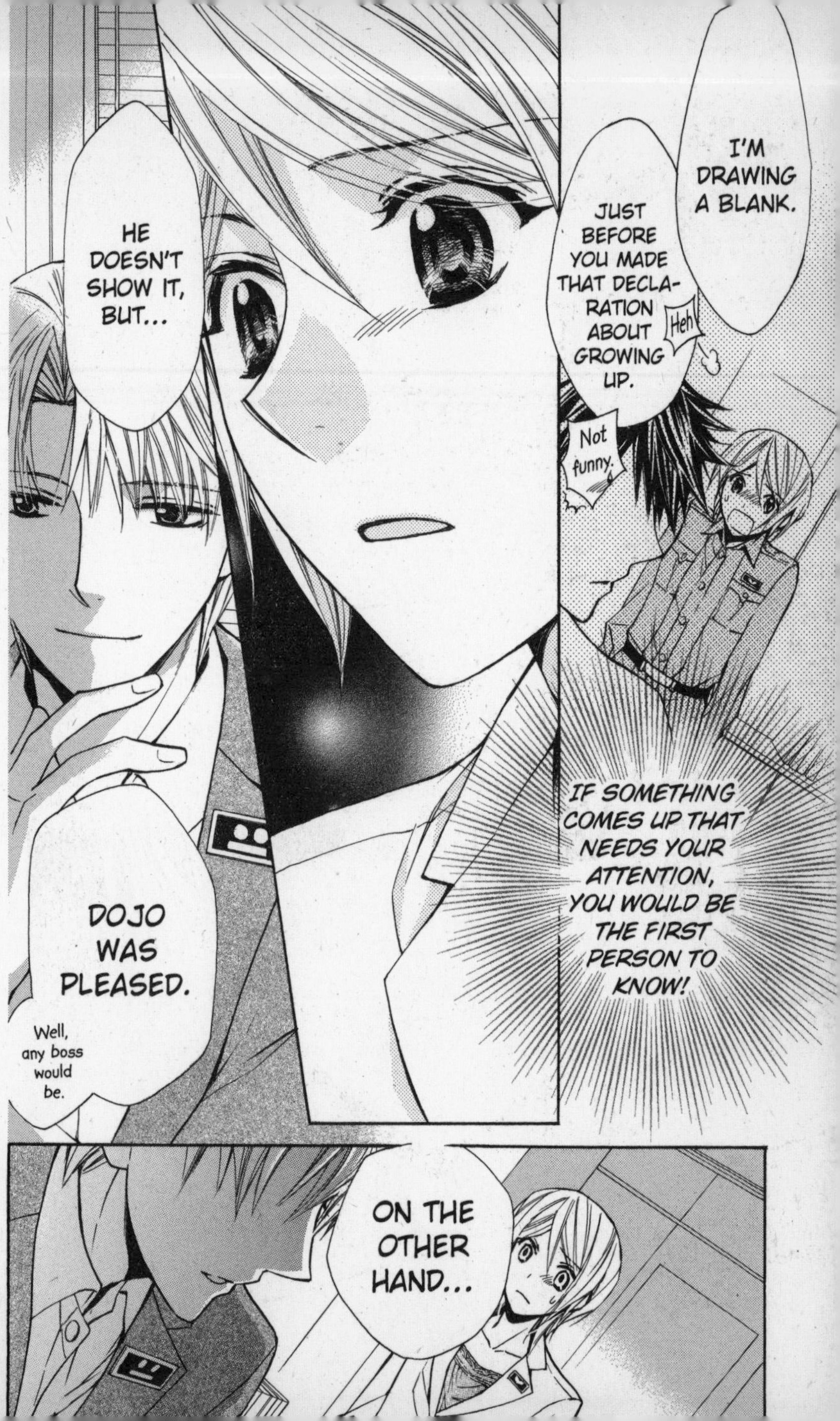
I'M DRAWING A BLANK.
JUST BEFORE YOU MADE THAT DECLARATION ABOUT GROWING UP.
Heh
Not funny.
IF SOMETHING COMES UP THAT NEEDS YOUR ATTENTION, YOU WOULD BE THE FIRST PERSON TO KNOW!
HE DOESN'T SHOW IT, BUT...
DOJO WAS PLEASED.
Well, any boss would be.
ON THE OTHER HAND...

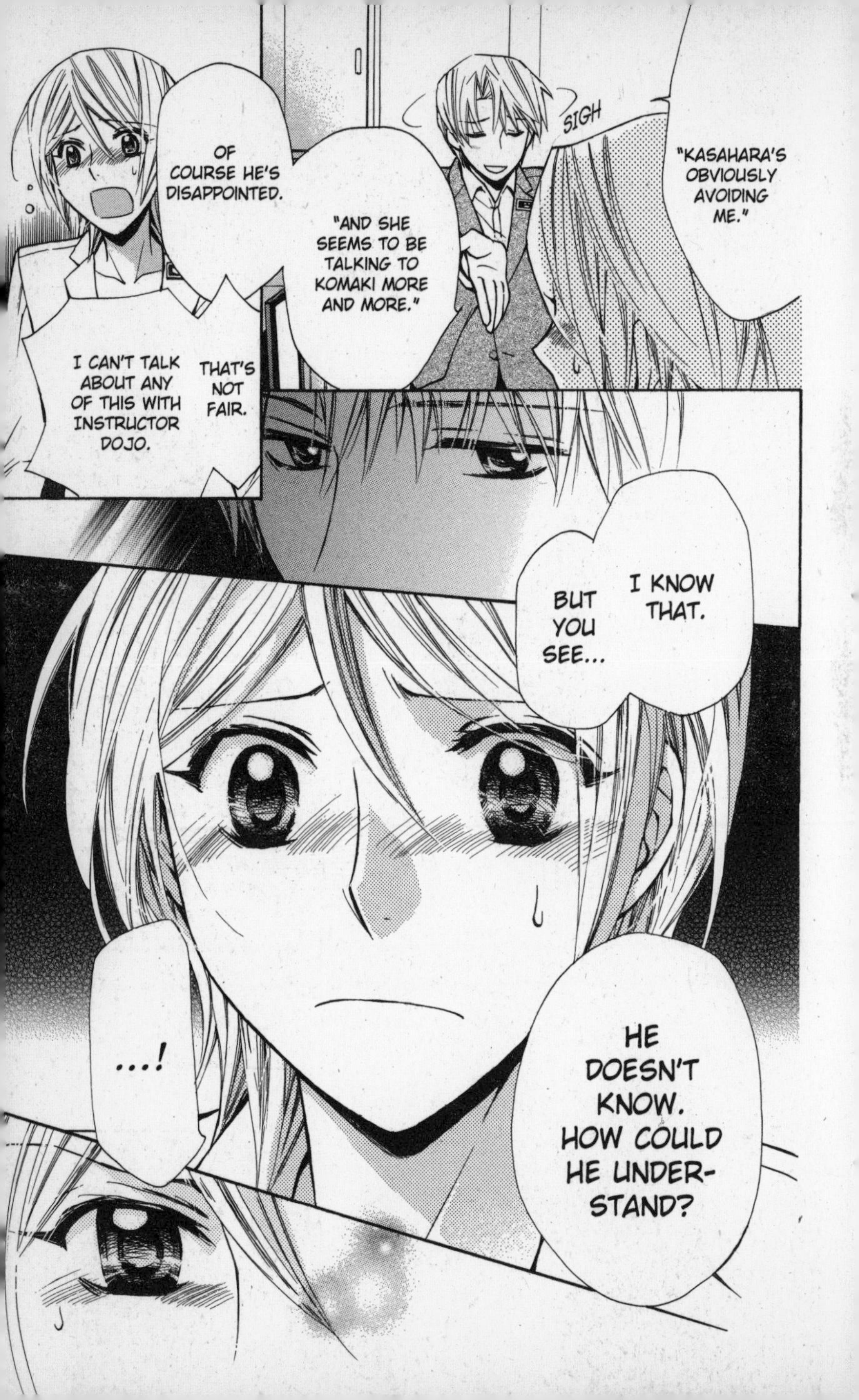
"KASAHARA'S OBVIOUSLY AVOIDING ME."
SIGH
"AND SHE SEEMS TO BE TALKING TO KOMAKI MORE AND MORE."
OF COURSE HE'S DISAPPOINTED.
THAT'S NOT FAIR.
I CAN'T TALK ABOUT ANY OF THIS WITH INSTRUCTOR DOJO.
I KNOW THAT.
BUT YOU SEE...
HE DOESN'T KNOW. HOW COULD HE UNDER-STAND?
...!

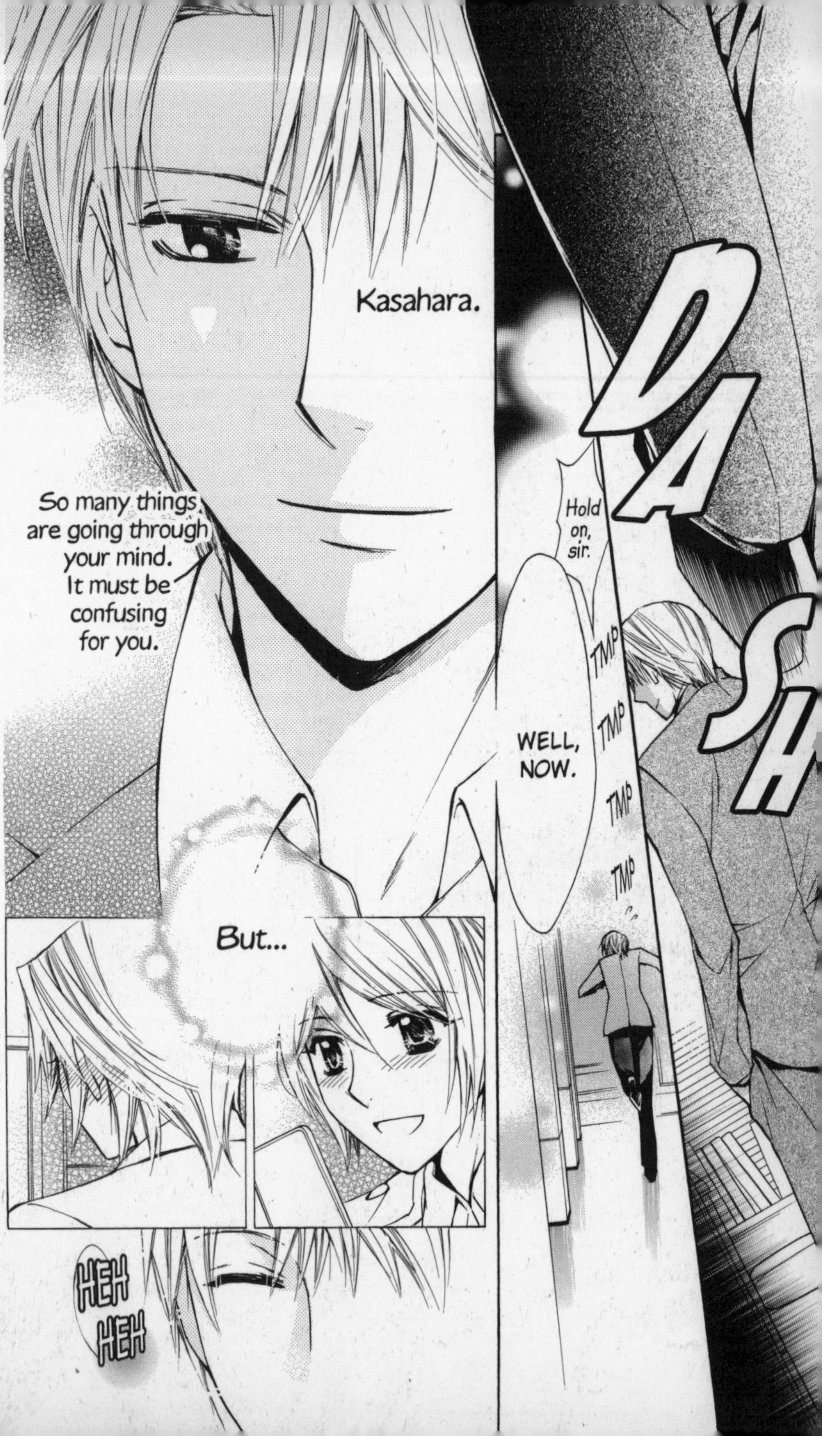
DASH
Hold on, sir.
WELL, NOW.
TMP
TMP
TMP
TMP
Kasahara.
So many things are going through your mind. It must be confusing for you.
But...
HEH HEH

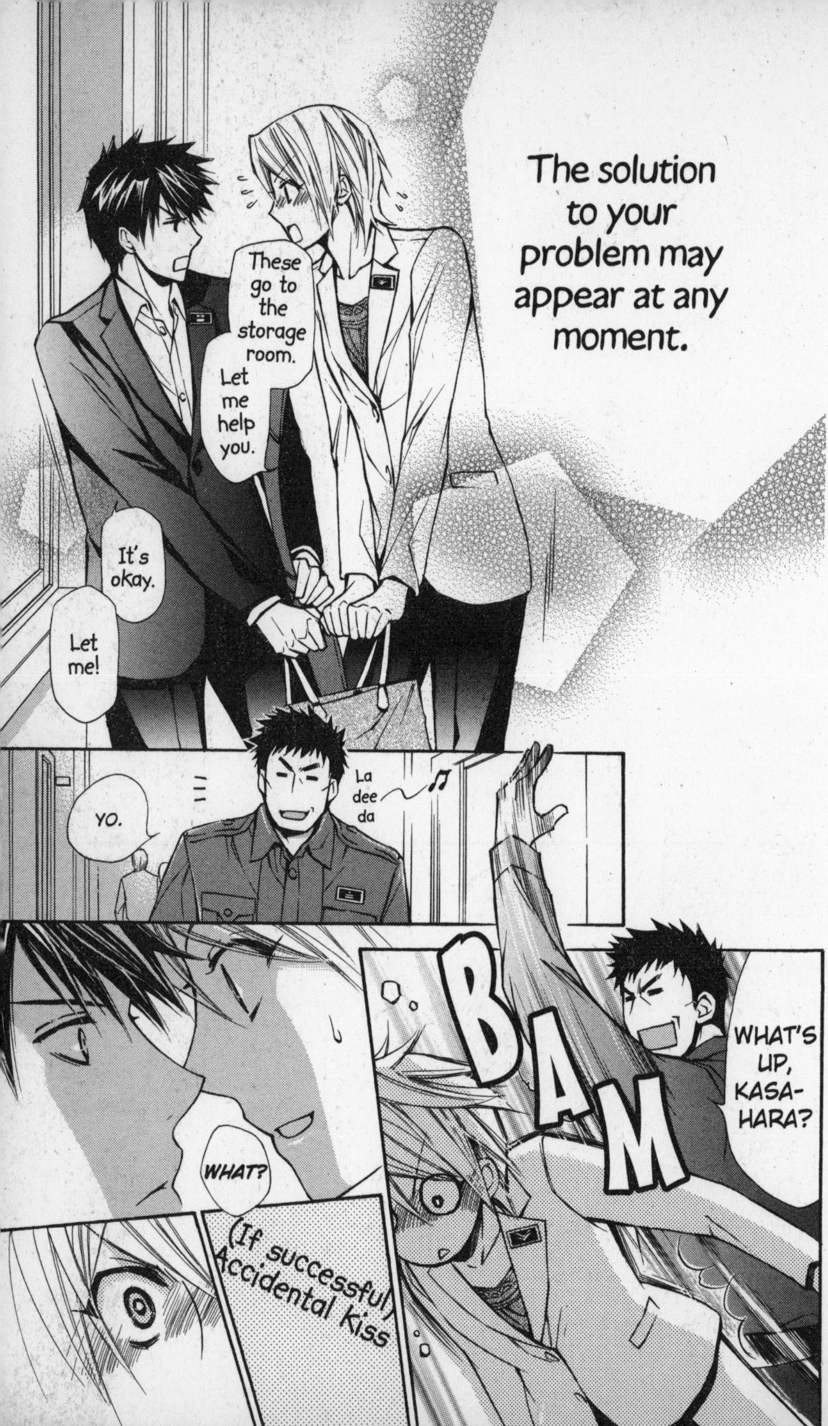
The solution to your problem may appear at any moment.
These go to the storage room.
Let me help you.
It's okay.
Let me!
La dee da
YO.
BAM
WHAT'S UP, KASA-HARA?
WHAT?
(If successful) Accidental Kiss

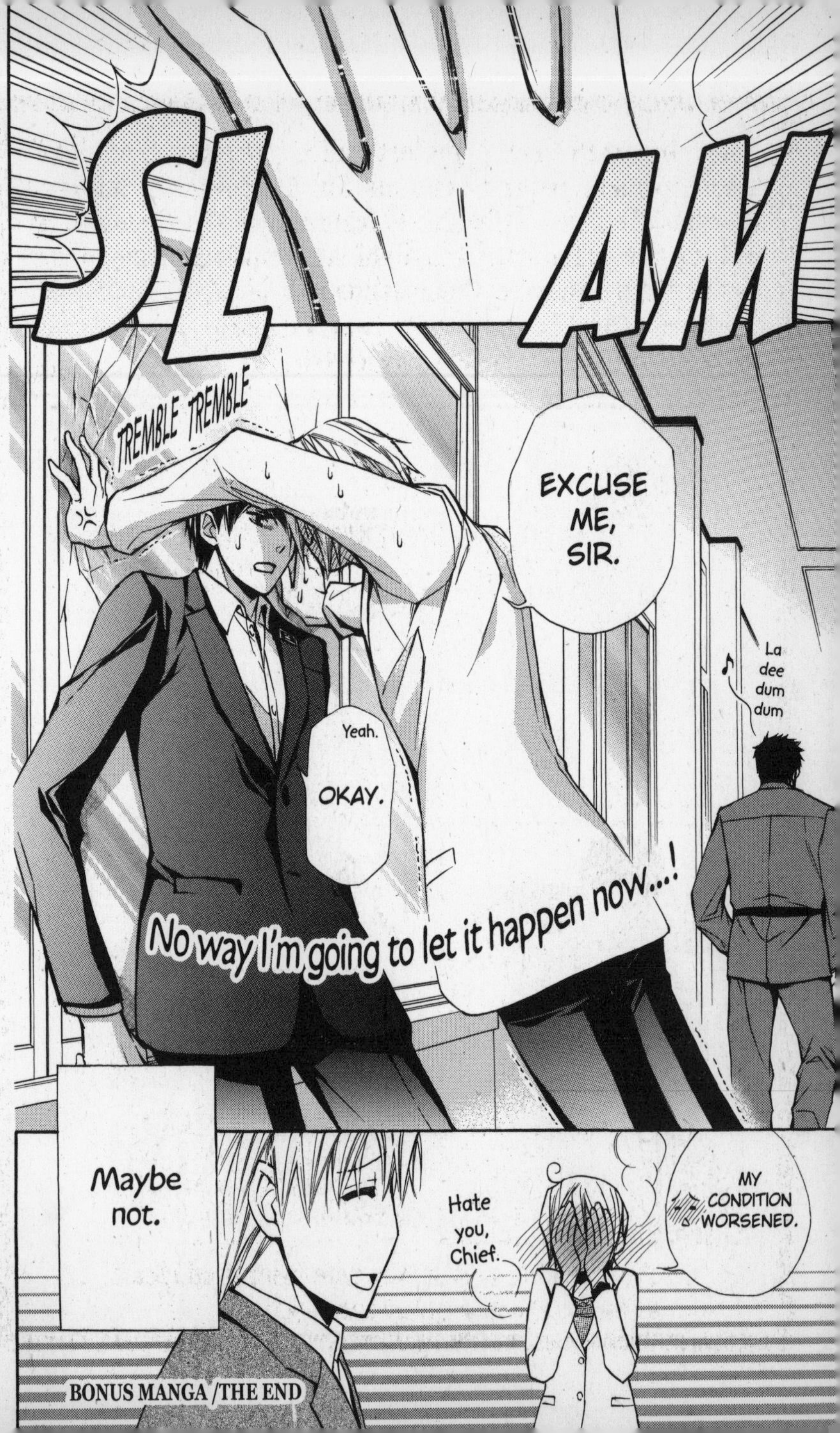
SLAM
EXCUSE ME, SIR.
La dee dum dum
Yeah.
OKAY.
TREMBLE TREMBLE
No way I'm going to let it happen now...!
MY CONDITION WORSENED.
Hate you, Chief.
Maybe not.
BONUS MANGA / THE END

LaLa Magazine had a project called "Dreamy Situations" where readers request concepts for the cover art for each chapter. The cover of Chapter 39 features *Alice in Wonderland*, a request from Sayarin from Aichi. Alice was a popular choice, but her idea of turning Chief Genda into The Queen of Hearts was particularly fascinating. Anyway, I'd like to share with you some of the great concepts we received.

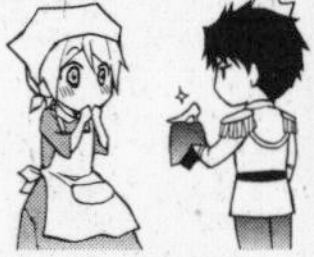

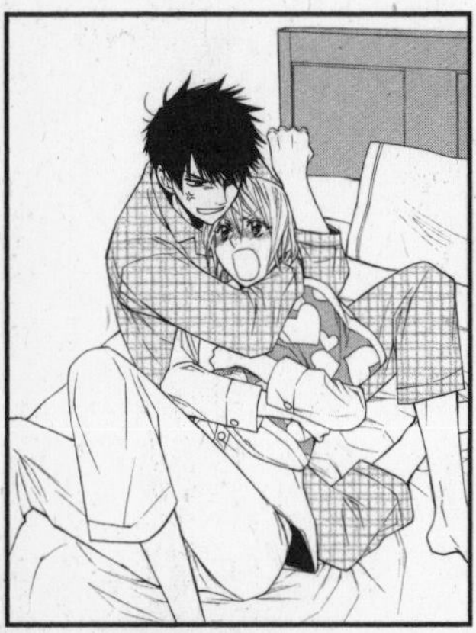

FRESHLY MARRIED IKU AND DOJO'S PILLOW TALK
KANCHA/KANAGAWA

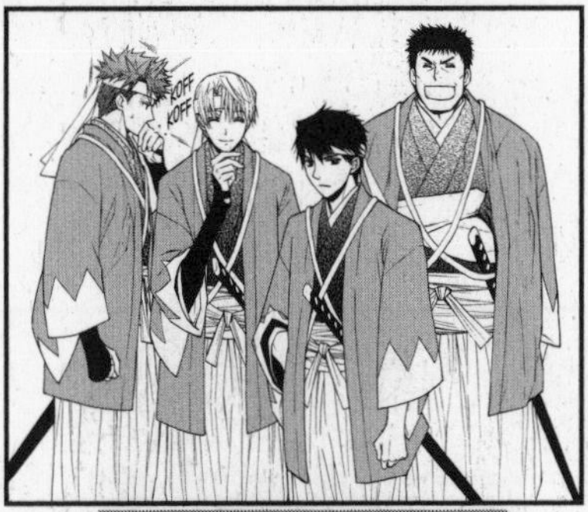
KOFF KOFF

AS SHINSENGUMI
MOMO-CHAN/OKAYAMA

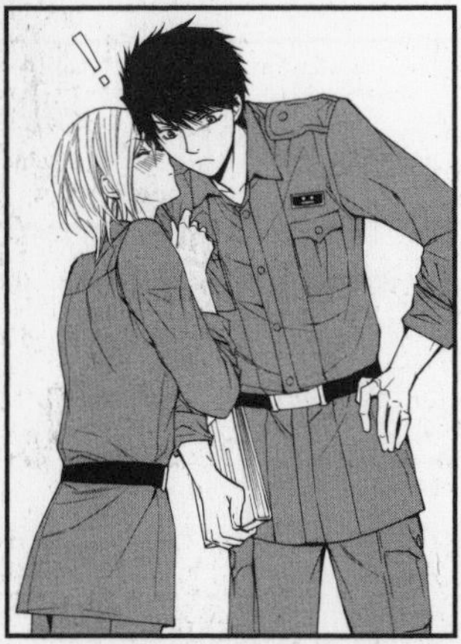

TALL DOJO
MAKI TERADA/OSAKA

A big thanks to everyone who submitted ideas!
It was fun to draw your concepts!

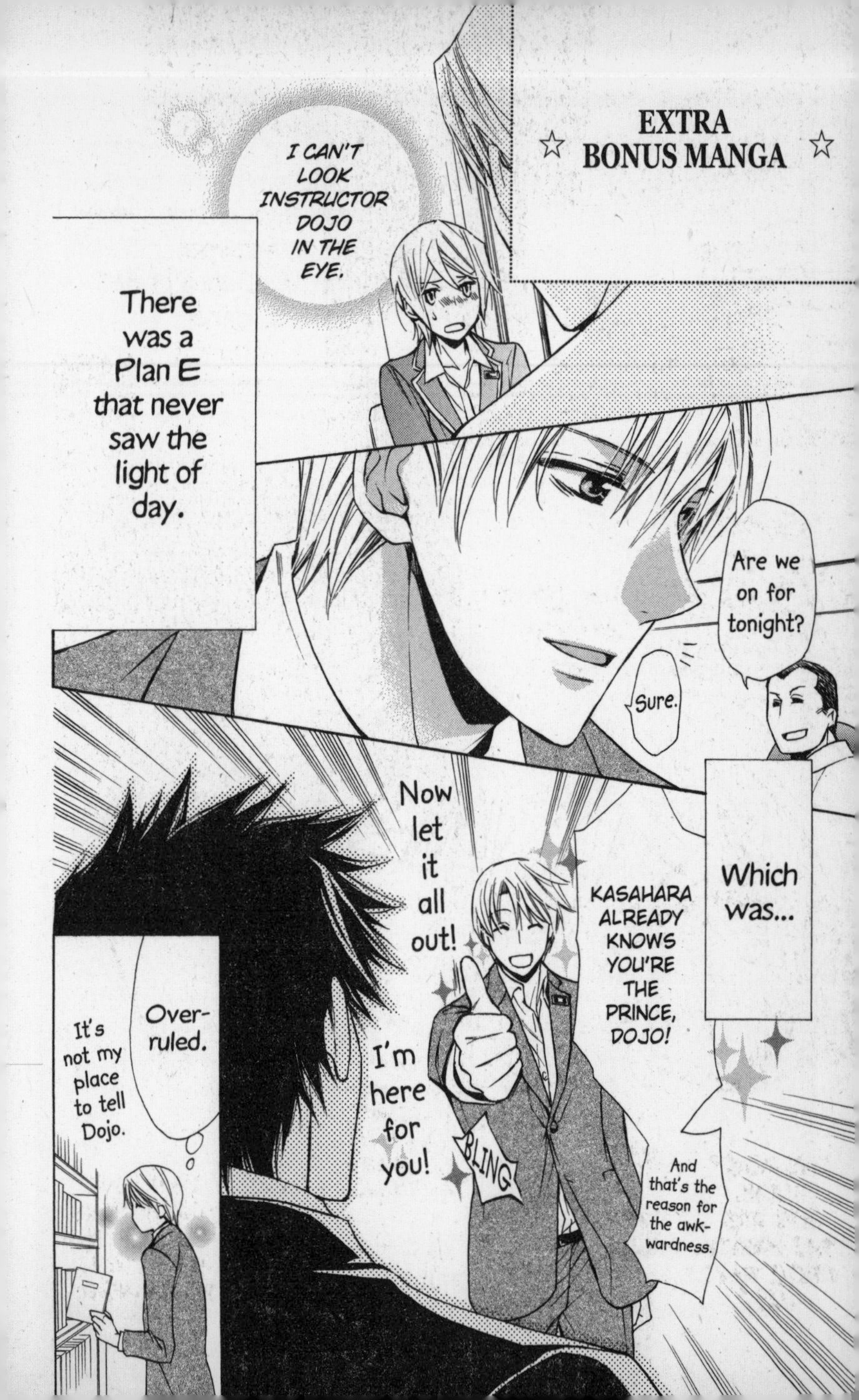
☆ EXTRA BONUS MANGA ☆
I CAN'T LOOK INSTRUCTOR DOJO IN THE EYE.
There was a Plan E that never saw the light of day.
Are we on for tonight?
Sure.
Which was...
KASAHARA ALREADY KNOWS YOU'RE THE PRINCE, DOJO!
Now let it all out!
I'm here for you!
BLING
And that's the reason for the awk-wardness.
Over-ruled.
It's not my place to tell Dojo.

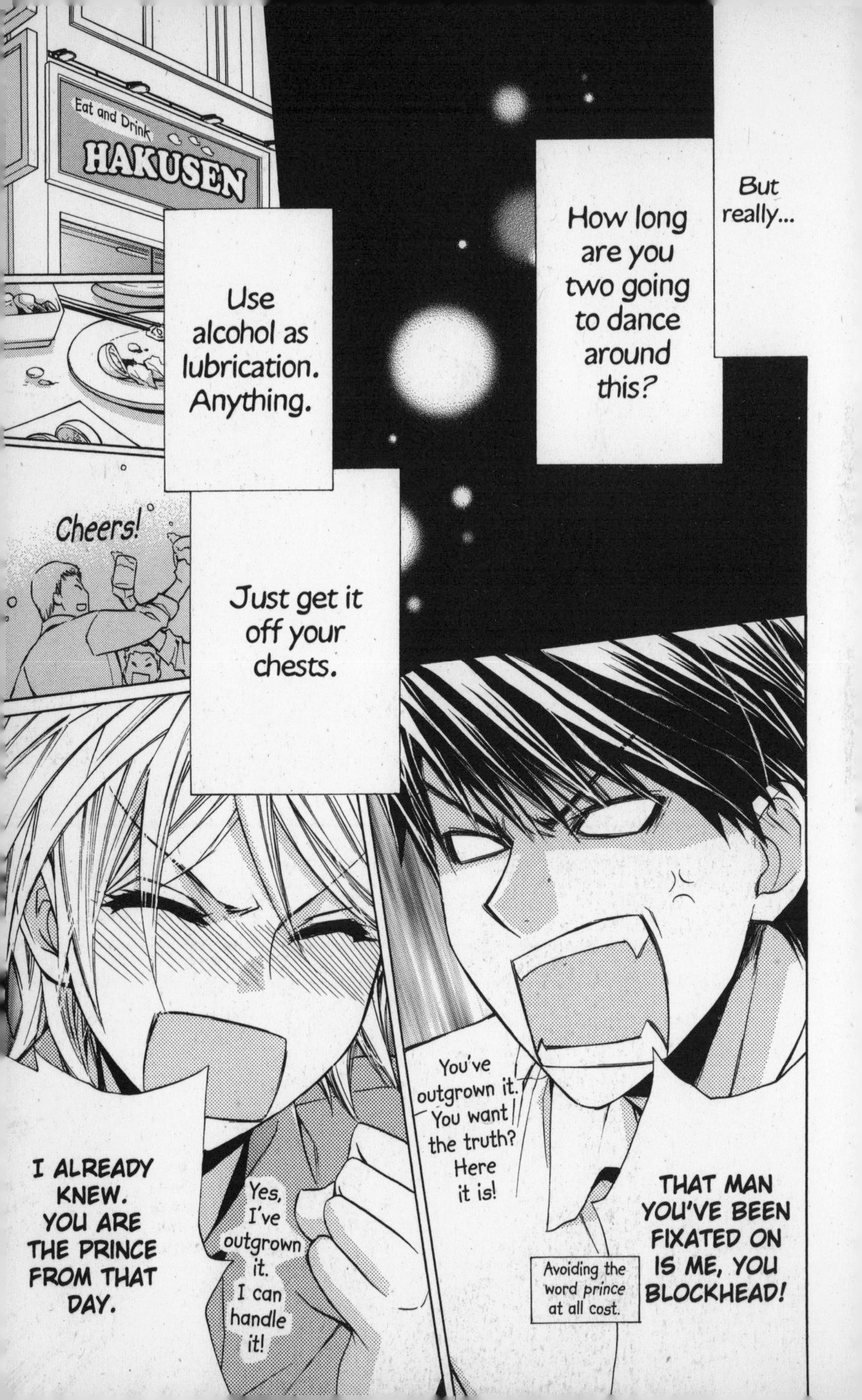
But really...
How long are you two going to dance around this?
Use alcohol as lubrication. Anything.
Just get it off your chests.
Eat and Drink
HAKUSEN
Cheers!
THAT MAN YOU'VE BEEN FIXATED ON IS ME, YOU BLOCKHEAD!
You've outgrown it. You want the truth? Here it is!
Avoiding the word prince at all cost.
Yes, I've outgrown it. I can handle it!
I ALREADY KNEW. YOU ARE THE PRINCE FROM THAT DAY.

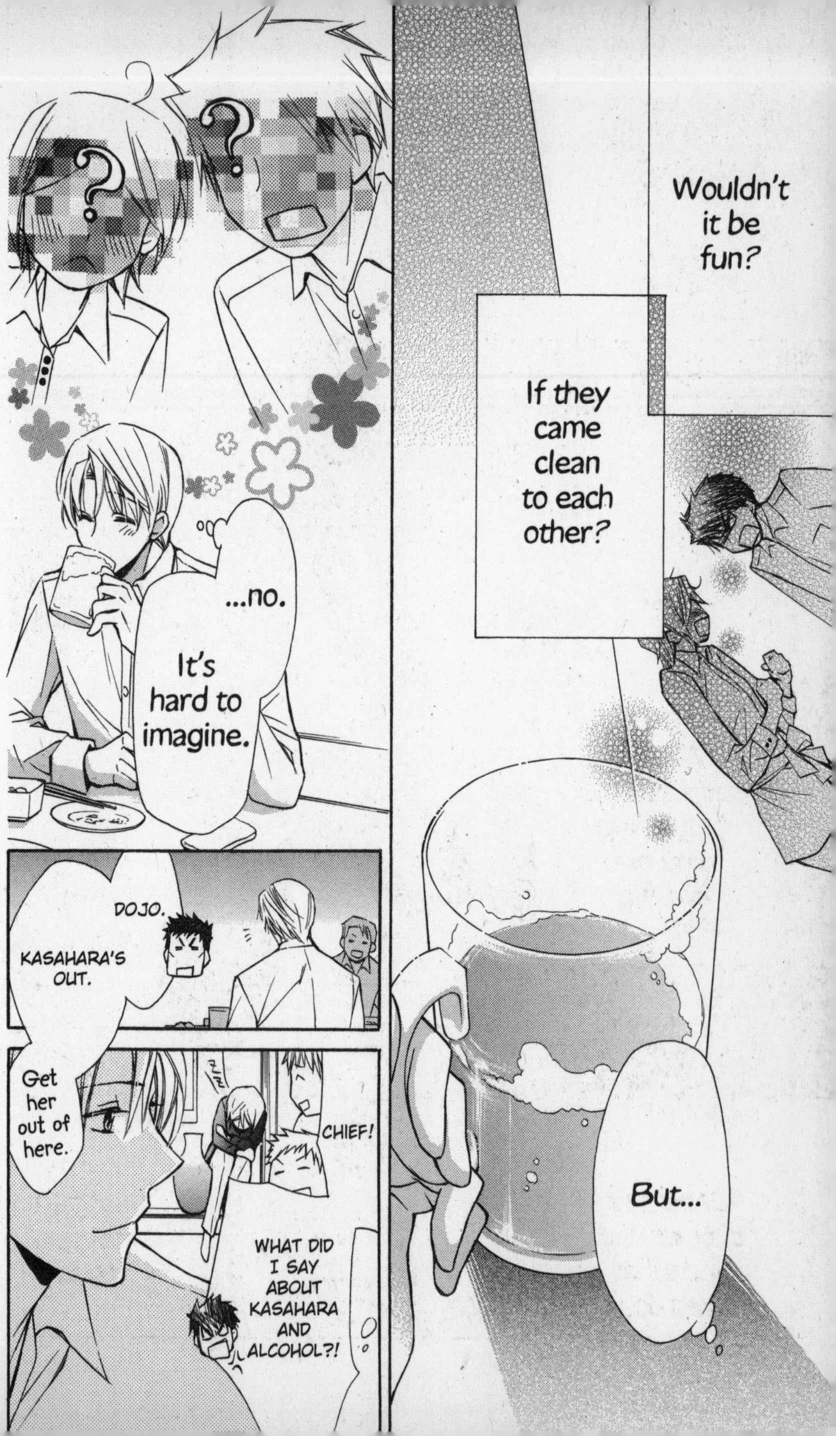
Wouldn't it be fun?
If they came clean to each other?
But...
...no.
It's hard to imagine.
DOJO.
KASAHARA'S OUT.
Get her out of here.
CHIEF!
WHAT DID I SAY ABOUT KASAHARA AND ALCOHOL?!

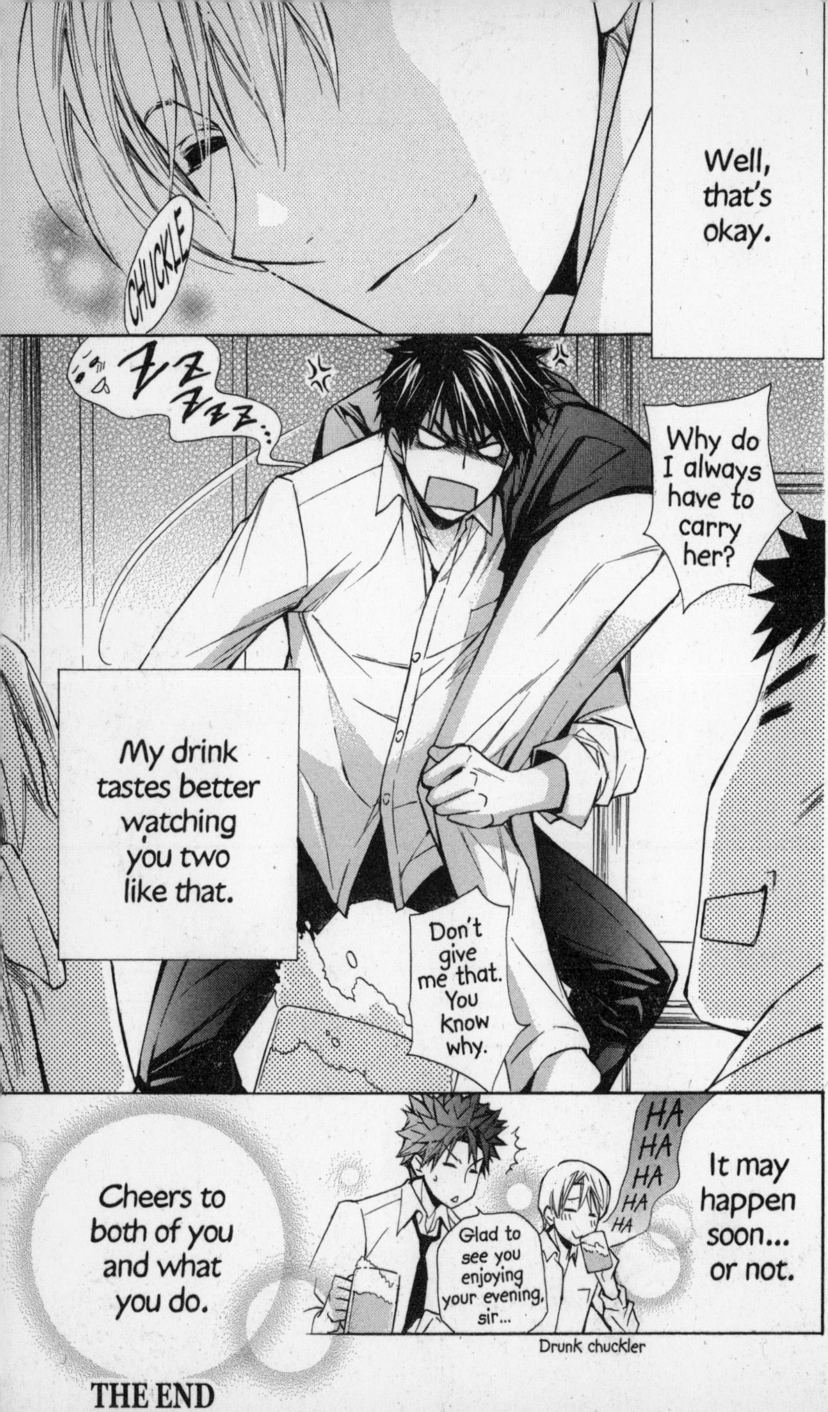
Well, that's okay.
CHUCKLE
Why do I always have to carry her?
ZZZZZ...
My drink tastes better watching you two like that.
Don't give me that. You know why.
HA HA HA HA HA HA
It may happen soon... or not.
Glad to see you enjoying your evening, sir...
Cheers to both of you and what you do.
Drunk chuckler

THE END

Special Thanks!!

Ms. Arikawa
Ms. Arikawa's editor (ASCII Media)
★
Mamada, Murakami, Aoki
★
My family
★
My editor, My former editor
★
Everyone who makes this series possible.
★★
Thanks so, so much!

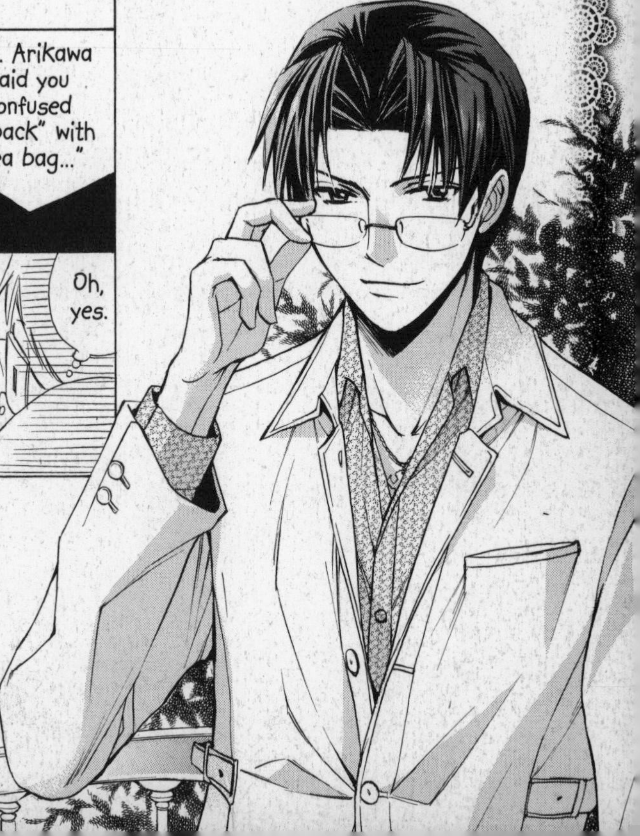

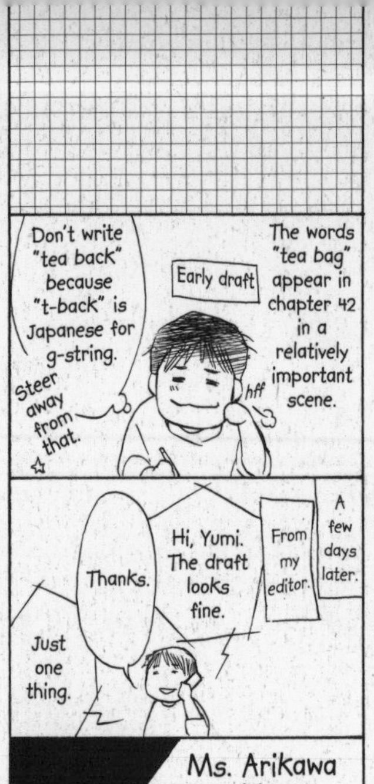

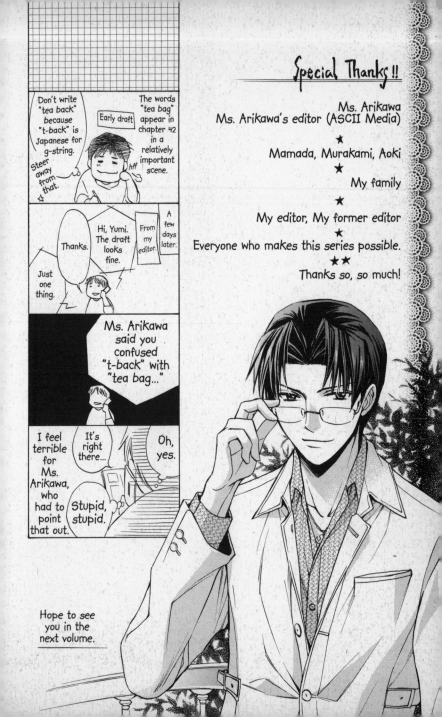

The words "tea bag" appear in chapter 42 in a relatively important scene.
Early draft
hff
Don't write "tea back" because "t-back" is Japanese for g-string.
Steer away from that.
A few days later.
From my editor.
Hi, Yumi. The draft looks fine.
Thanks.
Just one thing.
Ms. Arikawa said you confused "t-back" with "tea bag..."
Oh, yes.
It's right there...
Stupid, stupid.
I feel terrible for Ms. Arikawa, who had to point that out.

Hope to see you in the next volume.

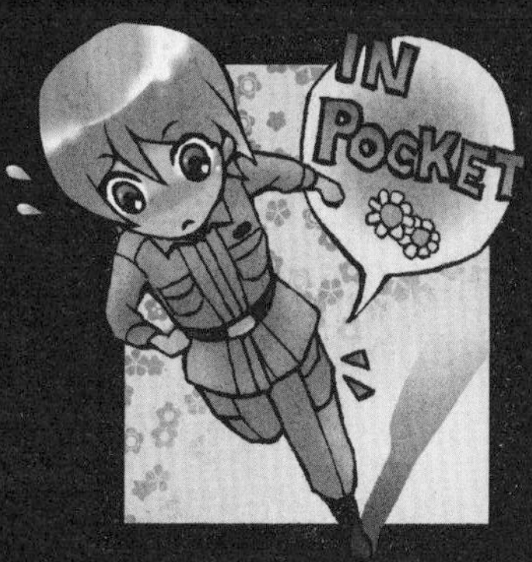
IN POCKET

Kiiro Yumi won the 42nd *LaLa* Manga Grand Prix Fresh Debut award for her manga *Billy Bocchan no Yuutsu* (Little Billy's Depression). Her latest series is *Toshokan Senso Love&War (Library Wars: Love & War)*, which runs in *LaLa* magazine in Japan and is published in English by VIZ Media.

Hiro Arikawa won the 10th Dengeki Novel Prize for her work *Shio no Machi: Wish on My Precious* in 2003 and debuted with the same novel in 2004. Of her many works, Arikawa is best known for the *Library Wars* series and her *Jieitai Sanbusaku* trilogy, which consists of *Sora no Naka* (In the Sky), *Umi no Soko* (The Bottom of the Sea) and *Shio no Machi* (City of Salt).

library wars

Volume 9
Shojo Beat Edition

Story & Art by **Kiiro Yumi**
Original Concept by **Hiro Arikawa**

ENGLISH TRANSLATION Kinami Watabe
ADAPTATION & LETTERING Sean McCoy
DESIGN Amy Martin
EDITOR Megan Bates

Toshokan Sensou LOVE&WAR by Kiiro Yumi and Hiro Arikawa

First published in Japan in 2012 by HAKUSENSHA, Inc., Tokyo.
English language translation rights arranged with HAKUSENSHA, Inc., Tokyo.

Printed in Canada

Published by VIZ Media, LLC
P.O. Box 77010
San Francisco, CA 94107

10 9 8 7 6 5 4 3 2 1
First printing, April 2013

www.shojobeat.com www.viz.com

RATED T+ FOR OLDER TEEN

PARENTAL ADVISORY
LIBRARY WARS: LOVE & WAR is rated T+ for Older Teen and is recommended for ages 16 and up. This volume contains alcohol use, adult language and violence.
ratings.viz.com

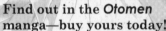

VIZMANGA
Read manga anytime, anywhere!

From our newest hit series to the classics you know and love, the best manga in the world is now available digitally. Buy a volume* of digital manga for your:

- iOS device (iPad®, iPhone®, iPod® touch) through the **VIZ Manga app**
- Android-powered device (**phone or tablet**) with a browser by visiting **VIZManga.com**
- **Mac or PC computer** by visiting **VIZManga.com**

VIZ Digital has loads to offer:

- 500+ ready-to-read volumes
- New volumes each week
- FREE previews
- Access on multiple devices! Create a log-in through the app so you buy a book once, and read it on your device of choice!*

To learn more, visit www.viz.com/apps

*Some series may not be available for multiple devices. Check the app on your device to find out what's available.

RATED
T
FOR OLDER
TEEN
ratings.viz.com

VIZ
MEDIA
viz.com/ap

This is the last page.

In keeping with the original Japanese comic format, this book reads from right to left—so action, sound effects, and word balloons are completely reversed. This preserves the orientation of the original artwork—plus, it's fun! Check out the diagram shown here to get the hang of things, and then turn to the other side of the book to get started!

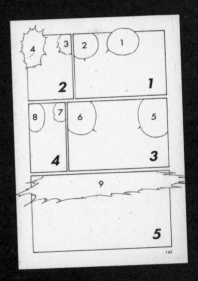